# The Function of Narrative Comments in the Gospel of John

# Interpreting Johannine Literature

The Interpreting Johannine Literature series is born from the desire of a group of Johannine scholars to bring rigorous study and explicit methodology into the teaching of these New Testament texts and their contexts. This series explores critical and perspectival approaches to the Gospel and Epistles of John. Historical- and literary-critical concerns are often augmented by current interpretive questions. Therefore, both a variety of approaches and critical self-awareness characterize titles in the series. Hermeneutical diversity and precision will continue to shed new light on the multi-faceted content and discourse of the Johannine Literature.

## Titles in the Series

*The Function of Narrative Comments in the Gospel of John: A Literary and Linguistic Analysis* (2025) by David A. Lamb

*The Johannine Community in Contemporary Debate* (2024) by Christopher W. Skinner and Christopher Seglenieks

*The Use of the Jewish Scriptures in the Johannine Passion Narrative: That the Scripture May Be Perfected* (2024) by David M. Allen

*Reading John through Johannine Lenses* (2021) by Stan Harstine

*Follow Me: The Benefits of Discipleship in the Gospel of John* (2020) by Mark Zhakevich

*What John Knew and What John Wrote: A Study in John and the Synoptics* (2020) by Wendy E. S. North

*Come and Read: Interpretive Approaches to the Gospel of John* (2019) edited by Alicia D. Myers and Lindsey S. Jodrey

# The Function of Narrative Comments in the Gospel of John

## A Literary and Linguistic Analysis

David A. Lamb

LEXINGTON BOOKS/FORTRESS ACADEMIC

*Lanham • Boulder • New York • London*

Lexington Books/Fortress Academic
Bloomsbury Publishing Inc, 1385 Broadway, New York, NY 10018, USA
Bloomsbury Publishing Plc, 50 Bedford Square, London, WC1B 3DP, UK
Bloomsbury Publishing Ireland, 29 Earlsfort Terrace, Dublin 2, D02 AY28, Ireland
www.rowman.com

Copyright © 2025 by The Rowman & Littlefield Publishing Group, Inc.

Scripture quotations in Greek are from *Nestle-Aland, Novum Testamentum Graece, 28th Revised Edition, edited by Barbara and Kurt Aland, Johannes Karavidopoulos, Carlo M. Martini, and Bruce M. Metzger in cooperation with the Institute for New Testament Textual Research, Münster/Westphalia, © 2012 Deutsche Bibelgesellschaft, Stuttgart. Used by permission.*

Scripture quotations in English are from the New Revised Standard Version Bible, Anglicized Edition © 1989, 1995 by the Division of Christian Education of the National Council of the Churches in the United States of America, and are used by permission. All rights reserved.

*All rights reserved.* No part of this publication may be: i) reproduced or transmitted in any form, electronic or mechanical, including photocopying, recording or by means of any information storage or retrieval system without prior permission in writing from the publishers; or ii) used or reproduced in any way for the training, development or operation of artificial intelligence (AI) technologies, including generative AI technologies. The rights holders expressly reserve this publication from the text and data mining exception as per Article 4(3) of the Digital Single Market Directive (EU) 2019/790.

British Library Cataloguing in Publication information available

**Library of Congress Cataloging-in-Publication Data**

Names: Lamb, David A., Revd., author.
Title: The function of narrative comments in the Gospel of John : a literary and linguistic analysis / David A. Lamb.
Description: Lanham : Lexington Books/Fortress Academic, [2025] I Series: Interpreting johannine literature I Includes bibliographical references and index. I Summary: "The Function of Narrative Comments in the Gospel of John is a comprehensive study of a major feature of the Fourth Gospel. It provides a clear and accessible overview of scholarship in this field, as well as providing fresh insights from contemporary literary and linguistic theories"— Provided by publisher.
Identifiers: LCCN 2024042716 (print) I LCCN 2024042717 (ebook) I ISBN 9781978715844 (cloth) I ISBN 9781978715851 (epub)
Subjects: LCSH: Bible. John—Criticism, Narrative. I Bible. John—Language, style. I Bible as literature.
Classification: LCC BS2615.52 .L35 2025 (print) I LCC BS2615.52 (ebook) I DDC 226.5/066—dc23/eng/20240930
LC record available at https://lccn.loc.gov/2024042716
LC ebook record available at https://lccn.loc.gov/2024042717

For product safety related questions contact productsafety@bloomsbury.com.

∞™ The paper used in this publication meets the minimum requirements of American National Standard for Information Sciences—Permanence of Paper for Printed Library Materials, ANSI/NISO Z39.48-1992.

# Contents

| | |
|---|---|
| Preface | vii |
| Acknowledgments | ix |
| List of Abbreviations | xi |
| Introduction | 1 |
| **1** Survey of Literature | 5 |
| **2** Terminology, Definitions, and Categorization | 57 |
| **3** An Annotated List of Narrative Comments in the Gospel of John | 99 |
| **4** The Process of Composition | 125 |
| **5** Whose Comments: The Narrator's or the Author's? | 163 |
| **6** Towards a Comparative Study | 205 |
| Conclusions: The Function of Narrative Comments in the Gospel of John | 241 |
| Bibliography | 249 |
| Index of Ancient Sources | 263 |
| Index of Modern Authors | 273 |
| About the Author | 277 |

v

# Preface

I am fascinated by words. Maybe this owes a lot to my being the child of a professor of modern European languages and a teacher of English literature. I am particularly interested in written words and have been a student of both literature and linguistics. I have also tried my hand at creative writing through poems and stories.

When I read the Gospel of John, I am captivated by words about "the Word" and I want to understand as best I can how to interpret these words. That is my motivation for writing this book.

However, although I am a words person, I know that visual images can also be powerful means of communication. On the cover of this book, I have used a photograph of a bronze sculpture called "The Water of Life." This remarkable work of art by the sculptor Stephen Broadbent shows the encounter between Jesus and the Samarian woman in John 4. It depicts an overflowing bowl of water being offered from one to the other. Around the base of the sculpture are Jesus words: "The water that I shall give will be an inner spring always welling up for eternal life" (John 4:14 NEB). "The Water of Life" stands in the cloister garden of Chester Cathedral (UK), where it was dedicated on 8 May 1994 by the then Dean of the Cathedral, Stephen Smalley, a notable Johannine scholar.

I chose this image for the cover of the book because I really like the sculpture. I also chose it because a phrase from John's account of the encounter between Jesus and the woman at the well, "Jews do not share things in common with Samaritans (John 4:9)," is a significant case study in my analysis of the narrative comments in John. Indeed, I suggest that those who regard these words as simply a later editorial aside may have a low view of the Samaritan woman's intellectual and linguistic capabilities. How we view the narrative comments in John has important implications for how we interpret the text.

vii

# Acknowledgments

For the past 10 years I have been an Honorary Research Fellow in Biblical Studies at the University of Manchester, UK, and I am grateful for the support of current and former colleagues there. I gave a paper entitled "Let the Reader Understand: The Function of 'Narrative Asides' in the Gospel of John: A Literary and Linguistic Analysis" at the Ehrhardt Seminar, University of Manchester in October 2015 and at the Johannine Literature Seminar of the British New Testament Conference in September 2016, and the feedback I received on both occasions stimulated my thinking in this area and eventually led to the writing of this book. During the course of writing, I have been particularly grateful for the support and advice I have received from Professor George Brooke, Professor Andrew Lincoln, Dr. Wendy North, Professor Thora Tenbrink, Professor Gilbert Van Belle, and the library staff at the University of Manchester, Bangor University (Gwynedd), Gladstone's Library (Hawarden), the National Library of Wales (Aberystwyth), and the British Library. I would also like to thank the following: Gayla Freeman, Megan White, and Jessica Smith, editors at Rowman & Littlefield Publishers, for their prompt replies to my various questions; the reviewer of the manuscript for a number of helpful suggestions; and Dr. Lesley Rickards for her proofreading of the text.

The illustration from the Codex Sinaiticus is used with the permission of The British Library, London, UK. Library shelf mark number: 43725. Reproduced from the *Codex Sinaiticus: Facsimile Edition* (2010) with the permission of Llyfrgell Genedlaethol Cymru/The National Library of Wales, Aberystwyth, UK.

All translations from other languages are my own, except where stated otherwise.

# List of Abbreviations

Abbreviations listed below only include those not in *The Society of Biblical Literature Handbook of Style*, 2nd edition (Atlanta: SBL Press, 2014). All other abbreviations are as in the *Handbook*.

BDR Friedrich Blass, Albert Debrunner, and Friedrich Rehkopf, *Grammatik des neutestamentlichen Griechisch*, 18th edition
FG Fourth Gospel
OED *Oxford English Dictionary*
NA27 *Novum Testamentum Graece*, Nestle-Aland, 27th edition
UBS4 *The Greek New Testament*, United Bible Societies, 4th edition

# Introduction

Writing in 1960, the NT scholar Merrill Tenney stated:

> Any casual reader of the Fourth Gospel soon becomes aware that its pages contain a great deal of explanatory material which is not directly involved in the progress of the narrative. This material is by no means irrelevant to the main thrust of the Gospel, but it is parenthetical. If it were omitted, the main theme of thought would remain largely unaltered, although the parenthetical material has a definite value for understanding the meaning of the Gospel. It is more extensive and varied than the notes that one finds occasionally in the Synoptics, and is worth special consideration in the interpretation of the meaning of *John*.[1]

It is this "parenthetical material" which forms the subject of this book. In a previous work I examined a set of "narrative asides" in the Gospel of John (2:21–22; 12:16; 19:35–37; 20:30–31; 21:23–25) in which there appears to be direct author-to-reader communication and in which the process of writing itself is consciously highlighted.[2] I was particularly interested in what these asides imply about the social context in which the Gospel was written, but studying them also raised for me questions of their definition (what exactly is an "aside"?) and of their relation to the process of composition (for example, are they the work of a later redactor?).

Reading what others, such as Tenney, have written about "narrative asides" in John has developed my interest in their overall function in the Gospel of John, an interest that I relate to my experience of both literary and linguistic approaches to NT studies. I began my academic career as an English literature student, but have ended up studying linguistics, while, in between, the bulk of my student and teaching work has been in NT and particularly Johannine

2                                   *Introduction*

studies. In this book, I intend to draw on a range of perspectives, both literary
and linguistic, in order to provide a comprehensive overview of the subject. I
also intend to present conclusions on the basis of my own and others' analyses of particular "narrative asides." In the course of the work, I use a variety
of terms for this literary/linguistic feature, but readers should note a gradual
shift from "asides" to "comments," corresponding to my growing sense that
these features are not so much parenthetical, but rather an essential part of
the text. Indeed, I remember once being asked by someone about to give a
public reading of a passage from the Gospel of John, if he should miss out the
words in brackets. His enquiry (inadvertently) raised issues about the purpose
of these words. Are they simply peripheral material that can be relegated to
footnotes as Raymond Brown once suggested?[3] Indeed, can they be omitted
altogether without any noticeable effect on an overall reading of the text, as
Tenney seems to imply? Or are they an integral part of the text, essential for
its correct interpretation?

In respect of the intended audience of this book, I have had in mind a keen
final-year undergraduate or a postgraduate student (levels that I have taught
at) and have tried to make my arguments clear and accessible, following
the example of Raymond Brown, one of my Johannine scholarship heroes.
I have a sneaking suspicion that in our current age of complex, competing,
and diverse NT methodologies, some scholars take delight in the obscurity
of their work and the superiority of their approach. By contrast, I try to hold
on to what some might consider the naïve belief that the best scholars make
things simple.

In chapter 1, I begin my study with a survey of the work of NT scholars on
Johannine asides over roughly the past 100 years, starting with an essay published by Rev. H. J. Flowers in 1921.[4] The focus is mostly on work published
in articles and monographs, although there is also some mention of sections
in commentaries and I also briefly look at various Greek grammars.

In chapter 2, I focus on the terminology, definition, and categorization of
asides, an area in which too much has probably been assumed rather than
argued for. I draw on insights from narrative, drama, and linguistic theory and
note that there is a considerable degree of complexity and uncertainty. This
is probably why authors have often shied away from consideration of these
issues. I provide my own definition of "narrative comments" that relates to
what lies outside the narrative framework of the Gospel.

I follow this, in chapter 3, with an annotated list of forty-five narrative
comments in John, which I regard as fitting my "outside the narrative framework" definition. I explain why I reject some asides/comments commonly
denoted as such by other scholars. I also include a brief list of comments
which I regard as internal to the narrative framework.

*Introduction* 3

Chapter 4 deals with the role of asides/comments in the process of the Gospel of John's composition. Did they arise at an oral stage of composition? Were they added at early "performances" of the narrative? Or are they later additions to the text, which reflect new and distinctive perspectives?

I then examine in some detail, in chapter 5, the role of the narrator and the author in respect of asides/comments. Whereas much recent work, drawing on narrative criticism, has focussed on the point of view of the narrator and questions of omniscience, intrusiveness, and reliability, I question whether is it helpful to make a distinction between the narrator and the author of the Gospel, even if we do not know who the (primary) author was. So, I think it is important to consider how real authors (real people) use language to engage with and persuade their readers and the function of parenthetical material in that process of communication. In this context, I refer to linguistic work on *metadiscourse*. I also include a case study on the category of comments often referred to as "translation asides," analysing their function in terms of the author-reader dynamic.

I have entitled my final chapter, chapter 6, "Towards a Comparative Study." I have used the word "towards" to indicate that this can only be a tentative investigation given the abundance of texts available for such comparative study and the importance of basing conclusions on the actual analysis of these texts. Indeed, I have chosen to limit my study mainly to an exploration of the use of asides/comments in some of the OT/Hebrew Bible (HB)'s historical writings and in the Synoptic Gospels. I am hesitant about comparing their use in John with their use in extrabiblical Greek writings, such as histories and biographies, given the lack of evidence of any direct dependence on such writings, but I do make some reference to various studies in this area. Clearly this is an area for further research.

Overall, I hope that this book will appeal not just to Johannine specialists, of any academic level, but to all those involved in NT studies (and beyond) who believe there is value in bringing together a variety of literary and linguistic methodologies, while keeping attention focussed on a close reading of texts. I do not claim to have made any startling new breakthroughs (I am not that sort of scholar), but I hope to have added to the work of others and to have provided a useful overview of what I have found a fascinating and worthwhile area of study.

## NOTES

1. Merrill C. Tenney, "The Footnotes of John's Gospel," *BSac* 117 (1960): 350.

2. David A. Lamb, *Text, Context and the Johannine Community: A Sociolinguistic Analysis of the Johannine Writings* (LNTS 477; London: Bloomsbury T & T Clark, 2014, 159–73.

3. Raymond E. Brown, *The Gospel According to John* (2 vols.; AB 29–29A; New York: Doubleday, 1966, 1970), 1:cxxxvi.

4. H. J. Flowers, "Interpolations in the Fourth Gospel," *JBL* 40, no. 3/4 (1921).

*Chapter 1*

# Survey of Literature

This chapter provides an overview of the main literature on asides in the Gospel of John, published mostly in articles and monographs, over the past 100 years. I have not included here discussion in commentaries unless the author has a specific section on asides, such as is found in the works of Bernard and Brown. Frequent reference will, however, be made to commentaries in the study of specific asides in subsequent chapters. Other works, including many earlier ones, are examined by Van Belle and readers may well profit from consulting his extensive survey.[1] The purpose of the overview in this chapter is to see what textual, literary, and linguistic issues are raised. These will then form the basis for further examination in the rest of this book. I begin with three contributions from the 1920s.

## FLOWERS (1921)

H. J. Flowers, in his 1921 essay "Interpolations in the Fourth Gospel," published in the *Journal of Biblical Literature*, examined phrases and sentences which he considered "superfluous" or "alien to the main thought of the Gospel" and therefore the work of a later writer.[2] He takes for granted that John 5:4 and 7:53–8:11 "do not belong to the true text of the Fourth Gospel" and argues that the same applies to chapter 21, which, owing to its lack of connection with chapter 20 (it "comes as a decided anti-climax") and its particular style, vocabulary, and contents, is a later addition to the Gospel.[3] He then looks for other "interpolations" which cannot be labelled as such on the "external evidence" of textual criteria.[4]

Flowers's main criteria for allocating certain phrases or sentences to a later editor or editors are twofold: (1) theological inconsistency; and (2) the

6    *Chapter 1*

"misinterpretation" of spiritual concepts. First, he sees examples of theological inconsistency in John 5:28–29, concerning οἱ ἐν τοῖς μνημείοις, and 6:39, 40, 44, 54, with their references to "the last day." All these he regards as interpolations on the basis that they reflect "primitive" eschatological ideas.[5] Another example is John 4:2: "and yet Jesus did not baptize, but his disciples," which Flowers sees as "a clear contradiction of the preceding verse" and "a clear case of the feeling of the Christian Church obtruding itself into the Gospel tradition."[6] He suggests that it may be a "marginal note by a scribe to explain away a difficulty and that the words slipped into the text."[7] Second, he sees examples of misinterpretation in 2:21–22; 7:39; 12:33; 18:9, where the editor has not understood the spiritual nature of Jesus' utterances and provides poor explanations of their meaning.[8] He states, "They are all cases in which an utterance of Jesus referring to timeless spiritual facts has been interpreted so as to refer to temporal events."[9]

Finally, Flowers examines 19:35, with its reference to ὁ ἑωρακώς, and concludes that it too is an editorial interpolation.[10] He sums up his overall argument in this way:

> Thus we have a tentative reconstruction of the Gospel; (1) the Gospel itself, chapters 1–20, depicting the life of Jesus in the light of the Prologue; (2) the appendix, written before the Gospel was published, by someone unknown; but this second man did not merely add the appendix. He saw fit to edit the Gospel; (3) the last two verses, 21 24, 25 and the attestation of 19 35 come from a body of men to authenticate the whole Gospel.[11]

Whether it is correct to speak of the Gospel as being "published," with its modern connotations, is questionable. However, Flowers's article does raise two important issues. First, his treating of asides as "interpolations" introduces the whole question of layers of redaction within the text. Second, the detection of conflicting voices in the narrative, leading to misinterpretations, relates to what later scholars have labelled the "unreliable narrator." Indeed, Flowers goes so far as to suggest that if we do accept the presence of later interpolations, "We are thus delivered from a great deal of contradiction and an equal amount of subtle exegesis."[12]

## GARVIE (1922)

A similar approach to that of Flowers, although with different conclusions, is taken by Alfred E. Garvie in *The Beloved Disciple: Studies of the Fourth Gospel*, published in 1922, which has chapters on "Comments by the Evangelist" and "The Redactor's Insertions."[13] Garvie believed that the Gospel had gone through a process of composition based on the "reminiscences and reflexions" of the *Witness*, but reproduced and commented on by the *Evangelist*, "a disciple of the witness," and subsequently added to by the *Redactor*, who contributes the appendix of Chapter 21 as well as a number of other insertions.[14] Although Garvie admits that it is not always possible to distinguish the work of these three figures, he provides a "tentative" analysis of the Gospel which divides the text into their respective contributions.[15]

In his chapter "Comments by the Evangelist," Garvie divides this material into six rough categories and provides examples of each. These categories are:

1. Comments that include quotations from or allusions to the OT, whereby speech or actions are viewed as the fulfilment of prophecy (2:17; 12:14–15, 37–41; 19:24, 36, 37; and, possibly, 17:12 and 19:28), a feature common to the Synoptics and the rest of the NT.
2. Comments which explain the meaning of Jesus' words, which were not understood at the time they were uttered, but only subsequently (2:21–22; 7:39; 8:27).
3. Explanations of Jesus' words or acts which betray the Evangelist's "own conception of the person of the Incarnate Word," with "a tendency to lay emphasis on the supernaturalness of Jesus' knowledge"[16] (1:48; 2:24–25; 4:44; 5:18; 13:1–3; and, possibly, 18:8–9).
4. Explanations of Jesus' words or acts that are put into the mouth of Jesus himself and which indicate the Evangelist's "own conception" of "the consciousness of Jesus"[17] (11:41; 13:19; 14:29).
5. Various other comments that Garvie finds difficult to classify: 11:51–52; 17:3; 18:31–33.
6. Longer passages which are more likely to be commentary by the Evangelist than reflections by the Witness: 3:31–36; 5:19–29.

Garvie's chapter on "The Redactor's Insertions" is mainly concerned with the inclusion of "Synoptic elements" in the Gospel by the Redactor.[18] However, he also refers to 19:35 as the Redactor's "protestation" of the "worthiness of the witness," identified as John, the son of Zebedee.[19]

Like Flowers, Garvie's study raises the issue of layers of redaction. It also introduces the *categorization* of comments, which has proved to be a feature of subsequent analyses. It is noticeable that Garvie's own analysis is based on his theological interpretation of the text regarding perceived later developments in christology and eschatology.[20] I note that Garvie finds in the Gospel "doctrine of a somewhat aggressive type."[21]

8                                  *Chapter 1*

## BERNARD (1928)

In the Introduction to his posthumously published two volumes on the Gospel
in the *International Critical Commentary* series, J. H. Bernard has sections on
"Non-Johannine Glosses" and "Evangelistic Comments."[22]

Regarding the "Non-Johannine Glosses," he suggests that there are several
passages, in addition to the generally recognized later addition of 7:53–8:11,
which "are probably due to editorial revision, being added after the Gospel
was finished, perhaps before it was issued to the Church."[23] These passages
are 4:1–2; 5:4; 6:23; and, possibly, 11:2 and 12:16, although Bernard is less
sure about these. Looking at the first three of these passages and referring to
the notes in his commentary, we see that Bernard rejects them all as original
on stylistic grounds. In addition, he makes the following observations. First,
4:2, the explanation that Jesus did not in fact perform baptism himself, but
delegated it to his disciples, "was added at a revision of the text, because of
the idea that it would detract from the dignity of Jesus to perform the ministry
of baptism, which even Paul was accustomed as a rule to leave to others."[24]
Second, 5:4, giving the reason why invalids waited by the pool of Bethzatha,
is "no part of the original text of Jn., but is a later gloss" and the verse is
"wholly omitted by ℵ B C* D W 33, the Old Syriac, the early Coptic versions
(including Q), and the true text of the Latin Vulgate."[25] Third, the town of
Tiberias referred to in 6:23 is not mentioned elsewhere in the NT and had
only recently been founded.[26] So, although "necessary to the narrative," it
"appears to be a later gloss."[27]

Although less sure about his other two suggestions for "non-Johannine
glosses," Bernard makes these comments. First, 11:2, which introduces Mary,
the sister of Lazarus, contains "two non-Johannine touches of style."[28] Second, 12:16, which states that it was only when Jesus "was glorified" that the
disciples understood the scripturally prophesied entry into Jerusalem, "reads
as if it was not due to the original evangelist, but to some one who had the
Synoptic, rather than the Johannine, story in his mind at this point."[29] It also
contains examples of non-Johannine style.[30]

In his section on "Evangelistic Comments," Bernard stresses that the "non-
Johannine glosses, must not be confused with the comments which Jn. makes,
as he proceeds, on his narrative, and on the words which he records."[31] Later
in his commentary, Bernard states, "A feature of the style of Jn. is his habit of
pausing to comment on words which he has recorded."[32] He lists a number of
such comments, such as explanations of Jesus' words (Jn. 2:21; 7:39; 12:33;
17:3); pointing out misunderstandings by the Jews (7:22; 8:27) and the disciples (11:13); noting how certain words of the Jews correspond to what Jesus
said about his death (4:44; 18:22); ascribing motives to Judas (12:6) and the
rulers (12:43); brief elucidations for those for whom the details would be new

*Survey of Literature*                                                                 9

(2:24; 4:9; 6:71; 7:5); and noting the irony of Caiaphas's unconscious prophecy (11:51). However, he also believes that the author's "general habit . . . is to pass over without comment . . . any obvious mistake or misapprehension as to the Person of Christ. These mistakes his readers will correct for themselves, while they need help in regard to obscure sayings."[33] In other words, while John will guide readers in some contexts, he will also leave readers to make their own judgements about Jesus.

Bernard's observations draw attention to three issues. Are there comments which can be definitively accepted as later additions ("glosses") on textual grounds? To what extent are the comments a feature of the author's narrative style? Why are some matters explained and others not—is John only a part-time guide?

From these three brief contributions from the 1920s, we move forward several decades to one particularly influential study.

## TENNEY (1960)

Merrill Tenney's article "The Footnotes of John's Gospel," published in *Bibliotheca Sacra* in 1960, is significant as the first study to systematically bring together an enumeration, classification, and interpretation of "explanatory material," which, although "parenthetical," is "by no means irrelevant to the main thrust of the Gospel."[34] On the contrary, it "has a definite value for understanding the meaning of the Gospel."[35] Regarding the innovative nature of his article, Tenney states, "To the best knowledge of this writer there is no separate treatment of this phenomenon to be found in the vast literature on the Fourth Gospel," despite the fact that the footnotes "offer a valuable insight into the design of the author, and provide some hints concerning the occasion for which the Gospel was written."[36] Indeed, the only explicit use he makes of the work of previous scholars are two references to Westcott's commentary.[37]

Although Tenney calls the explanatory material "footnotes," he clarifies that in his article: "The word does not have the meaning in the sense of the numbered references that one finds in the text of a modern book of research."[38] He states that they "are more nearly 'glosses' or 'asides' which the writer introduced to make his story more lucid, or to explain the cause or motive for some act."[39] He further defines the Gospel's footnotes in this way: "They are sentences or paragraphs of explanatory comment, interjected into the running narrative of the story and obviously intended to illumine some casual reference, or to explain how some important statements should be understood."[40] He detects 59 such footnotes (more or less), which he divides into ten categories. I have indicated the number of examples he gives of each category in brackets and provided a brief explanation.

10                                        *Chapter 1*

1.  Footnotes of translation (8 or 9)
    These either give the meaning in Greek of Hebrew or Aramaic terms or
    else state the equivalent Hebrew term for a Greek place name.
2.  Footnotes of time and place (10)
    Geographical or chronological references.
3.  Customs (1)
    Explanations of Jewish customs that are "not part of the running narra-
    tive."[41] "For the Jews have no dealing with the Samaritans" (4:9) is the
    only example of this.

As Tenney believes that the footnotes can contribute to an understanding of
the Gospel's social context ("the occasion for which the Gospel was written"), it is worth noting here the value he attaches to these first three categories. He suggests that the explanatory *translations* (1:38, 41, 42; 4:25; 9:7;
19:13, 17; 20:16, 24) and the explanations of place and custom indicate that
whereas the author is familiar with Palestinian culture, his intended audience
(or some part of it) is not.[42] For example, referring to the footnote in 4:9 ("the
Jews have no dealing with the Samaritans"), Tenney believes that this observation "shows that the writer knew the Palestinian viewpoint, and that he was
writing for persons who lived elsewhere."[43]

4.  Footnotes reflecting the author (6)
    Tenney includes in this category the use of "we" and "I" in 1:14, 16 and
    21:24–25, as well as the references to the "disciple whom Jesus loved" in
    13:23 and 21:23 and to the witness in 19:35.
5.  Recollections of the disciples (6)
    These are closely linked to the author's references to himself. Indeed,
    they overlap with the "we" passages in 1:14, 16.[44] Otherwise, they refer
    to the later reflection by the disciples on deeds of Jesus that they did not
    understand at the time.
6.  Notes explanatory of situations or actions (14)
    This is the category with most examples. Tenney states that these "have
    no special doctrinal purpose," but "add to the color or to the understand-
    ing of the action described."[45] However, he includes 20:30–31, which
    would seem to have doctrinal significance.
7.  Enumeration or summary (3)
    These are the numbering of the "signs" in 2:11 and 4:54, with the obser-
    vation that, "Although we might expect that [the writer] would continue
    these notices of the order of the signs, he does not."[46] Tenney also includes
    in this category the reference to the numbering of the post-resurrection
    appearances in 21:14. In regard to the purpose of these, he states, "The
    enumeration of footnotes is quite in keeping with the general method and

*Survey of Literature*

11

structure of the Gospel. Few though they are, they show that the author was methodical, and that he intended to treat his subject matter in orderly and climactic fashion."[47] Of course, this does not answer the question as to why the numbering of the "signs" is not continued.

8. Identification of persons (5)

These enable the hearer or reader to identify certain characters that were either previously mentioned in John's own narrative or whose names may be significant in other ways. These characters are: Nicodemus; Mary, the sister of Lazarus;[48] Malchus; Caiaphas; and Barabbas.

9. Knowledge of Jesus (3)

Passages that "emphasize the supernatural quality of Jesus' knowledge": 6:6, 64; 13:11.[49]

10. Long theological notes (3)

These are 3:16–21; 3:31–36; and 12:37–43, which may be considered as commentary, but are possibly too long to be treated as footnotes.

These 59 examples are set out in a chart, classified into the ten categories and also by a rough indication of the text's divisions.[50]

Tenney's study, which in many ways sets the agenda for future work in this area, raises a number of important issues.

First, it marks a shift away from a focus on redaction. Tenney emphasizes that the footnotes "are not interpolations" but "an essential part of the inspired text of the Gospel."[51] This is linked to his understanding of the authorship of the Gospel, for although, in his analysis of the "Footnotes reflecting the author," Tenney states that he is not setting out a case for the authorship of the Gospel in this article, he nevertheless understands the author to be a personal witness of the events of Jesus' life, who "claimed firsthand knowledge of the facts that he was discussing."[52] Moreover, in his "Summary and Conclusion," Tenney highlights the value of the footnotes as a witness to the authorship of the Gospel, concluding, "All the evidence that the footnotes afford favors the traditional authorship by John, leaving room for assistance by others in the actual process of writing."[53] Indeed, he goes so far as to say that, "Perhaps the greatest value [*sc.* of the footnotes] for the modern reader lies in their disclosure of the personal thinking of the author."[54] So, although Tenney denies that the question of authorship is the focus of his paper, his conclusion that the Gospel (including the footnotes) is almost certainly composed by the Apostle John, with minimal scribal assistance, takes the focus away from a process of redaction.[55]

Second, Tenney's study raises the question: In what sense is this material actually parenthetical? Tenney acknowledges that it is not always easy to know "whether the author is interjecting an observation, or whether the narrative itself is diffuse."[56] His definition of "footnotes" as "sentences or

12                                     *Chapter 1*

paragraphs of explanatory comment, interjected into the running narrative of the story"[57] needs further clarification in terms of what he means by "interjected."

Third, it highlights the significance of the parenthetical material for the interpretation of the Gospel. It forms an important part of the author's didactic strategy:

> The footnotes show also something of the purpose of the author in communicating with his audience. He wanted them to understand the Jewish terms that were used, and he tried to keep the leading threads of his thought clear in their minds by the use of cross references. Names, places, occasions, and situations were explained so that the message might be unhindered.[58]

Fourth, it alludes to the *style* of the author. In acknowledging the difficulty of deciding what material should be regarded as parenthetical owing to the "diffuse" nature of the narrative, he suggests that this may be a reflection of "the oral style of its author."[59] In his "Summary and Conclusion," he expands on this: "The random occurrence of these comments and the diversity of their nature convey the impression that they may have been oral parentheses in material that was either repeated frequently in public teaching or that was dictated to an amanuensis for writing, or both."[60]

Future works on the form and function of the asides are indebted to Tenney's pioneering study.


## BROWN (1966, 2003)

In the Introduction to his *Anchor Bible Commentary* on the Gospel, the first volume of which was published in 1966, Raymond Brown has a section on various "Notable Characteristics in Johannine Style." This includes a paragraph on "Explanatory Notes" in which he states, "In the Gospel we often find explanatory comments, inserted into the running narrative of the story."[61] He lists various functions of these explanatory comments, with examples given: the explanation of names (1:38, 42) and symbols (2:21; 12:33; 18:9); the correction of possible misapprehensions (4:2; 6:6); reminders for the reader of related events (3:24; 11:2); and the reidentification of characters in the plot (7:50; 21:20). He suggests that "if it would not lead to confusion, they might well be placed at the bottom of the page as footnotes."[62]

Brown also states, "These notes are often indicative of the editing process at work in the composition of the Gospel."[63] However, in his revised text for the new *Introduction*, published posthumously in 2003 under the editorship of Francis Maloney, he is less certain about this "editing process" and more open to the idea of the explanatory notes having a narrative function rather than simply being later additions to the text:

> It is difficult to decide whether these notes reflect an editing process, wherein the same writer at a later time or a later writer decides that (new?) readers/hearers need help in order to understand. . . . Narrative critics insist upon the essential function of these so-called "notes" *within the text* as "explicit" or "implicit" commentary upon the discourse of the story.[64]

We are left unsure of Brown's own position here, although he does suggest that the movement of the Johannine Community from Palestine to the Gentile world, possibly Ephesus, may have made it necessary to explain words with Semitic roots (as in 1:38, 41,42).[65] In his "An Overview of Johannine Studies" for the new *Introduction*, Brown does show a growing appreciation for literary critical approaches as a necessary corrective to historical criticism, a way of "bringing the scales of interpretation back to a better balance by emphasizing the importance of following the logic of the text itself."[66] Given this reappraisal, it seems reasonable to suggest that Brown would no longer advise relegating the explanatory comments to footnotes at the bottom of the page.

## OLSSON (1974)

Birger Olsson's 1974 publication *Structure and Meaning in the Fourth Gospel: A Text-Linguistic Analysis of John 2:1–11 and 4:1–42* is an early example of a NT scholar applying linguistic and literary insights from what is now commonly labelled a "discourse analysis" perspective.[67] Using a somewhat eclectic approach, but drawing particularly on the work of Eugene Nida, he focusses on two passages in the Gospel for detailed analysis. In the course of this, he makes various observations regarding the narrator's "comments" or "remarks." For example, concerning 2:11, he states that this verse "takes the form of a parenthetical comment and thus reveals something of the narrator's view of the events he describes."[68] However, its use of distinction Johannine vocabulary and themes (signs, revelation, glory, belief) indicates that it is "an integral part of the Gospel as a whole."[69] He also observes that the use of "the introductory deictic adjective ταύτην directs the attention back to the preceding account and combines it into a single unit" and that this is a common feature of the "comments" in John.[70]

14 *Chapter 1*

In relating the use of such comments to the *point of view* of the narrator, Olsson is careful to observe, "The fiction of the last two centuries reveals a highly sophisticated use of the possibilities inherent in the narrative situation; in literary analysis the concept *point of view* has therefore been subjected to far-reaching theoretical discussion and further development."[71] He adopts a simple definition of point of view as "the position from which the narrative is presented to the reader" and he broadly concurs with David Wead that this is "a post resurrection point of view."[72]

In a chapter on "The Interpretative Character of the Text and the Paraclete," Olsson has a specific section on "The Remarks of the Narrator."[73] Here, he states that apart from Tenney's article, "there is no special work on these 'footnotes', although such an investigation could provide valuable information on the structure of the Gospel, on the evangelist's 'horizon' and on the situation(s) of the text."[74] He refers to 65 such "remarks," as well as noting that there are "a series of phrases and sentences where it is difficult to decide whether they should be regarded as remarks or as an integral part of the narrative."[75] He states that the remarks are found throughout the Gospel, "but are extremely rare in speech sections, which may be considered an indication that the speeches themselves act as interpretative comments by the evangelist."[76]

Like Tenney he places the "footnotes" into various categories: translations; identification of individuals; data of time, place and customs; summarizing; explanations of speeches and events; and longer theological expositions. He notes some of their grammatical characteristics, such as clauses with γάρ, those beginning with ταῦτα or τοῦτο, and those with ἦν as the verb.[77] He also notes certain common stylistic features, such as the use of the expressions "that the Scriptures/Jesus' words should be fulfilled"; "this he/they said"; "he/they knew/did not know"; and "that is, in translation."[78] He believes that the abundance of footnotes throughout the Gospel, their variety of function and lack of definite form, along with "the difficulty of delimiting remarks from the text," all indicate they are "an integrated part of the Gospel."[79] So, although these factors may indicate that "the Johannine text has a long prehistory, and that the notes were added on different occasions," Olsson is keener to stress that these factors are primarily "an indication that the Johannine text as whole has an interpretative character."[80]

Olsson completes his section on the remarks by looking more closely at two passages, 2:13–22, the cleansing of the Temple, and 12:12–16, the entry into Jerusalem, where the narrator's comments (2:21–22 and 12:16) speak of the disciples' understanding before and after Jesus' "hour" and bring to the fore the importance of remembering (through the agency of the Paraclete) and its application to "*the Jesus sayings, the Jesus events* and *the Scriptures*."[81]

This relates to his earlier discussion of the "post resurrection" point of view of the narrator.

Although Olsson does not provide the detailed investigation of the comments or footnotes which he suggests could provide valuable information on the Gospel's structure, the evangelist's "horizon," and the situation/s of the text, he does nevertheless raise these issues and, in particular, he stresses the integration of the comments into the text as a whole as part of its overall interpretative purpose, reflecting the distinctive point of view of the narrator.

## O'ROURKE (1979)

In an article published in *Novum Testamentum* in 1979, "Asides in the Gospel of John," John J. O'Rourke reconsiders Tenney's essay, alongside insights gleaned from the commentaries of Brown (1966, 1970), Bultmann (ET 1971), Lindars (1972), Morris (1971), Sanders and Mastin (1968), and Wickenhauser (3rd ed., 1961). O'Rourke's own definition of "asides" or "editorial comments" is: "The criterion for determining the presence of such asides is this: Their omission would not affect greatly the flow of the narrative, but is [*sic*] should be noted that some asides may be important for the achievement of an important goal of the evangelist."[82]

O'Rourke follows Tenney's system of classification, but rejects or reclassifies some of Tenney's examples and adds a number of his own, resulting in an extension of the number of asides from 59 to 109, although 18 of these are marked as "doubtful." Like Tenney, he sets out his results in a chart, while pointing out that there is some overlap in the categories.[83] He notes that there are no asides in chapters 15 to 17 ("which are entirely presented as the words of Our Lord") and that "there does appear some connection with the amount of narrative in a given chapter and the likelihood of the appearance of asides."[84] He provides a further chart which attempts to set out the number of "Asides per Verse" compared with the "Percentage of Narrative" for each chapter in which asides occur.[85] From his observation that the highest number of asides per verse is found in chapter 21, he concludes that this chapter "stands out from the rest of the Gospel, and this criterion could be indicative of another author at work."[86] However, he does concede that his "criterion of asides per verse has to be used cautiously, since the asides differ from one another at times considerably by their length."[87]

Finally, O'Rourke observes that although sources were used in the composition of the Gospel, it is "impossible to determine whether or not a given aside already existed as such in a source which was then taken over without change into the Gospel as we now have it."[88]

16                              *Chapter 1*

It seems to me that O'Rourke's article, with its close dependence on that of Tenney, does not add much to the discussion other than reopening and perhaps complicating the issue of redaction. He also introduces some basic statistical analysis, regarding the proportion of asides to the amount of narrative, but he acknowledges the limitations of this approach.

## CULPEPPER (1983)

Alan Culpepper's pioneering study of the Gospel, *Anatomy of the Fourth Gospel: A Study in Literary Design* (1983), which employs insights from literary-critical theory to complement historical, sociological, and theological approaches to the Gospel, does not have a specific chapter on "narrative asides," but they do form a major component of his chapter on "The Implied Reader."[89]

In a chapter on "Narrator and Point of View," Culpepper outlines the distinctions narrative critics make between the author, the implied author, and the narrator, but concludes that in the case of the Gospel, "there is no reason to suspect any difference in the ideological, spatial, temporal, or phraseological points of view" of these.[90] (This is quite different from the conflicting voices observed by Flowers in his 1921 essay, even if Flowers had no concept of narrative-critical categories.) However, Culpepper's focus is on the role of the narrator, which he describes as follows:

> In John, the narrator is the one who speaks in the prologue, tells the story, introduces the dialogue, provides explanations, translates terms, and tells us what various characters knew or did not know. In short, the narrator tells us what to think. Because he, or she, makes comments to the reader which interrupt the flow of the narrative, the narrator is *intrusive*.[91]

In reference to the narrator's "comments to the reader," Culpepper refers to the studies by Tenney and O'Rourke and observes that "the distinction between narration and commentary is a precarious one. Commentary can be suggested or implied in the course of the narration, and even 'intrusive' commentary is not always clearly distinguishable."[92] Nevertheless, in his chapter on "The Implied Reader," Culpepper uses the narrator's "explanatory comments" as the primary way of building up a picture of the intended audience of the Gospel. By analysing references to persons, places, languages, Judaism's beliefs and practices (including OT references), and events external to the narrative, he concludes that "a remarkably coherent and consistent picture of the intended reader emerges from the narrator's comments."[93] He states, "Analysis of the gospel's indications of its intended audience confirms, or at least complements, much of the recent research which has concluded that John was written for a particular community of believers."[94] However, Culpepper does concede that "a characterization of the narratee could be used in the debate over the actual, historical audience only on the assumptions that the narratee accurately represents the intended audience and that the author's judgments about his actual audience were also accurate."[95]

What Culpepper's work particularly contributes to the study of comments is an emphasis on reading the Gospel of John as a text in itself rather than a composite document ("the gospel as it stands rather than its sources")[96] and on the need to consider the roles of author/implied author/narrator in relationship to the roles of reader/implied reader/narratee. This will be discussed in more detail in chapter 5 of this book. For now, I note that Culpepper has made a number of assumptions, such as his categorization of the comments as "explanatory" and his reading of the narrative within a particular historical context, that of a Johannine community.

## VAN BELLE (1985)

The fullest examination of the asides is Gilbert Van Belle's monograph *Les Parenthèses dans L'Évangile de Jean: Aperçu Historique et Classification, Texte Grec de Jean* (1985), with a supplementary essay, "Les Parenthèses Johanniques," published in 1992, which will be considered later.[97] *Les Parenthèses* is a work of painstaking scholarship that deserves to be examined at some length. It is important to note that the term *parenthèses* can, as with the English translation "parentheses," be used both for sentences, clauses, or phrases which form a digression from the surrounding text and for the punctuation marks, brackets, that are used to indicate these.

The starting point for Van Belle's work is Johan Konings's Leuven University licentiate dissertation, "De bemerkingstof in het evangelie volgens Johannes" (The commentary in the Gospel according to John).[98] Konings's analysis of various categories and stylistic features leads him to stress the literary unity of the text, rather than the comments being secondary additions, a conclusion that is followed by Van Belle.[99] *Les Parenthèses* is divided into three parts: first, a survey of previous authors' examples of parentheses; second, an extensive cumulative list and categorization of these examples, as well as a survey of further authors; and third, an arrangement of the Greek text to indicate Van Belle's own selection of parentheses. Each of these three parts is considered here in more detail.

18                                    *Chapter 1*

In the first part of *Les Parenthèses,* Van Belle provides a survey of discussions of the parentheses over several centuries in editions of the Greek text, grammars of NT Greek, and commentaries and other studies.[100]

He compares eight editions of the Greek text in their use of punctuation (brackets and dashes or hyphens) to indicate parentheses in the Gospel, from the *Textus Receptus* (Stephanus's third edition of 1550) to Westcott and Hort's 1881 edition, noting that subsequent versions of the text employ almost exactly the same layout as Westcott and Hort, including those of Nestle up to the 25th edition (1963) and the UBS *The Greek New Testament* up to the third edition (1975).[101] He then sets out in a table instances of parentheses indicated in the eight editions from Stephanus to Westcott and Hort, alongside the use of such punctuation indicators in the Vulgate and the Revised Standard Version (second edition of 1971) translations.[102] The number of parentheses varies from 9 in Tischendorf's first edition of 1842 to 30 in Knapp's fifth edition of 1840.[103] There is a tendency for more recent editions to have fewer indications of parenthesis. Van Belle concludes:

> Ce tableau met en évidence une grande diversité dans le choix des passages mis entre parenthèses ou entre tirets dans le seul évangile de Jn. Quelle que soit leur manière de procéder à chacun, les éditions ont dû rencontrer au moins deux questions : où y a-t-il réellement parenthèse ? Et où l'emploi de signes particuliers (parenthèses ou tirets) est-il nécessaire pour la désigner? (This table is evidence of a great diversity in the choice of passages put between brackets or dashes just in the Gospel of John. Whatever their way of proceeding with each case, the editions have had to deal with at least two questions: where is there really a parenthesis? And where is it necessary to use particular signs (brackets or dashes) to indicate it?)[104]

Van Belle goes on to note that grammarians reproach editors for too much subjectivity in the choice of signs of parenthesis and that they, by contrast, seek to define the notion of parenthesis independently of the textual editions.[105] This introduces his examination of a number of works on Greek grammar from the 18th century to the first half of the 20th century: Adam Benedict Spitzner, *Commentatio philologica de parenthesi libris sacris Veteris et Novi Testamenti accommodata* (1773); George B. Winer, *Grammatik des neutestamentlichen Sprachidioms als sichere Grundlage der neutestamentlichen Exegese bearbeitet* (5th edition, 1844); Christian G. Wilke, *Die Neutestamentlichen Rhetorik, ein Seitenstück zur Grammatik des neutestamentlichen Sprachidioms* (1843) and *Die Hermeneutik des Neuen Testaments systematisch dargestellt* (1843–44); Friedrich Blass, *Grammatik des neutestamentlichen Griechisch* (1896), as well as subsequent editions

*Survey of Literature* 19

(Blass and Debrunner, 1913; Blass, Debrunner, and Rehkopf, 1976); Gunnar Rudberg, "Parentesen i Nya Testamentet" (1940).[106] He also refers to a short work by Eduard Schwyzer, published in 1939, *Die Parenthese im engern und im weitern Sinne*, which considers various aspects of the parenthesis in Greek and other literatures.[107]

From this examination, Van Belle concludes that, in grammatical terms, the parenthesis cannot simply be equated with a subordinate or appositional clause, rather it must be "une phrase indépendante grammaticalement des éléments entre lesquels elle s'insère, même si elle conserve avec eux un rapport logique" (a phrase grammatically independent from the elements between which it is inserted, even if it keeps a logical relationship with them).[108] So, it differs from anacoluthon in that, despite the interruption which it causes, it does not destroy the general order of a sentence.[109] Overall, his enquiry into the grammars shows that the notion of parenthesis is not very strongly established and it carries a range of meaning.[110] The number of parentheses considered in the grammars is more limited than those indicated in the Greek editions.

The third part of Van Belle's survey covers commentaries and other studies from Johann Albrecht Bengel, *Gnomon Novi Testamenti* (1742) to Birger Olsson, *Structure and Meaning in the Fourth Gospel* (1974).[111] In all, the works of 25 scholars are surveyed, which include the writings of various 18th- and 19th-century German scholars; the commentaries of Bernard, Bultmann (in considerable detail), Schnackenburg, and Brown; and the writings of Flowers, Garvie, Tenney, O'Rourke, and Olsson, which I have considered above. He also includes Abbott, *Johannine Grammar* (1906) in this section, although it would seem to belong more naturally to his section on the grammars. Somewhat disappointingly, Van Belle does not draw any overall conclusions from this survey.

In the second part of *Les Parenthèses Johanniques,* Van Belle provides a "cumulative list" of all the parentheses noted in the various texts, grammars, commentaries and other studies that he has surveyed (or is about to survey). These examples of parenthesis are classified into the three separate categories of content, grammar, and style. He then supplements his initial survey of editions, grammars, commentaries, and other studies with summaries of the works of other scholars who have related the parentheses to their interpretation of the Gospel. Finally, he provides a detailed analysis of John 4:9 as a case study. Each of these sections is considered here in more detail.

In his *Liste cumulative des parenthèses*, Van Belle records 700 instances with the aid of a somewhat elaborate coding system linked to the texts, grammars, commentaries, and other studies.[112] It must be noted that there is considerable overlap in this cumulative list. So, for example, one verse may

20                                    Chapter 1

be listed as a complete example or as part of a longer passage or else divided into various clauses.

Following his cumulative list, he sorts the instances of parenthesis into different categories. The first of these classifications is "according to contents," in which there are 17 categories:[113]

1. Translation of Hebrew or Aramaic words
2. Explanation of Jewish customs
3. Indication or description of persons
4. Indication or description of place
5. Indication or description of time
6. Explanation of the words of Jesus or another person
7. Explanation of the actions of Jesus or another person
8. Lack of understanding by the disciples or other persons
9. Belated understanding by the disciples
10. Fulfilment of Scripture or the words of Jesus
11. Reference to a passage which precedes or follows
12. Correction
13. Concluding note
14. Reflection inserted "after the event" in the narrative
15. Extended theological reflection
16. "Reference" to the author of the Gospel
17. Supernatural knowledge by Jesus

This is followed by 29 categories of grammatical classification arranged according to the use of particular particles and conjunctions, pronouns, and other syntactical elements, such as asyndeton, apposition, genitive absolute, ellipsis, and anacoluthon.[114]

In his third classification, "les caractéristiques stylistiques," he provides no fewer than 415 examples.[115] Here, he follows the method, order, and enumeration of the list published by Frans Neirynck in *Jean et les Synoptiques* (1979), which is itself an adaptation of that of Boismard and Lamouille (1977).[116] Quite what is the purpose of such an extensive list of stylistic features is not made clear.

Next, Van Belle examines the works of a number of 19th- and 20th-century scholars, who have related the parentheses to their interpretation of the Gospel. This can be seen as a supplement to his survey of commentaries and other studies in the first part of *Les Parenthèses*, and it is not altogether clear why he chose to separate the two surveys. The scholars in this section are divided into two broad groups: those who, following a literary-critical methodology,[117] divide the text into layers of composition and redaction and relate perceived parentheses to particular layers of this process; and those who,

*Survey of Literature* 21

seeking to defend the unity of the text, regard the parentheses as primarily an aspect of the author's style.

In the first group, Van Belle cites the works of 23 scholars, from Alexander Schwiezer (1841) to Craig Evans (1982). He notes that Schweizer attributes a number of parentheses to an *Überarbeiter* on the basis that they interrupt the thread of the narration, they exhibit a non-Johannine style, and/or their contents are opposed to the rest of the Gospel.[118] The attribution of parentheses to later redactors or interpolators is particularly noticeable in the exchange of ideas between Julius Wellhausen and Eduard Schwartz, following Schwartz's series of articles on the *Aporien im vierten Evangelium*, published at the University of Göttingen in 1907–1908.[119] Wellhausen's division of the text into a *Grundschrift* and later additions by a variety of editors, who are responsible for the majority of the parentheses, is taken up by later scholars such as Macgregor, who in his 1928 commentary, states, "Parenthetical comments occur which so clearly misunderstand the real point of the context as to prove that they are due to a later hand."[120] Fortna, in his 1970 work on the Signs Source, attributes parentheses both to this original source and to the Evangelist.[121] Becker, in his 1979–1981 commentary, attributes some parentheses to the Signs Source or the Passion Source, others to the Evangelist or to the *kirchliche Redaktion*, or else describes them as simply "glosses."[122]

In the opposing group are the works of 16 scholars, which Van Belle separates into those that have reacted against the tendency to attribute parentheses to an interpolator or redactor, ranging from Schwegler (1842) to Carson (1982), and (a subset) those that have adopted an approach drawn specifically from modern literary theory, namely Wead (1970), Culpepper (1983), and Nicholson (1983).[123] In these works that have reacted against redactional "literary-criticism," there is a stress on the unity of style throughout the text (with the possible exception of chapter 21) and a rejection of the idea that perceived contradictions between the main narrative and some asides must be the result of a later redaction. For example, Lagrange states in his 1924 article defending the Gospel's unity:

> S'il y avait vraiment dans le texte de Jo. des contradictions, et qu'on ne puisse les attribuer à un seul auteur, il serait, nous l'avons dit, très invraisembable [*sic*] de les attribuer à un éditeur-arrangeur, dont ce serait le métier de les faire disparaître, non de les introduire, et il faudrait en effet regarder les deux passages comme appartenant à deux documents. (If there really were contradictions in the text of John, that could not be attributed to a single author, it would be, we have said, very unlikely that they could be attributed to an editor-arranger, whose job would be to make them disappear, not introduce them, and it would be necessary in fact to regard the two passages as belonging to two documents.)[124]

22                                    *Chapter 1*

Ruckstuhl objects to Bultmann's use of "footnotes" as one of his criteria for a literary-critical reading of the text. Rather they should be interpreted as *Erläuterungen* or *Begründungen* that accord with the logical thinking of the author and which are characteristic of the style of the Gospel. Similarly, Wead, writing from a narrative perspective, argues for the complete assimilation of sources into the final text: "If the author has used sources, written or oral, they were so molded by him and he was so selective in his choice of material that he composed a work distinctly his own."[125]

In the conclusion to his survey of scholars who have related the parentheses to their interpretation of the Gospel, including the narrative approaches of Wead, Culpepper, and Nicholson, it is made clear that Van Belle is convinced by those who have argued for the essential unity of the text, that the use of parentheses is an important characteristic of the author's style, and that an examination of lexical and grammatical features supports the understanding that they are an integral part of the text rather than later additions.[126] Their essential function is one of guiding and teaching: "l'évangéliste aide ses lecteurs à bien comprendre les événements qu'il raconte et les idées qu'il enseigne" (the evangelist helps his readers to understand well the events he recounts and the ideas he teaches).[127] Indeed, they provide "une clef d'interprétation" (a key for interpretation) for a unified work, rather than "une clef de la critique littéraire" (a key for literary criticism).[128] Against the objection that they might reflect the *sociolect* of a Johannine School rather than the *idiolect* of an individual author, Van Belle argues that the parentheses include the principal themes of Johannine theology and have an essential role in the structure of the Gospel by looking backward and forward within the narrative. Moreover, following Ruckstuhl's lead, he suggests that they agree with the logical thinking of the author, "dont le progression de pensée est lente" (whose thought progression is slow), hence the need for corrections and cross-references with the aim of warning readers that they should understand properly what has been written.[129] It seems to me that perhaps only the last of these arguments actually supports the idea that the remarks are the work of a particular individual.

In the final chapter of this section, Van Belle provides a detailed analysis of the phrase οὐ γὰρ συγχρῶνται Ἰουδαῖοι Σαμαρίταις in John 4:9 as a test case to support his claim that the parentheses should be treated as an integral part of the text. This phrase is chosen as it is absent from two uncials, Codex Sinaiticus (original reading) and Codex D, and some early versions. However, Van Belle rejects, on stylistic and thematic grounds, the conviction of some commentators that this is a later addition to the text.[130] I will consider the phrase in more detail in chapter 4.

In the final part of *Les Parenthèses Johanniques*, the author sets out the Greek text of the Gospel (using the Nestle-Aland 26th edition) in such a way as to "rendre visible d'un seul coup d'oeil la construction de la phrase

*Survey of Literature* 23

at la structure de la péricope" (make obvious at a glance the construction of the sentence and the structure of the pericope).[131] He also indicates his own choice of parentheses by the use of brackets (or else hyphens/dashes to indicate "une parenthèse a l'intérieur d'une parenthèse" or the second part of a double parenthesis).[132] Regrettably, he does not provide a separate list or enumeration of his own choice of parentheses. By my reckoning, there are 176.[133]

Van Belle has provided the most substantial and extensively researched work on the asides in the Gospel of John. It has not been without its critics. For example, Steven Sheeley comments:

> One must give a great deal of credit to Van Belle for the meticulous and comprehensive nature of his work. His survey of the literature has rendered any similar undertaking obsolete. That Van Belle chose to restrict his inquiry into the parenthetical remarks in John to a survey, however, without following some of the avenues for understanding and interpretation that were opened by many of those whom he surveyed is disappointing.[134]

Charles Hedrick, in his review of the book, praises it as "a much needed history-of-research foundation for the study of 'parentheses,'" but criticizes the author for devoting "so little space . . . to his own critical analysis," for failing to give a "critical definition of the 'parentheses,'" and for not noting the "specific criteria by which he identifies them."[135]

However, despite such criticisms, *Les Parenthèses* not only provides a comprehensive survey of literature, but also brings to the fore a number of important issues for the study of asides in the Gospel. The first of these is the difficulty of establishing a clear definition of this feature, whether in terms of grammar, style, or content. Indeed, the sheer number of asides that commentators have suggested, alongside the range of associated grammatical and stylistic features, is evidence of this difficulty, Second, there is a strong challenge to the belief that the asides are clear indicators of levels of redaction in the text. Rather, on the grounds of both style and content, they can be viewed as an integral part of an individual author's work: "Il est difficile, semble-t-il, d'attribuer les parenthèses à une autre main qu'à celle d'évangéliste" (It seems that it is difficult to attribute the parentheses to another hand than that of the evangelist).[136] Third, Van Belle suggests that the primary function of the asides is that of guiding the reader to a correct understanding of the Gospel.

## BJERKELUND (1987)

In the monograph *Tauta Egeneto: Die Präzierungssätze im Johannesevangelium*, published in 1987, the Norwegian scholar Carl Bjerkelund examines

24                                    *Chapter 1*

a subset of comments which he labels *Präzierungssätze* (precision-making sentences/clauses).[137] He uses various terms for comments generally, including "Bemerkungen," "Randbemerkungen," "Notizen" and "Fußnoten," but it is primarily with the *Präzierungssätze* that he is concerned, and his contention is "daß man sich durch diese Sätze der Gedankenwelt des Johannesevangeliums nähern konnte" (that through these clauses one could approach the thought-world of the Gospel of John).[138]

*Tauta Egeneto* was mostly written before the publication of Van Belle's 1985 book, although Bjerkelund does briefly summarize it in a footnote.[139] In his opinion, the weakness of Van Belle's work is that he lists too many examples, which he believes to be partly the result of the scholars Van Belle surveys failing to draw a sharp distinction between parentheses that are a result of redaction and those that are integral to the text.[140] He considers in more detail the work of Tenney, O'Rourke, and Olsson.[141] Generally, he is critical of Tenney and O'Rourke for not providing formal principles for their selection and classification of asides. He is more favourably disposed towards Olsson's attempt to consider both form and function, while noting Olsson's admission that there is great variety of these. As Bjerkelund comments: "Wie wir sehen, bilden die Fußnoten bei Johannes ein ziemlich sperriges und unsystematisches wissenschaftliches Untersuchungsfeld. Ihre Vielfalt stellt eine schwierige Forschungsaufgabe dar." (As we see, the footnotes in John provide quite an unwieldy and unsystematic field for scholarship. Their variety presents a difficult task for research.)[142]

However, Bjerkelund believes that there is little point in restricting work on the footnotes simply to a discussion of their classification, rather it is better to focus on one particular group of footnotes for deeper investigation.[143] So, following Olsson's observation that a number of the comments in the Gospel begin with forms of the demonstrative pronoun (specifically ταῦτα or τοῦτο), Bjerkelund selects a group of these for closer scrutiny.[144] The 12 *Präzierungssätze* he examines are from 1:28; 2:11; 2:21–22; 4:54; 6:59; 7:39; 8:20: 10:6; 11:51; 12:16, 33, 41. (It should be noted that 2:21–22 is something of an odd one out in that it begins with ἐκεῖνος, referring to Jesus.) From the first of these sentences, 1:28, Ταῦτα ἐν Βηθανίᾳ ἐγένετο πέραν τοῦ Ἰορδάνου, ὅπου ἦν ὁ Ἰωάννης βαπτίζων, he derives the title *Tauta Egeneto* for his work and he uses it to define the *Präzierungssätze* as referring to previous pericopes, which are then treated with greater precision.[145] The purpose of these *Präzierungssätze* is to state where or when something happened and/ or to explain its significance.[146] For example, 1:28 provides the location and also clarifies the account of John the Baptist in 1:19–28: the author highlights the Baptist's public ministry and gives a unity to the whole pericope, from which some commentators regard the reference to the Pharisees in 1:24 as indicative of redaction.[147] Similarly, 2:11 confirms the location and explains

## Survey of Literature

the purpose of Jesus' actions at the wedding in Cana (2:1–10).[148] And so on. In some respects, Bjerkelund is carrying out a form critical analysis following in the footsteps of Dibelius and Bultmann.[149]

Before examining the *Präzierungssätze* and the pericopes to which they refer in more detail, Bjerkelund provides a chapter on comparisons from outside the New Testament, specifically in the works of Josephus and Philo and parts of the Samaritan literature. He sees the closest parallels in Josephus and the Samaritan literature where they comment on passages from the OT books, specifically the historical narratives.[150] Given the uncertainty of the dating of the Samaritan works he cites and the fact that they were written in Hebrew, Aramaic, or Arabic rather than Hellenistic Greek, these may not be the best parallels for Bjerkelund to employ.[151] Moreover, while he sees the comparisons with Josephus and the Samaritan literature as providing a broader foundation for his study, he, in fact, makes little use of these parallels in his subsequent thesis.

In a chapter on the challenge of the *Präzierungssätze* to traditional historical-critical analysis of the Gospel, Bjerkelund accepts that there are layers of composition in the Gospel. However, he stresses (as he does throughout his monograph) that the *Präzierungssätze* belong to one and the same layer of composition: they are the work of the Evangelist and not comments worked into the text by later redactors.[152]

From his detailed study of the *Präzierungssätze* and their corresponding pericopes, Bjerkelund draws a number of conclusions. First, the *Präzierungssätze* are distinguished from other comments in John, with their brief explanations of Jewish customs, people and place names, by their deliberate link to particular pericopes. Moreover, whatever complex source traditions lie behind these pericopes, the *Präzierungssätze* are comments on the whole pericopes to which they refer.[153] Second, the pericopes to which the *Präzierungssätze* refer have a certain "offizielle Prägung" (formal characteristic). That is, they share certain common features which contribute to the public witness to Jesus, rather than only dealing with his interactions with his disciples.[154] Third, following on from this, he argues that even if they occur in polemical sections of the Gospel, the specific pericopes he deals with are not polemical in nature, but rather they focus on the revelation of Jesus's lordship.[155] Fourth, the *Präzierungssätze* and the pericopes to which they relate have a major compositional function in the Gospel.[156] Fifth, the pericopes contain a marked concentration of the OT citations occurring in the first part of the Gospel.[157] He finishes by saying, "Unsere Überzeugung, daß die P-Sätze keine unwichtigen Fußnoten sind, hat sich verstärkt. Die Sätze sind Beitrag einer Seite, die entscheidenden Einfluß auf das Evangelium hatte, nicht nur formal sondern auch theologisch." (Our conviction that the *Präzierungssätze* are not unimportant footnotes

26                                    *Chapter 1*

has strengthened. The sentences are contributed by a source which had a crucial influence on the Gospel, not just from the point of view of form but also theologically.)[158]

In addition to these conclusions, Bjerkelund provides a chapter on the relationship of the *Präzierungssätze* to the "Erfüllungszitaten" (fulfilment quotations) that are found in John's passion narrative and which relate the OT scriptures to the ministry of Jesus.[159]

Finally, he makes a number of additional remarks. First, he urges that greater attention be given to the asides generally, especially as they mark important turning points in the narrative, and that particular attention should be given to the *Präzierungssätze*, for, if his thesis that they belong to one compositional layer in the Gospel is correct, they have a major structural function in the interpretation of the text.[160] Second, while he accepts that there is a Johannine community whose circumstances are reflected in the origin and development of the Gospel and he references J. L. Martyn's *History and Theology in the Fourth Gospel* (1968) with regard to this, he believes that the work of the redactor (the Evangelist) who composed the *Präzierungssätze* is of greater importance than the community and its milieu.[161] Third, he recognizes that there are long chains of thought (*lange Gedankenketten*) running through the Gospel which reflect its theological motives and he regards his analysis of the *Präzierungssätze* as contributing to an understanding of these. However, he also observes that the Evangelist is concerned for the dating and location of concrete historical events rather than just making abstract connections (*gedanklichen Zusammenhänge*).[162] Fourth, regarding the question of the extent of symbolism and double meaning in the Gospel, Bjerkelund notes the significance of geographical names and notes. However, he believes that geographical references in the *Präzierungssätze* must be interpreted on an entirely literal basis owing to the clear boundaries between narrative and asides in the Gospel.[163] Fifth, he uses the example of the precision-making character of the aside in John 10:6, in the middle of the parables of the good shepherd, as a way of highlighting how John's method differs from that of the Synoptics and the way they present Jesus' parables.[164] Finally, he sees common ground both structurally and theologically between the *Präzierungssätze*, found in the first part of the Gospel, and the *Reflexionszitate* (equivalent to *Erfüllungszitaten*) in the second part.[165]

I make two main observations on Bjerkelund's detailed study. First, in order to draw a relationship between form and function in the asides, he has concentrated on a particular group, the *Präzierungssätze*, a subset of the varied and extensive footnotes found in the Gospel, which he regards as central to the author's purpose. While not rejecting the notion of a process of redaction in the Gospel, he repeatedly insists that these belong to one compositional layer in the Gospel and therefore have a major structural function in

*Survey of Literature* 27

the interpretation of the text. Second, he has identified his subset of footnotes on a grammatical basis—that is, the use of the demonstrative pronoun. However, somewhat surprisingly, he makes almost no mention of the "first ending" of the Gospel (20:31), with its ταῦτα demonstrative pronoun (ταῦτα δὲ γέγραπται ἵνα πιστεύ[σ]ητε ὅτι . . .), where a parallel could be drawn between Bjerkelund's 12 *Präzierungssätze* and their corresponding pericopes and this ending's relation to the rest of the Gospel. Perhaps he makes too much of his division of the Gospel into a first part (chapters 1–12), which contains the *Präzierungssätze*, and a second part (chapters 13–21), which contains the "fulfilment citations."

Overall, I suggest that the value of Bjerkelund's analysis is that it sees at least some of the asides as integral to the author's purpose and having a major interpretative function. However, his argument about the tight relationship between these asides and particular pericopes is not entirely convincing and he is over-optimistic in saying, "die Grenzen zwischen dem erzählten Stoff und den Randbemerkungen im Joh klar und scharf sind" (the boundaries between the narrative material and the asides in John are clear and sharp).[166]


## LOMBARD (1987)

A revised version of Herman A. Lombard's inaugural lecture as Professor of New Testament Studies at the Faculty of Theology in the University of South Africa was published in *Hervormde Teologiese Studies* in 1987 as "John's Gospel and the Johannine church: A mirror of events within a text or/and a window on events within a church." In this article, Lombard analyses "narrator's commentary (footnotes, asides)" from the perspectives of both the historico-critical method and literary criticism and concludes that "a referential correlation exists between the worlds within and outside the text."[167] Lombard's study is important for our thesis in that he appears to be the first scholar to make a distinction between a purely "literary" approach to analysing narrative comments and one that attempts to use them to determine the historical realities that lie behind the text, in particular what they might suggest about a "Johannine church." He states, "The ultimate methodological issue at stake is whether one should use the text of JG as a WINDOW through which a church is perceived outside the text, or as a MIRROR in which a church is observed within the world of the text of JG."[168]

Lombard lists 203 footnotes in the same 10 categories proposed by Tenney, although he does not explain "the perspective of textpragmatics and communication," which guides his process of selection.[169] In his analysis and interpretation, his focus is on "what indications these footnotes provide for

28                                Chapter 1

identifying the character of a Johannine church within the text."[170] Much of
Lombard's article is taken up with discussion of the competing hermeneutical
methodologies he deals with, and he concludes that the footnotes can provide
insight into both the Johannine church as a literary construct for its implied
readers and, for its real readers, the actual church that lies behind the text.[171]
He argues that religio-historical texts, such as the Gospel of John, "make an
appeal to the intertextual and extratextual readers."[172] To this, he adds the
comment: "Religious texts are by no means a-contextual; neither are they
neutral or incompetent. Being a religious text, JG had a relevant intentionality
towards the implied and real readers of the first century."[173]

Referring to the work of Tenney, O'Rourke, and Culpepper, Lombard
moves towards a definition of the footnotes by stating, "This commentary
was originally made by the narrator, every time he purposely interrupted
the flow of the narrative to change to a different mode or tense."[174] This narrator "figures as a well-informed, omniscient and omnipresent personality
who informs the reader of concealed and profound issues—a kind of inside
informer!"[175] However, the footnotes not only provide extra information for
the reader, they "also function as bearers of the plot-development in the narrative and draw the reader's attention to some of the dramatic moments of
the narrated events."[176]

Lombard's study is helpful for raising the issue of whether the asides can
provide indications of the historical context of the Gospel, although here
more is assumed than argued for, and he is also aware of their essentially
narrative function as markers of significant moments in the story.


## HEDRICK (1990)

In an essay published in 1990, Charles W. Hedrick summarizes the work
of Garvie, Tenney, O'Rourke, Culpepper, and Van Belle, as well as briefly
mentioning Bjerkelund, and he sets out a table of the first four authors' asides
alongside his own selection.[177] He asserts that the author of John "has a more
sophisticated compositional technique" than the synoptic writers and that he
"frequently resorts to a particular narrative device to control the story so as
to insure that the reader gains a 'proper' understanding of it."[178] He notes that
this device has been labelled explanatory comments, asides, footnotes, and
parentheses, and he provides his own definition, which he regards as a "refining" of Tenney's definition: "It is comprised of intrusive word(s), sentence(s),
or paragraph(s) of explanatory or clarifying commentary included in the narrative as direct address to the reader. In general, it is characterized by 'telling'
about the story as opposed to the 'showing' of the story."[179]

*Survey of Literature*                29

Hedrick states that this narrative feature is common in ancient literature and he lists a number of Greek and Roman novels, without actually providing examples from them.[180] He refers to the rhetorical categories of *parenthesis, apostrophe, digression,* and *amplification* that are described in the writings of Aristotle, Cicero, and Quintilian.[181] He further notes that "explanatory 'asides'" are a common feature of the synoptic gospels and Acts.[182]

Hedrick's definition proposes a distinction between *telling* and *showing* in John, whereby intrusions into the narrative can be seen as temporarily suspending the dramatic showing of the story. At their "most extreme" these intrusions can be labelled *hermeneiai* (ἑρμηνεία), a term Hedrick derives from the use of the verb ἑρμηνεύω (interpret, explain) and its cognates in 1:38, 41, 42; 9:7.[183] He does, however, concede that some of these explanations are simply required "for the clarity of the 'showing'" (giving 2:1 as an example) and, hence, "are not *digressions* in a narrow sense; they are novelistic features that belong properly to the showing of the story."[184] Indeed, there does seem to be a degree of ambiguity in Hedrick's definition of the asides as solely relating to a distinction between *telling* and *showing*, for after setting out his own list of 121 asides in 15 categories, he goes on to make a further distinction between explanations that "simply clarify aspects of the story being shown in the dramatic presentation, and hence function *inside* the dramatic presentation" and those that "take on a much greater distance from the story being shown."[185] The focus in the rest of his essay is on the latter type of *hermeneiai*, which he sees as belonging to "a second narrative world," stating, "This second more distant narrative voice seems much more self-conscious as a personality vis-à-vis that voice that merely intensifies the visualization of the dramatic presentation of the story."[186]

Through three case studies, examining 2:21–22; 4:2; and 7:21–22 and their co-texts, and drawing on modern literary-critical theory's notions of the *implied author* and the *unreliable narrator*, Hedrick proposes that there is a divergence between the author of the asides and the narrator of the main narrative: "Is it not possible that the (implied) author's 'heavy-handed' use of intrusive commentary is due to the fact that the story that the principal narrator shows in the Gospel of John actually subverts the (implied) author's (later) understanding of the story?"[187]

He sees parallels for the functioning of two such contradictory voices in both modern and ancient texts, giving the examples of Graham Greene, *The Power and the Glory*; Achilles Tatius, *Clitophon and Leucippe*; and Ezra-Nehemiah.[188]

Although Hedrick rejects critical scholarship's proposed later redaction of the text, his interest is in the two conflicting voices in the Gospel, and it seems clear that his own sympathy lies with the original narrator of the story of Jesus and not the author of the *hermeneiai* with their misplaced interpretations of this story.

30                                    Chapter 1

Overall, Hedrick's essay is helpful for its attempt at definition, although there is a measure of ambiguity in this; for its reference to the use of explanatory comments in other Graeco-Roman literature; and for its use of insights from literary theory, such as the distinction between *telling* and *showing* and the concept of an *unreliable narrator* (or, in this case, an unreliable author), insights which will be considered in more detail in chapter 5.


## NEIRYNCK (1991)

Frans Neirynck was for many years Professor of New Testament Exegesis at Leuven, where Van Belle was his assistant in the 1970s and 1980s.[189] In some brief notes intended as a supplement to Van Belle, *Les Parenthèses*, Neirynck refers to a number of commentaries, grammars, monographs, and essays, including those of Bjerkelund (1987) and Hedrick (1990).[190] He draws particular attention to the suggestion by Abbott (1906) that the pluperfect tense in John "often expresses a parenthesis, or a statement out of its chronological place, of the nature of an after-thought."[191] He then proceeds to look at John 18:24: ἀπέστειλεν οὖν αὐτὸν ὁ Ἄννας δεδεμένον πρὸς Καϊάφαν τὸν ἀρχιερέα (Annas then sent him bound to Caiaphas the high priest: RSV), pointing out that the aorist ἀπέστειλεν was understood by some earlier scholars (16th to 19th century) to function as a pluperfect and is translated thus in the AV ("Now Annas *had sent* him . . ."), with the implication that this verse should be considered a parenthetical remark. Neirynck's brief notes, characterized by his customary depth of knowledge, are useful in highlighting possible grammatical indications of parentheses.


## VAN BELLE (1992)

Appropriately in a Festschrift for his mentor, Frans Neirynck, Van Belle provides his own update, "Les Parenthèses Johanniques," in which he responds to works published since *Les Parenthèses* (1985), including a number of reviews of the book. The essay is divided into two main sections.

In the first section, "Les parenthèses et la narratologie," Van Belle focuses on those who have studied "le commentaire explicite" in John. He provides outlines of the articles by Lombard and Hedrick discussed above.[192] He briefly notes the observations by Jeffrey Lloyd Staley (1988) on the rhetorical function of the translation asides in John 1:38, 41, 42 in underlining of the reliability and intermediary role of the narrator.[193] He also refers to the commentary by the Dutch scholar Sjef van Tilborg (1988) and an article by him on communicative processes in John published in *Neotestamentica*

## Survey of Literature                                              31

(1989).[194] In his commentary, van Tilborg makes reference to the "auctoriële opmerkingen" (authorial comments) as one of the three levels of discourse which the author uses to communicate with the reader. Van Belle rejects van Tilborg's criticism of his own work that it makes no reference to any literary theory.[195] Van Belle also provides a fuller overview of an unpublished doctoral thesis by Chuck Pourciau on "The Use of Explicit Commentary in the Gospels of Luke and John" (1990).[196] From his survey of these five writers, Van Belle notes that the narrator is very "intrusive" throughout the Gospel of John (Pourciau) and that through the asides the narrator addresses the implied reader directly (van Tilborg).[197] He concludes, "Cela signifie que le procédé littéraire des parenthèses est d'une grande importance pour l'interprétation de l'évangile de Jn" (This indicates that the literary device of the parentheses is very important for the interpretation of the Gospel of John).[198] He expands on this by noting that the parentheses provide information on the plot and theological themes of the Gospel, as well as making the account "plus vivant et plus concret."[199] Moreover, the studies discussed contribute to his conviction that the Gospel can be regarded as a literary unity.[200]

In the second section, "Les parenthèses et le style johannique," Van Belle again takes up a defence of the Gospel's unity in the face of objections from literary critical scholars such as Robert Fortna.[201] He then considers the definition and classification of parentheses. Regarding definition, he notes the criticism of several reviewers of *Les Parenthèses* that he failed to provide a clear definition and he responds by reviewing his methodology of examining the editions of the text, grammars, commentaries, and other studies. In effect, Van Belle's method is inductive: he starts with the data of existing scholarship and he acknowledges that "la notion de parenthèse n'est pas très fermement établie et qu'elle est susceptible d'une extension plus ou moins large" (the concept of parenthesis is not very firmly established and it is liable to be extended more or less).[202] Indeed, he concludes that "la notion même de 'parenthèse' reste floue et qu'au fond la parenthèse est une question d'exégèse" (the very concept of "parenthesis" remains vague and basically the parenthesis is a question of exegesis).[203]

He then updates his survey of relevant literature with a look at recent editions of the Greek text and English translations up to the New Revised Standard Version (1990) and observations on grammatical issues by Quacquarelli (1986), Hedrick (1990), Thielman (1991), and Neirynck (1992).[204] I have referred already to the essays by Hedrick and Neirynck. It is worth adding that in his review of *Les Parenthèses*, Antonio Quacquarelli accuses Van Belle of having given insufficient attention to the nature of ancient rhetoric and he emphasizes its oral characteristics, so that parentheses can only be distinguished by the modulation of the voice or, from the reader's perspective, the rhythm of the prose.[205] Thielman, in an essay on the literary

32                                    *Chapter 1*

characteristics of religious discourse in antiquity, refers to the ambiguities, clarifications, variations, and apparent contradictions in the Gospel, which he suggests, "shroud the document with a mystery which was entirely appropriate to religious writing in the ancient world."[206]

In his deliberations on the characteristic style of John, Van Belle considers the work of Ruckstuhl and Bjerkelund, while also noting the contributions of a number of other writers.[207] He highlights Ruckstuhl's 1987 article, "Zur Antithese Idiolekt-Soziolekt im johanneischen Schrifttum," which draws on Culpepper and Van Belle's own work to support the literary unity of the Gospel.[208] He then gives particular attention to the monograph by Bjerkelund discussed above, noting particularly Bjerkelund's refusal to attribute the Johannine *Präzierungssätze* to different compositional layers within the Gospel.[209] In summary, Van Belle notes, "plusieurs auteurs sont d'avis que 'les parenthèses' font partie du style même de l'évangéliste" (several authors are of the opinion that "the parentheses" are part of the evangelist's actual style).[210]

In his comments on classification, Van Belle recaps his method of organizing the parentheses into the three categories of contents, grammar, and style and he responds to a number of criticisms of his approach.[211]

In a brief final section, he gives a few notes on the phrase οὐ γὰρ συγχρῶνται Ἰουδαῖοι Σαμαρίταις in John 4:9, which was used as a case study in *Les Parenthèses*. He observes that the majority of recent authors regard it as a genuine parenthesis by the narrator/author rather than a gloss or later redaction.[212]

Overall, this update by Van Belle and his response to various criticisms help consolidate his belief that the parentheses are integral to the text and part of the author's overall strategy of guiding the reader, although he still concedes that a formal definition is problematic.


## SHEELEY (1992)

Various studies of asides in the Gospel of John are considered in a work whose focus is on other NT writings, Steven Sheeley, *Narrative Asides in Luke-Acts*, a reworking of his doctoral thesis supervised by Culpepper and published in 1992.[213] In addition to Culpepper, Sheeley acknowledges the specific influence of Hedrick's work on his own thesis, although he is critical of Hedrick's sharp dichotomy between the reliable narrator of authentic tradition and the unreliable commentator correcting the narrative through asides.[214]

In his introductory chapter, Sheeley includes a summary of earlier work on the Gospel of John. He refers to Tenney's seminal contribution with its emphasis on criteria and categories and O'Rourke's contribution in the same vein.[215] He then deals with the introduction of insights from modern literary criticism in the writings of Nicholson, Culpepper, and Hedrick, while also providing an overview of Van Belle's *Les Parenthèses*, although, as noted earlier, he is disappointed with Van Belle's perceived lack of conclusions.[216]

More than any previous NT scholar, Sheeley spends time considering the definition and function of narrative asides. He draws on insights from both ancient rhetoricians (specifically Quintilian) and modern literary critics (Booth, Genette, Chatman, Rimmon-Kenan) in order to develop his own conclusions.[217] From Quintilian, he derives three figures of speech used in the description of ancient rhetoric which relate to narrative asides. These are:

| | |
|---|---|
| *Parenthesis*: | "the interruption of the continuous flow of our language by the insertion of some remark"; |
| *Apostrophe*: | "the act of turning aside from addressing the judge in the courtroom to address some other person"; |
| *Parekbasis* (digression): | "interrupting the logical presentation of one's case in order to deal with a related theme."[218] |

From modern literary critics, who are more concerned with the function of asides than their definition, he derives a focus on *narrative voice*. Here, Sheeley states that the issues of concern are the "presence or perceptibility of the narrator in the text" and the question of "narrative levels": how much does the narrator intrude into the narrative in order to attract the reader's attention.[219] These issues seem to me to be essentially the same.

On the basis of Quintilian's definitions and the narratologists' exploration of the function of the narrative voice, Sheeley offers his own definition:

> Narrative asides may be defined as parenthetical remarks addressed directly to the reader which interrupt the logical progression of the story, establishing a relationship between the narrator and the narratee which exists outside the story being narrated. They provide commentary on the act of telling the story or on some aspect of the story itself. They include such things as self-conscious narration, prologues, postscripts and appeals to the reader.[220]

He rejects the idea that asides can be determined on grammatical grounds, although "the use of a vocative and the presence of second person address without a dramatized narratee may indicate the existence of a narrative aside."[221]

He believes that the asides can serve a number of different functions and he provides a taxonomy in four broad categories, which are split into various sub-categories:

34                                    *Chapter 1*

1. "Material which is necessary for the reader to understand the story." That is: explanations of action or speech; the introduction of a setting or character; the translation of unfamiliar terms; the providing of the story's context; commentary on the story and characters; the explanation of customs foreign to the reader.
2. "General information for the reader." This is not necessary for the reader's understanding of the story, but can include information of interest such as "etiologies, moral and philosophical discourses, aphorisms, comments on human nature, comments on nature itself, and general human customs."
3. Asides "which provide an inside view into the minds and thoughts of a character."
4. "Self-conscious narration," including "asides which comment on the narrator's relation to the story, the narrator's relation to the reader, or the reader's relation to the story."[222]

Sheeley's monograph is particularly noticeable for the parallels which he draws with contemporaneous Graeco-Roman literature.[223] In his second chapter, he examines the use of asides in 11 texts drawn from the genres of romance (novel), historiography, and biography from the period 100 BC/BCE to AD/CE 250. The texts he uses are:

Romances:    Longus, *Daphis and Chloe*; Apuleius, *The Golden Ass*; Achilles Tatius, *Leucippe and Clitophon*.
Histories:    1 Maccabees; 2 Maccabees; Josephus, *Jewish War*; Suetonius, *Lives*; Tacitus, *Annals*.
Biographies:  Philostratus, *Life of Apollonius*; Philo, *Life of Moses*; Lucian, *Demonax*.

In his survey of complete texts (for the romances) or more limited selections (for the longer histories and biographies), Sheeley applies his definition and taxonomy of asides, leading him to a number of broad conclusions, which are: (i) that explanatory asides to help the reader understand the story are used more extensively in the romances and histories than in the biographies; (ii) that there is more use of asides to provide general information in the biographies, perhaps "due to the tendency of biography toward entertainment or edification"; (iii) that there is extremely limited use of asides to provide "inside views" in all three genres; and (iv) that although self-conscious narration is found in all three genres, it is a particular feature of the biographies and some of the histories.[224] However, he qualifies these conclusions by emphasizing, "In order to characterize the three genres of ancient narratives based on their use of narrative asides one must be careful to paint in very

Survey of Literature

large strokes, keeping in mind the fact that the narrators show remarkably individual characteristics, no matter what the genre."[225]

This is followed, in chapters 3 and 4, by his overview of asides in the Gospel of Luke and Acts and a consideration of their function in relation to the plot, narrator, and audience of these writings. Regarding the Gospel of Luke, Sheeley lists 23 asides and states, "Most of the asides are used to provide commentary or information which the reader finds necessary in order to interpret the story in the way in which the narrator desires it to be interpreted."[226] So, the emphasis is on explanatory asides. He sees self-conscious narration as limited to the Prologue (Luke 1:1–4) and three other instances (2:22–23; 5:24; 14:35). Overall, the function of the asides in both Luke and Acts is to impact on the thematic development of the plot, through their occurrence at points of significance; to reinforce and affirm the authority and reliability of the narrators, particularly in the "prefaces" of these two writings; and to bring to the fore the presence of the narrator and consequently remind the reader that a story is being told; and, perhaps, above all, "to guide the readers into the correct interpretation of events."[227]

In his general conclusions regarding Luke, Acts and contemporaneous Graeco-Roman literature, Sheeley stresses that although his study revealed a certain correlation between particular categories of aside and the genre of texts, there was also considerable fluidity, so that "the differences between narrators within the same genre suggested that much of a narrator's use of asides was dependent on his or her personality and approach to the story rather than any generic constraints."[228]

Sheeley's monograph offers a clear, restrained, and readable application of aspects of narrative theory to an overview of the function of asides in two NT texts. His taxonomy is helpful in adopting the four broad categories of necessary explanatory information, information of general interest, inside views, and self-conscious narration, which are then subdivided as necessary in the actual examination of texts. This seems to me of more value than the longer lists of categories in Tenney and Van Belle, which are not related to overall function. In addition, Sheeley's systematic comparative methodology, which draws on a range of contemporaneous genres, is important in drawing attention to the variety of ways in which a narrator can make use of asides in relation to the overall purpose of a text.

## THATCHER (1994)

In a brief and breezy article published in *Bibliotecha Sacra*, 34 years after Tenney's article in the same journal, Tom Thatcher looks at the categorizations

36 *Chapter 1*

used by Tenney and O'Rourke and argues that their "broad, mixed categories are too indistinct to be helpful."[229] He also states, "Tenney's concept of a 'footnote' or 'aside' is vague," and he is critical of Tenney's combining of "function" with "formal features."[230] He is, for example, critical of Tenney's category of "theological notes," saying, "What makes narrative material 'theological'?"[231] So, regarding definition, Thatcher employs Wayne Booth's "acclaimed distinction between telling and showing" to state that asides "are always what the author tells."[232] In place of the perceived inadequate labelling used by Tenney and O'Rourke, Thatcher proposes a categorization of asides that is based on their function in the text.[233] Like Sheeley, he suggests four broad functional categories, which are then subdivided on the basis of content. Thatcher's categories are:

1. *Staging.* That is, explaining the physical context in which an event occurs, with reference to space, time, "objects available for use," or climate. The "objects available for use" are the stone water jars at the wedding at Cana (2:6); Simon Peter's sword (18:10); and the jar of sour wine at the crucifixion (19:29), but it is hard to know what justification there is for this particular choice of objects or how they fit into the "staging" of the narrative. I also note that Thatcher qualifies his space and time sub-categories by choosing to disregard places which are the objects of verbs of motion and also "statements of general sequence."[234]
2. *Defining.* This is used for translations and also for "character labels," which "establish identity or personal qualities, pointing out the significance of an individual or explaining his or her behavior."[235] These labels can be either "preliminary," to introduce a character, or "reminiscent," to reintroduce a character who had already appeared, an example being the labelling of Judas as the betrayer (6:71; 12:4; 13:2).[236]
3. *Explaining discourse.* This "may include the reason . . . for what a speaker said or its significance," such as refusing to speak openly about Jesus for fear of "the Jews" or "the Pharisees" (7:13; 9:22; 12:42).[237]
4. *Explaining actions.* Again this may include either the reason for an action or its significance.[238] In the case of both *explaining discourse* and *explaining actions*, Thatcher does concede that "significance" is a difficult sub-category to apply and it may reach across his other main categories, such as *staging*.[239]

Thatcher then provides a table of 191 asides listed in these four broad categories and sub-categories. He also mentions two instances in which Jesus' inner emotions are revealed (11:33, 38), but he is unclear about their primary function, so they are not included in his table.

*Survey of Literature* 37

This is an article written with confidence and, as with Sheeley, it may well be beneficial to assign asides to broad functional categories. However, it would have helped if Thatcher had provided more reasons for his definition and categories, other than simply stating, "Since Tenney's essay and O'Rourke's revision, narrative criticism has further specified the nature and value of asides" and then making reference solely to Booth's telling-showing distinction.[240]

## LEE (2002)

Dal Lee's *The Narrative Asides in the Book of Revelation* is a revision of his doctoral thesis, supervised by David Aune at Chicago Theological Seminary.[241] Like Sheeley's monograph, it provides an overview of studies of asides in the Gospel of John, although focussed on another NT writing. Specifically, Lee looks at the writings of Tenney, O'Rourke, Van Belle, and Hedrick, as well as Sheeley on Luke-Acts.[242]

Lee attempts to give precision to the definition and classification of narrative asides, although he acknowledges that this is not an easy task.[243] Using insights from poetics, drama criticism, and film theory, he constructs a methodology which sees asides as interventions by the (implied) author to be distinguished from the rest of the text which belongs to the narrator.[244] These asides "can be parenthesized, not because they can be omitted or unimportant [*sic*] but because the continuous narrative act is temporarily stopped for authorial intervention"; they are also "often explanatory and supplementary to the main line of the text"; and they are frequently indicated by "an abrupt change of tense, verb form . . . , mood, words . . . and point of view."[245]

Of particular interest is Lee's comparison of asides to such devices as the stage whisper and the monologue in plays or the use of a "voice-over" in films.[246]

## BAUCKHAM (2007)

In an essay on "Historiographical Characteristics of the Gospel of John," published in 2007, Richard Bauckham includes a section on "Narrative Asides (or Parentheses)."[247] Bauckham accepts the theses of Richard Burridge and Dirk Frickenschmidt that the Gospels are historiographical biographies rather than *sui generis*.[248] He challenges the dominant scholarly view that the Gospel of John is theology rather than history by highlighting the various features that it shares in common with Graeco-Roman historiography. In addition to narrative asides, these features are: a concern for precise

38                                      *Chapter 1*

topography and chronology, a judicious selectivity in the choice of material, eyewitness testimony, and the use of appropriately constructed discourses and dialogues.[249] He concludes, "The evidence we have examined in this study strongly suggests that to its contemporaries the Gospel of John would have looked considerably more like historiography than the Synoptic Gospels would."[250]

In his section on narrative asides, Bauckham draws on the work of O'Rourke, Culpepper, Van Belle, Hedrick, and Sheeley. He follows Sheeley in defining narrative asides as "intrusions of the narrator's voice into the narrative, commenting on the story or telling about the story rather than telling the story."[251] Using the lists found in Hedrick's 1990 article, he states that the asides in the Gospel "are very numerous, and highly characteristic of John."[252] They are used for a broad range of purposes, such as:

> to indicate the location or time of an event, to translate Hebrew or Aramaic words, to explain Jewish customs, to cite Old Testament passages, to clarify the inner thoughts, motivations, and feelings of characters, to explain what the words of Jesus or another character mean, and to comment on the significance of events, especially with the benefit of a perspective later than that of the characters in the narrative.[253]

Bauckham asserts, "Such parentheses, used for broadly the same range of purposes, are common in Greco-Roman historiography and biography."[254] However, the examples he gives are restricted to referencing Sheeley and Bjerkelund, and he wonders if it is "a symptom of the often isolated character of Johannine scholarship that there has been so little comparison of the functions of narrative asides in John with those in other ancient narrative literature."[255] Nonetheless, he suggests that "the frequency and variety of the asides in John's Gospel align it more closely than the Synoptic Gospels with Greco-Roman historiography."[256]

It seems to me that Bauckham's summary of narrative asides in John is of particular value in drawing attention to the need for further comparative study on asides.

## KÖSTENBERGER (2009)

In *A Theology of John's Gospel and Letters*, Andreas J. Köstenberger has a section on "Johannine Literary Devices," which includes an overview of "Narrative 'Asides.'"[257] Köstenberger cites the studies by Tenney, O'Rourke, Van Belle, Hedrick, Thatcher, and Bauckham, as well as referring to a list by the 19th-century German scholar Karl August Credner in his *Einleitung in das Neue Testament*.[258]

*Survey of Literature* 39

He provides the text of 80 asides, plus references to other examples, in 12 categories. I have noted the number of asides in each category:

1. Translations of Aramaic or Hebrew terms (8)
2. Explanations of Palestinian topography (3)
3. Explanations of Jewish customs (5)
4. References to Jesus' supernatural insight or foreknowledge of events or to God's providential ordering of events (9)
5. References to characters or events mentioned earlier in the narrative (11)
6. References to the fulfilment of scripture or of Jesus' words (6)
7. References to a failure to understand (11)
8. Clarifications of the meaning of statements made by Jesus or others (14)
9. Statements "in relation to the Gospel tradition" (4) (That is, material in the Synoptic Gospels or the "tradition" associated with them.)
10. Numbering of events in the narrative (2)
11. Extended commentary (3:16–21, 31–36) (2)
12. Other clarifying or explanatory statements (5)

He observes that while narrative asides are found in the other gospels, they are particularly frequent in John and they display a considerable amount of variety.[259] In terms of their overall function, he states, "they enable the narrator to steer his readers to his desired conclusion."[260] He expands on this by saying, "The plethora of Johannine 'asides' thus fulfill an important narratological function in facilitating an informed reading of the gospel and preventing the reader from being sidelined because of missing data required for a successful decoding of the narrative."[261]

He also notes that "several of the Johannine asides (including several back references) enhance the cohesiveness of the narrative and constitute it as a closely interwoven textual fabric."[262] For example, he picks up on Culpepper's observation of how significant terms related to Jesus' death ("the hour," "glorify," "Spirit/spirit," "put out of the synagogue") used in the asides, are taken up again in the Farewell Discourse.[263]

Since Köstenberger's work, interest in the asides seems to have waned somewhat in Johannine scholarship, although examples continue to be noted in the many commentaries being published.

## GRAMMARS: AN UPDATE TO VAN BELLE

I have already noted Van Belle's comments regarding the grammarians' criticism of the editors of the Greek New Testament for showing too much

40                                    *Chapter 1*

subjectivity in their choice of indications of parenthesis.[264] In this section, I provide a brief supplement to Van Belle's survey of grammars.

## Robertson (1919)

Van Belle does not summarize the work of A. T. Robertson (1863–1934), although he does quote from it on one occasion: "At bottom the parenthesis in the text is a matter of exegesis."[265] Robertson provides some brief notes in his grammar in a section entitled "The Parenthesis."[266] He observes that a parenthetical clause, "inserted in the midst of the sentence without proper syntactical connection, is quite common in the N.T."; that "the term is somewhat loosely employed applied to clauses that really do not interrupt the flow of thought"; and that "certainly not every explanatory remark is to be regarded as parenthetical."[267] He cites the γάρ clauses in John 7:39 and 9:30 as examples of explanatory remarks that are not parenthetical.[268] However, the relative clauses in John 1:38 and 41, which provide interpretations of Ῥαββεί and Μεσσίαν, can be regarded as parenthetical.[269] Robertson is unsure whether ὄνομα αὐτῷ Ἰωάνης (Jn. 1:6) and Νικόδημος ὄνομα αὐτῷ (Jn. 3:1) should be considered parenthetical or "merely a form of apposition."[270] He sees an example of parenthesis in John 4:7ff. (presumably referring to verse 8), where the οὖν of v.9 "may look back beyond the parenthesis"; and further examples in 10:35 (καὶ οὐ δύναται λυθῆναι ἡ γραφή) and "the sharp interruption" in 4:1–3 (presumably verse 2).[271] Noting "the wide difference of opinion concerning the parenthesis," he concludes, as Van Belle noted, that "at bottom the parenthesis in the text is a matter of exegesis."[272]

## Blass, Debrunner, and Funk (1961)/Blass, Debrunner, and Rehkopf (2001)

Robert W. Funk's English translation of Blass and Debrunner, *Grammatik des neutestamentlichen Griechisch* (BDF), was published in 1961. It was based on the 9th and 10th editions of the German work (1954, 1959) and included a number of revisions proposed by Debrunner himself prior to his death in 1958. I have compared Funk's edition with the 18th edition of the German work as revised by Friedrich Rehkopf and published in 2001 (BDR).[273]

BDF deal with "The Parenthesis" in the section on "Sentence Structure," noting, "Normal sentence structure may be interrupted in two ways: parenthesis, i.e. a grammatically independent thought thrown into the midst of the sentence; and anacoluthon, i.e. the failure to carry through the structure of the sentence as originally conceived."[274]

Their definition of the function of the parenthesis is somewhat awkward, seeing it as a sudden afterthought which has to be fitted into the text: "The parenthesis . . . usually originates in a need which suddenly crops up to enlarge upon a concept or thought where it appears in the sentence; or it may be due to the difficulty of adapting an afterthought which suddenly comes to mind to the structure of the sentence as it was begun."[275] They distinguish parentheses from nominative absolutes "introducing proper names or as temporal designations which form an essential part of the thought and occupy the proper place in the sentence."[276] They also note that while parentheses can become anacoluthon if "an insertion disturbs the structure of the sentence as a whole," they can also take "the form of a relative clause without interrupting the structure of the sentence."[277]

BDR make a distinction between harder (*härter*) and lighter (*leichter*) forms of parenthesis:

> Als härteste Form unterbricht die Parenthese als ein vollständiger Satz die Konstruktion des schon angefangenen Satzes. Meistens handelt es sich aber—als die leichtere Form—um einen kurzen und überblickbaren Einschub, der die Konstruktion des Gastsatzes nicht empfindlich zu stören vermag. (In its hardest form, the parenthesis interrupts the sentence already started as a complete clause. However, it is generally—in its lighter form—a short and detectable insertion that does not severely disrupt the construction of the host sentence.)[278]

They note that the "harte Parenthesen" are frequent in the Pauline epistles and no less frequent in other NT writings, giving John 2:9 and 4:2 as examples.[279]

## Runge (2010)

In *Discourse Grammar of the Greek New Testament*, Steven Runge has a chapter on "Metacomments."[280] He provides a "working definition" of these: "When speakers stop saying what they are saying in order to comment on what is going to be said, speaking abstractly about it."[281] He adds that "metacomments look forward to what is coming, commenting on it in a way that does not substantially contribute to the propositional content."[282] Although Runge asserts that "metacomments are not a form of parenthetical comment, since the latter focus on something off topic, such as background information,"[283] there is a clear overlap between metacomments as he defines them and some of the discussion of asides in our survey. This is particularly evident in the distinction between showing and telling highlighted by Hedrick and Thatcher, but is also reflected in the proleptic function of some asides, as stated, for example, by Van Belle ("Reference to a passage which . . . follows") and in

42 Chapter 1

the perceived redundancy of some asides in terms of their contribution to the narrative (hence the suggestion that they can be relegated to "footnotes"). One of the examples of a metacomment given by Runge is the clause in Mark 13:14: ὁ ἀναγινώσκων νοείτω (let the reader understand), which is put in brackets in the New Revised Standard Version (NRSV) and given a similar parenthetical status in other translations. Runge states, "The pragmatic effect of inserting the metacomment here is to create a dramatic pause by addressing the reader directly regarding the apocalyptic events being described."[284]

## Van Emde Boas, Rijksbaron, Huitink, and Bakker (2019)

In *The Cambridge Grammar of Classical Greek*, the most recent extensive reference grammar of classical Greek published in English, there are some brief notes on "Parentheses" in the section on "Elements Interrupting or Outside the Syntax of a Sentence."[285] The authors state, "Sentences may be interrupted by other sentences—**parentheses**. These are often relatively short, and frequently contain some form of comment."[286] They also observe, "Parenthetical sentences or clauses are also used to introduce, beforehand, important information which relates to the host sentence that is still to come."[287] This suggests that parentheses can have a proleptic function as well as commenting on material already narrated.

## Von Siebenthal (2019)

In Heinrich von Siebenthal's recently published comprehensive *Ancient Greek Grammar for the Study of the New Testament*, there is a reference to the definition and function of "Parenthesis" in the section on "Figures involving word or clause order."[288] He states, "The term 'parenthesis' . . . refers to a grammatically independent insertion into a text component whose context is to elucidate. . . . As it regularly interrupts the flow of a sentence, a parenthesis typically leads to a hyperbaton. . . . It occurs fairly frequently in the NT."[289]

He also notes the parenthetic nature of phrases using the vocative: "Grammatically speaking a vocative phrase is outside the surrounding sentence structure (it is parenthetical . . . ). It has no syntactic role (as a sentence constituent); it does, however, have a communicative function; it (deictically) points to an entity in the extralinguistic situation."[290]

I give more attention to the communicative function of parenthetical clauses in chapter 5.

## CONCLUSIONS: ISSUES ARISING

This survey of the literature has highlighted a number of insights into the extent, nature, and possible functions of the "asides" in the Gospel of John. It has also left us with various textual, literary, and linguistic questions, which will form the basis for further examination in the rest of this book. It seems to me that the major issues arising from the survey are these:

## Terminology, Definition, and Categorization

It is generally recognized that "asides" (or whatever term authors use) are a significant feature of the Gospel of John. As Tenney observed, "The parenthetical material . . . is more extensive and varied than the notes that one finds occasionally in the Synoptics, and is worth special consideration in the interpretation of the meaning of *John*."[291] However, we have noted that only a few of the authors we have surveyed have attempted to provide a formal definition of this literary feature, notably Hedrick and Sheeley and the various grammars, so that we encounter a wide range of terms (footnotes, asides, parentheses, comments, and so on) and an extensive and varying list of their functional categories. Van Belle's cumulative and admittedly overlapping list of 700 examples strongly implies that there is a considerable subjective element in determining what an "aside" is. We need to ask if there are any objective criteria for distinguishing asides from the main narrative of the text. So, for example, can they be identified, at least partly, on lexical or syntactical grounds, as Van Belle, Bjerkelund, and Neirynck have argued?

This survey has also raised the issue of categorization, which I suggested began with Tenney's survey. Long lists of categories are found in the works of Tenney, O'Rourke, Van Belle, Hedrick, and Köstenberger. However, I suggested that Sheeley's taxonomic approach may, in fact, be of greater value. The following chapter will examine in more detail the terminology, definition, and categorization of asides, and I will attempt to provide and justify my own choices.

## Process of Composition

We noted that the earlier scholars in our survey (Flowers, Garvie, Bernard) all raised the issue of the relation of the asides to layers of redaction within the text. The use of terms such as "interpolations" (Flowers) or "glosses" (Bernard) imply that they are the work of an editor or editors adding material to an existing text. Moreover, Flowers claimed to detect conflicting voices in the narrative, leading to misinterpretations. This anticipates what later scholars have labelled the "unreliable narrator."

The attribution of asides to a process of redaction has continued to be a theme amongst commentators, but from roughly the 1960s onwards there has been more focus on a synchronic approach and an increasing interest in the *literary* function of asides. I observed that Tenney (1960) shifted focus

44 Chapter 1

away from redaction, regarding the footnotes not as "interpolations" but "an essential part of the inspired text of the Gospel."[292] I also noted Brown's shift in emphasis from seeing the explanatory notes as being part of an editorial process to their possible narrative function. However, as we have seen in the case of Hedrick, this shift has not removed consideration of the possibility of conflicting voices within the narrative. Moreover, as I will point out in chapter 4, some scholars continue to emphasize layers of redaction in the composition of the Gospel. In that chapter, I will look at diachronic and synchronic approaches to the text and the influence these have on our understanding of the function of asides in the Gospel.

## The Author and the Narrator

The rise of literary (that is, narratological) approaches to the interpretation of the Gospel has raised issues of the relation between the *author* and the *narrator*. For a scholar such as Tenney, the footnotes were an important indicator of the thinking of the actual author, as well as being a reflection of his style of writing (or speaking). For others, such as Olsson, parenthetical comments indicate the *point of view* of the *narrator*. Lombard was first scholar to clearly raise the question of whether the asides reveal something about the context of situation of a real author and readers, thus serving as a "window" through which we can see an actual Johannine church, or else as a "mirror" into a narrative world. This is a significant matter to be dealt with in our understanding of the function of the asides in the Gospel. In chapter 5, I will compare literary and linguistic (specifically sociolinguistic) approaches to the asides.

## Comparative Study

I noted, in this chapter, Bauckham's comment regarding the lack of "comparison of the functions of narrative asides in John with those in other ancient narrative literature."[293] While Hedrick makes reference to the use of explanatory comments in Graeco-Roman novels, the Synoptics, and Acts, and Bauckham himself refers to Graeco-Roman historiography, only Bjerkelund and Sheeley make detailed comparative studies. Bjerkelund compares his remarks with a "precision-making" function to similar features in the works of Josephus, Philo, and the Samaritan literature. Sheeley makes comparisons of the asides in Luke and Acts with those in Graeco-Roman romances, histories, and biographies.

To attempt a comprehensive study of the function of asides in literature written prior to or roughly at the same time as the Gospel of John would be an immense task. It therefore seems reasonable to me to focus on their use in the OT/HB and the Synoptics, texts which the author of John was either certainly

## Survey of Literature

45

(in the case of the former) or possibly (in the case of the latter) aware of. I will also make some note of the use of asides/comments in certain Greek historical writings, even if the author of John made no direct use of these. For, while many parallels can undoubtedly be found in Graeco-Roman literature, it would seem to be of most benefit to concentrate on the biblical texts and discover what a survey of these adds to our understanding of the function of asides in John. This is my aim for chapter 6.

## NOTES

1. Gilbert Van Belle, *Les Parenthèses dans L'Évangile de Jean: Aperçu Historique et Classification, Texte Grec de Jean* (SNTA 11; Leuven: Leuven University Press, 1985), 3–57, 156–206.

2. Flowers, "Interpolations," 152.

3. Flowers, "Interpolations," 146–51.

4. Flowers, "Interpolations," 152. He cites the phrase οὐ γὰρ συγχρῶνται Ἰουδαῖοι Σαμαρείταις (Jn. 4:9) as an example of an interpolation that can be determined on the basis of "external evidence."

5. Flowers, "Interpolations," 152–53.

6. Flowers, "Interpolations," 153.

7. Flowers, "Interpolations," 154. We have no textual evidence to support this suggestion.

8. Flowers, "Interpolations," 154–56.

9. Flowers, "Interpolations," 156.

10. Flowers, "Interpolations," 156–58.

11. Flowers, "Interpolations," 158.

12. Flowers, "Interpolations," 156.

13. Alfred E. Garvie, *The Beloved Disciple: Studies of the Fourth Gospel* (London: Hodder and Stoughton, 1922). The volume was based on two series of articles published in the journal *The Expositor.*

14. Garvie, *Beloved Disciple*, xxi–xxii.

15. Garvie, *Beloved Disciple*, xxvii–xxviii.

16. Garvie, *Beloved Disciple*, 16, 17.

17. Garvie, *Beloved Disciple*, 18.

18. Garvie, *Beloved Disciple*, 38–39.

19. Garvie, *Beloved Disciple*, 39.

20. Garvie, *Beloved Disciple*, 22–29.

21. Garvie, *Beloved Disciple*, 27. I suspect that his perception of the Evangelist's (or Redactor's) presentation of Jesus does not accord with Garvie's own ecumenical tendencies. Jesus is not quite an English gentleman.

22. John Henry Bernard, *A Critical and Exegetical Commentary on the Gospel According to St. John*, ed. A. H. McNeile (2 vols.; ICC; Edinburgh: T & T Clark, 1928), 1:xxxiii–xxxiv.

46        *Chapter 1*

23. Bernard, *Gospel*, 1:xxxiii. I have the same reservations about the Gospel being "issued" as I have of Flowers's description of it being "published." These are modern concepts.

24. Bernard, *Gospel*, 1:133–34. The Pauline reference is to 1 Cor. 1:14–17.

25. Bernard, *Gospel*, 1:228.

26. Bernard, *Gospel*, 1:189. He notes that Tiberias is also mentioned in 6:1 (referring to "the Sea of Tiberias" as another name for the Sea of Galilee), although not the later mention in 21:1 (also to "the Sea of Tiberias"). I assume he means that it is a Johannine term not found in the other NT writings.

27. Bernard, *Gospel*, 1:189.

28. Bernard, *Gospel*, 2:372.

29. Bernard, *Gospel*, 1:xxxiii; cf. 2:427.

30. Bernard, *Gospel*, 2:427.

31. Bernard, *Gospel*, 1:xxxiii–xxxiv.

32. Bernard, *Gospel*, 1:7.

33. Bernard, *Gospel*, 1:xxxiv.

34. Tenney, "Footnotes," 350.

35. Tenney, "Footnotes," 350.

36. Tenney, "Footnotes," 350.

37. Tenney, "Footnotes," 354n2; 361n3. These are almost certainly references to Westcott's commentary on the Greek text, edited by his son Arthur Westcott and published posthumously in 1908, rather than his earlier commentary based on the Authorized Version and published as a separate volume in 1882. However, the book title and page reference Tenney gives on page 354, note 2 appears to be incorrect for either commentary.

38. Tenney, "Footnotes," 350.

39. Tenney, "Footnotes," 350.

40. Tenney, "Footnotes," 350–51.

41. Tenney, "Footnotes," 354.

42. Tenney, "Footnotes," 352–54.

43. Tenney, "Footnotes," 354.

44. Tenney does not indicate this particular overlap of categories in his summarizing chart (364).

45. Tenney, "Footnotes," 357.

46. Tenney, "Footnotes," 358.

47. Tenney, "Footnotes," 359.

48. Tenney, "Footnotes," 359–60. Tenney is aware that Mary is identified as the one who had anointed Jesus with perfume (11:2) without any prior reference being made to her. The anointing is not described till 12:3. He concludes that "the Fourth Gospel was composed as a conscious supplement to the Synoptic tradition, and that common knowledge of its main narrative was taken for granted" (360).

49. Tenney, "Footnotes," 360. Observant readers will note that Tenney's chart (364) indicates four such examples. However, 12:37–43 has been mistakenly included in this category.

50. Tenney, "Footnotes," 364.

Survey of Literature 47

51. Tenney, "Footnotes," 362.

52. Tenney, "Footnotes," 354–55.

53. Tenney, "Footnotes," 363.

54. Tenney, "Footnotes," 363.

55. Tenney does not actually mention the "Apostle," but that is the clear implication of what he says.

56. Tenney, "Footnotes," 351.

57. Tenney, "Footnotes," 350–51.

58. Tenney, "Footnotes," 363.

59. Tenney, "Footnotes," 351.

60. Tenney, "Footnotes," 362. Despite their "random occurrence," which is presumably an indication of their distribution in the text, Tenney does note that none occur in 13:31–17:26 (351).

61. Brown, *Gospel*, 1:cxxxvi.

62. Brown, *Gospel*, 1:cxxxvi.

63. Brown, *Gospel*, 1:cxxxvi.

64. Raymond E. Brown, *Introduction to the Gospel of John*, ed. Francis J. Maloney, ABRL (New York: Doubleday, 2003), 290.

65. Brown, *Introduction*, 290.

66. Brown, *Introduction*, 30.

67. Birger Olsson, *Structure and Meaning in the Fourth Gospel: A Text-Linguistic Analysis of John 2:1–11 and 4:1–42*, trans. Jean Gray; ConBNT 6 (Lund: CWK Gleerup, 1974).

68. Olsson, *Structure and Meaning*, 63.

69. Olsson, *Structure and Meaning*, 63.

70. Olsson, *Structure and Meaning*, 63.

71. Olsson, *Structure and Meaning*, 92.

72. Olsson, *Structure and Meaning*, 92, 93. He is referring to David W. Wead, *The Literary Devices in John's Gospel*, Theologische Dissertationen 4 (Basel: Friedrich Reinhardt Kommissionsverlag, 1970).

73. Olsson, *Structure and Meaning*, 262–66.

74. Olsson, *Structure and Meaning*, 262.

75. Olsson, *Structure and Meaning*, 262.

76. Olsson, *Structure and Meaning*, 262. He gives 3:16–21, 31–36; 5:19–47; 12:44–50 as examples of these "speech sections."

77. Olsson, *Structure and Meaning*, 262. In the case of "ἦν as the verb," he is referring specifically to its use as the first word in the clause. The examples he gives are 1:44; 11:2; 18:13f., 40; 19:31; 21:7.

78. Olsson, *Structure and Meaning*, 262–63.

79. Olsson, *Structure and Meaning*, 263n32.

80. Olsson, *Structure and Meaning*, 263.

81. Olsson, *Structure and Meaning*, 266.

82. John J. O'Rourke, "Asides in the Gospel of John," in *The Composition of John's Gospel: Selected Studies from Novum Testamentum*, compiled by David E.

48                                 *Chapter 1*

Orton (Leiden: Brill, 1999), 206. Repr. from *Novum Testamentum* 21, no. 3 (1979): 210–19.

83. O'Rourke, "Asides," 211–13.

84. O'Rourke, "Asides," 213.

85. O'Rourke, "Asides," 213. His methodology for this (e.g., the definition and precise boundaries of an "aside") are not set out, which makes the value of this statistical exercise somewhat open to question.

86. O'Rourke, "Asides," 213.

87. O'Rourke, "Asides," 214.

88. O'Rourke, "Asides," 214.

89. R. Alan Culpepper, *Anatomy of the Fourth Gospel: A Study in Literary Design* (Philadelphia: Fortress Press, 1983). It should be stressed that Culpepper uses "literary-critical" with reference to the contemporary study of fictional literature, especially the novel, not in the sense of the search for the sources and layers of redaction more associated with the *Literaturkritik* of German biblical scholarship.

90. Culpepper, *Anatomy*, 43.

91. Culpepper, *Anatomy*, 17.

92. Culpepper, *Anatomy*, 17–18.

93. Culpepper, *Anatomy*, 224.

94. Culpepper, *Anatomy*, 225. It should be noted that such "recent research" would include the author's own work on "the Johannine school": R. Alan Culpepper, *The Johannine School: An Evaluation of the Johannine-School Hypothesis Based on an Investigation of the Nature of Ancient Schools* (SBLDS 26; Missoula: Scholars Press, 1975). A very different conclusion is reached by Klink using the same material as Culpepper: Edward W. Klink III, *The Sheep of the Fold: The Audience and Origin of the Gospel of John* (SNTSMS 141; Cambridge: Cambridge University Press, 2007), 157–81.

95. Culpepper, *Anatomy*, 212.

96. Culpepper, *Anatomy*, 5.

97. Van Belle, *Les Parenthèses*; Gilbert Van Belle, "Les Parenthèses Johanniques," in *The Four Gospels, 1992: Festschrift Frans Neirynck*, ed. Frans Van Segbroeck et al., 3 vols., BETL 100 (Leuven: Leuven University Press, 1992), 3:1901–33.

98. Van Belle, *Les Parenthèses*, vii. Part of this dissertation was reworked and incorporated into Konings's 1972 doctoral thesis, *Het johanneïsche verhaal in de literaire kritiek* (The Johannine narrative in literary criticism), which has not been published (51–52).

99. See Van Belle, *Les Parenthèses*, 51–56 for a summary of Konings's dissertation.

100. Van Belle, *Les Parenthèses*, 3–57.

101. Van Belle, *Les Parenthèses*, 3–6.

102. Van Belle does not state which edition of the *Biblia Sacra Vulgata* he uses. The full list of Greek texts is: Stephanus' third edition of the "Textus Receptus" (1550); Eliezer's various editions of the same text (1624–78); Schulz's printing of Griesbach's third edition (1827), Bloomfield's third edition (1839), Knapp's fifth

Survey of Literature 49

edition (1840), Lachmann (1842), Tischendorf (1841), Westcott–Hort (1881). Various other editions are mentioned in the text and footnotes.

103. Van Belle, *Les Parenthèses*, 8–9.

104. Van Belle, *Les Parenthèses*, 7.

105. Van Belle, *Les Parenthèses*, 7.

106. Van Belle, *Les Parenthèses*, 10–18. Gunnar Rudberg (1880–1954) was an internationally renowned Swedish classical philologist.

107. Van Belle, *Les Parenthèses*, 11.

108. Van Belle, *Les Parenthèses*, 14.

109. Van Belle, *Les Parenthèses*, 17.

110. Van Belle, *Les Parenthèses*, 18.

111. Van Belle, *Les Parenthèses*, 19–57.

112. Van Belle, *Les Parenthèses*, 61–104.

113. Van Belle, *Les Parenthèses*, 106–12.

114. Van Belle, *Les Parenthèses*, 113–24.

115. Van Belle, *Les Parenthèses*, 124–55.

116. Van Belle, *Les Parenthèses*, 124. See Frans Neirynck, *Jean et les Synoptiques: Examen critique de l'exégèse de M.-E. Bosimard*, BETL 49 (Leuven: Leuven University Press, 1979), 41–66; Marie-Emile Boismard and Arnaud Lamouille, *Synopse des quatre Évangiles en français III: L'évangile de Jean* (Paris: Éditions du Cerf, 1977), 491–514.

117. "Literary-critical" is being used here as roughly equivalent to "historical-criticism" (*Literaturkritik*) and should be distinguished from modern "literary criticism" or narratology. It seems to me that Piñero and Peláez, in their splendid introduction to New Testament study, are right to consider "literary criticism" as "a common denominator of source, form and redaction criticism, since the three methods work on the basis of literary arguments," rather than restricting its meaning to source criticism alone. Antonio Piñero and Jesús Peláez, *The Study of the New Testament: A Comprehensive Introduction*, trans. David E. Orton and Paul Ellingworth (Leiden: Deo, 2003), 354.

118. Van Belle, *Les Parenthèses*, 157.

119. Van Belle, *Les Parenthèses*, 161.

120. Van Belle, *Les Parenthèses*, 168. See G. H. C. Macgregor, *The Gospel of John* (London: Hodder and Stoughton, 1928), xliv.

121. Van Belle, *Les Parenthèses*, 174–76.

122. Van Belle, *Les Parenthèses*, 185–87.

123. Van Belle, *Les Parenthèses*, 187–206.

124. Van Belle, *Les Parenthèses*, 191. See Marie-Joseph Lagrange, "Où en est la dissection littéraire du quatrième évangile?" *Revue Biblique* 33, no. 3 (1924), 329. There is a typo in Van Belle's quotation: "invraisembable" for "invraisemblable."

125. Van Belle, *Les Parenthèses*, 200. See Wead, *Literary Devices*, 9.

126. Van Belle, *Les Parenthèses*, 209–10.

127. Van Belle, *Les Parenthèses*, 206.

128. Van Belle, *Les Parenthèses*, 210. He mentions Boismard regarding the idea that the parentheses are "une clef de la critique littéraire." He does not provide an

50 Chapter 1

exact citation, but the reference is to the appendix of stylistic features in Boismard and Lamouille, *Synopse*, 491–514.

129. Van Belle, *Les Parenthèses*, 208–9.

130. Van Belle, *Les Parenthèses*, 211–35.

131. Van Belle, *Les Parenthèses*, 239.

132. Van Belle, *Les Parenthèses*, 239.

133. Hedrick states that Van Belle's list has 165+ examples. Charles W. Hedrick, "Authorial Presence and Narrator in John: Commentary and Story," in *Gospel Origins and Christian Beginnings: In Honor of James M. Robinson*, ed. James E. Goehring et al. (Sonoma: Polebridge Press, 1990), 75.

134. Steven M. Sheeley, *Narrative Asides in Luke-Acts*, JSNTSup 72 (Sheffield: Sheffield Academic Press, 1992), 20. I hope that my own survey is not obsolete!

135. Charles W. Hedrick, "Review of Gilbert Van Belle, *Les Parenthèses dans L'Évangile de Jean: Aperçu Historique et Classification, Texte Grec de Jean*," *JBL* 106, no. 4 (1987), 720, 721.

136. Van Belle, *Les Parenthèses*, 209.

137. Carl J. Bjerkelund, *Tauta Egeneto: Die Präzisierungssätze im Johannesevangelium*, WUNT 40 (Tübingen: Mohr Siebeck, 1987).

138. Bjerkelund, *Tauta Egeneto*, vii.

139. Bjerkelund, *Tauta Egeneto*, 5–6n2.

140. Bjerkelund, *Tauta Egeneto*, 6n2.

141. Bjerkelund, *Tauta Egeneto*, 5–11.

142. Bjerkelund, *Tauta Egeneto*, 11.

143. Bjerkelund, *Tauta Egeneto*, 11.

144. Bjerkelund, *Tauta Egeneto*, 12–14. It should be noted that in two of Bjerkelund's examples the demonstrative pronoun is used adjectively (8:20; 10:6). The use of forms of οὗτος is also one of the features that Van Belle includes in his grammatical classification (*Les Parenthèses*, 116).

145. Bjerkelund, *Tauta Egeneto*, 2.

146. Bjerkelund, *Tauta Egeneto*, 14.

147. Bjerkelund *Tauta Egeneto*, 73–76.

148. Bjerkelund, *Tauta Egeneto*, 76–80.

149. Bjerkelund, *Tauta Egeneto*, 20–21.

150. Bjerkelund, *Tauta Egeneto*, 54.

151. There may have been Hellenistic Greek texts of Samaritan origin, but we do not have them. See Alan D. Crown, "Samaritan Literature and Its Manuscripts," *BJRL* 76, no. 1 (1994): 22–24.

152. See, for example, Bjerkelund, *Tauta Egeneto*, 4, 71, 127, 148.

153. Bjerkelund, *Tauta Egeneto*, 127–28.

154. Bjerkelund, *Tauta Egeneto*, 128.

155. Bjerkelund, *Tauta Egeneto*, 129–30. I have here combined Bjerkelund's conclusions 3 and 4 into one.

156. Bjerkelund, *Tauta Egeneto*, 130.

157. Bjerkelund, *Tauta Egeneto*, 131.

158. Bjerkelund, *Tauta Egeneto*, 132.

*Survey of Literature* 51

159. Bjerkelund, *Tauta Egeneto*, 133–45.
160. Bjerkelund, *Tauta Egeneto*, 148.
161. Bjerkelund, *Tauta Egeneto*, 148–49.
162. Bjerkelund, *Tauta Egeneto*, 149.
163. Bjerkelund, *Tauta Egeneto*, 149.
164. Bjerkelund, *Tauta Egeneto*, 150.
165. Bjerkelund, *Tauta Egeneto*, 150–51.
166. Bjerkelund, *Tauta Egeneto*, 149.
167. Herman A. Lombard, "John's Gospel and the Johannine church: A Mirror of Events within a Text or/and a Window on Events within a Church," *HvTSt* 43, no. 3 (1987), 395. Van Belle provides a brief summary of Lombard's article in "Les Parenthèses Johanniques" (1904–5).
168. Lombard, "John's Gospel," 397.
169. Lombard, "John's Gospel," 400.
170. Lombard, "John's Gospel," 400.
171. Lombard, "John's Gospel," 397–99, 408–11.
172. Lombard, "John's Gospel," 410.
173. Lombard, "John's Gospel," 410.
174. Lombard, "John's Gospel," 399.
175. Lombard, "John's Gospel," 399.
176. Lombard, "John's Gospel," 400.
177. Hedrick, "Authorial Presence," 74–75, 77–81. See 75n7 for mention of Bjerkelund.
178. Hedrick, "Authorial Presence," 74.
179. Hedrick, "Authorial Presence," 76.
180. Hedrick, "Authorial Presence," 76. He provides the titles of two Roman and six Greek texts (76n14).
181. Hedrick, "Authorial Presence," 75–76.
182. Hedrick, "Authorial Presence," 76.
183. Hedrick, "Authorial Presence," 76.
184. Hedrick, "Authorial Presence," 76. He does not include Jn. 2:1 in his list of asides, nor is it found in those of the other scholars he sets out in his table (77).
185. Hedrick, "Authorial Presence," 82–83.
186. Hedrick, "Authorial Presence," 83.
187. Hedrick, "Authorial Presence," 93.
188. Hedrick, "Authorial Presence," 89–92.
189. Neirynck was also director of Johan Konings's Leuven licentiate dissertation, "De bemerkingstof in het evangelie volgens Johannes" (Commentary in the Gospel of John), the starting point for Van Belle's 1985 study.
190. Frans Neirynck, "Parentheses in the Fourth Gospel," in *Frans Neirynck. Evangelica II: 1982–1991 Collected Essays*, ed. F. Van Segbroeck, 693–98; BETL 99 (Leuven: Leuven University Press, 1991).
191. Neirynck, "Parentheses," 693. See Edwin A. Abbott, *Johannine Grammar* (London: Adam and Charles Black, 1906), 348–49. Abbott gives the examples of the use of the pluperfect in 3:24; 4:8; 9:22; 11:19, 30, 57 and states, "This tense takes the

52 *Chapter 1*

reader, as it were, behind the scenes" (349). I include 3:24; 4:8; 9:22; 11:57 in my list of internal comments in chapter 3.

192. Van Belle, "Les Parenthèses Johanniques," 1904–5, 1911–15.

193. Van Belle, "Les Parenthèses Johanniques," 1906, 1916. See Jeffrey Lloyd Staley, *The Print's First Kiss: A Rhetorical Investigation of the Implied Reader in the Fourth Gospel*, SBLDS 82 (Atlanta: Scholars Press, 1988), 81–83.

194. Van Belle, "Les Parenthèses Johanniques," 1906. See Sjef van Tilborg, *Johannes, Belichting van het bijbelboek* (Boxtel: KBS, 1988); and Sjef van Tilborg, "The Gospel of John: Communicative Processes in a Narrative Text," *Neotestamentica* 23 (1989): 19–31.

195. Van Belle, "Les Parenthèses Johanniques," 1907n28.

196. Van Belle, "Les Parenthèses Johanniques," 1907–11. See Chuck Aaron Pourciau, "The Use of Explicit Commentary in the Gospels of Luke and John" (PhD diss., New Orleans Baptist Theological Seminary, 1990; ProQuest Dissertations Publishing, Publication No: 9026805).

197. Van Belle, "Les Parenthèses Johanniques," 1915. See Pourciau, "Explicit Commentary," 113; Van Tilborg, "Communicative Processes," 22.

198. Van Belle, "Les Parenthèses Johanniques," 1915.

199. Van Belle, "Les Parenthèses Johanniques," 1915–16.

200. Van Belle, "Les Parenthèses Johanniques," 1916.

201. Van Belle, "Les Parenthèses Johanniques," 1917.

202. Van Belle, "Les Parenthèses Johanniques," 1917–18.

203. Van Belle, "Les Parenthèses Johanniques," 1918.

204. Van Belle, "Les Parenthèses Johanniques," 1918–22.

205. Van Belle, "Les Parenthèses Johanniques," 1920.

206. Van Belle, "Les Parenthèses Johanniques," 1921. See Frank Thielman, "The Style of the Fourth Gospel and Ancient Literary Concepts of Religious Discourse," in *Persuasive Artistry: Studies in New Testament Rhetoric in Honor of George A. Kennedy*, ed. Duane F. Watson, JSNTSup 20 (Sheffield: Sheffield Academic Press, 1991), 169–70, 179.

207. Van Belle, "Les Parenthèses Johanniques," 1922–27.

208. Van Belle, "Les Parenthèses Johanniques," 1922–23.

209. Van Belle, "Les Parenthèses Johanniques," 1926.

210. Van Belle, "Les Parenthèses Johanniques," 1923.

211. Van Belle, "Les Parenthèses Johanniques," 1929–32.

212. Van Belle, "Les Parenthèses Johanniques," 1932–33.

213. Sheeley, *Narrative Asides*, 14–24.

214. Sheeley, *Narrative Asides*, 9, 22–24.

215. Sheeley, *Narrative Asides*, 14–17.

216. Sheeley, *Narrative Asides*, 17–25. Sheeley observes that Nicholson employs Tenney's criteria and categories, but also introduces insights from narrative criticism— for example, the use of dramatic irony (17–18). In fact, Nicholson only uses some of Tenney's categories in his own list of about 105 asides, of which he is confident about only 69, with the others being "less clearly distinguished" or "possible." See Godfrey

C. Nicholson, *Death as Departure: The Johannine Descent-Ascent Schema*, SBLDS 63 (Chico: Scholars Press, 1983), 32–33.

217. Sheeley, *Narrative Asides*, 31–39.

218. Sheeley, *Narrative Asides*, 31–32. The references are to Quintilian, *Institutio Oratoria*, trans. H. E. Butler, LCL (Cambridge, MA: Harvard University Press, 1921), 4.3.23; 4.1.63; 4.3.12–14.

219. Sheeley, *Narrative Asides*, 32–34.

220. Sheeley, *Narrative Asides*, 36; cf. 177.

221. Sheeley, *Narrative Asides*, 36. Van Belle is critical of Sheeley for rejecting grammatical (and stylistic) criteria as one aspect of the identification of asides. See Gilbert Van Belle, "Review of Steven M. Sheeley, *Narrative Asides in Luke-Acts*," *Ephemerides Theologicae Lovanienses* 71, no. 4 (1995): 467. Van Belle concludes his review of Sheeley, by saying, "Personally, I would prefer to identify and classify the asides not only according to their function and content, but primarily according to their style and grammatical construction" (468).

222. Sheeley, *Narrative Asides*, 37–38.

223. I note (as Van Belle did in his review) that Sheeley makes no reference to Bjerkelund's comparative studies in *Tauta Egeneto*.

224. Sheeley, *Narrative Asides*, 93–96.

225. Sheeley, *Narrative Asides*, 95.

226. Sheeley, *Narrative Asides*, 118. Eighteen of his asides belong to the category of "Material necessary to understand the story"; one to "General information"; two to "Inside views"; and four to "Self-conscious narration" (98). The text of his list of asides is set out in an appendix (186–88). There is an overlap of categories in two of his asides (2:22–23; 9:45).

227. Sheeley, *Narrative Asides*, 175–76.

228. Sheeley, *Narrative Asides*, 178.

229. Tom Thatcher, "A New Look at Asides in the Fourth Gospel," *Bibliotheca Sacra* 151 (1994): 429.

230. Thatcher, "New Look at Asides," 429.

231. Thatcher, "New Look at Asides," 429.

232. Thatcher, "New Look at Asides," 430.

233. Thatcher, "New Look at Asides," 428–30.

234. Thatcher, "New Look at Asides," 43n14.

235. Thatcher, "New Look at Asides," 431.

236. Thatcher, "New Look at Asides," 431.

237. Thatcher, "New Look at Asides," 432.

238. Thatcher, "New Look at Asides," 432–23.

239. Thatcher, "New Look at Asides," 433.

240. Thatcher, "New Look at Asides," 429–30.

241. Dal Lee, *The Narrative Asides in the Book of Revelation* (Lanham, MD: University Press of America, 2002). Lee is currently Professor of New Testament at the Department of Christian Studies, Hannam University, Korea.

242. Lee, *Narrative Asides*, 18–25.

243. Lee, *Narrative Asides*, 37.

54                *Chapter 1*

244. "We differentiate the commentator as telling the narrative asides from the narrator who is considered as one telling all the rest of the story" (Lee, *Narrative Asides*, 49). Lee uses the label "the commentator" as equivalent to the (implied) author (see, e.g., 156).

245. Lee, *Narrative Asides*, 117–18.

246. Lee, *Narrative Asides*, 43, 44.

247. Richard Bauckham, *The Testimony of the Beloved Disciple: Narrative, History, and Theology in the Gospel of John* (Grand Rapids: Baker Academic, 2007), 104–5. The essay was originally published in slightly different form in *New Testament Studies* 53:1 (2007): 17–36.

248. Bauckham, *Testimony*, 94–95.

249. Bauckham, *Testimony*, 95–112.

250. Bauckham, *Testimony*, 112.

251. Bauckham, *Testimony*, 104.

252. Bauckham, *Testimony*, 105.

253. Bauckham, *Testimony*, 105.

254. Bauckham, *Testimony*, 105.

255. Bauckham, *Testimony*, 105n45. He admits that he has not been able to consult Bjerkelund.

256. Bauckham, *Testimony*, 105.

257. Andreas J. Köstenberger, *A Theology of John's Gospel and Letters* (Grand Rapids: Zondervan, 2009), 135–41.

258. Köstenberger, *Theology*, 135n34. I am not quite sure why Köstenberger cites Credner. The reference is to two sets of examples in Credner's list of stylistic characteristics in John, one of which lists examples of referrals back (*Rückweisungen*) to what happened earlier and the other explanatory comments (*Bemerkungen*) by the author. Karl August Credner, *Einleitung in das Neue Testament: Erster Theil* (Halle: Waisenhauses, 1836), 226–27. These are noted in Van Belle, *Les Parenthèses*, 24–25. (Only the first volume of Credner's introduction was published.)

259. Köstenberger, *Theology*, 135, 140.

260. Köstenberger, *Theology*, 135.

261. Köstenberger, *Theology*, 140.

262. Köstenberger, *Theology*, 140–41.

263. Köstenberger, *Theology*, 141n38.

264. Van Belle, *Les Parenthèses*, 7.

265. Van Belle, *Les Parenthèses*, 7.

266. A. T. Robertson, *A Grammar of the Greek New Testament in the Light of Historical Research*, 3rd ed. (New York: Hodder and Stoughton, 1919), 433–35. Robertson's Grammar was first published in 1914. The third edition was a major revision. Two further editions were published (1923, 1931), but these contain only minor corrections.

267. Robertson, *Grammar*, 433.

268. Robertson, *Grammar*, 433.

269. Robertson, *Grammar*, 433. NA28 and UBS5 have Ῥαββί in Jn. 1:38.

270. Robertson, *Grammar*, 434.

# Survey of Literature 55

271. Robertson, *Grammar*, 434.

272. Robertson, *Grammar*, 435.

273. Friedrich Blass, Albert Debrunner, and Robert W. Funk, *A Greek Grammar of the New Testament and Other Early Christian Literature* (Chicago: University of Chicago Press, 1961); Friedrich Blass, Albert Debrunner, and Friedrich Rehkopf, *Grammatik des neutestamentlichen Griechisch*, 18th ed. (Göttingen: Vandenhoeck and Ruprecht, 2001). The 19th edition of BDR (2020) differs from the 18th edition only in format not in wording.

274. Blass, Debrunner, Funk, *Greek Grammar*, 239.

275. Blass, Debrunner, Funk, *Greek Grammar*, 242.

276. Blass, Debrunner, Funk, *Greek Grammar*, 243.

277. Blass, Debrunner, Funk, *Greek Grammar*, 243. They give Jn. 1:38 as an example of the latter.

278. Blass, Debrunner, Rehkopf, *Grammatik*, 393.

279. Blass, Debrunner, Rehkopf, *Grammatik*, 393, 393n3. In a short section on "Interpolation of sentences: Parenthesis," Turner suggests, "The NT parentheses are harsher than would be permitted in a Greek stylist, especially those in Paul . . . , which may be due to dictation of the letters." Nigel Turner, *Syntax*, Vol. 3 of James Hope Moulton, *A Grammar of New Testament Greek* (Edinburgh: T & T Clark, 1963), 342.

280. Steven E. Runge, *Discourse Grammar of the Greek New Testament: A Practical Introduction for Teaching and Exegesis* (Peabody, MA: Hendrickson, 2010), 101–24.

281. Runge, *Discourse Grammar*, 101.

282. Runge, *Discourse Grammar*, 101n1.

283. Runge, *Discourse Grammar*, 101n1.

284. Runge, *Discourse Grammar*, 112.

285. Evert van Emde Boas, Albert Rijksbaron, Luuk Huitink, and Mathieu de Bakker, *The Cambridge Grammar of Classical Greek* (Cambridge: Cambridge University Press, 2019), 320. The other elements they refer to are forms of address, exclamations, interjections, list entries, and headings/titles (321).

286. Van Emde Boas et al., *Cambridge Grammar*, 320.

287. Van Emde Boas et al., *Cambridge Grammar*, 321.

288. Heinrich von Siebenthal, *Ancient Greek Grammar for the Study of the New Testament* (Oxford: Peter Lang, 2019), 552–53.

289. Von Siebenthal, *Ancient Greek Grammar*, 552. He defines "hyperbaton" as occurring "when two expressions that syntactically belong together are separated by the interposition of one or more expressions" (552).

290. Von Siebenthal, *Ancient Greek Grammar*, 224.

291. Tenney, "Footnotes," 350.

292. Tenney, "Footnotes," 362.

293. Bauckham, *Testimony*, 105n45.

*Chapter 2*

# Terminology, Definitions, and Categorization

So, what exactly is the phenomenon that we are dealing with in this book? For although, as we have seen in the previous chapter, scholars have interacted to some extent with others' work and there is a measure of common ground in their discussions, there is also considerable variation in their assessment of the extent of the phenomenon (how many asides are there?) and in its terminology, definition, and categorization. The purpose of this chapter is to consider in more detail each of these aspects of the phenomenon. I begin with an overview of the terminology employed by the scholars covered in the survey.

## TERMINOLOGY USED BY SCHOLARS AND SOME DEFINITIONS

Of the early writers investigated in the previous chapter, Flowers uses the term "interpolations," Garvie speaks of the "comments" of the Evangelist and the "insertions" of the Redactor, Bernard of the Evangelist's "comments" and the non-Johannine "glosses." There would, therefore, seem to be a distinction here between those terms (interpolations, insertions, glosses) which imply that the highlighted clauses or sentences are added to an existing text by another writer and the term "comments" used of clauses or sentences attributed to the primary author of the text.

Tenney's main term is "footnotes." He also uses "glosses," "asides," and "comments," as well as referring to "explanatory material which is . . . parenthetical." Tenney does not, however, make a distinction between original and added material. For him, the footnotes "are not interpolations," but "an essential part of the inspired text of the Gospel."[1] So, although the term "glosses"

57

58                                   *Chapter 2*

would seem to imply later interpolations by another writer, Tenney regards
them as additions by the original author to clarify the text.[2]

Of the writers considered between the particularly influential works of
Tenney and Van Belle, the focus is on the explanatory nature of the material.
Brown speaks of explanatory "notes" or "comments," which may nevertheless indicate a process of editing.[3] He flirts with the idea of treating them
as "footnotes." Olsson refers to the narrator's "comments" or "remarks," as
well as drawing on Tenney's term "footnotes." O'Rourke speaks of "asides"
or editorial "comments." Culpepper surveys the explanatory "comments" of
the narrator.

Van Belle's major work is *Les Parenthèses dans L'Évangile de Jean* and
it is the term "parenthèses" that he uses throughout, alongside the occasional
use of "remarques." I noted that *parenthèses* can, as with the English translation "parentheses," be used both for sentences, clauses, or phrases which form
a digression from the main text and also for the punctuation marks (brackets)
used to indicate these. Unlike other scholars up to this time, Van Belle does
make a brief attempt to define his chosen terminology by citing Quintilian,
the first century AD/CE Roman advocate and teacher of rhetoric:

> Illa quoque ex eodem genere possunt videri: unum quod interpositio-
> nem, vel interclusionem dicimus, Graeci παρένθεσιν, παρέμπτωσιν
> vocant, dum continuationi sermonis medius aliqui sensus intervenit
> (*Institutio Oratoria*, 9.3.23).[4] (The following may also be thought to
> belong to the same genus: (1) What we call *interpositio* or *interclusio*,
> and the Greeks *parenthesis* or *paremptosis*, namely the insertion of a
> phrase in the middle of a continuous utterance.)[5]

In his 1992 essay, Van Belle also makes some use of the terms "à-côtés"
and "apartés" (asides), in addition to "parenthèses" and "remarques."[6]

Bjerkelund uses the terms "Bemerkungen" (comments, remarks), "Randbemerkungen" (marginal notes), "Notizen" (notes), and "Fußnoten" (footnotes),
alongside his focus on the "Präzierungssätze" (precision-making sentences/
clauses). We can compare this with other terms used by German commentators. So, for example, Van Belle notes a wide range of expressions used in the
commentaries of Bultmann (1941) and Schnackenburg (1965, 1971, 1975),
which I have arranged in a rough typological order (and provided translations
where necessary):

Bultmann:

- Anmerkungen (comments), Bemerkungen;
- Erläuterungen (explanations), Ausdeutung (interpretation), Interpretament,
  Interpretation;

*Terminology, Definitions, and Categorization*     59

- Parenthesen;
- Reflexionen;
- Rückverweisungen (referrals back);
- Einfügungen (insertions); Glossen, Zusätze (additions).[7]


Schnackenburg:

- Kommentare, Bemerkungen;
- Erklärungen, Erläuterungen (explanations); Interpretament;
- Abschweifungen (digressions);
- Parenthesen, Zwischenbemerkungen (interjections);
- Reflexionen;
- Abschlussbemerkungen, Schlussbemerkungen (closing remarks);
- Rahmenbemerkungen (framing remarks);
- Rückverweise (referrals back);
- Einfügungen (insertions); Hinzufügungen, Zufügungen, Zusätze (additions).[8]

Lombard (following Tenney) uses the terms "footnotes," as well as referring to "commentary" by the author/narrator. Hedrick is somewhat circumspect in giving a name to this "particular narrative device." He notes some of the terms used by others and refers to "asides" and "explanations," but his main focus is on the term "hermeneiai" (from the Greek ἑρμηνεία), which he defines as "characterized by a suspension of the dramatic showing of the story and the intrusion of a 'voice' that stands some distance from the story, reflecting on it from that distant and different perspective."[9]

Sheeley's monograph is called *Narrative Asides in Luke-Acts* and the terms "narrative asides" or simply "asides" are used consistently throughout. Sheeley devotes more space than other writers to the definition of this narrative feature, drawing on ancient rhetoricians and modern narrative critics. I will return to his definition later in this chapter.

Thatcher sticks to the term "aside" as "a direct statement that tells the reader something," drawing, like Hedrick (and, to a lesser extent, Sheeley), on Wayne Booth's distinction between telling and showing.[10] Bauckham uses the terms "narrative asides" and "parentheses."

The grammarians surveyed in chapter 1 focus on the definition and function of "parentheses," although I also noted Runge's observations on "metacomments."

From this survey of terminology, we can draw a number of conclusions. First, those scholars who emphasize the redactional process in the text use terms such as *interpolations, insertions, glosses*; *Einfügungen,*

60                                    *Chapter 2*

*Hinzufügungen, Zufügungen, Züsatze, Glossen*. Other terms, such as Bult-mann's *Rückverweisungen* and Schnackenburg's *Schlussbemerkungen, Abschlussbemerkungen, Rahmenbemerkungen*, and *Rückverweise*, may also indicate later redactions to an existing text. The process of composition will be considered in detail in chapter 4. Second, those who focus on the dynamics of the text from the perspective of modern literary criticism favour the term (*narrative*) *asides*, while also referring to *comments, remarks*, and *notes*. Third, the terms *footnotes* and *parentheses* are somewhat harder to categorize and could belong equally to a redactional process or to the voice of the narra-tor. Fourth, the explanatory nature of the material is emphasized by the terms *commentary, explanations*, and *hermeneiai* (Hedrick's label).

## THE KEY TERMS: FOOTNOTES, PARENTHESES, ASIDES

I suggest that the key terms, as a result of the influence of the works in which they are used, are *footnotes* (Tenney), *parentheses* (Van Belle), and *narra-tive asides* (Sheeley). I will make some observations about these at this point and then discuss them and other terms at greater length subsequently. The first thing to note is that all three of these terms are *spatial metaphors*. *Foot-notes* can literally be found at the foot of the page, but they can also imply something of lesser significance. *Parentheses* are literally what are "placed in beside" (from the Hellenistic Greek παρένθεσις), similar to *interpolations* and *insertions*, but can again imply something that is of lesser significance. *Asides* has the literal implication of what is not spoken directly to a hearer, but uttered in an alternative direction. This can be most obviously observed in a dramatic setting (theatre, television, film), where the speaker turns from the addressees to speak directly to the audience or camera.

*Footnotes* is the term which Tenney uses in the title of his 1960 essay, but, as we have seen, he is not using this in a literal sense and he states that *glosses* or *asides* may be more appropriate terms. Brown also considers (but rejects) the idea of footnotes, although he draws attention to E. V. Rieu's use of them in his translation of the Gospels. In fact, Rieu's usage of footnotes is quite limited and somewhat inconsistent. Only some of the "translation asides" in John 1:38, 41, 42; 4:25; 6:1 and the observation "though it was not Jesus himself but his disciples that baptized" in 4:2 are actually placed in footnotes, while other "asides" are either placed in brackets (e.g., 14:22) or else not marked at all (e.g., the "translation asides" in 20:16, 24).[11]

The footnote with its graphic depiction of information communicated to the reader at a different level and quite often with a different audience in mind is a relatively modern concept, connected to the development of the printed text.[12] For that reason it would seem to be of limited value as an explanatory term for a literary device found originally in manuscripts. However, it does raise the issue of whether the original writer/s of the Gospel had different audiences in mind.

*Parentheses* is the term used by Van Belle in his comprehensive monograph and I noted his attribution of it to Quintilian. It is a major term in our field of study and can be regarded as the most technical expression, widely used in literary and linguistic studies alongside the cognate term *parentheticals*. It also provides, as we have seen, an overlap between content and one of the methods for indicating this in written form, by using the punctuation signs known as parentheses (or brackets). This is defined by the *Oxford English Dictionary* (*OED*) as "the upright curves ( ) used to mark off a word or clause inserted parenthetically; round brackets."[13] Such brackets (or what Erasmus called *lunulae*, referring to the fact that they recall the shape of the crescent moon) date from the late 14th century.[14]

Parenthetical material can also be indicated by hyphens/dashes or commas, so that the *OED* defines a *parenthesis* as "a word, clause, or sentence inserted as an explanation, aside, or afterthought into a passage with which it has not necessarily any grammatical connection, in writing usually marked off by brackets, dashes, or commas."[15] However, as marking a clause with commas is a less reliable guide to the presence of parenthetical material, it is easier to take note of cases marked with brackets or hyphens/dashes, as in the following examples in John from one of the modern Greek texts, Nestle-Aland, *Novum Testamentum Graece*, 28th edition (NA28), and one recent translation of the Gospel, the NRSV.[16]

Ὡς οὖν ἔγνω ὁ Ἰησοῦς ὅτι ἤκουσαν οἱ Φαρισαῖοι ὅτι Ἰησοῦς πλείονας μαθητὰς ποιεῖ καὶ βαπτίζει ἢ Ἰωάννης—καίτοιγε Ἰησοῦς αὐτὸς οὐκ ἐβάπτιζεν ἀλλ' οἱ μαθηταὶ αὐτοῦ—

Now Jesus learned that the Pharisees had heard that he was gaining and baptising more disciples than John—although in fact it was not Jesus who baptised, but his disciples—(4:1–2)

καὶ εἶπεν αὐτῷ· ὕπαγε νίψαι εἰς τὴν κολυμβήθραν τοῦ Σιλωάμ (ὃ ἑρμηνεύεται Ἀπεσταλμένος). ἀπῆλθεν οὖν καὶ ἐνίψατο καὶ ἦλθεν βλέπων.

saying to him, 'Go, wash in the pool of Siloam' (which means Sent). Then he went and washed and came back able to see. (9:7)

Sheeley's work on *Narrative Asides* in Luke and Acts has brought the term *asides* to the fore, and I have grouped it with *comments*, *remarks*, and *notes* in the conclusions above drawn from my survey of terminology. In

62                                    *Chapter 2*

his introduction to the Gospel, Gary Burge highlights this term, referring to
"asides" or "reader helps" and suggesting that "we are more informed than
the apostles when we read this Gospel because John is slipping us notes."[17]
This picture of the author wanting the reader to be well-informed is also
found in several of Wendy North's writings. Acknowledging her debt to
Van Belle's "definitive study," she proposes that John makes extensive use
of "parentheses" or "asides," including "readers' helps" and "in general
shepherds [his audience] along through the narrative, fussing the while with
explanatory comments on why things happen quite as they do."[18] Indeed,
she concludes, "when it comes to getting his message across to his readers,
John is a born pedant; everything necessary is explicitly communicated, false
impressions are carefully ruled out, and nothing is left to chance."[19]

However, not all of the parenthetical material in the Gospel is explanatory,
nor does the narrator only provide such explanations by means of "asides."
As Sheeley states, "Narrative asides cannot be limited to explanatory or
clarifying functions. They serve other functions as well. At the same time
they cannot contain all of the explanatory commentary in a narrative. Not all
commentary is spoken in aside to the reader. Narrative asides provide only a
portion of the narrator's comments to the reader."[20]

This leads us to further consideration of the complex area of the definition
of parentheses/asides.


## DEFINITION OF ASIDES: AN INDUCTIVE APPROACH?

It would seem evident from the fact that Van Belle lists 700 examples in his
cumulative list of parentheses drawn from textual editions, grammars, commentaries, and other studies over a period of roughly 200 years that there is
a considerable subjectivity in determining precisely what is meant by parenthetical material in the Gospel of John. Indeed, I suggest that one of the
major problems with the study of this material is the lack of precise definition
offered by scholars. In this section I examine some of the definitions offered
by the scholars surveyed in chapter 1 and compare them with definitions
found in the fields of modern literary criticism and of linguistics. I also offer
my own definitions and reasons for them.

I propose that most commentators have actually deliberately shied away
from offering a precise definition. Rather they have adopted an inductive
approach: certain phrases or sentences appear to stand out from the main
narrative, so they are then grouped together and given a label. There may be
some value in this approach, so rather than starting with definitions, I first
note some widely accepted examples that are indicated by punctuation. Like
Van Belle, I list here instances of phrases or sentences that are put in brackets

Terminology, Definitions, and Categorization 63

or set apart with dashes in editions of the Greek text, in this case in three of the most recent Greek texts: NA28 (2012), UBS5 (2014), and *The Greek New Testament: SBL Edition* (SBLGNT) (2010).[21]
NA28 has just one phrase/sentence in brackets and three in dashes.

In brackets:

9:7: (ὃ ἑρμηνεύεται Ἀπεσταλμένος)

In dashes:

4:2 (whole verse): —καίτοιγε Ἰησοῦς αὐτὸς οὐκ ἐβάπτιζεν ἀλλ᾽ οἱ μαθηταὶ αὐτοῦ—
7:22: —οὐχ ὅτι ἐκ τοῦ Μωϋσέως ἐστὶν ἀλλ᾽ ἐκ τῶν πατέρων—
10:12: —καὶ ὁ λύκος ἁρπάζει αὐτὰ καὶ σκορπίζει—

I note that the editors of NA28 have dropped one phrase put in brackets in NA27 (1993), namely 20:16 (ὃ λέγεται Διδάσκαλε).
UBS5 has the same three phrases/sentences in dashes as NA28 (4:2; 7:22; 10:12), but not the phrase in brackets (9:7). Both 9:7 and 20:16 are in brackets in UBS4 (1983), which suggests a decision to move away from this form of parenthesizing in the later edition.
SBLGNT has six phrases/sentences in brackets and three in dashes, as follows:

In brackets:

1:15 (whole verse): (Ἰωάννης μαρτυρεῖ περὶ αὐτοῦ καὶ κέκραγεν λέγων· Οὗτος ἦν ⸀ὃν εἶπον⸱· Ὁ ὀπίσω μου ἐρχόμενος ἔμπροσθέν μου γέγονεν, ὅτι πρῶτός μου ἦν·)
1:38: (ὃ λέγεται μεθερμηνευόμενον Διδάσκαλε)
1:41: (ὅ ἐστιν μεθερμηνευόμενον χριστός)
1:42: (ὃ ἑρμηνεύεται Πέτρος)
9:7: (ὃ ἑρμηνεύεται Ἀπεσταλμένος)
20:16: (ὃ λέγεται Διδάσκαλε)

In dashes:

4:2 (whole verse): —καίτοιγε Ἰησοῦς αὐτὸς οὐκ ἐβάπτιζεν ἀλλ᾽ οἱ μαθηταὶ αὐτοῦ—
7:22: —οὐχ ὅτι ἐκ τοῦ Μωϋσέως ἐστὶν ἀλλ᾽ ἐκ τῶν πατέρων—
10:12: —καὶ ὁ λύκος ἁρπάζει αὐτὰ καὶ σκορπίζει—

64                                    *Chapter 2*

These correspond to the use of brackets and dashes in Westcott and Hort's 1881 edition, the starting point for the SBLGNT text, and I observe that NA28 and UBS5 have the same use of dashes, although not of brackets.[22] Westcott-Hort also has John 4:9 in square brackets, primarily to indicate the editors' uncertainty about the text, but it may also suggest an aside. Westcott comments, "These words, which are omitted by an important group of ancient authorities, are, if genuine, an explanatory note of the Evangelist."[23]

In his article on "Parentheticals" in the *Encyclopedia of Language and Linguistics*, Burton-Roberts states, "What all [parentheticals] have in common, observationally, is that they are marked off from their hosts by some form of punctuation in writing or special intonation contour in speech." [24] However, there are few, if any, punctuation marks in the early Greek manuscripts and, as Metzger notes, "Not until the eighth or ninth century AD did Greek scribes begin to be more or less systematic in the use of punctuation marks."[25] So, we are relying on a tradition of later editorial judgement regarding the use of brackets and hyphens/dashes in isolating examples of asides in the Greek editions. Moreover, when we compare the examples in the three recent editions with those surveyed by Van Belle, we see a trend towards far fewer indications of parenthetical material by punctuation.[26]

However, even in the small number of asides marked in these modern editions, we can see that they are parenthetical in different ways. So, for example, looking just at the four asides in NA28, I think we can readily accept as remarks of the author (or narrator) the "translation aside" in 9:7 and the "explanation" in 4:2 that it was not actually Jesus himself who was baptizing, an apparent correction of the report conveyed to the Pharisees that "Jesus was baptizing more disciples than John" (4:1). However, the other two examples (7:22; 10:12) can be attributed to the speaker within the narrative, that is Jesus himself, who would, presumably, from a historical perspective, have used a "special intonation contour in speech" (Burton-Roberts), rather than these being comments by the author (or narrator). These different levels of *voice* in the narrative are something that we will need to investigate at greater depth.

When we compare recent English translations with the modern Greek editions, we find that there a greater number of asides is indicated. Thus, the NRSV has 21 phrases or sentences in brackets and 4 in dashes, as follows:

In brackets:

1:15: (*whole verse*) (John testified to him and cried out, 'This was he of whom I said, "He who comes after me ranks ahead of me because he was before me."')
1:38: (which translated means Teacher)
1:41: (which is translated Anointed)
1:42: (which is translated Peter)

2:9: (though the servants who had drawn the water knew)

4:8: (*whole verse*) (His disciples had gone to the city to buy food.)

4:9: (Jews do not share things in common with Samaritans.)

4:25: (who is called Christ)

4:44: (*whole verse*) (for Jesus himself had testified that a prophet has no honour in the prophet's own country)

7:5: (*whole verse*) (For not even his brothers believed in him.)

7:22: (it is, of course, not from Moses, but from the patriarchs)

9:7: (which means Sent)

12:4: (the one who was about to betray him)

12:6: (*whole verse*) (He said this not because he cared about the poor, but because he was a thief; he kept the common purse and used to steal what was put into it.)

14:22: (not Iscariot)

18:32: (*whole verse*) (This was to fulfil what Jesus had said when he indicated the kind of death he was to die.)

19:28: (in order to fulfil the scripture)

19:35: (*whole verse*) (He who saw this has testified so that you also may believe. His testimony is true, and he knows that he tells the truth.)

20:16: (which means Teacher)

20:24: (who was called the Twin)

21:19: (He said this to indicate the kind of death by which he would glorify God.)

In dashes

3:24: —John, of course, had not yet been thrown into prison.[27]

4:2: —although it was not Jesus himself but his disciples who baptized—

10:35: —and the scripture cannot be annulled—

13:23: —the one whom Jesus loved—

(I note that some other phrases are introduced with a dash, but do not appear to be asides, for example, 5:3; 10:12, despite Van Belle's noting them as such.)[28]

It is worth noting that more asides are indicated in the NRSV than in the Revised Standard Version (RSV, 2nd edition, 1971), which has 16 phrases or sentences in brackets and one in dashes. The main difference from the NRSV is that the RSV marks fewer whole sentences as asides: 4:8, 44; 7:5; 18:32; 19:35 are not marked as such, although part of 19:35 is marked with dashes ("—his testimony is true, and he knows that he tells the truth—"). It does have one aside not marked in the NRSV: 19:31 "(for that sabbath was a high day)." Tracing the "standard version" lineage further back, the King James Version

66                                    *Chapter 2*

(KJV, Standard Text Edition, 1769) has 14 asides marked in brackets. These include 6 of those marked in the NRSV (1:38; 2:9; 4:2 [in dashes in the NRSV]; 4:8; 7:22; 9:7), 1 marked in the RSV but not in the NRSV (19:31), and 7 found in neither the NRSV or RSV, as follows:

> 1:14: (and we beheld his glory, the glory as of the only begotten of the Father,)
> 6:23: (*whole verse*) (Howbeit there came other boats from Tiberias nigh unto the place where they did eat bread, after that the Lord had given thanks:)
> 7:39: (*whole verse*) (But this spake he of the Spirit, which they that believe on him should receive: for the Holy Ghost was not yet given; because that Jesus was not yet glorified.)
> 7:50: (he that came to Jesus by night, being one of them,)
> 11:2: (*whole verse*) (It was that Mary which anointed the Lord with ointment, and wiped his feet with her hair, whose brother Lazarus was sick.)
> 21:7: (for he was naked,)
> 21:8: (for they were not far from land, but as it were two hundred cubits,)

I note that the King James Version (Standard Text Edition, 1769) (KJV) marks more whole sentences than the RSV does and also that there is no direct correspondence between the three versions (NRSV, RSV, KJV), although there is some overlap. The increase in the number of asides marked by punctuation in the English translations contrasts with the trend in the Greek editions. However, the parenthesized phrases or sentences in the editions and translations do not include what many would regard as major narrative insertions such as the summaries of the purpose of the Gospel in John 20:30–31 and 21:24–25. Such sentences may be compared to the Prologue to the Gospel of Luke (1:1–4), in which the author sets forward a specific reason for writing. Such extended comments, although in some way distinct from the main narrative, do not fit so well into brackets or dashes. The same applies to the Gospel of John's own Prologue (1:1–18).

What both the asides marked in the Greek editions and in the English translations suggest is a variety of functions, including "translation" and explanation, and varying degrees of how intrusive the author or narrator is in the text. For example, the asides in 7:22 and 10:12 can simply be attributed to the character speaking (Jesus), whereas the summary statement in 19:35 would appear to be a more direct communication between the narrator and reader. Consideration of these issues will have a bearing on the definitions that we give from both literary and linguistic perspectives.

# Terminology, Definitions, and Categorization

## DEFINITIONS USED BY SCHOLARS

Having looked at the parenthetical material marked in the modern Greek texts and some English translations, I turn again now to the definitions offered by the scholars surveyed in chapter 1.

Tenney defines *footnotes* as "sentences or paragraphs of explanatory comment, interjected into the running narrative of the story."[29] However, to take as an example the parenthesized material in the NRSV, we can see that this comprises mostly clauses or phrases rather than sentences and that there are no paragraphs, such as 20:30–31 and 21:24–25, marked in this way. Nor can all the asides be regarded as "explanatory," as Sheeley has indicated. For example, in what sense is 1:15 ("John testified to him and cried out, 'This was he of whom I said, "He who comes after me ranks ahead of me because he was before me."'") an explanation? Its bracketing in the SBLGNT and NRSV (and RSV) looks more like a case of the editors seeing it as in some way not fitting into the surrounding text, a xenolith enclosed in the larger rock of the Prologue.

Van Belle has been criticized for not providing a clear definition of *parentheses*.[30] His response is that given the lack of unanimity even amongst the editors of the Greek texts as to what constitutes a parenthesis, he refuses to be bound to a particular grammatical definition that could not be consistently applied to the various instances in John.[31]

Hedrick's "refining" of Tenney's definition leads him to the observation that the narrative feature "is comprised of intrusive word(s), sentence(s), or paragraph(s) of explanatory or clarifying commentary included in the narrative as direct address to the reader. In general, it is characterized by 'telling' about the story as opposed to the 'showing' of the story."[32] Hedrick is correct in noting that such parenthetical material may consist of words (although possibly not a single word) rather than just longer units of text. However, he has kept Tenney's emphasis on the explanatory function of the material in his use of the term *hermeneiai*.

Sheeley, in his work on *narrative asides* in Luke and Acts, is critical of others for failing to provide a definition and he offers this: "Narrative asides may be defined as parenthetical remarks addressed directly to the reader which interrupt the logical progression of the story, establishing a relationship between the narrator and the narratee which exists outside the story being narrated."[33] However, to define "asides" as "parenthetical remarks" is somewhat tautological and it is not easy to determine what interrupts "the logical progression of the story" or to agree to what extent the "asides" are, in fact, a more direct address to the reader than the rest of the text.

Hedrick and Sheeley, and also Thatcher, share an emphasis on the distinction between the main narrative's *showing* and the asides' *telling*. This showing/

68                                  *Chapter 2*

telling distinction is drawn from the work of Wayne Booth and subsequent narratologists.[34] I will consider in greater depth this distinction between showing
and telling, or what some narratologists label as *mimesis* and *diegesis*, in chapter 5.[35] For, as Jo-Ann Brant states, "The examination of the many narrative
asides becomes a significant data set in the discussion of Johannine diegesis."[36]

However, even at this point, I think it is worth raising the question of how
clear-cut the distinction between showing and telling is in the Gospel, taking into account Booth's awareness that *showing* is a form of *telling*, which
leads him to state, "the author's judgment is always present."[37] For example,
in John 4:9 we read:

> The Samaritan woman said to him, "How is it that you, a Jew, ask a
> drink of me, a woman of Samaria?" (Jews do not share things in com-
> mon with Samaritans.)

Are the bracketed words those of the narrator (hence *telling*), as most commentators judge, or simply the words of the Samaritan woman (and therefore
part of the *showing*)? Either way the information is imparted to the reader
and maybe a telling/showing distinction is not particularly significant at this
point, as Calvin recognized in his 1553 commentary:

> *For the Jews have no dealings with Samaritans.* I think the woman
> spoke these words. Others take them as an interpolation by the Evange-
> list in explanation. It is of little importance which meaning you choose,
> but it seems to me to fit in best that the woman is jeering at Christ like
> this: "Oh! You're sure it's all right to ask me for a drink, when you think
> we are so irreligious?" If any prefer the other interpretation, I shall not
> argue about it.[38]

Indeed, it may be more helpful to speak in terms of *direct* or *indirect* address,
a distinction made by Thomas Boomershine, who, writing from a performance
perspective, states, "In storytelling, by contrast with drama, the performer is
first and foremost him or herself and is always addressing the audience, sometimes directly and sometimes indirectly."[39] These are complex issues and will
be examined further later. For now, I make the following conclusions from
the relatively few definitions provided by scholars. First, the footnotes/paren-
theses/asides in the Gospel of John make some form of interjection/intrusion/
interruption into the narrative. However, it is not easy to determine the force of
this interjection. As Van Belle points out, it is a question of exegesis. Second,
the principal function of these interjections is an explanatory one. However
as Sheeley observes, this is not their sole function. Third, they may indicate
a more direct form of address to the reader by *telling* rather than *showing*.

*Terminology, Definitions, and Categorization* 69

Fourth, following on from the previous point, they may also help to establish a relationship between the author and reader (or narrator and narratee).

## DEFINITIONS IN LITERARY THEORY

As we have seen, insofar as scholars have used a theoretical underpinning for their definitions of parenthetical material, it is drawn largely from the world of modern literary criticism, hence the emphasis on the role of the *narrator* and the use of the term *narrative asides*. In fact, this particular term is not widely used in narratology, the focus being rather on *focalization* or the *point of view* or *voice* of the narrator. James L. Resseguie, in his helpful glossary of New Testament narrative criticism, defines an *aside* as a device whereby a "narrator may . . . provide commentary on characters or events that gives the reader/hearer information that may or may not be available to the characters in the story."[40] In support of his use of this term, he cites other NT scholars, namely Sheeley (1992) and Rhoads and Michie's influential study on the narrative of the Gospel of Mark, but not the standard works on narratology.[41]

When we turn to some of the reference works on narratology, we find definitions of *commentary*, rather than asides or parentheses. For example, Gerald Prince provides the following definition of *commentary* in his *A Dictionary of Narratology* (2003):

A commentarial excursus by the narrator; an author's intrusion; a narratorial intervention going beyond the identification or description of existents and the recounting of events. In commentary, the narrator explains the meaning or significance of a narrative element, makes value judgments, refers to worlds transcending the characters' world, and/ or comments on his or her own narration. Commentary can be simply ornamental; it can fulfill a rhetorical purpose; and it can function as an essential part of the dramatic structure of the narrative.[42]

This definition refers to the intrusive nature of comments by the author or narrator and their explanatory function, but also draws attention to the fact that they can make "value judgments" and can be "an essential part" of the narrative. I am less sure what Prince means by asserting that commentary can be "simply ornamental."

In the *Routledge Encyclopedia of Narrative Theory* (2005), Ansgar Nünning has articles on "Commentary" and "Metanarrative Comment."[43] He draws on his research on the role of the narrator in George Eliot's novels to define "Commentary" as, "a general category designating those speech acts by a narrator that go beyond providing the facts of the fictional world and the recounting of

70                                   *Chapter 2*

events. (For this reason they are also occasionally identified as 'authorial intrusions' or 'interventions.')"[44] He distinguishes the narrator's comments from description, report, summary, the representation of speech and direct address to the reader and, using Chatman's distinction between *story* and *discourse* (roughly equivalent to a chronological series of events and the way these are actually presented), he makes a further division between comment on the story which "can explain or interpret an event, a character's motivation, or the significance of a narrative element (interpretation), express his or her personal values and moral opinions (judgement), or express 'gnomic' and philosophical statements (generalisation)" and comment on the discourse which "includes self-reflexive and self-conscious references to the act or process of narration."[45] Nünning labels such comment on discourse as *metanarrative*. Presumably an example of this would be John 19:35: "(He who saw this has testified so that you also may believe. His testimony is true, and he knows that he tells the truth)." Nünning concludes by stating that all commentary can be either "explicit or implicit" and that "it can fulfil a variety of functions: it can be merely ornamental, but it can also serve important rhetorical or ideological purposes."[46] In that such commentary conveys the narrator's *voice*, it "can project an image of the narrator as honest, insincere, or morally untrustworthy."[47]

Like Prince, Nünning expresses the intrusive nature of comments and the fact that, alongside an explanatory function, they can convey the values of the narrator. His use of the category of *metanarrative* draws attention to a particular type of comment that is "self-reflexive and self-conscious," a category that is used by Sheeley in his analysis of asides in Luke-Acts. Again, like Prince, Nünning speaks of commentary that is "merely ornamental," alongside commentary that has an important function in the narrative.

## DEFINITIONS IN DRAMATIC THEORY

Although the term *aside* is not used in narratology, there have been various studies of *asides* in drama and it is worth considering some of the terms and definitions provided. I mentioned earlier that *aside* is a spatial metaphor that can most obviously be observed in a dramatic setting, where the speaker turns from the addressees to speak directly to the audience or camera.

In *Actors and Audience: A Study of Asides and Related Conventions in Greek Drama* (1977), David Bain provides the following definition: "When X and Y are on stage together, an aside is any utterance by either speaker not intended to be heard by the other and not in fact heard or properly heard by him."[48] He further refines this by saying, "To detect an aside one must first consider the intention behind a remark and then examine its effect. If it is taken up by the next speaker in such a way as to suggest that he has heard it properly, it is not an aside whatever the intention behind it."[49] In other words, an aside must be both intended for the audience alone and treated as such by other actors on stage.

Bain's definition of an aside can be viewed in relation to *dramatic irony*, whereby the audience is aware of information hidden to characters within the play, which can have either a comic or a tragic effect. This is also known as *parabasis*, a term derived from the function of the chorus in fifth century BC/BCE Athenian "Old Comedy," or "breaking the fourth wall," a description used in contemporary theatre and film studies. The implications of dramatic irony for the Gospel have been explored by Jo-Ann Brant, amongst others, and will be considered in more detail in chapter 5.[50]

Manfred Pfister, in his classic study of dramatic theory *The Theory and Analysis of Drama* (1988), describes three types of *aside*: the *monological aside*, the *aside ad spectores*, and the *dialogical aside*. The first two of these can be compared with the soliloquy, which "is based primarily on a convention, an unspoken agreement between author and receiver, which—unlike conditions prevailing in the real world—allows a dramatic figure to think aloud and talk to itself."[51] Indeed, in that "the speaker is neither alone on stage, nor does he imagine he is alone, nor has he forgotten that he is in the presence of others," the aside is "a convention that contravenes the circumstances of real life even more than the conventionalised soliloquy."[52] This "conventionalised monological aside" enables "the author to present the figure's thoughts directly . . . or to convey information on the intentions of a figure or the background to a particular situation in an economic way."[53] The second type, the *aside ad spectores*, is used to explicitly communicate with the audience, often to comic effect, and can provide information about the background to a dramatic situation and the speaker's plans.[54] The third type, the *dialogical aside*, is unlike the soliloquy in that it involves more than one actor in conversation with "the convention that although a speech is heard by the audience it is not 'heard' by certain characters on stage."[55]

Again, Pfister's definitions of asides raise the issue of dramatic irony, in this case suggesting its possible "comic effect." It is also noteworthy that his definition of the monological aside includes the observation that it can "convey information . . . in an economic way." In other words, one function of asides is to enable an author to provide important information to the hearer in a more concise way by telling rather than showing.

The functional implications of the definitions of *comments* in narratology and *asides* in dramatic theory will be considered in more detail in chapter 5.

## DEFINITIONS IN LINGUISTICS

As suggested earlier, where scholars have some theoretical underpinning for their definitions of *asides*, it is drawn mainly from modern literary criticism.

However, I believe that it is also important to look at the question of definition from the perspective of linguistics, given that the Gospel of John was not composed as literary fiction, a point I will return to later.

I noted above Burton-Roberts's observation that all parentheticals "are marked off from their hosts" by punctuation in writing or "special intonation contour in speech."[56] (Here, "hosts" is used to refer to those expressions which, in some fashion, contain the parenthetical clauses.) However, he acknowledges that the term *parentheticals* "covers a disparate and problematic range of phenomena" and the relationship between parentheticals and their hosts is a contested one.[57] This contested relationship concerns the extent to which parentheticals have a syntactical connection to their host clauses/sentences, which in many cases requires "special levels of syntactical representation, special assumptions and/or categories."[58] This debate on the relationship between parentheticals and their hosts is expanded by Nicole Dehé and Yordanka Kavalova in the introduction to their edited collection of essays on *Parentheticals* (2007).[59] They describe parentheticals as "a motley crew" and also acknowledge that "in linguistic research, parentheticals represent a rather peripheral and often neglected phenomenon."[60] However, they do offer the following definition:

> Parentheticals are expressions that are linearly represented in a given string of utterance (a host sentence), but seemingly independent at the same time. . . . Parentheticals typically function as modifiers, additions to or comments on the current talk. They often convey the attitude of the speaker towards the content of the utterance, and/or the degree of speaker endorsement.[61]

Dehé and Kavalova consider the relationship between parentheticals and their hosts in both syntactical and semantic/pragmatic terms, in addition to considering prosody (the sound of spoken parentheticals). Regarding syntax, they present a range of views from the "radical orphanage approach" of Liliane Haegman, who, they state, "argues that parentheticals are orphan constituents which are syntactically unattached at all levels of representation," to those who adopt an "integrated approach" in order "to account for linearization and certain syntactic relations that exist between the parenthetical and its host in the syntactic structure."[62]

Dehé and Kavalova also cite an example from Burton-Roberts of a parenthetical that may be an "instance of disfluency"—that is, where there is neither syntactic nor discourse relation to the host clause:

> The main point—*why not have a seat?*—is outlined in the middle paragraph.[63]

Such instances of disfluency (in this case presumably a comment addressed to a late arrival at a lecture) are more characteristic of spoken than written discourse and Dehé and Kavalova rightly question whether such interruptions

Terminology, Definitions, and Categorization 73

can justifiably be defined as parentheticals.[64] I do not observe any example of such "disfluency" in the Gospel of John. The nearest equivalent in the other Gospels would, I think, be the phrase "let the reader understand" (ὁ ἀναγινώσκων νοείτω) in Mark 13:14, a phrase which has generated considerable debate amongst commentators. However, even here there would seem to be some discourse relation to the preceding clause ("But when you see the desolating sacrilege set up where it ought not to be") and this connection is made clearer in the parallel in Matthew 24:15, which describes "the desolating sacrilege" as "standing in the holy place, as was spoken of by the prophet Daniel," so that the reader's understanding depends on knowledge of the relevant text in Daniel. In the Gospel of John, all parenthetical material has both a syntactic and discourse relation to the host clause. Sometime the syntactic link is quite weak, such as the parenthesis "and the scripture cannot be annulled" (καὶ οὐ δύναται λυθῆναι ἡ γραφή) in John 10:35, but even here there is at least a superficial link in the connective conjunction καί.

Recent work within linguistics continues to indicate a lack of consensus as to whether parentheticals can actually be defined in syntactic terms. Thus, Marlies Kluck, Dennis Ott, and Mark de Vries, who have written extensively on parentheticals, state, "Beyond the intuitive identification of parenthetical insertions, there is little agreement as to what precisely the defining characteristics of parenthesis are."[65] They go on to say:

> Even if we take for granted that we can more or less reliably identify parenthetical expressions, crucial questions arise about the nature of parentheses. From a syntactic point of view, for instance, we can ask whether parenthetical constituents are *structurally* integrated into the clause they are related to, or whether this integration takes place only at some extra-grammatical (discursive) level.[66]

Kluck, Ott, and Vries's own approach is to relate parentheticals to *ellipsis*— that is, where parts of the "surface form" of expressions are "omitted from the explicit signal (sound or sign) such that the meaning of these omitted parts can be reliably and systematically recovered."[67] Thus, syntactic connections between a parenthetical and its host clause can (in most cases?) be reconstructed. For example, in the case of John 10:35, mentioned above, we can derive a syntactic connection between the parenthetical and the host sentence on the basis of syntactical ellipsis:

> εἰ ἐκείνους εἶπεν θεοὺς πρὸς οὓς ὁ λόγος τοῦ θεοῦ ἐγένετο, καὶ οὐ δύναται λυθῆναι ἡ γραφή, ὃν ὁ πατὴρ ἡγίασεν καὶ ἀπέστειλεν εἰς τὸν κόσμον ὑμεῖς λέγετε ὅτι βλασφημεῖς, ὅτι εἶπον· υἱὸς τοῦ θεοῦ εἰμι;

> If those to whom the word of God came were called "gods"—and the scripture cannot be annulled—can you say that the one whom the Father

74                                    *Chapter 2*

has sanctified and sent into the world is blaspheming because I said, "I
am God's Son"? (10:35–36)

Here the ellipsis relates to the previous sentence:

ἀπεκρίθη αὐτοῖς [ὁ] Ἰησοῦς· οὐκ ἔστιν γεγραμμένον ἐν τῷ νόμῳ ὑμῶν
ὅτι ἐγὼ
εἶπα· θεοί ἐστε;

Jesus answered, "Is it not written in your law, 'I said, you are gods'?"
(10:34)

The verb γράφω in the phrase οὐκ ἔστιν γεγραμμένον . . . ; (Is it not
written . . . ?) in v.34 is echoed in the parenthetical clause in v.35 by the noun
ἡ γραφή (scripture). We can represent this process of ellipsis in this way:

1.  "I said, you are gods" is written in the law.
2.  What is written in the law equals "the scripture" (This is the ellipted syn-
    tactical link.)
3.  The scripture cannot be broken.
4.  Therefore, the sentence "I said, you are gods" cannot be broken.

This is a stronger syntactical link than the simple use of the connective conjunction καί, the opening word of the parenthetical.

Overall, from this brief survey of linguistic definitions, I note that
most linguistic studies tend to analyse small units of text within spoken
discourse and focus on the relationship between parentheticals and their
hosts. They acknowledge that the definition of parentheticals is complex
and contested, but that they have in most cases a syntactic relationship to
their hosts (even if through the use of ellipsis), while still in some way
appearing independent. In terms of function, they can modify, add to, or
comment on their hosts and, in doing so, can reflect the attitude of the
speaker/author.

## A TEMPORAL AND SPATIAL DEFINITION?

In a previous work, I provided my own definition of asides through reference to a *temporal* or *spatial* dimension. Comparing my definition to that of
Sheeley, I wrote, "My own, briefer, proposal is to define narrative asides as
referring to what lies outside the narrative framework of the text in a temporal
or spatial sense."[68] This proposed definition picks up on a phrase of Sheeley
referring to that "which exists outside the story being narrated," which can

## Terminology, Definitions, and Categorization

be compared to what North describes as "outside the 'time capsule' of the narrative itself."[69] This is essentially a definition based on content rather than one that takes account of grammatical features.

To clarify the terms *temporal* and *spatial*, I gave examples of what I understood as belonging outside the narrative framework in a temporal sense: "If the author refers to existing scriptures, these belong to a time before the narrative framework of the GJ, and when he says ταῦτα δὲ γέγραπται ἵνα πιστεύ[σ]ητε ὅτι Ἰησοῦς ἐστιν ὁ Χριστὸς ὁ υἱὸς τοῦ θεοῦ (Jn. 20:31), then this relates to a time after the narrative framework."[70] I also gave examples of what I understood as belonging outside and inside the narrative framework in a spatial sense:

> By "spatial" I include *explanatory* asides, such as the translation of words, where the narrator steps out of the narrative framework to provide extra information. I would not include explanations which, while somewhat out of sequence with the main narrative flow, are nonetheless part of the immediate action. For example, I would not count Jn. 4:8 as an aside.[71]

However, there are some problems with this attempt at a brief but all-encompassing definition based on content, namely:

1. What exactly is meant by the "narrative framework"?
2. How does the narrator "step out" of this narrative framework?
3. Is it necessary to exclude asides that are inside the narrative framework?

### THE NARRATIVE FRAMEWORK: A TEMPORAL DEFINITION

The first part of my definition refers to what lies outside the narrative framework from a *temporal* perspective. So, if we give John's narrative a definite starting point and end point, then phrases or sentences which refer to words or actions before or after this framework can be regarded as in some way separate from it. We might agree that a clear starting point for the Gospel's narrative framework is the ministry of John the Baptist from John 1:19 onwards, corresponding to the Gospel of Mark's starting point (Mark 1:4), although we also need to take into account the references to the Baptist in 1:6–8, 15, which seem embedded like xenoliths in the carved rock of the Prologue. A definite end point is Jesus' call to Peter to follow him in 21:22, the last action in the Gospel involving Jesus. However, as Bauckham perceptively points out, "John incorporates history into metahistory. These mere two-and-half years of this-worldly history are framed by reference to the beginning of time

76                                    *Chapter 2*

at the outset of the Prologue, and to the end of time, in Jesus' last words in the Epilogue (21:23)."[72] He regards this as significant, given that "ancient historical theory stressed the need to define the most appropriate starting point and the most appropriate finishing point for a history," so that "for a truly universal history, a metahistory, John has chosen the earliest possible starting point (creation), before which quite literally no previous event could be imagined, and the latest possible end point, the one that brings all history to a fully satisfying conclusion (the Parousia)."[73] Similarly, Brant states, "John's management of time is not simply about coherence and structure but about creating an experience of the sacred that entails the collapsing of the past and future into atemporal eternity."[74] She cites Jesus' statement "before Abraham was, I am" (8:58) and Jesus' "I am sayings" as examples of John's blending of tenses to create this "sense of eternal time."[75]

So, maybe the narrative in John starts at the very beginning with creation itself, a very good place to start? Certainly, the way we define the starting point (and end point) of the Gospel will affect our definition of asides/comments that lie outside the temporal framework. So, in the Prologue, are 1:6–8, 15, the references to John the Baptist, the intrusions? Or are 1:1–5, 9–14, 16–18, the "christological hymn," intrusions into the narrative of Jesus' life that begins, like Mark, with the account of the Baptist? It seems that we might have here the sort of ambiguous image or reversible figure beloved of Gestalt psychology.

My own judgement is that for the purpose of defining asides/comments, we should stick to the narrative framework of Jesus' earthly ministry. So, despite the fact that 1:6–8 (and 9), and 15, are put in brackets in Brown's commentary, they are certainly not extraneous to the Gospel's narrative.[76] Rather they help provide a kind of chiaroscuro effect in this opening passage: John is not the light, but he points to the "true light" (1:7–9). I would actually define the rest of the Prologue (1:1–5, 8–14, 16–18) as the asides or, to use a better term, comments, in that they provide the author's explanatory material lying behind the narrative which follows. This may appear a somewhat paradoxical choice in that most commentators consider the references to John as the asides. I admit that the issue is a complex one and maybe the Prologue belongs in a category of its own. I think what we can agree on is that elsewhere there are *temporal* asides where reference is made to things before or after Jesus' earthly ministry. As already noted, I gave 20:31 as an example of something relating to *after* the narrative framework (the call to believe in Jesus) and stated that where the author refers to existing scriptures, these belong to a time *before* the narrative framework. Examples of these references to the scriptures which are fulfilled in the ministry of Jesus are:

2:17:          ἐμνήσθησαν οἱ μαθηταὶ αὐτοῦ ὅτι γεγραμμένον ἐστίν· ὁ ζῆλος
               τοῦ οἴκου σου καταφάγεταί με.
               His disciples remembered that it was written, "Zeal for your house will consume me."

## Terminology, Definitions, and Categorization

**12:14–15:** εὑρὼν δὲ ὁ Ἰησοῦς ὀνάριον ἐκάθισεν ἐπ᾽ αὐτό, καθώς ἐστιν γεγραμμένον· μὴ φοβοῦ, θυγάτηρ Σιών· ἰδοὺ ὁ βασιλεύς σου ἔρχεται, καθήμενος ἐπὶ πῶλον ὄνου

Jesus found a young donkey and sat on it; as it is written: "Do not be afraid, daughter of Zion. Look, your king is coming, sitting on a donkey's colt!"

**12:38–41:** ἵνα ὁ λόγος Ἡσαΐου τοῦ προφήτου πληρωθῇ ὃν εἶπεν· κύριε, τίς ἐπίστευσεν τῇ ἀκοῇ ἡμῶν; καὶ ὁ βραχίων κυρίου τίνι ἀπεκαλύφθη; διὰ τοῦτο οὐκ ἠδύναντο πιστεύειν, ὅτι πάλιν εἶπεν Ἡσαΐας· τετύφλωκεν αὐτῶν τοὺς ὀφθαλμούς. . . . ταῦτα εἶπεν Ἡσαΐας ὅτι εἶδεν τὴν δόξαν αὐτοῦ, καὶ ἐλάλησεν περὶ αὐτοῦ.

This was to fulfil the word spoken by the prophet Isaiah: "Lord, who has believed our message, and to whom has the arm of the Lord been revealed?" And so they could not believe, because Isaiah also said, "He has blinded their eyes. . . ." Isaiah said this because he saw his glory and spoke about him.

**19:24:** εἶπαν οὖν πρὸς ἀλλήλους· μὴ σχίσωμεν αὐτόν, ἀλλὰ λάχωμεν περὶ αὐτοῦ τίνος ἔσται· ἵνα ἡ γραφὴ πληρωθῇ [ἡ λέγουσα]· διεμερίσαντο τὰ ἱμάτιά μου ἑαυτοῖς καὶ ἐπὶ τὸν ἱματισμόν μου ἔβαλον κλῆρον.

So they said to one another, "Let us not tear it, but cast lots for it to see who will get it." This was to fulfil what the scripture says, "They divided my clothes among themselves, and for my clothing they cast lots."

**19:28:** Μετὰ τοῦτο εἰδὼς ὁ Ἰησοῦς ὅτι ἤδη πάντα τετέλεσται, ἵνα τελειωθῇ ἡ γραφή, λέγει· διψῶ.

After this, when Jesus knew that all was now finished, he said (in order to fulfil the scripture), "I am thirsty."

**19:36–37:** ἐγένετο γὰρ ταῦτα ἵνα ἡ γραφὴ πληρωθῇ· ὀστοῦν οὐ συντριβήσεται αὐτοῦ. καὶ πάλιν ἑτέρα γραφὴ λέγει· ὄψονται εἰς ὃν ἐξεκέντησαν.

These things occurred so that the scripture might be fulfilled, "None of his bones shall be broken." And again another passage of scripture says, "They will look on the one whom they have pierced."

78                                      *Chapter 2*

These are the references by the author/narrator (as opposed to references made by Jesus or others) citing or alluding to what is written in
the Hebrew scriptures.[77] They derive from the evangelist's "omniscient"
post-resurrection perspective that allows him to interpret the words and
acts of Jesus and his disciples in relation to the fulfilment of scripture,
as Van Belle points out:

> Parce qu'il parle d'un point de vue situé dans le temps d'après la résurrection,
> l'évangéliste est "omniscient" et par conséquent capable d'interpréter les
> mots et les actes de Jésus et d'autres personnages, de souligner la connais-
> sance surnaturelle de Jésus, l'incompréhension et la compréhension tardive
> des disciples et d'interpréter la vie de Jésus à la lumière de l'accomplissement
> de l'Ecriture. (Because he speaks from a point of view situated in the time
> after the resurrection, the evangelist is "omniscient" and as a result able to
> interpret the words and deeds of Jesus and other characters, to underline
> the supernatural knowledge of Jesus, the lack of understanding and belated
> understanding of the disciples, and to interpret the life of Jesus in the light of
> the fulfilment of Scripture.)[78]

There would also appear to be a number of other temporal asides in the
Gospel, in addition to the already mentioned 20:31, where reference is being
made to a period after Jesus' earthly ministry. Thus, in 2:21–22, we have
the author/narrator's explanation of what Jesus was referring to when he had
spoken of raising up the destroyed temple in three days (2:19):

> ἐκεῖνος δὲ ἔλεγεν περὶ τοῦ ναοῦ τοῦ σώματος αὐτοῦ. ὅτε οὖν ἠγέρθη ἐκ
> νεκρῶν, ἐμνήσθησαν οἱ μαθηταὶ αὐτοῦ ὅτι τοῦτο ἔλεγεν, καὶ ἐπίστευσαν
> τῇ γραφῇ καὶ τῷ λόγῳ ὃν εἶπεν ὁ Ἰησοῦς.
>
> But he was speaking of the temple of his body. After he was raised
> from the dead, his disciples remembered that he had said this; and they
> believed the scripture and the word that Jesus had spoken.

Similarly, in 12:16, the author/narrator makes the following observation concerning Jesus' entry into Jerusalem (12:12–15):

> ταῦτα οὐκ ἔγνωσαν αὐτοῦ οἱ μαθηταὶ τὸ πρῶτον, ἀλλ' ὅτε ἐδοξάσθη
> Ἰησοῦς τότε ἐμνήσθησαν ὅτι ταῦτα ἦν ἐπ' αὐτῷ γεγραμμένα καὶ ταῦτα
> ἐποίησαν αὐτῷ.
>
> His disciples did not understand these things at first; but when Jesus was
> glorified, then they remembered that these things had been written of
> him and had been done to him.

## Terminology, Definitions, and Categorization 79

We can also compare these to the author/narrator's interpretation, in 7:39, of Jesus' words at the Festival of Tabernacles "Let anyone who is thirsty come to me and let the one who believes in me drink" (7:37–38):

τοῦτο δὲ εἶπεν περὶ τοῦ πνεύματος ὃ ἔμελλον λαμβάνειν οἱ πιστεύσαντες εἰς αὐτόν· οὔπω γὰρ ἦν πνεῦμα, ὅτι Ἰησοῦς οὐδέπω ἐδοξάσθη.

Now he said this about the Spirit, which believers in him were to receive; for as yet there was no Spirit, because Jesus was not yet glorified.

These explanations also clearly come from a post-resurrection perspective, as David Wead emphasizes in his examination of the author's "point of view," part of his study of literary devices in the Gospel.[79] Of course, the resurrection itself and some of the post-resurrection events lie within the temporal narrative, which ends with the final appearance of the resurrected Jesus to the disciples at the Sea of Tiberias and Jesus' call to Peter to follow him. However, the comments in 2:21–22 and 12:16 may well relate to a post-resurrection period beyond the narrative framework. Similarly, while the reference to believers' receiving the Holy Spirit (7:39) could be seen as part of the narrative, on the assumption that is what happens to the disciples when the resurrected Jesus breathes on them (20:22), the comment in 7:39 may well relate to a time period beyond the narrative framework. Indeed, Wead stresses that the promise of the Holy Spirit is for all believers and is only fulfilled at Pentecost.[80]

In regard to comments and the temporal framework, what should we make of the commonly denoted aside in 4:44 regarding Jesus' move from Samaria to Galilee (4:43–45)?

αὐτὸς γὰρ Ἰησοῦς ἐμαρτύρησεν ὅτι προφήτης ἐν τῇ ἰδίᾳ πατρίδι τιμὴν οὐκ ἔχει.

(for Jesus himself had testified that a prophet has no honour in the prophet's own country)

As commentators have noted, "a prophet has no honour in his own town/country" appears to be a common proverb, which is found in the Synoptics (Matthew 13:57; Mark 6:4; Luke 4:24) and the *Gospel of Thomas* 31. Michaels states, "Similar sayings are widely attested in the ancient world."[81] In the Synoptics it is applied to Jesus' home town of Nazareth in Galilee, but the reference to Galilee in John would seem awkward given that he is (initially, at least) welcomed there (4:45). This has led some scholars to see own town/country as a reference here to Jerusalem/Judea, where Jesus had set out from while travelling through Samaria, rather than Nazareth/Galilee, his destination. For example, Barrett accepts that, for John, Jerusalem is the

80 *Chapter 2*

place of Jesus' rejection, "the proper scene on which the Messiah must teach, work, and die."[82] However, it is, from a temporal perspective, part of the narrative framework and, according to the narrator, it is Jesus himself who has stated these words (αὐτὸς γὰρ Ἰησοῦς ἐμαρτύρησεν), so I would not include it in my list of temporal asides.

## THE NARRATIVE FRAMEWORK:
## A SPATIAL DEFINITION

The other aspect of my definition refers to what lies outside the narrative framework in a *spatial* sense, by which I mean explanatory comments, where the narrator "steps out" of the box of the narrative framework to provide extra information for the reader. I distinguish this from explanations which, although out of sequence with the main narrative, are nonetheless part of the immediate action. I will consider the latter under the heading of "Asides/ Comments within the Narrative Framework."

We need to ask how the narrator "steps out" of the narrative framework, for although it is in some of the asides that the narrator is most intrusive, there still remains an element of subjectivity in making a judgement as to what is explanation (*telling*) rather than narrative (*showing*). I have already referred to the distinction between telling and showing made by Hedrick, Sheeley, and Thatcher in their definitions and cited 4:9 ("Jews do not share things in common with Samaritans") as an example of a sentence that is commonly denoted as an aside, but where the telling/showing distinction may not be clear-cut. In this case, the distinction depends on whether the words should be interpreted as spoken by the Samaritan woman or as a comment by the author. A similar ambiguity occurs with passages such as 3:13 (or 16) to 21, where we cannot be sure if the author wants to present these as the words of Jesus or his own explanation. The RSV makes the editorial decision to put quotation marks at the end of verse 15, indicating that this is where Jesus finishes speaking; although it notes, "Some interpreters hold that the quotation continues through verse 21." The NRSV does the reverse: quotation marks at the end of verse 21 and a footnote to say that some interpreters conclude at verse 15. Brown states, "The attempt to attribute a certain number of verses to Jesus and a certain number to the evangelist is, in our opinion, impossible."[83] By contrast, Schnackenburg believes, "Verses 13–21 do not form part of the Gospel narrative, but come from a kerygmatic exposition of the evangelist which was originally independent."[84] Similarly, Theobald describes this passage as "Ein johanneisches »Lehrstück«" (a Johannine "teaching unit").[85]

The same ambiguity and editorial uncertainty about where to put quotation marks occurs in 3:31–36, where it is unclear if these words should be attributed to John the Baptist or the author (or Jesus himself). In this instance, both the RSV and the NRV place quotation marks at the end of verse 30, but include a footnote to the effect that some interpreters hold that the quotation continues to the end of verse 36. Brown suggests that verses 31–36 are a discourse of Jesus that an editor has inserted after the words of John the Baptist.[86] Similarly, Theobald states, "Die *Sprache* des Stücks ist die des johanneischen Christus."[87]

In other cases, it is much clearer that it is the author/narrator speaking and the words cannot be attributed to Jesus or another character within the narrative. This is true of the "translation" of Aramaic or Hebrew terms, a category of asides commonly used by scholars. It is also true of the Prologue (excluding the references to John the Baptist), the reference to eyewitness testimony in 19:35, and the concluding summaries in 20:30–31 and 21:24–25.

However, in other instances, even when the words clearly belong to the narrator and cannot be attributed to a character within the narrative, I suggest that we cannot necessarily state that the narrator has stepped out of the box of the narrative framework. For example, what should we make of the geographical indication in 1:28, "This took place in Bethany across the Jordan where John was baptizing," which is listed as an aside by Van Belle and Hedrick, and as a possible aside by O'Rourke? Tenney does not include 1:28 in his list of "Footnotes of time and place" and notes, "Not every geographical or chronological reference, of which there are many in John, can be called a footnote. Some of them are woven firmly into the texture of the main narrative; but others which are seemingly added as subsequent comments fall into this classification."[88] The criterion Tenney provides for distinguishing the latter is that they "identify or qualify some main action by a reference to place or time which is significant in the experience of the author, and which he feels he must explain for the sake of his audience."[89] The instances of "Footnotes of time and place" he lists are 6:23; 7:2; 8:20; 9:14; 10:22–23; 11:30; 19:31, 42; 21:8.[90]

My own observation is that it is difficult for a writer to tell a narrative without giving geographical or chronological indications and, of Tenney's examples, only 8:20 ("He spoke these words while he was teaching in the treasury of the temple, but no one arrested him, because his hour had not yet come") stands out from the narrative because of its reference to Jesus' "hour," a recurring motif which receives its meaning only through a grasp of the whole narrative. My tendency in reading the text is to accept phrases or sentences as part of the narrative or dialogue unless they seem clearly intended as direct address to the reader. This raises again the issue of how intrusive the narrator is, something which literary critics have focussed on and to which I will return.

82                                    *Chapter 2*

## ASIDES/COMMENTS INSIDE THE
## NARRATIVE FRAMEWORK

In my proposed definition of asides I chose to exclude what belongs *inside* the narrative framework. I cited 4:8, "(His disciples had gone to the city to buy food)," as an example. This is put in brackets in the KJV and NRSV, although not in the RSV. It is included in the lists of asides given by Van Belle, Hedrick, and Köstenberger, although not those of Tenney or O'Rourke, and it is treated as parenthetical by a number of commentators.[91] I suggest that it is an integral part of the narrative of Jesus' encounter with the Samaritan woman in 4:4–42, a distinct literary unit, and it accounts for why Jesus is (probably) alone with the woman at the well.[92] The disciples are not mentioned again until verse 27, when we are told that they arrive on the scene and are astonished that Jesus is speaking with a woman. The woman then returns to Sychar and Jesus' subsequent discourse is with the disciples (verses 31–38).

Barrett describes 4:8 as a "stage direction" and notes that "the story is neatly contrived dramatically," whether or not verse 8 was inserted by the evangelist into a traditional story.[93] Thyen calls it, "eine notwendige ‚szenische Bemerkung'" (a necessary "staging remark").[94] Michaels, too, emphasizes the dramatic purpose of the verse, in that it sets the stage for the disciples' return and their shock.[95] Theobald describes the narrative function of v.8 as "die Nebenhandlung von V. 27–38 vorzubereiten" (to prepare the subplot of vv. 27–38).[96] These seem to me important observations that relate to my earlier discussion of asides in drama, and they suggest that 4:8 is not a later addition to an existing source but an integral aspect of the author's style.

Brant calls the verse "an important analepsis (flashback)" provided by the narrator to explain why Jesus asks the woman and not one of his disciples for a drink.[97] Elsewhere, Brant states that the Gospel's narrator "frequently employs analepsis (reference to a past act) and prolepsis (reference to a future act)," which she sees as an example of taking advantage "of the reader's privileged vantage point of standing outside story time."[98] In relation to the first of these categories, analepsis, I have already noted Bultmann's use of the term *Rückverweisungen*.[99] Schnackenburg uses the similar term *Rückverweise* and Thyen *Rückblicken*. In his list of asides, Köstenberger includes the category entitled "References to Characters or Events Mentioned Earlier in the Narrative," of which he provides 11 instances.[100] Van Belle has a more extensive list of "Référence à un passage qui précède ou qui suit" (Reference to a passage which precedes or which follows), that is, examples of both analepsis and prolepsis.[101] He includes 14 examples of parentheses looking back and seven examples looking forward that are additional to those in Köstenberger's list.

These instances of analepsis and prolepsis occur with some frequency in the Gospel and are a noteworthy category of asides/parentheses in the view of many scholars, so I wonder if I am right to exclude them from my temporal/spatial definition solely because they lie within the narrative framework, albeit out of sequence with the narrative's linear progression? It is certainly the case that quite frequently in the Gospel, the narrator directs the reader to earlier material to aid clarification. Commenting on this as a feature of the parentheses, Wendy North affirms that "as a narrator, John is given to much repetition, which is all part of the care package. . . . [H]e ensures that his readers do not lose the thread of his argument by constantly reminding them of the story so far and repeating material they already know from earlier in the Gospel."[102] I suggest that this "care package" is, in fact, a common aspect of storytelling. We may or may not like the author of John's somewhat discursive (or what Tenney calls "diffuse") style, moving back and forth during the narrative, picking up and sometimes clarifying earlier details, but the comments made lie within the narrative framework, not outside it. Some would regard such out-of-sequence remarks as a feature of John's meandering, parenthetical style. Indeed, Tenney suggests that it is an indication of the oral teaching of an old man.[103] However, the discursive style helps to create an interest in the narrative, so that it does not consist simply of a dull linear progression. It also allows for the development of ideas and a deepening of the reader's understanding. A clear example of this involves the mentions of Nicodemus in 7:50 and 19:39:

λέγει Νικόδημος πρὸς αὐτούς, ὁ ἐλθὼν πρὸς αὐτὸν [τὸ] πρότερον, εἷς ὢν ἐξ αὐτῶν
Nicodemus, who had gone to Jesus before, and who was one of them, asked

ἦλθεν δὲ καὶ Νικόδημος, ὁ ἐλθὼν πρὸς αὐτὸν νυκτὸς τὸ πρῶτον
Nicodemus, who had at first come to Jesus by night

In both cases the *Rückverweisungen* (ὁ ἐλθὼν πρὸς αὐτὸν [τὸ] πρότερον and ὁ ἐλθὼν πρὸς αὐτὸν νυκτὸς τὸ πρῶτον) refer back to the introduction of Nicodemus in 3:1–2:

Ἦν δὲ ἄνθρωπος ἐκ τῶν Φαρισαίων, Νικόδημος ὄνομα αὐτῷ, ἄρχων τῶν Ἰουδαίων· οὗτος ἦλθεν πρὸς αὐτὸν νυκτὸς . . .
"Now there was a Pharisee named Nicodemus, a leader of the Jews. He came to Jesus by night . . .

84                                            *Chapter 2*

The *Rückverweisungen* in 7:50 and 19:39 appear to act as stage asides, prompts to the listener to remind us that Nicodemus was the one who actively came to Jesus, albeit at night. Zumstein calls 7:50 an example of analepsis and 19:39 an explanatory gloss.[104] It is, I think, significant that 19:39 picks up on the temporal marker νυκτός (by night) used of Nicodemus's initial visit to Jesus and that the same term is also used in some variant readings of 7:50. Given the repeated symbolism of dark and light in the Gospel, the author is probably saying more about Nicodemus here by the use of νυκτός than just identifying who he is. As Brown observes, "John consistently recalls this detail . . . because of its symbolic import," with darkness and night symbolizing "the realm of evil, untruth, and ignorance."[105] There are other, perhaps more obvious, ways in which Nicodemus could have been identified for an audience listening to the narrative at both 7:50 (variant readings) and 19:39. For example, he could have been referred to as the Pharisee who had conversed with Jesus about the meaning of being born again/anew.

The Nicodemus *Rückverweisungen* are included in Köstenberger's list of "References to Characters or Events Mentioned Earlier in the Narrative" and it is probably helpful to consider all the examples Köstenberger gives, alongside the passages referred back to:[106]

| | |
|---|---|
| 4:46 | 2:1–11: the wedding at Cana |
| 6:23 | 6:1–15: Jesus feeds the crowd with bread |
| 7:50 | 3:1–2: Nicodemus comes to Jesus |
| 9:13, 18, 24 | 9:1–7: the healing of the man born blind |
| 10:40 | 1:28: the place where John was baptizing |
| 12:1–2, 9, 17 | 11:1–44: the raising of Lazarus from the dead |
| 18:14: | 11:49–51: Caiaphas's "prophecy" |
| 18:26 | 18:10: Peter cuts off the ear of the high priest's servant |
| 19:39 | 3:1–2: Nicodemus comes to Jesus |
| 20:8 | 20:4: the other disciple who reached the tomb first |
| 21:20 | 13:23–25: the disciple who asked Jesus about his betrayer |

Some of these references occur so soon after the original passage (notably 6:23; 9:13, 18, 24; 20:8) that they can hardly be considered reminders. The same applies to most of the other examples provided by Van Belle—for example, 1:40 referring back to 1:37.[107] However, other of Van Belle's examples may have more significance despite the short gap between the reference and referent. A case in point is 1:24, which refers back to 1:19, but narrows down "the Jews" who send a delegation to John the Baptist to "the Pharisees," (unless there is a second separate delegation).[108]

## Terminology, Definitions, and Categorization 85

However, it seems to me that we need to take into account the gap between the *Rückverweisungen* and the material they refer to in assessing what is an internal aside. For example, in the case of the asides Λάζαρος, ὃν ἤγειρεν ἐκ νεκρῶν Ἰησοῦς (Lazarus whom Jesus had raised from the dead) (12:1) and τὸν Λάζαρον . . . ὃν ἤγειρεν ἐκ νεκρῶν (Lazarus . . . whom he had raised from the dead) (12:9), which look back to the dramatic account of Lazarus's raising in 11:1–44, with the short gap of an intervening passage (11:45–57), are we to assume that the audience have left for a break in the course of the narration, so that they had forgotten who Lazarus was and need him to be reintroduced for the next section of the story, beginning with the temporal indicator, "Six days before the Passover" (12:1)? Or are these asides simply emphasizing the enormity of what Jesus had done? Or are we dealing with a somewhat clumsy piece of editing? Commentators are divided over this. Brown labels the phrase in 12:1 an "editorial gloss," indicated by the repetition of "Jesus" from earlier in the same verse, and regarding 12:9 he states, "The Lazarus motif with persistent identification ('whom he had raised from the dead') is mentioned only in the editorial framework."[109] From another perspective, Lincoln suggests, "The narrator ensures that readers will see the links with what has preceded it by an explicit and somewhat heavy-handed identification of Lazarus as the one whom Jesus had raised from the dead."[110] Michaels sees "a certain redundancy to the clause 'whom he had raised from the dead,' for the reader already knows this."[111] Brant refers to the phrase in 12:1 as an "analeptic epithet" to tie 12:1–8 to the previous episode, but also sees a deeper significance, namely that it "constructs a ritual space" whereby the resurrected Lazarus is able to attend his own funeral rites.[112] I am not sure about Brant's interpretation, but it does suggest to me that the asides in 12:1, 9 do not need to be dismissed as editorial glosses.

In considering the "narrative distance" between intertextual references, we also have to take into account the possibility that the author is alluding to characters and events from earlier traditions, including the synoptic traditions, in which case the asides/parentheses/ comments can no longer be regarded as just *internal*. A notable example of this is the possible *prolepsis* in 11:2:

ἦν δὲ Μαριὰμ ἡ ἀλείψασα τὸν κύριον μύρῳ καὶ ἐκμάξασα τοὺς πόδας αὐτοῦ ταῖς θριξὶν αὐτῆς
Mary was the one who anointed the Lord with perfume and wiped his feet with her hair

The account of this incident does not occur until 12:3, which leads Brown to state, "This verse is clearly a parenthesis added by an editor" and that "it refers to a scene in ch. xii which has not yet been narrated."[113] However, other scholars see in 11:2 either a retelling of the synoptic traditions recorded in

86                                   *Chapter 2*

Mark 14:3–9 (with its parallel in Matthew 26:6–13) and/or Luke 7:36–50, or else a recalling of a separate tradition known to John's readers. For example, Barrett says, "John points forward to the incident he describes in 12.1–8; but it seems clear that he is able to presuppose that his readers were already familiar with it; this implies that they were Christians, and knew the synoptic tradition (or a tradition closely akin to it)."[114] This is not a new idea. Westcott states, "This verse obviously presupposes . . . a general knowledge of the Evangelic history."[115] Bultmann calls it "a gloss of the ecclesiastical redactor" whose purpose is to identify the Mary named here with the synoptic traditions.[116]

Bauckham rejects the idea that 11:2 is a redactional gloss, rather it serves as an "explanatory parenthesis . . . directed at readers/hearers of John who already knew Mark's Gospel."[117] Wendy North does not regard it as an example of prolepsis, arguing cogently that "11:2 does not direct the reader forward to the story in 12.1–8. Rather, it functions to bring to mind an event of which the reader is already aware, either through oral teaching or, possibly, from hearing an earlier version of the Gospel."[118] Theobald, who describes the verse as "ein außertextliches Vorwissen der Leser" (an existing knowledge on the part of the reader beyond the text), believes that we can only speculate on the basis for this knowledge.[119] Overall, we can conclude that 11:2 is quite possibly not an *internal* aside.

To sum up my thoughts on asides/comments within the narrative framework, I suggest that the frequent use of analepsis in the Gospel is a feature of the author's style and it helps provide explanations for the reader. The less frequent use of prolepsis may not provide clarification for the reader in the way that analepsis does, but it can have a stylistic function in creating interest in the narrative. Whether these instances of analepsis and prolepsis are the result of editorial glossing or else an indication of oral traditions lying behind the text will be considered in more detail in the next chapter, looking at the process of composition. We need to take into account the "narrative distance" between intertextual references, and we also need to be aware that some of these perceived internal references may in fact be alluding to earlier gospel traditions, including the synoptic traditions. Overall, it seems to me that the internal asides/comments should be treated separately from those asides/comments which lie outside the temporal/spatial framework of the narrative. This leads me on to a consideration of the categorization of these *external* asides/comments.

## CATEGORIZATION

Returning to the NRSV's 25 phrases or sentences in brackets or dashes that I listed earlier, I suggest the following headings to give a sense of the variety of asides/comments which the editors of this translation consider in some way set apart from the narrative:

| | |
|---|---|
| Looking forward (Prolepsis): | 1:15 (cf. 1:30); 12:4 (cf. 13:21–30; 18:1–5) |
| Reference to existing tradition? | 3:24; 4:44 |
| Explanation or clarification of the narrative: | 2:9; 4:2; 4:8; 7:5; 7:22; 10:35; 12:6; 13:23; 14:22; 18:32; 21:19 |
| "Translations" of Hebrew/Aramaic terms: | 1:38, 41, 42; 4:25; 9:7; 20:16, 24 |
| Explanation of Jewish customs: | 4:9 |
| Reference to the fulfilment of scripture: | 19:28 |
| Authority of the narrator (or witness): | 19:35 |

The majority of these comments have an explanatory function, with some relating to other writings such as the Hebrew scriptures and (possibly) the synoptic traditions. However, other functions are exhibited, such as the assertion of the authority of the author or witness in 19:35.

In my survey of existing scholarship, I noted that the practice of categorizing the comments in the Gospel of John started in earnest with Tenney's essay (1960), although Garvie (1922) had provided six rough categories. Tenney's categorization was adopted by O'Rourke (1979), and developed by Van Belle (1985), Hedrick (1990), and Köstenberger (2009), with Thatcher (1994) providing a radically different approach.

Tenney and O'Rourke's 10 categories are:[120]

1. Footnotes of translation
2. Footnotes of time and place
3. Customs
4. Footnotes reflecting the author
5. Recollections of the disciples
6. Notes explanatory of situations or actions
7. Enumeration or summary
8. Identification of persons
9. Knowledge of Jesus
10. Long theological notes

Van Belle uses 17 categories "according to contents" alongside his grammatical and stylistic classifications:[121]

1. Translation of Hebrew or Aramaic words
2. Explanation of Jewish customs
3. Indication or description of persons
4. Indication or description of place

88                                    *Chapter 2*

5.  Indication or description of time
6.  Explanation of the words of Jesus or another person
7.  Explanation of the actions of Jesus or another person
8.  Lack of understanding by the disciples or other persons
9.  Belated understanding by the disciples
10. Fulfilment of Scripture or the words of Jesus
11. Reference to a passage which precedes or follows
12. Correction
13. "Notice de conclusion" (that is, marking the end of a particular section)
14. Reflection inserted 'after the event' in the narrative
15. Extended theological reflection
16. Reference to the author of the Gospel
17. Supernatural knowledge by Jesus

Hedrick has 15 categories,[122] in which the narrator:

1.  Locates particular events with a topographical site
2.  Explains Hebrew and Aramaic words
3.  Explains the time of an event
4.  Explains Jewish religious customs
5.  Clarifies, or further explains, the significance or success of events or sayings
6.  Cites (and sometimes explains) or alludes to OT passages as proof texts that clarify events or sayings
7.  Explains the "true" meaning, cause, or intent of a saying of Jesus
8.  Clarifies the inner motivation and inner feelings of Jesus
9.  Adds new information to clarify a preceding statement
10. Provides the Hebrew term for a given location
11. Explains thoughts, motives, and character of personalia in the story
12. Makes a brief statement indicating a passage of time, change of location, or indicates a brief interlude in the action of the story
13. Identifies personalia in the story
14. Clarifies distances between locations
15. Cites sayings of Jesus as "proof texts"

Köstenberger has 12 categories:[123]

1.  Translations of Aramaic or Hebrew terms
2.  Explanations of Palestinian topography
3.  Explanations of Jewish customs
4.  References to Jesus' supernatural insight or foreknowledge of events or to God's providential ordering of events

*Terminology, Definitions, and Categorization* 89

5. References to characters or events mentioned earlier in the narrative
6. References to the fulfilment of scripture or of Jesus' words
7. References to a failure to understand
8. Clarifications of the meaning of statements made by Jesus or others
9. Statements in relation to the Gospel tradition
10. Numbering of events in the narrative
11. Extended commentary
12. Other clarifying or explanatory statements

Thatcher's dissatisfaction with Tenney and O'Rourke's lists of categories leads him to a more overarching approach using the broad categories of Staging, Defining, Explaining discourse, and Explaining actions, although he then applies various sub-categories to these and he also acknowledges that it is not always clear which categories some of his asides should be assigned to.[124]

I think we need to ask whether, other than satisfying scholars' natural tendency towards order, these categories actually help us to understand an overall function for the comments, if such an overall function can in fact be determined? The common denominators in the lists above seem to me to be:

- Explanation of words, places, times and customs
- Theological insights into words and events
- Self-awareness of the author/narrator
- Reference to external scriptures and traditions
- A holding together of the narrative, for example, though the (re-)identification of characters and the enumerating of events (that is, internal comments)

We can compare these with the four broad categories that Sheeley employs in his analysis of asides in Luke-Acts and comparative literature:

- Material which is necessary for the reader to understand the story
- General information for the reader
- Asides "which provide an inside view into the minds and thoughts of a character"
- Self-conscious narration, including "asides which comment on the narrator's relation to the story, the narrator's relation to the reader, or the reader's relation to the story"[125]

I will consider these categories in greater detail in relation to the role of the narrator and the author in chapter 5. For now, I also want to draw attention to Seymour Chatman's hierarchy of narrator prominence, which Scott Richardson draws on in his insightful study of the narrator in the writings of

90                                    *Chapter 2*

Homer.[126] Richardson uses this "scale of narrative features ranging from the most covert signs of the narrator's presence to the most overt" to structure his analysis of the "Homeric narrator" in seven broad categories: summaries, pauses in the story while the discourse is continued, versions of the characters' speech, rearrangement of the order of events, special (superhuman) abilities, commentary on the story, and commentary on the discourse (self-conscious commentary).[127] These categories would seem to overlap with those of the various Johannine scholars, for example, special (superhuman) abilities corresponding to "supernatural knowledge by Jesus" (Van Belle) or "references to Jesus' supernatural insight or foreknowledge of events" (Köstenberger). It would therefore be helpful to broadly follow Richardson's procedure and categorize the comments in the GJ in a "covert to overt scale"— that is, the "degrees of intrusion" by the narrator/author—alongside my own broad distinction between comments inside (temporal and spatial) and outside the narrative framework. I will attempt to do this after further consideration of the literary and linguistic functions of the comments.


## CONCLUSIONS


What this chapter has highlighted is a considerable degree of complexity and uncertainty regarding the terminology, definition, and categorization of asides/parentheses/comments. Nevertheless, I believe that it is possible to draw some broad conclusions before going on to consider the particular functions of this phenomenon in the Gospel of John.

I noted the great variety of *terminology* used for those phrases and sentences which commentators regard as in some way distinct from their co-text. Some of these terms emphasize a perceived redactional process in the composition of the text, terms such as *interpolations, insertions, glosses,* and more consideration of the implication of this will be given in the following chapter. Other terms reflect the influence of modern literary criticism and consideration of the point of view of the narrator, terms such as *asides, comments* and *remarks.* I suggested that the terms *footnotes* and *parentheses* could belong equally to these two perspectives, the redactional process or the narrator's voice. Finally, the predominantly explanatory nature of the phenomenon is stressed by the terms *commentary, explanations,* and *hermeneiai* (Hedrick). *Asides* is probably the term which become most widespread in NT studies, perhaps because of the influence of Sheeley's *Narrative Asides in Luke-Acts.* It is used, for example, by Michaels in his commentary.[128] However, the problem with the term *asides* and other spatial metaphors such as *footnotes* or *parentheses* is that they imply that these phrases and sentences are of lesser value than the "real" narrative. Some scholars may argue that this is indeed the case, but I think it is important to employ a more neutral term such as *comments*, and this is the term that I will use most frequently from now on. Whether they should be considered as comments of the *author* or the *narrator* will need further examination of their literary and linguistic function.

I also noted the reluctance on the part of scholars to provide a precise *definition* of asides/parentheses/comments and that where definitions are offered by NT scholars, for example by Hedrick and Sheeley, there remains a degree of ambiguity. From the various definitions offered, I proposed that in the Gospel of John they make some form of interjection/intrusion/interruption into the narrative, although there remains a significant subjective element in determining the force of this interjection. Although their principal function is an explanatory one, this is not their sole function. They also indicate a more direct form of address to the reader by *telling* rather than *showing* and they may help to establish a relationship between the author/narrator and reader/narratee.

I also considered the range of definitions in literary, dramatic, and linguistic theory, noting that they can fulfil a rhetorical function in conveying the values of the narrator and that they can be used as part of a strategy of dramatic irony. However, their definition remains complex and contested, especially with regard to a grammatical/syntactical definition.

I offered my own temporal and spatial definitions in relation to the narrative framework of the Gospel and distinguished between internal and external asides/comments, questioning whether the examples of analepsis and prolepsis that are internal to the narrative can truly be considered as asides.

Finally, I made a brief look at *categorization*, referring to the lists given by Tenney, O'Rourke, Van Belle, Hedrick, and Köstenberger and comparing them to the broader categories used by Thatcher and Sheeley. I concluded that general agreement could be found in the categories of explanation (words, places, times, and customs), a holding together of the narrative, theological insights, reference to external sources, and the self-awareness of the author/narrator. I also concluded that there was value in considering a scale of how overt or covert the author/narrator comes across in the asides/comments, following Scott Richardson's study of the narrator in Homer.

## NOTES

1. Tenney, "Footnotes," 362.
2. Tenney, "Footnotes," 350.
3. As noted above, Brown is less confident of this editing process in his revised *Introduction* (2003).

92                                    *Chapter 2*

4. Van Belle, *Les Parenthèses*, 10.

5. Translation from Quintilian, *The Orator's Education, Volume IV: Books 9–10*, ed. and trans. Donald A. Russell, LCL 127 (Cambridge, MA: Harvard University Press, 2002), 113.

6. See, for example, Van Belle, "Les Parenthèses Johanniques," 1915, 1921.

7. Van Belle, *Les Parenthèses*, 35–42, referencing Rudolf Bultmann, *Das Evangelium des Johannes*, (Göttingen: Vandenhoeck & Ruprecht, 1941). Van Belle notes Bultmann's uncertainty as to whether some of the *Anmerkungen* should be attributed to the original sources or are added by the Evangelist or the ecclesiastical redactor (36–37).

8. Van Belle, *Les Parenthèses*, 47–50, referencing Rudolf Schnackenburg, *Das Johannesevangelium*, 3 vols., HTKNT 4 (Freiburg: Herder, 1965, 1971, 1975).

9. Hedrick, "Authorial Presence," 76.

10. Thatcher, "New Look at Asides," 430.

11. E.V. Rieu, *The Four Gospels: A New Translation from the Greek* (London: Penguin, 1952), 193–250. Rieu does not use versification, so I have followed the NRSV's versification here.

12. The historian Anthony Grafton, in his quirky survey of footnotes, traces their origins to around 1700 or slightly earlier in the work of Pierre Bayle (1647–1706), but states, "Footnotes flourished most brightly in the eighteenth century, when they served to comment ironically on the narrative in the text as well as support its veracity." Anthony Grafton, *The Footnote: A Curious History* (London: Faber and Faber, 1997), 191, 229; cf. Anthony Grafton, "The Footnote from De Thou to Ranke," *History and Theory* 33, no. 4, (1994), 72.

13. *Oxford English Dictionary*, s.v. "parenthesis (n.)," December 2023, https://doi.org/10.1093/OED/3479361568.

14. Malcolm Beckwith Parkes, *Pause and Effect: An Introduction to the History of Punctuation in the West* (Aldershot: Scholar Press, 1992), 48–49.

15. *Oxford English Dictionary*, s.v. "parenthesis (n.)," December 2023, https://doi.org/10.1093/OED/3479361568.

16. *Novum Testamentum Graece*, ed. Barbara Aland, Kurt Aland, Johannes Karavidopoulos, Carlo M. Martini, Bruce M. Metzger, 28th rev. edition (Stuttgart: Deutsche Bibelgesellschaft, 2012).

17. Gary M. Burge, *Interpreting the Gospel of John: A Practical Guide*, 2nd ed. (Grand Rapids: Baker Academic, 2013), 93.

18. Wendy E. S. North, *A Journey Round John: Tradition, Interpretation and Context in the Fourth Gospel*, LNTS 534 (London: Bloomsbury T & T Clark, 2015), 148, 149; cf. Wendy E. S. North, "Why Should Historical Criticism Continue to Have a Place in Johannine Studies?" in *What We Have Heard: The Past, Present, and Future of Johannine Studies*, ed. Tom Thatcher (Waco: Baylor University Press, 2007), 20.

19. North, *Journey Round John*, 149.

20. Sheeley, *Narrative Asides*, 36.

21. *The Greek New Testament*, ed. Barbara Aland, Kurt Aland, Johannes Karavidopoulos, Carlo M. Martini, Bruce M. Metzger, Holgar Strutwolf, Institute for New Testament Textual Research, 5th rev. ed. (Stuttgart: Deutsche Bibelgesellschaft/

# Terminology, Definitions, and Categorization          93

United Bible Societies, 2014); *The Greek New Testament: SBL Edition*, ed. Michael W. Holmes (Atlanta: SBL/Bellingham: Logos Bible Software, 2010).

22. The editor, Michael Holmes, comments, "Punctuation generally follows that of Westcott and Hort" (*SBLGNT*, xiv). The other editions used by SBLGNT are: Tregelles (1857–79), Richard J. Goodrich and Albert L. Lukaszewski, *A Reader's Greek New Testament* (Grand Rapids: Zondervan, 2003), and Maurice A. Robinson and William G. Pierpont (eds.), *The New Testament in the Original Greek: Byzantine Textform 2005* (Southborough, MA: Chilton, 2005).

23. Brooke Foss Westcott, *The Gospel According to St. John: The Greek Text with Introduction and Notes*, ed. Arthur Westcott, 2 vols. (London: John Murray, 1908), 1:147.

24. Noel Burton-Roberts, "Parentheticals," in *Encyclopedia of Language and Linguistics*, ed. Keith Brown, 2nd ed., 14 vols. (Amsterdam: Elsevier, 2006), 9:180.

25. Bruce M. Metzger, "Persistent Problems Confronting Bible Translators," *Bibliotheca Sacra* 150 (1993): 278; cf. Bruce M. Metzger, *Manuscripts of the Greek Bible: An Introduction to Greek Palaeography* (New York: Oxford University Press, 1981), 31–32.

26. See Van Belle, *Les Parenthèses*, 8–9.

27. This marks the end of a paragraph, so there is no dash after the clause.

28. Van Belle, "Les Parenthèses Johanniques," 1919n92.

29. Tenney, "Footnotes," 350.

30. Hedrick, review of Van Belle, 720–21. Van Belle himself notes similar criticisms by Bjerkelund, F. Grob, and Y. Simoens ("Les Parenthèses Johanniques," 1917).

31. Van Belle, "Les Parenthèses Johanniques," 1918.

32. Hedrick, "Authorial Presence," 76.

33. Sheeley, *Narrative Asides*, 36; cf. 177.

34. See Wayne Booth, *The Rhetoric of Fiction*, 2nd ed. (Chicago, IL: University of Chicago Press, 1983), 3–20. (The first edition was published in 1961.) See also Seymour Chatman, *Story and Discourse: Narrative Structure in Fiction and Film* (Ithaca, NY: Cornell University Press, 1978), 32.

35. It is important to note that the terms *mimesis* and *diegesis*, which derive from Plato's *Republic*, are used in significantly different ways by narratologists. See Jeremy Hawthorn, *A Glossary of Contemporary Literary Theory*, 4th ed. (London: Arnold, 2000), 78–81.

36. Jo-Ann A. Brant, "The Fourth Gospel as Narrative and Drama," in *The Oxford Handbook of Johannine Studies*, ed. Judith M. Lieu and Martinus C. de Boer (Oxford: Oxford University Press, 2018), 190.

37. Booth, *Rhetoric*, 20.

38. Jean Calvin, *Calvin's Commentaries: The Gospel according to St John 1–10*, trans. T. H. L. Parker, ed. David W. Torrance and Thomas F. Torrance (Edinburgh: Saint Andrew Press, 1959), 90.

39. Thomas E. Boomershine, "The Medium and Message of John: Audience Address and Audience Identity in the Fourth Gospel," in *The Fourth Gospel in First*

94 *Chapter 2*

*Century Media Culture*, ed. Anthony Le Donne and Tom Thatcher, LNTS 426 (London: Bloomsbury T & T Clark, 2011), 101.

40. James L. Resseguie, "A Glossary of New Testament Narrative Criticism with Illustrations," *Religions* 10, no. 3 (2019): 7. https://doi.org/10.3390/rel10030217.

41. Resseguie's reference is to the most recent edition of Rhoads and Michie's study (which was originally published in 1982): David Rhoads, Joanna Dewey, and Donald Michie, *Mark as Story: An Introduction to the Narrative of a Gospel*, 3rd ed. (Minneapolis: Fortress Press, 2012). Their understanding of asides is expressed in this way: "At points throughout the story, the narrator seems to pause and—ever so briefly—address the audience more directly by providing commentary on the story, commentary that is not part of the events themselves and that often includes information not available to some or all of the characters in the story (42)."

42. Gerald Prince, *A Dictionary of Narratology*, rev. ed. (Lincoln: University of Nebraska Press, 2003), 25.

43. Ansgar Nünning, "Commentary," "Metanarrative Comment," in *Routledge Encyclopedia of Narrative Theory*, ed. David Herman, Manfred Jahn, and Marie-Laure Ryan (New York: Routledge, 2005), 74, 304–5.

44. Nünning, "Commentary," 74. See Ansgar Nünning, *Grundzüge eines kommunikationstheoretischen Modells der erzählerischen Vermittlung: die Funktion der Erzählinstanz in den Romanen George Eliots* (Horizonte: Studien zu Texten und Ideen der europäischen Moderne 2; Trier: Wissenschaftlicher Verlag Trier, 1989).

45. Nünning, "Commentary," 74.

46. Nünning, "Commentary," 74.

47. Nünning, "Commentary," 74.

48. David Bain, *Actors and Audience: A Study of Asides and Related Conventions in Greek Drama* (Oxford: Oxford University Press, 1977), 17. He gives a "modern example" of Othello's comment regarding Desdemona, "O, hardness to dissemble!" (*Othello* III.iv.34), which is said with her on stage but not "heard" by her (17).

49. Bain, *Actors and Audience*, 17.

50. See Jo-Ann A. Brant, *Dialogue and Drama: Elements of Greek Tragedy in the Fourth Gospel* (Peabody, MA: Hendrickson, 2004), 72–73; Brant, "Fourth Gospel," 198–99.

51. Manfred Pfister, *The Theory and Analysis of Drama*, trans. John Halliday (Cambridge: Cambridge University Press, 1988), 131.

52. Pfister, *Drama*, 138. The "conventionalised monological aside" can be distinguished from what Pfister calls "a motivated monological aside," which is a "short, unpremeditated and spontaneous exclamation in reaction to a particular situation" and "remains within the naturalist bounds of plausibility" (138–39).

53. Pfister, *Drama*, 138.

54. Pfister, *Drama*, 139–40.

55. Pfister, *Drama*, 140.

56. Burton-Roberts, "Parentheticals," 180.

57. Burton-Roberts, "Parentheticals," 179.

58. Burton-Roberts, "Parentheticals," 179.

59. Nicole Dehé and Yordanka Kavalova, "Parentheticals: An Introduction," in *Parentheticals*, ed. Dehé and Kavalova, Linguistik Aktuell/Linguistics Today 106 (Amsterdam: John Benjamins, 2007), 1–22.

60. Dehé and Kavalova, "Parentheticals," 1.

61. Dehé and Kavalova, "Parentheticals," 1.

62. Dehé and Kavalova, "Parentheticals," 5. See Liliane Haegeman, "Parenthetical Adverbials: The Radical Orphanage Approach," in *Dislocated Elements in Discourse: Syntactic, Semantic, and Pragmatic Perspectives*, ed. Benjamin Shaer, Philippa Cook, Werner Frey, and Claudia Maienborn (New York: Routledge, 2009), 331–47.

63. Dehé and Kavalova, "Parentheticals," 8, citing Burton-Roberts, "Parentheticals," 180. However, as Burton-Roberts points out, the positioning of the parenthetical is still constrained by the host clause.

64. Dehé and Kavalova, "Parentheticals," 9.

65. Marlies Kluck, Dennis Ott, and Mark de Vries, "Incomplete parenthesis: An overview," in *Parenthesis and Ellipsis: Cross-Linguistics and Theoretical Perspectives*, ed. Marlies Kluck, Dennis Ott, and Mark de Vries, Studies in Generative Grammar 121 (Berlin: De Gruyter, 2015), 3.

66. Kluck, Ott, and Vries, "Incomplete parenthesis," 3.

67. Kluck, Ott, and Vries, "Incomplete parenthesis," 1.

68. Lamb, *Text, Context*, 156.

69. Sheeley, *Narrative Asides*, 36; Wendy E. Sproston North, *The Lazarus Story within the Johannine Tradition*, JSNTSup 212 (Sheffield: Sheffield Academic Press, 2001), 32.

70. Lamb, *Text, Context*, 156–57.

71. Lamb, *Text, Context*, 156–57n64.

72. Bauckham, *Testimony*, 102.

73. Bauckham, *Testimony*, 102n33.

74. Brant, "Fourth Gospel," 192.

75. Brant, "Fourth Gospel," 192.

76. Brown, *Gospel*, 1:3–4. 1:15 is bracketed in Westcott and Hort, RSV, NRSV, and other versions.

77. However, as commentators have noted, it is not always obvious which texts are being referenced. So, for example, 12:14–15 is a loose citation of Zech. 9:9 LXX (and Zeph. 3:16?). Jesus cites or alludes to the Scriptures in 6:45; 7:38; 10:34–35; 13:18; 15:25; John the Baptist in 1:23; the crowd in 6:31. Bruce Schuchard, in an examination of the form and function of these citations, argues that they have an explanatory function: "The evangelist's chief purpose in citing the Old Testament is to elucidate the person and the work of Jesus, especially the death of Jesus." Bruce G. Schuchard, "Form versus Function: Citation Technique and Authorial Intention in the Gospel of John," in *Abiding Words: The Use of Scripture in the Gospel of John*, ed. Alicia D. Myers and B. G. Schuchard, SBLRBS 81 (Atlanta: SBL Press, 2015), 41.

78. Van Belle, *Les Parenthèses*, 209.

79. David W. Wead, *The Literary Devices in John's Gospel*, rev. ed., ed. Paul N. Anderson and R. Alan Culpepper (Eugene: Wipf & Stock, 2018), 6.

96                                   *Chapter 2*

80. Wead, *Literary Devices*, rev. ed., 9.

81. J. Ramsey Michaels, *The Gospel of John*, NICNT (Grand Rapids: Eerdmans, 2010), 272n4.

82. Charles K. Barrett, *The Gospel According to St. John*, 2nd ed. (London: SPCK, 1978), 246. See Donald A. Carson, "Current Source Criticism of the Fourth Gospel: Some Methodological Questions," *JBL* 97, no. 3 (1978): 424n50 for a range of alternative interpretations.

83. Brown, *Gospel*, 1:136.

84. Rudolf Schnackenburg, *The Gospel According to St. John*, trans. Kevin Smyth, 3 vols., Herder's Theological Commentary on the New Testament (London: Burns & Oates, 1968, 1980, 1982), 1:361.

85. Michael Theobald, *Das Evangelium nach Johannes: Kapitel 1–12*, RNT (Regensburg: Friedrich Pustet, 2009), 266.

86. Brown, *Gospel*, 1:160.

87. Theobald, *Das Evangelium*, 289.

88. Tenney, *Footnotes*, 353. We can compare these "Footnotes of time and place" to Thatcher's "Staging asides" under the sub-categories of "space" and "time." Thatcher includes 1:28 as one of his "space" asides ("New Look at Asides," 434).

89. Tenney, *Footnotes*, 353.

90. Tenney, *Footnotes*, 353. He does express some uncertainty about 7:2.

91. Bernard comments that "the use of parenthesis" here "is quite in Jn.'s style" (*Gospel* 1:136). Bultmann attributes 4:8 to the Evangelist. Rudolf Bultmann, *The Gospel of John: A Commentary*, trans. George R. Beasley-Murray, ed. Rupert W. N. Hoare and John K. Riches (Philadelphia: Westminster Press, 1971), 175. Brown puts it in brackets, but makes no comment (*Gospel* 1:166). Schnackenburg calls it "an afterthought" (*Gospel*, 1:424). Wengst speaks of the evangelist inserting a remark. Klaus Wengst, *Das Johannesevangelium*, 2nd ed., 2 vols., Theologischer Kommentar zum Neuen Testament 4 (Stuttgart: Kohlhammer, 2004, 2007), 1:166.

92. We assume that Jesus was alone with the woman, although this is not actually stated and it is possible that there were other people there. The impression is that Jesus and the woman were the only two present. Westcott suggests the possibility that, of the disciples, John may have remained and hence been an eyewitness (Westcott, *Gospel*, 1:147).

93. Barrett, *Gospel*, 232.

94. Hartwig Thyen, *Das Johannesevangelium*, HNT 6 (Tübingen: Mohr Siebeck, 2005), 246.

95. Michaels, *Gospel*, 238–39; Theobald, *Das Evangelium*, 310.

96. Theobald, *Das Evangelium*, 310.

97. Jo-Ann A. Brant, *John*, Paideia Commentaries on the New Testament (Grand Rapids: Baker Academic, 2011), 83.

98. Brant, "Fourth Gospel," 192. She gives 11:2 as an example of prolepsis.

99. Van Belle notes that this is the only category of aside mentioned in the index to Bultmann's 1941 commentary (*Les Parenthèses*, 39).

100. Köstenberger, *Theology*, 137–38.

101. Van Belle, *Les Parenthèses*, 110–11.

## Terminology, Definitions, and Categorization 97

102. North, *Journey Round John*, 17.

103. Tenney, "Footnotes," 362.

104. Jean Zumstein, *L'Évangile selon Saint Jean*, 2 vols., CNT: Deuxième Série 4 (Geneva: Labor et Fides, 2007, 2014), 1:274.

105. Brown, *Gospel*, 1:130. However, Brown also acknowledges: "On a purely natural level, the nighttime visit may have been a stealthy expedient 'for fear of the Jews' (xix 38); or it may reflect the rabbinic custom of staying up at night to study the Law" (1:130). The second option seems less likely to me. Cf. Zumstein, *L'Évangile*, 2:263, re the "fear of the Jews" interpretation.

106. Adapted from Köstenberger, *Theology*, 137–38.

107. Van Belle, *Les Parenthèses*, 110.

108. For various interpretations of the delegation/s and their historical likelihood, see Michaels, *Gospel*, 101n29, and Craig S. Keener, *The Gospel of John: A Commentary*, 2 vols. (Peabody, MA: Hendrickson, 2003), 1:431–33.

109. Brown, *Gospel*, 1:448, 456. Re the repetition of the name "Jesus" in 12:1, cf. Bernard, *Gospel*, 2:415; Theobald, *Das Evangelium*, 774. By contrast, Westcott believes, "There is a solemn emphasis in the repetition of the Lord's name" in 12:1 (*Gospel*, 2:110).

110. Andrew T. Lincoln, *The Gospel According to St John*, BNTC (London: Continuum, 2005), 337.

111. Michaels, *Gospel*, 663.

112. Brant, *John*, 179.

113. Brown, *Gospel*, 1:423.

114. Barrett, *Gospel*, 390.

115. Westcott, *Gospel*, 2:80.

116. Bultmann, *Gospel*, 396n1.

117. Richard Bauckham, "John for Readers of Mark," in *The Gospels for All Christians: Rethinking the Gospel Audiences*, ed. Richard Bauckham (Edinburgh: T & T Clark, 1998), 161. See also 161–65.

118. North, *Journey Round John*, 101; cf. 184; cf. Lincoln, *Gospel*, 318.

119. Theobald, *Das Evangelium*, 725–26.

120. Tenney, "Footnotes," 352–62; O'Rourke, "Asides," 205–6.

121. Van Belle, *Les Parenthèses*, 106–12.

122. Hedrick, "Authorial Presence," 82.

123. Köstenberger, *Theology*, 136–40.

124. Thatcher, "New Look at Asides," 431–33.

125. Sheeley, *Narrative Asides*, 37–38.

126. Scott Richardson, *The Homeric Narrator* (Nashville: Vanderbilt University Press, 1990). See Chatman, *Story and Discourse*, 196–262.

127. Richardson, *Homeric Narrator*, 7.

128. Michaels refers to the work of Garvie, Tenney, Culpepper, Van Belle, and Hedrick, as well as noting that Ferrar Fenton's 1903 Bible translation made use of brackets for "narrative asides" in John (*Gospel*, 119n7).

*Chapter 3*

# An Annotated List of Narrative Comments in the Gospel of John

This is a numbered list of narrative comments in the Gospel of John based on my own definitions set out in the previous chapter. These are comments which I regard as *external* to the narrative framework in contrast to those that are *internal* to the framework, which I have listed separately. The external comments are further classified as belonging outside the narrative in a *temporal* sense or in a *spatial* sense, although in some cases there is an overlap between these two sub-categories and I have given these a combined *temporal/spatial* designation. I have cited the comments in full, using both NA28 and the NRSV. I have used the abbreviations *v* or *vv* to indicate where these citations are a whole verse or whole verses. Where the citations consist only of a phrase or sentence within a verse, readers will need to check the co-text themselves.

In most cases I have also added explanations to justify the choices I have made. I would stress that my definitions and categorization are not perfect and we cannot entirely avoid a subjective element in the choice of asides/parentheses/comments, so others may not agree with my selection.

## EXTERNAL COMMENTS: TEMPORAL AND SPATIAL

The first three narrative comments are the Prologue (1:1–18) with the omission of the references to John the Baptist in vv. 6–8 and 15.[1] I have discussed my reasons for this selection, which inverts the more usual choice of the references to John as the asides in the Prologue, in chapter 2.

# Chapter 3

1. 1:1–5vv: Temporal/Spatial

Ἐν ἀρχῇ ἦν ὁ λόγος, καὶ ὁ λόγος ἦν πρὸς τὸν θεόν, καὶ θεὸς ἦν ὁ λόγος. Οὗτος ἦν ἐν ἀρχῇ πρὸς τὸν θεόν. Πάντα δι' αὐτοῦ ἐγένετο, καὶ χωρὶς αὐτοῦ ἐγένετο οὐδὲ ἕν. ὃ γέγονεν ἐν αὐτῷ ζωὴ ἦν, καὶ ἡ ζωὴ ἦν τὸ φῶς τῶν ἀνθρώπων· καὶ τὸ φῶς ἐν τῇ σκοτίᾳ φαίνει, καὶ ἡ σκοτία αὐτὸ οὐ κατέλαβεν.

In the beginning was the Word, and the Word was with God, and the Word was God. He was in the beginning with God. All things came into being through him, and without him not one thing came into being. What has come into being in him was life, and the life was the light of all people. The light shines in the darkness, and the darkness did not overcome it.

2. 1:9–14vv: Temporal/Spatial

Ἦν τὸ φῶς τὸ ἀληθινόν, ὃ φωτίζει πάντα ἄνθρωπον, ἐρχόμενον εἰς τὸν κόσμον. ἐν τῷ κόσμῳ ἦν, καὶ ὁ κόσμος δι' αὐτοῦ ἐγένετο, καὶ ὁ κόσμος αὐτὸν οὐκ ἔγνω. Εἰς τὰ ἴδια ἦλθεν, καὶ οἱ ἴδιοι αὐτὸν οὐ παρέλαβον. ὅσοι δὲ ἔλαβον αὐτόν, ἔδωκεν αὐτοῖς ἐξουσίαν τέκνα θεοῦ γενέσθαι, τοῖς πιστεύουσιν εἰς τὸ ὄνομα αὐτοῦ, οἳ οὐκ ἐξ αἱμάτων οὐδὲ ἐκ θελήματος σαρκὸς οὐδὲ ἐκ θελήματος ἀνδρὸς ἀλλ' ἐκ θεοῦ ἐγεννήθησαν. Καὶ ὁ λόγος σὰρξ ἐγένετο καὶ ἐσκήνωσεν ἐν ἡμῖν, καὶ ἐθεασάμεθα τὴν δόξαν αὐτοῦ, δόξαν ὡς μονογενοῦς παρὰ πατρός, πλήρης χάριτος καὶ ἀληθείας.

The true light, which enlightens everyone, was coming into the world. He was in the world, and the world came into being through him; yet the world did not know him. He came to what was his own, and his own people did not accept him. But to all who received him, who believed in his name, he gave power to become children of God, who were born, not of blood or of the will of the flesh or of the will of man, but of God. And the Word became flesh and lived among us, and we have seen his glory, the glory as of a father's only son, full of grace and truth.

3. 1:16–18vv: Temporal/Spatial

ὅτι ἐκ τοῦ πληρώματος αὐτοῦ ἡμεῖς πάντες ἐλάβομεν καὶ χάριν ἀντὶ χάριτος· ὅτι ὁ νόμος διὰ Μωϋσέως ἐδόθη, ἡ χάρις καὶ ἡ ἀλήθεια διὰ Ἰησοῦ Χριστοῦ ἐγένετο. θεὸν οὐδεὶς ἑώρακεν πώποτε· μονογενὴς θεὸς ὁ ὢν εἰς τὸν κόλπον τοῦ πατρὸς ἐκεῖνος ἐξηγήσατο.

From his fullness we have all received, grace upon grace. The law indeed was given through Moses; grace and truth came through Jesus Christ. No one has ever seen God. It is God the only Son, who is close to the Father's heart, who has made him known.

## An Annotated List of Narrative Comments in the Gospel of John    101

4.     1:38: Spatial
ὃ λέγεται μεθερμηνευόμενον Διδάσκαλε
(which translated means Teacher)

This is the first of what are commonly designated "translation asides," although I believe that this may be something of a misnomer, as I discuss in more detail in chapter 5. The other comments in this category that I have listed are 1:41, 42; 4:25; 9:7; 19:13, 17; and 20:16. I have not included the references to Thomas as the Twin (Δίδυμος) in 11:16; 20:24; and 21:2.

5.     1:41: Spatial
ὅ ἐστιν μεθερμηνευόμενον Χριστός
(which is translated Anointed)

6.     1:42: Spatial
ὃ ἑρμηνεύεται Πέτρος
(which is translated Peter)

7.     2:11v: Spatial
Ταύτην ἐποίησεν ἀρχὴν τῶν σημείων ὁ Ἰησοῦς ἐν Κανὰ τῆς Γαλιλαίας καὶ ἐφανέρωσεν τὴν δόξαν αὐτοῦ, καὶ ἐπίστευσαν εἰς αὐτὸν οἱ μαθηταὶ αὐτοῦ.
Jesus did this, the first of his signs, in Cana of Galilee, and revealed his glory; and his disciples believed in him.

This is the first of the two instances when the author/narrator numbers signs. The other is 4:54. Precisely why only these two signs are numbered has intrigued many scholars. Bultmann believed that it was derived from enumeration in his proposed "σημεῖα-source."[2] I suggest other possible reasons in chapter 4.

8.     2:17v: Temporal
Ἐμνήσθησαν οἱ μαθηταὶ αὐτοῦ ὅτι γεγραμμένον ἐστίν· ὁ ζῆλος τοῦ οἴκου σου καταφάγεταί με.
His disciples remembered that it was written, "Zeal for your house will consume me."

This is an example of a reference to the existing scriptures, which belong to a time before the narrative framework, but which are fulfilled in the ministry of Jesus. Here the reference is to Psalm 69:9.

102                                    *Chapter 3*

9.      2:21–22vv: Temporal/Spatial

ἐκεῖνος δὲ ἔλεγεν περὶ τοῦ ναοῦ τοῦ σώματος αὐτοῦ. ὅτε οὖν ἠγέρθη ἐκ νεκρῶν, ἐμνήσθησαν οἱ μαθηταὶ αὐτοῦ ὅτι τοῦτο ἔλεγεν, καὶ ἐπίστευσαν τῇ γραφῇ καὶ τῷ λόγῳ ὃν εἶπεν ὁ Ἰησοῦς.

But he was speaking of the temple of his body. After he was raised from the dead, his disciples remembered that he had said this; and they believed the scripture and the word that Jesus had spoken.

The spatial element is the author/narrator's explanation that Jesus was speaking metaphorically. The temporal element lies in the fact that the disciples may only have remembered Jesus' statement in a period after the end of the narrative framework.

10.     2:24–25vv: Spatial

αὐτὸς δὲ Ἰησοῦς οὐκ ἐπίστευεν αὐτὸν αὐτοῖς διὰ τὸ αὐτὸν γινώσκειν πάντας καὶ ὅτι οὐ χρείαν εἶχεν ἵνα τις μαρτυρήσῃ περὶ τοῦ ἀνθρώπου· αὐτὸς γὰρ ἐγίνωσκεν τί ἦν ἐν τῷ ἀνθρώπῳ.

But Jesus on his part would not entrust himself to them, because he knew all people and needed no one to testify about anyone; for he himself knew what was in everyone.

See my comment on 6:6 regarding insight into the mind of Jesus.

11.     3:16–21vv

Οὕτως γὰρ ἠγάπησεν ὁ θεὸς τὸν κόσμον, ὥστε τὸν υἱὸν τὸν μονογενῆ ἔδωκεν, ἵνα πᾶς ὁ πιστεύων εἰς αὐτὸν μὴ ἀπόληται ἀλλ' ἔχῃ ζωὴν αἰώνιον. οὐ γὰρ ἀπέστειλεν ὁ θεὸς τὸν υἱὸν εἰς τὸν κόσμον ἵνα κρίνῃ τὸν κόσμον, ἀλλ' ἵνα σωθῇ ὁ κόσμος δι' αὐτοῦ. ὁ πιστεύων εἰς αὐτὸν οὐ κρίνεται· ὁ δὲ μὴ πιστεύων ἤδη κέκριται, ὅτι μὴ πεπίστευκεν εἰς τὸ ὄνομα τοῦ μονογενοῦς υἱοῦ τοῦ θεοῦ. αὕτη δέ ἐστιν ἡ κρίσις ὅτι τὸ φῶς ἐλήλυθεν εἰς τὸν κόσμον καὶ ἠγάπησαν οἱ ἄνθρωποι μᾶλλον τὸ σκότος ἢ τὸ φῶς· ἦν γὰρ αὐτῶν πονηρὰ τὰ ἔργα. πᾶς γὰρ ὁ φαῦλα πράσσων μισεῖ τὸ φῶς καὶ οὐκ ἔρχεται πρὸς τὸ φῶς, ἵνα μὴ ἐλεγχθῇ τὰ ἔργα αὐτοῦ· ὁ δὲ ποιῶν τὴν ἀλήθειαν ἔρχεται πρὸς τὸ φῶς, ἵνα φανερωθῇ αὐτοῦ τὰ ἔργα ὅτι ἐν θεῷ ἐστιν εἰργασμένα.

For God so loved the world that he gave his only Son, so that everyone who believes in him may not perish but may have eternal life. Indeed, God did not send the Son into the world to condemn the world, but in order that the world might be saved through him. Those

*An Annotated List of Narrative Comments in the Gospel of John*     103

who believe in him are not condemned; but those who do not believe are condemned already, because they have not believed in the name of the only Son of God. And this is the judgement, that the light has come into the world, and people loved darkness rather than light because their deeds were evil. For all who do evil hate the light and do not come to the light, so that their deeds may not be exposed. But those who do what is true come to the light, so that it may be clearly seen that their deeds have been done in God.

In support of my decision to list this as commentary rather than include it as part of Jesus' speech, I note the view of Westcott, who wrote, "This section is a commentary on the nature and mission of the Son. . . . It adds no new thoughts, but brings out the force of the revelation already given in outline (1–15) by the light of Christian experience. It is therefore likely (from its secondary character, apart from all other considerations) that it contains the reflections of the Evangelist, and is not a continuation of the words of the Lord."[3] Piñero and Peláez describe this "movement of the dialogue into an exposition" as a "stylistic feature of John, which shows how his theological concern overrides his narrative intention."[4]

12.     3:31–36vv: Spatial

Ὁ ἄνωθεν ἐρχόμενος ἐπάνω πάντων ἐστίν· ὁ ὢν ἐκ τῆς γῆς ἐκ τῆς γῆς ἐστιν καὶ ἐκ τῆς γῆς λαλεῖ. ὁ ἐκ τοῦ οὐρανοῦ ἐρχόμενος [ἐπάνω πάντων ἐστίν·] ὃ ἑώρακεν καὶ ἤκουσεν τοῦτο μαρτυρεῖ, καὶ τὴν μαρτυρίαν αὐτοῦ οὐδεὶς λαμβάνει. ὁ λαβὼν αὐτοῦ τὴν μαρτυρίαν ἐσφράγισεν ὅτι ὁ θεὸς ἀληθής ἐστιν. ὃν γὰρ ἀπέστειλεν ὁ θεὸς τὰ ῥήματα τοῦ θεοῦ λαλεῖ, οὐ γὰρ ἐκ μέτρου δίδωσιν τὸ πνεῦμα. ὁ πατὴρ ἀγαπᾷ τὸν υἱὸν καὶ πάντα δέδωκεν ἐν τῇ χειρὶ αὐτοῦ. ὁ πιστεύων εἰς τὸν υἱὸν ἔχει ζωὴν αἰώνιον· ὁ δὲ ἀπειθῶν τῷ υἱῷ οὐκ ὄψεται ζωήν, ἀλλ᾽ ἡ ὀργὴ τοῦ θεοῦ μένει ἐπ᾽ αὐτόν.

The one who comes from above is above all; the one who is of the earth belongs to the earth and speaks about earthly things. The one who comes from heaven is above all. He testifies to what he has seen and heard, yet no one accepts his testimony. Whoever has accepted his testimony has certified this, that God is true. He whom God has sent speaks the words of God, for he gives the Spirit without measure. The Father loves the Son and has placed all things in his hands. Whoever believes in the Son has eternal life; whoever disobeys the Son will not see life, but must endure God's wrath.

104                          *Chapter 3*

Again, in support of my decision to include this as comment rather than speech, I note Westcott's observation, "This section contains reflections of the Evangelist on the general relation of the Son to the forerunner, and to the teachers of the earlier Dispensation generally. The Baptist had spoken figuratively in the language of the Old Testament of what Christ was, and so directed his disciples to acknowledge Him. The Evangelist, looking over the long interval of years, reaffirms in clearer words the witness of the herald, and shows how it has been fulfilled."[5]

13.     4:25: Spatial
        ὁ λεγόμενος Χριστός
        (who is called Christ)

14.     4:54v: Spatial
        Τοῦτο [δὲ] πάλιν δεύτερον σημεῖον ἐποίησεν ὁ Ἰησοῦς ἐλθὼν ἐκ τῆς Ἰουδαίας εἰς τὴν Γαλιλαίαν.

        Now this was the second sign that Jesus did after coming from Judea to Galilee.

This is the second of the two numbered signs, following 2:11. It could be considered as an *internal* comment, looking back to the earlier sign.

15.     5:16–18vv: Spatial
        καὶ διὰ τοῦτο ἐδίωκον οἱ Ἰουδαῖοι τὸν Ἰησοῦν, ὅτι ταῦτα ἐποίει ἐν σαββάτῳ. ὁ δὲ [Ἰησοῦς] ἀπεκρίνατο αὐτοῖς· ὁ πατήρ μου ἕως ἄρτι ἐργάζεται κἀγὼ ἐργάζομαι· διὰ τοῦτο οὖν μᾶλλον ἐζήτουν αὐτὸν οἱ Ἰουδαῖοι ἀποκτεῖναι, ὅτι οὐ μόνον ἔλυεν τὸ σάββατον, ἀλλὰ καὶ πατέρα ἴδιον ἔλεγεν τὸν θεὸν ἴσον ἑαυτὸν ποιῶν τῷ θεῷ.

        Therefore the Jews started persecuting Jesus, because he was doing such things on the sabbath. But Jesus answered them, "My Father is still working, and I also am working." For this reason the Jews were seeking all the more to kill him, because he was not only breaking the sabbath, but was also calling God his own Father, thereby making himself equal to God.

Jesus' words in this paragraph, Ὁ πατήρ μου ἕως ἄρτι ἐργάζεται κἀγὼ ἐργάζομαι, relate to the preceding episode, the healing of the paralyzed man (5:1–15), as well as providing the basis for the Jewish authorities' accusation that he was making himself equal with God, an accusation which is repeated in their own words in 10:33. The words also serve to introduce the discourse which follows (5:19–47). So, it is difficult to separate them from the author/

An Annotated List of Narrative Comments in the Gospel of John       105

narrator's commentary. Brown calls Jesus' words in verse 17 "a lapidary saying."[6]

16.    6:1: Spatial
       τῆς θαλάσσης . . . τῆς Τιβεριάδος.
       also called the Sea of Tiberias

This name for the Sea of Galilee would seem to belong in the same category as the "translation asides" (1:38, 41, 42, etc.), although in this case it is an alternative name not a translation. The town of Tiberias is mentioned in 6:23 and the Sea of Tiberias again in 21:1. The name is not found elsewhere in the NT. Tiberias had only recently been founded (early or mid-20s AD/CE) by the time of Jesus' ministry, which leads some scholars to regard this as an explanatory gloss intended for readers at the end of the first century.[7] Haenchen states that the same editor who added the supplement of chapter 21 "also supplemented the text here by adding the new name to the old."[8] However, even if the description "the Sea of Tiberias" did not come into common use until late in the first century, this, as Barrett points out, "does not affect the historicity of John's account; he supplies the up-to-date term for the convenience of his readers."[9]

17.    6:6v: Spatial
       τοῦτο δὲ ἔλεγεν πειράζων αὐτόν· αὐτὸς γὰρ ᾔδει τί ἔμελλεν ποιεῖν.
       He said this to test him, for he himself knew what he was going to do.

This is one of a number of comments in chapter 6 (including verses 15 and 64), where the author/narrator shows insight into the mind of Jesus. Hedrick categorizes this as clarifying "the inner motivation and inner feelings of Jesus" and Sheeley describes it as an "inside view of some person within the story."[10] The comments in 2:24–25; 13:1, 3, 11; and 18:4 also belong to this category. However, as Sheeley points out, not all such insights can be categorized as asides.[11] For example, I am doubtful about including 6:61 (εἰδὼς δὲ ὁ Ἰησοῦς ἐν ἑαυτῷ ὅτι γογγύζουσιν περὶ τούτου οἱ μαθηταὶ αὐτοῦ . . .) as a comment reflecting an "inside view," given that the disciples' complaint is made explicit in 6:60. Insight into characters' emotions and motivations will be considered in more detail in respect of the *point of view* of the narrator in chapter 5.

18.    6:15v: Spatial
       Ἰησοῦς οὖν γνοὺς ὅτι μέλλουσιν ἔρχεσθαι καὶ ἁρπάζειν αὐτὸν ἵνα ποιήσωσιν βασιλέα, ἀνεχώρησεν πάλιν εἰς τὸ ὄρος αὐτὸς μόνος.

106                                    *Chapter 3*

When Jesus realized that they were about to come and take him
by force to make him king, he withdrew again to the mountain by
himself.

19.     6:64: Spatial

ᾔδει γὰρ ἐξ ἀρχῆς ὁ Ἰησοῦς τίνες εἰσὶν οἱ μὴ πιστεύοντες καὶ τίς
ἐστιν ὁ παραδώσων αὐτόν.

For Jesus knew from the first who were the ones that did not believe,
and who was the one that would betray him.

20.     7:39v: Temporal

τοῦτο δὲ εἶπεν περὶ τοῦ πνεύματος ὃ ἔμελλον λαμβάνειν οἱ
πιστεύσαντες εἰς αὐτόν· οὔπω γὰρ ἦν πνεῦμα, ὅτι Ἰησοῦς οὐδέπω
ἐδοξάσθη.

Now he said this about the Spirit, which believers in him were to
receive; for as yet there was no Spirit, because Jesus was not yet
glorified.

It is not clear whether the reception of the Spirit by believers forms part of
John's narrative framework. In 20:22, Jesus breathes on the (10?) gathered
disciples and says to them, "Receive the Holy Spirit." However, this is not
the same as "believers" in general, and there is also an element of ambiguity regarding the extent Jesus's glorification, specifically whether or not to
include the ascension. I am inclined to take this as a comment belonging
outside the narrative from a temporal perspective.

21.     9:7: Spatial

(ὃ ἑρμηνεύεται Ἀπεσταλμένος)

(which means Sent)

22.     11:13v: Spatial

εἰρήκει δὲ ὁ Ἰησοῦς περὶ τοῦ θανάτου αὐτοῦ, ἐκεῖνοι δὲ ἔδοξαν ὅτι
περὶ τῆς κοιμήσεως τοῦ ὕπνου λέγει.

Jesus, however, had been speaking about his death, but they thought
that he was referring merely to sleep.

This seems to be a straightforward correction of a linguistic misunderstanding
on the part of the disciples relating to the use of the verb κοιμάω in 11:11–12,
which can mean "sleep" or "die." The same semantic ambiguity can be found
in the Hebrew and Aramaic root שׁכב.[12] As Michaels points out, "The Gospel

*An Annotated List of Narrative Comments in the Gospel of John* 107

writer intervenes in his customary way to explain what may have been obvious to most readers. . . . For the moment, readers of the Gospel—even the less perceptive ones who needed the narrative aside—are one step ahead of the disciples in the story."[13] This is an instance of dramatic irony: the audience is better informed than the characters in the plot.

23.     11:51–52vv: Spatial
τοῦτο δὲ ἀφ' ἑαυτοῦ οὐκ εἶπεν, ἀλλὰ ἀρχιερεὺς ὢν τοῦ ἐνιαυτοῦ ἐκείνου ἐπροφήτευσεν ὅτι ἔμελλεν Ἰησοῦς ἀποθνήσκειν ὑπὲρ τοῦ ἔθνους, καὶ οὐχ ὑπὲρ τοῦ ἔθνους μόνον ἀλλ' ἵνα καὶ τὰ τέκνα τοῦ θεοῦ τὰ διεσκορπισμένα συναγάγῃ εἰς ἕν.

He did not say this on his own, but being high priest that year he prophesied that Jesus was about to die for the nation, and not for the nation only, but to gather into one the dispersed children of God.

Another instance of dramatic irony.

24.     12:6v: Spatial
εἶπεν δὲ τοῦτο οὐχ ὅτι περὶ τῶν πτωχῶν ἔμελεν αὐτῷ, ἀλλ' ὅτι κλέπτης ἦν καὶ τὸ γλωσσόκομον ἔχων τὰ βαλλόμενα ἐβάσταζεν.

(He said this not because he cared about the poor, but because he was a thief; he kept the common purse and used to steal what was put into it.)

The statement that Judas Iscariot was a thief who used to steal from the common purse is part of the narrative, but the observation that he did not care about the poor is an insight into this character's mind and therefore qualifies as an external comment. Brant calls it a "glimpse into the private world of Judas's intent."[14]

25.     12:14–15v: Temporal
καθώς ἐστιν γεγραμμένον· μὴ φοβοῦ, θυγάτηρ Σιών· ἰδοὺ ὁ βασιλεύς σου ἔρχεται, καθήμενος ἐπὶ πῶλον ὄνου.

as it is written: "Do not be afraid, daughter of Zion. Look your king is coming, sitting on a donkey's colt."

Following the statement that Jesus found a young donkey (ὀνάριον) and sat on it (12:14a), this is another reference to the fulfilment of existing scriptures, here a version of Zechariah 9:9, possibly combined with Zephaniah 3:14–16 (and/or Isaiah 40:9).

108     *Chapter 3*

26.     12:16v: Temporal

ταῦτα οὐκ ἔγνωσαν αὐτοῦ οἱ μαθηταὶ τὸ πρῶτον, ἀλλ᾽ ὅτε ἐδοξάσθη Ἰησοῦς τότε ἐμνήσθησαν ὅτι ταῦτα ἦν ἐπ᾽ αὐτῷ γεγραμμένα καὶ ταῦτα ἐποίησαν αὐτῷ.

His disciples did not understand these things at first; but when Jesus was glorified, then they remembered that these things had been written of him and had been done to him.

As is the case with 7:39, this belongs outside the narrative framework if Jesus' glorification includes the ascension. It certainly necessitates a post-resurrection perspective.

27.     12:33v: Spatial

τοῦτο δὲ ἔλεγεν σημαίνων ποίῳ θανάτῳ ἤμελλεν ἀποθνήσκειν.

He said this to indicate the kind of death he was to die.

This follows Jesus' declaration, "And I, when I am lifted up from the earth, will draw all people to myself" (12:32). Given that a primary function of the narrative comments is an explanatory one, there is a frustrating ambiguity in this particular comment. The fact that the remark is referenced again in 18:32 in the context of the Jewish authorities' deputation to Pilate with the indication that Jesus' "kind of death" would be a Roman punishment and not a Jewish one, suggests that it is death by crucifixion that 12:33 has in mind.[15] However, there may also be the suggestion here that his death would by salvatory—drawing people to himself.[16]

28.     12:38–41vv: Temporal

ἵνα ὁ λόγος Ἡσαΐου τοῦ προφήτου πληρωθῇ ὃν εἶπεν· *κύριε, τίς ἐπίστευσεν τῇ ἀκοῇ ἡμῶν; καὶ ὁ βραχίων κυρίου τίνι ἀπεκαλύφθη;* διὰ τοῦτο οὐκ ἠδύναντο πιστεύειν, ὅτι πάλιν εἶπεν Ἡσαΐας· *τετύφλωκεν αὐτῶν τοὺς ὀφθαλμοὺς καὶ ἐπώρωσεν αὐτῶν τὴν καρδίαν, ἵνα μὴ ἴδωσιν τοῖς ὀφθαλμοῖς καὶ νοήσωσιν τῇ καρδίᾳ καὶ στραφῶσιν, καὶ ἰάσομαι αὐτούς.* ταῦτα εἶπεν Ἡσαΐας ὅτι εἶδεν τὴν δόξαν αὐτοῦ, καὶ ἐλάλησεν περὶ αὐτοῦ.

This was to fulfil the word spoken by the prophet Isaiah: "Lord, who has believed our message, and to whom has the arm of the Lord been revealed?" And so they could not believe, because Isaiah also said, "He has blinded their eyes and hardened their heart, so that they might not look with their eyes, and understand with their heart and turn—and I would heal them." Isaiah said this because he saw his glory and spoke about him.

*An Annotated List of Narrative Comments in the Gospel of John*    109

Further references to the fulfilment of existing scriptures, here explicitly to the prophet Isaiah (53:1 LXX and a version of 6:10). The author/narrator makes clear the belief that Isaiah was prophesying about Jesus. Elsewhere Isaiah is quoted by John the Baptist (1:23), but I would not include this as a narrative comment as it belongs to the Baptist's dialogue. The same applies to Jesus' quotations of scripture in 6:45; 10:34; and 15:25.

29.    13:1: Temporal/Spatial

Πρὸ δὲ τῆς ἑορτῆς τοῦ πάσχα εἰδὼς ὁ Ἰησοῦς ὅτι ἦλθεν αὐτοῦ ἡ ὥρα ἵνα μεταβῇ ἐκ τοῦ κόσμου τούτου πρὸς τὸν πατέρα.

Now before the festival of the Passover, Jesus knew that his hour had come to depart from this world and go to the Father.

The first of a series of insights into the mind of Jesus in chapter 13 (including verses 3 and 11).

30.    13:3v: Temporal/Spatial

εἰδὼς ὅτι πάντα ἔδωκεν αὐτῷ ὁ πατὴρ εἰς τὰς χεῖρας καὶ ὅτι ἀπὸ θεοῦ ἐξῆλθεν καὶ πρὸς τὸν θεὸν ὑπάγει

Jesus, knowing that the Father had given all things into his hands, and that he had come from God and was going to God

31.    13:11v: Spatial

ᾔδει γὰρ τὸν παραδιδόντα αὐτόν· διὰ τοῦτο εἶπεν ὅτι Οὐχὶ πάντες καθαροί ἐστε.

For he knew who was to betray him; for this reason he said, "Not all of you are clean."

32.    18:4: Spatial

Ἰησοῦς οὖν εἰδὼς πάντα τὰ ἐρχόμενα ἐπ᾽ αὐτὸν

Then Jesus, knowing all that was to happen to him

Another insight into the mind of Jesus.

33.    18:32v: Spatial

ἵνα ὁ λόγος τοῦ Ἰησοῦ πληρωθῇ ὃν εἶπεν σημαίνων ποίῳ θανάτῳ ἤμελλεν ἀποθνήσκειν.

(This was to fulfil what Jesus had said when he indicated the kind of death he was to die.)

110                                            *Chapter 3*

An example of analepsis, looking back to Jesus' declaration in 12:32 and the comment in 12:33. It could be considered an *internal* aside, but the theme of fulfilment is stressed here.

34.       19:13: Spatial
          Ἑβραϊστὶ δὲ Γαββαθα
          or in Hebrew Gabbatha

35.       19:17: Spatial
          ὃ λέγεται Ἑβραϊστὶ Γολγοθα
          which in Hebrew is called Golgotha

36.       19:24v: Temporal
          ἵνα ἡ γραφὴ πληρωθῇ [ἡ λέγουσα]· *διεμερίσαντο τὰ ἱμάτιά μου ἑαυτοῖς καὶ ἐπὶ τὸν ἱματισμόν μου ἔβαλον κλῆρον.*
          This was to fulfill what the scripture says, "They divided my clothes among themselves, and for my clothing they cast lots."

Another reference to the existing scriptures, in this case to Psalm 21:19 LXX.

37.       19:28v: Temporal
          Μετὰ τοῦτο εἰδὼς ὁ Ἰησοῦς ὅτι ἤδη πάντα τετέλεσται, ἵνα τελειωθῇ ἡ γραφή, λέγει· διψῶ.
          After this, when Jesus knew that all was now finished, he said (in order to fulfil the scripture), "I am thirsty."

Another reference to the existing scriptures, although precisely which is hard to determine. Barrett says of Psalm 69:21, "There can be little doubt that this is the γραφή in mind."[17] However, as Michaels points out, it is not a quotation from this verse and other texts in the Psalms may be more relevant, such as 42:1–2 and 63:1.[18] The phrase εἰδὼς ὁ Ἰησοῦς ὅτι ἤδη πάντα τετέλεσται could also be considered a comment (in the *spatial* category), indicating insight into the mind of Jesus, but I think it is a reasonable assumption on the part of the narrator that Jesus' death was very near and Jesus would realize that.

38.       19:35v: Temporal/Spatial
          καὶ ὁ ἑωρακὼς μεμαρτύρηκεν, καὶ ἀληθινὴ αὐτοῦ ἐστιν ἡ μαρτυρία, καὶ ἐκεῖνος οἶδεν ὅτι ἀληθῆ λέγει, ἵνα καὶ ὑμεῖς πιστεύ[σ]ητε.
          (He who saw this has testified so that you also may believe. His testimony is true, and he knows that he tells the truth.)

*An Annotated List of Narrative Comments in the Gospel of John*   111

The temporal categorizing depends to some extent on who the eyewitness referred to here is. Most commentators believe it is the Beloved Disciple, but I have argued elsewhere that it most likely refers to the soldier who pierced Jesus' side with a spear (19:34).[19] If it is the Beloved Disciple, then "his testimony" can be understood as in some sense the very words of this account and so part of the narrative. If it is the soldier, then presumably his testimony is subsequent to the narrative plot.

39.   19:36–37vv: Temporal

ἐγένετο γὰρ ταῦτα ἵνα ἡ γραφὴ πληρωθῇ· Ὀστοῦν οὐ συντριβήσεται αὐτοῦ. καὶ πάλιν ἑτέρα γραφὴ λέγει· Ὄψονται εἰς ὃν ἐξεκέντησαν.

These things occurred so that the scripture might be fulfilled, "None of his bones shall be broken." And again another passage of scripture says, "They will look on the one whom they have pierced."

The second citation is from Zechariah 12:10 (probably in a Hebrew version).[20] The first may come from a number of passages, the most likely being Exodus 12:46 LXX, a reference to the Passover lamb, and/or Psalm 34:20.

40.   20:9v: Temporal

οὐδέπω γὰρ ᾔδεισαν τὴν γραφὴν ὅτι δεῖ αὐτὸν ἐκ νεκρῶν ἀναστῆναι.

for as yet they did not understand the scripture, that he must rise from the dead

Another reference to the fulfilment of scripture, but in this case no specific passage is quoted. Barrett suggests, "It may be that the reference (like that of 1 Cor. 15:4) is to the Old Testament generally."[21] Michaels draws attention to the reference to "all the scriptures" in Luke 24:27.[22]

41.   20:16: Spatial

ὃ λέγεται Διδάσκαλε

(which means Teacher)

42.   20:30–31vv: Spatial

Πολλὰ μὲν οὖν καὶ ἄλλα σημεῖα ἐποίησεν ὁ Ἰησοῦς ἐνώπιον τῶν μαθητῶν [αὐτοῦ], ἃ οὐκ ἔστιν γεγραμμένα ἐν τῷ βιβλίῳ τούτῳ· ταῦτα δὲ γέγραπται ἵνα πιστεύ[σ]ητε ὅτι Ἰησοῦς ἐστιν ὁ Χριστὸς ὁ υἱὸς τοῦ θεοῦ, καὶ ἵνα πιστεύοντες ζωὴν ἔχητε ἐν τῷ ὀνόματι αὐτοῦ.

Now Jesus did many other signs in the presence of his disciples, which are not written in this book. But these are written so that you may come to believe that Jesus is the Messiah, the Son of God, and that through believing you may have life in his name.

112                              *Chapter 3*

The first of two summarizing "conclusions" to the Gospel. Many scholars believe that this was the original ending to the Gospel, with chapter 21 and its conclusion in verses 23–25 added later. This is a hotly contested issue and there is no definite textual evidence to support the widely held belief that chapter 21 is an addition.[23] Regarding this "ending," Cynthia Long Westfall, in a study analysing the linguistic category of *prominence* in Hellenistic Greek, uses the "purpose statement" of 20:31 as "a clear example of a particular sort of discourse staging, where the author steps outside of the structure, and draws attention to its organization and theme."[24]

43.    21:14v: Spatial

τοῦτο ἤδη τρίτον ἐφανερώθη Ἰησοῦς τοῖς μαθηταῖς ἐγερθεὶς ἐκ νεκρῶν.

This was now the third time that Jesus appeared to the disciples after he was raised from the dead.

Tenney refers to this enumeration as an example of the author's methodical style.[25] Most scholars assume the two previous appearances to the disciples were those recorded in 20:19–29, with the appearance to Mary Magdalene in 20:11–18 not included as this was an appearance to one individual alone. However, Michaels states the case for including the appearance to Mary.[26]

44.    21:19: Temporal/Spatial

τοῦτο δὲ εἶπεν σημαίνων ποίῳ θανάτῳ δοξάσει τὸν θεόν.

(He said this to indicate the kind of death by which he would glorify God.)

This is similar to the comment about Jesus' death in 12:33 and the reference to the fulfilment of the comment in 18:32. However, in contrast to Jesus' crucifixion, an account of the manner of Peter's death is not part of John's narrative, so 21:19 lies outside the narrative in a temporal sense. The fact that Peter's death would bring glory to God is a spatial comment, an interpretation by the author/narrator, which echoes the glory of the "hour" of Jesus' crucifixion (12:28; 13:31; 17:1).

# An Annotated List of Narrative Comments in the Gospel of John    113

45.    21:23–25vv: Temporal/Spatial

ἐξῆλθεν οὖν οὗτος ὁ λόγος εἰς τοὺς ἀδελφοὺς ὅτι ὁ μαθητὴς ἐκεῖνος οὐκ ἀποθνῄσκει· οὐκ εἶπεν δὲ αὐτῷ ὁ Ἰησοῦς ὅτι οὐκ ἀποθνῄσκει ἀλλ'· ἐὰν αὐτὸν θέλω μένειν ἕως ἔρχομαι [, τί πρὸς σέ]; Οὗτός ἐστιν ὁ μαθητὴς ὁ μαρτυρῶν περὶ τούτων καὶ ὁ γράψας ταῦτα, καὶ οἴδαμεν ὅτι ἀληθὴς αὐτοῦ ἡ μαρτυρία ἐστίν. Ἔστιν δὲ καὶ ἄλλα πολλὰ ἃ ἐποίησεν ὁ Ἰησοῦς, ἅτινα ἐὰν γράφηται καθ' ἕν, οὐδ' αὐτὸν οἶμαι τὸν κόσμον χωρῆσαι τὰ γραφόμενα βιβλία.

So the rumour spread in the community that this disciple would not die. Yet Jesus did not say to him that he would not die, but, "If it is my will that he remain until I come, what is that to you?" This is the disciple who is testifying to these things and has written them, and we know that his testimony is true. But there are also many other things that Jesus did; if every one of them were written down, I suppose that the world itself could not contain the books that would be written.

This is the most striking example of narrator/author intrusion into the narrative. It contains the first-person plural verb οἴδαμεν (v.24) and the only example of a first-person singular verb in the narrative framework: οἶμαι (v.25).[27] These verses have come to the fore in redaction-critical study. Some understand verses 24–25 as a later scribal addition, with the "we" of verse 24 as referring to a Johannine community/circle/school and the "I" of verse 25 as a particular individual within that group.[28] I suggest that too much is made of the plural/singular difference: οἴδαμεν may imply a single author wishing to include readers rather than it indicating a community composition.[29] (In this respect, I think that NRSV's translation of εἰς τοὺς ἀδελφούς in verse 23 as "in the community" is misleading.) Regarding οἶμαι, Köstenberger, after a comparative study of the term with contemporaneous extrabiblical literature, using examples from Diodorus of Sicily, Dionysius of Halicarnassus, Josephus and Plutarch, concludes:

> the term οἶμαι is a literary term frequently used by historians reflecting authorial modesty in stating a claim or opinion. It is commonly part of authorial discourse, not infrequently at the beginning or conclusion of a literary unit or at points of transition. In its extrabiblical instances the term regularly forms an inextricable part of the author's argument that cannot be easily separated from the larger context by source or redaction-critical means.[30]

In other words, the author of the Gospel may simply be adopting a relatively common stylistic feature here.

114                                    *Chapter 3*

These forty-five narrative comments represent those instances which fit my definition of what belongs outside the narrative in a temporal and/or spatial sense. Of these, I have placed nine in the category *temporal*, twenty-seven in the category *spatial*, and nine in the category *temporal/spatial*, as indicated in table 3.1.

My list shows some evidence of "clusters" of narrative comment, with most occurring in chapters 1 and 2, 6, 11 to 13, and 19 to 21. This differs from Tenney's remark that "the footnotes do not seem to be massed at any particular point in the Gospel, but are evenly distributed throughout its text."[31] On the other hand, I have not listed any comments at all in John 13:12–17:26, which corresponds to Tenney's observation: "One curious gap appears, however: from 13:31 through 17:26 there is not one explanatory note. Perhaps the writer thought that the discourse of Jesus and His prayer should not be interrupted, or else that His words were sufficiently self-explanatory."[32]

Most of the comments are whole sentences and do not, therefore, fit the linguistic definition of phrases or clause within a host sentence. Those that do are mostly relative clauses.

## COMMONLY DENOTED ASIDES NOT INCLUDED

I am quite willing to admit that there is an element of subjectivity in my selection and others may wish to add to this list. However, I think there are reasonable grounds for not including some instances that are commonly denoted as asides/comments. So, for example, I have not included in my list of *external* narrative comments those sentences or phrases marked with dashes or brackets in the NRSV which I regard as integral to the narrative or discourse. These are:

1:15v:   (John testified to him and cried out, "This was he of whom I said, 'He who comes after me ranks ahead of me because he was before me.'")

As, I have argued above, John the Baptist's words belong to the narrative framework. It is the surrounding verses (1:1–5, 7–14, 16–18) which are commentary on the narrative.

2:9:     (though the servants who had drawn the water knew)

I do not regard this as an external comment in that the narrator/author is not disclosing information that the reader is not already aware of. However, it does serve to draw the reader closer to the narrator/author in sharing an

## An Annotated List of Narrative Comments in the Gospel of John    115

**Table 3.1.** A list of the (external) narrative comments in the Gospel of John showing the categories of temporal, spatial, and temporal/spatial. Whole verse(s) are indicated by v/vv.

|    |    | Temporal | Spatial | Temporal/Spatial |
|----|----|----------|---------|------------------|
| 1 | 1:1–5vv | | | X |
| 2 | 1:9–14vv | | | X |
| 3 | 1:16–18vv | | | X |
| 4 | 1:38<br>ὃ λέγεται μεθερμηνευόμενον Διδάσκαλε<br>(which translated means Teacher) | | X | |
| 5 | 1:41<br>ὅ ἐστιν μεθερμηνευόμενον Χριστός<br>(which is translated Anointed) | | X | |
| 6 | 1:42<br>ὃ ἑρμηνεύεται Πέτρος<br>(which is translated Peter) | | X | |
| 7 | 2:11v | | X | |
| 8 | 2:17v | X | | |
| 9 | 2:21–22vv | | | X |
| 10 | 2:24–25vv | | X | |
| 11 | 3:16–21vv | | X | |
| 12 | 3:31–36vv | | X | |
| 13 | 4:25<br>ὁ λεγόμενος Χριστός<br>(who is called Christ) | | X | |
| 14 | 4:54v | | X | |
| 15 | 5:16–18vv | | X | |
| 16 | 6:1<br>τῆς θαλάσσης . . . τῆς Τιβεριάδος<br>also called the Sea of Tiberias | | X | |
| 17 | 6:6v | | X | |
| 18 | 6:15v | | X | |
| 19 | 6:64<br>ᾔδει γὰρ . . . παραδώσων αὐτόν.<br>For Jesus knew . . . betray him. | | X | |
| 20 | 7:39v | X | | |
| 21 | 9:7<br>(ὃ ἑρμηνεύεται Ἀπεσταλμένος)<br>(which means Sent) | | X | |
| 22 | 11:13v | | X | |
| 23 | 11:51–52vv | | X | |
| 24 | 12:6v | | X | |

*(continued)*

116 Chapter 3

**Table 3.1. (continued)**

| | | Temporal | Spatial | Temporal/Spatial |
|---|---|---|---|---|
| 25 | 12:14–15v<br>καθώς ἐστιν γεγραμμένον . . . ἐπὶ πῶλον ὄνου.<br>as it is written . . . on a donkey's colt. | X | | |
| 26 | 12:16v | X | | |
| 27 | 12:33v | | X | |
| 28 | 12:38–41vv | X | | |
| 29 | 13:1<br>Πρὸ δὲ . . . πρὸς τὸν πατέρα<br>Now before . . . to the Father | | | X |
| 30 | 13:3v | | | X |
| 31 | 13:11v | | X | |
| 32 | 18:4<br>Ἰησοῦς οὖν . . . ἐπ᾿ αὐτὸν<br>Then Jesus . . . to him | | X | |
| 33 | 18:32v | | X | |
| 34 | 19:13<br>Ἑβραϊστὶ δὲ Γαββαθα.<br>or in Hebrew Gabbatha | | X | |
| 35 | 19:17<br>ὃ λέγεται Ἑβραϊστὶ Γολγοθα<br>which in Hebrew is called Golgotha | | X | |
| 36 | 19:24v | X | | |
| 37 | 19:28<br>Μετὰ τοῦτο . . . ἵνα τελειωθῇ ἡ γραφή<br>After this . . . "I am thirsty." | X | | |
| 38 | 19:35v | | | X |
| 39 | 19:36–37vv | X | | |
| 40 | 20:9v | X | | |
| 41 | 20:16<br>ὃ λέγεται Διδάσκαλε<br>(which means Teacher) | | X | |
| 42 | 20:30–31vv | | X | |
| 43 | 21:14v | | X | |
| 44 | 21:19<br>τοῦτο δὲ εἶπεν . . . τὸν θεόν.<br>(He said this . . . God.) | | | X |
| 45 | 21:23–25vv | | | X |

*An Annotated List of Narrative Comments in the Gospel of John* 117

insight which is not revealed to the steward (ὁ ἀρχιτρίκλινος). As Brant suggests, "There is ironic pleasure when someone who is ostensibly in charge is in the dark and when the servants who are not the wedding guests become the insiders," and she understands the comment as an ironic glimpse "of the reversal of the social order," which is prominent in the Synoptics.[33] The reader can share this "ironic pleasure," so the phrase can be considered an example of dramatic irony and possibly be categorized as an *internal* comment.

3:24:     —John, of course, had not yet been thrown into prison.

Many commentators regard this as either a correction of or harmonization with the synoptic traditions (Mark 1:14; 6:17; Matthew 4:12; 14:3; Luke 3:19–20).[34] However, Barrett rejects the idea that it is a correction, as does Bauckham.[35] Michaels describes it as "a parenthetical aside," that "comes belatedly, as an afterthought."[36] However, even though John does not record any other mention of the Baptist's imprisonment, it is intrinsic to the narrative framework and, therefore, an *internal* aside/comment.

I am not sure where the NRSV gets its "of course" from. It is not in the RSV and, as far as I am aware, is not found in any of the Greek texts. NA28 reads: οὔπω γὰρ ἦν βεβλημένος εἰς τὴν φυλακὴν ὁ Ἰωάννης.

4:2:     —although it was not Jesus himself but his disciples who baptized—

I consider this to be an *internal* comment and I discuss it in more detail in chapter 4.

4:8v:     (His disciples had gone to the city to buy food.)

Again, an *internal* comment, which appears slightly out of sequence, as it would seem to follow on more naturally from verse 6, setting the scene for Jesus' encounter with the Samaritan woman. Barrett calls it a "stage direction."[37] Michaels labels it an "afterthought."[38] Brant describes it as "an important analepsis (flashback)."[39]

4:9:     (Jews do not share things in common with Samaritans.)

As I have already suggested, this may be an example of *showing*, as part of the Samaritan woman's reply to Jesus' request for a drink, rather than *telling* and, therefore, not a comment. I discuss it in more detail in chapter 4.

118                                    *Chapter 3*

4:44v:   (for Jesus himself had testified that a prophet has no honour in the
         prophet's own country)

Michaels calls this a "narrative aside."[40] I have already indicated in chapter 2
that I do not count it as an external comment as, from a temporal perspective,
it is part of the narrative framework and, according to the narrator, it is Jesus
himself who stated these words. It is not an example of analepsis as it does
not refer to a previous statement in the Gospel, although there may be echoes
of the synoptic traditions (Mark 6:4; Matthew 13:57; Luke 4:24).

7:5v:    (For not even his brothers believed in him.)

I am not sure how to categorize this sentence. It depends what sort of belief/
trust/faith the author has in mind. In some ways the remark could be considered integral to the narrative: Jesus' brothers are just not sure what to make
of him and they think he needs some guidance at this point. They do not trust
his judgement.[41] On the other hand it could be a more general comment on the
presence or absence of faith, such a key theme in the Gospel, and, therefore,
an *external* comment, which is temporal if the author is aware of the brothers'
later faith in Jesus (as depicted in Acts 1:14). This temporal understanding
may have prompted Codex Bezae (D) and a few other manuscripts' addition
of τότε at the end of the sentence.[42]

7:22:    (it is, of course, not from Moses, but from the patriarchs)

I regard this as part of Jesus' dialogue with the Jewish crowd and not a comment by the narrator/author. It would seem highly unlikely for the author to
"correct" Jesus.[43]

10:35:   —and the scripture cannot be annulled—

This example of syntactical ellipsis is typical of spoken parentheses and I
have analysed it in the previous chapter. It belongs to the words of Jesus not
those of the narrator. Indeed the phrase is integral to Jesus' argument.

12:4:    (the one who was about to betray him)

This is one of a number of "labels," which the author uses to clarify which
disciple is being referred to. Here the reference is to Judas Iscariot. The other
examples are: 11:16; 20:24; 21:2 (Thomas); 14:22 (the "other" Judas); and

*An Annotated List of Narrative Comments in the Gospel of John*     119

13:23; 19:26; 20:2; 21:7, 20 (the "Beloved Disciple"). I note that in some cases the NRSV has marked these with parenthetical punctuation, in other cases not. 12:4 can also be considered an example of analepsis, looking back to 6:64–71, and hence an internal aside/comment.

13:23:   —the one whom Jesus loved—

The first of the references to the "Beloved Disciple." Traditionally, commentators have identified this disciple as John the son of Zebedee, but this view is contested (at great length) in modern scholarship.[44]

14:22:   (not Iscariot)

20:24:   (who was called the Twin)

NRSV places this label in brackets, but not the other references to Thomas as the Twin (Δίδυμος) in 11:16 and 21:2. KJV and RSV puts none of these in brackets and it is hard to see the justification for the NRSV editors' decision here.

## SOME INTERNAL ASIDES/COMMENTS

In chapter 3, in my discussion of the possible category of *internal* asides/comments in the Gospel, I commented on the author's frequent use of analepsis and occasional use of prolepsis. I also stated that we need to take into account the "narrative distance" between these intertextual references and be aware that some of these perceived internal references may, in fact, be alluding to earlier traditions, including the synoptic traditions. Of the commonly denoted asides marked in the NRSV, which I did not accept as *external*, I noted the following as examples of *internal* comments:

3:24:    —John, of course, had not yet been thrown into prison.

4:2:     —although it was not Jesus himself but his disciples who baptized—

4:8v:    (His disciples had gone to the city to buy food.)

12:4:    (the one who was about to betray him)

120                                    *Chapter 3*

I would also include as internal comments the other "labels" (in addition to 12:4) used to clarify which disciple is being referred to in 11:16; 13:23; 14:22; 19:26; 20:2, 24: 21:2, 7, 20.

I propose that other significant internal comments are:

7:30     ὅτι οὔπω ἐληλύθει ἡ ὥρα αὐτοῦ
         because his hour had not yet come

This is the first reference in the narrative framework to Jesus' "time" or "hour" (ὥρα), used "to designate a particular and significant period in Jesus' life" (Brown).[45] There are frequent references in Jesus' own dialogue (2:4; 4:21, 23; 5:25, 28–29; 12:23, 27; 16:25, 32; 17:1).[46] However, there are only two other references by the narrator:

8:20     ὅτι οὔπω ἐληλύθει ἡ ὥρα αὐτοῦ
         because his hour had not yet come

13:1     εἰδὼς ὁ Ἰησοῦς ὅτι ἦλθεν αὐτοῦ ἡ ὥρα
         Jesus knew that his hour had come

These three comments are examples of prolepsis and analepsis connecting with the use of ὥρα in the dialogue.

9:22–23vv  ταῦτα εἶπαν οἱ γονεῖς αὐτοῦ ὅτι ἐφοβοῦντο τοὺς Ἰουδαίους·
           ἤδη γὰρ συνετέθειντο οἱ Ἰουδαῖοι ἵνα ἐάν τις αὐτὸν ὁμολογήσῃ
           Χριστόν, ἀποσυνάγωγος γένηται. διὰ τοῦτο οἱ γονεῖς αὐτοῦ
           εἶπαν ὅτι ἡλικίαν ἔχει, αὐτὸν ἐπερωτήσατε.
           His parents said this because they were afraid of the Jews; for
           the Jews had already agreed that anyone who confessed Jesus
           to be the Messiah would be put out of the synagogue. Therefore
           his parents said, "He is of age; ask him."

Michaels states, "At this point the Gospel writer breaks in with a narrative aside."[47] At first glance ἤδη γὰρ συνετέθειντο οἱ Ἰουδαῖοι ἵνα ἐάν τις αὐτὸν ὁμολογήσῃ Χριστόν, ἀποσυνάγωγος γένηται looks like a temporal aside, referring to a previous decision by the Jewish authorities, although it is only now that this information is revealed by the author/narrator.[48] However, the authorities' decision clearly belongs within the narrative time-frame, not outside it. It is similar to the observation in 11:57 that the authorities "had given orders that anyone who knew where Jesus was should let them know."

# An Annotated List of Narrative Comments in the Gospel of John   121

18:9v   ἵνα πληρωθῇ ὁ λόγος ὃν εἶπεν ὅτι οὓς δέδωκάς μοι οὐκ ἀπώλεσα ἐξ αὐτῶν οὐδένα.

This was to fulfil the word that he had spoken, "I did not lose a single one of those whom you gave me."

This seems to be a reference back to Jesus' words in 6:39; 10:28; and (especially) 17:12, although it is not a precise quotation of these words.

7:50:   λέγει Νικόδημος πρὸς αὐτούς, ὁ ἐλθὼν πρὸς αὐτὸν [τὸ] πρότερον, εἷς ὢν ἐξ αὐτῶν

Nicodemus, who had gone to Jesus before, and who was one of them, asked

19:39:   ἦλθεν δὲ καὶ Νικόδημος, ὁ ἐλθὼν πρὸς αὐτὸν νυκτὸς τὸ πρῶτον

Nicodemus, who had at first come to Jesus by night

These are both examples of analepsis, looking back to the account of Nicodemus coming to Jesus in 3:1–2. I discussed their significance in chapter 2.

There are other cross-references in the narrative, such as 10:40's mention of "the place where John had been baptizing" (compare with 1:28) and 18:14's reminder that Caiaphas was the one who had advised the Jewish leaders (compare with 11:49–52), but I think that these hardly merit the description of narrative asides/comments. They do, however, contribute to the author's structuring of the narrative.

## NOTES

1. This separation of the references to John the Baptist is complicated by the overlap in vocabulary and thought between vv.7–8 and v.9. Brown chooses to put all three verses in brackets (*Gospel*, 1:3).
2. Bultmann, *Gospel*, 118, 209.
3. Westcott, *Gospel*, 1:118–19.
4. Piñero and Peláez, *Study of the New Testament*, 494.
5. Westcott, *Gospel*, 1:130.
6. Brown, *Gospel*, 1:213.
7. Bernard, *Gospel*, 1:172; Macgregor, *Gospel*, 127.
8. Ernst Haenchen, *A Commentary on the Gospel of John,* trans. Robert W. Funk, ed. Robert W. Funk and Ulrich Busse, 2 vols., Hermeneia (Philadelphia: Fortress Press, 1984), 1:270; cf. Schnackenburg, *Gospel*, 2:13.
9. Barrett, *Gospel*, 273.
10. Hedrick, "Authorial Presence," 82; Sheeley, *Narrative Asides*, 38.

122                           *Chapter 3*

11. Sheeley, *Narrative Asides*, 38.

12. Carson states, "Although sleep as a metaphor for death is common in Christian theology, it is less common (though not unknown) in the Old Testament and in the Judaism of the second temple period." Donald A. Carson, *The Gospel According to John* (Leicester: Inter-Varsity Press, 1991), 409. He implies that this less common usage may have contributed to the disciples' misunderstanding. However, George Brooke points out that it is difficult to judge the extent of the metaphorical use of שׁכב in early Aramaic, given the amount of textual material that survives and uncertainty as to how readers would have understood the term. He cites an example in Qumran Aramaic from 11QtgJob, col. 24, where the term appears to mean "to die" (George J. Brooke, email message to author, February 27, 2024).

13. Michaels, *Gospel*, 621; cf. Brant: "The narrator's clarification of Jesus's meaning serves more to underscore the disciples' confusion than to inform the audience of Jesus's intent" (*Gospel*, 173). Carson is more kindly disposed towards the disciples and provides a number of reasons for their misunderstanding (*Gospel*, 409).

14. Brant, *Gospel*, 180.

15. See, for example, Michaels, *Gospel*, 700–701; Zumstein, *L'Évangile*, 1:406.

16. So Brown, *Gospel*, 1:468–69.

17. Barrett, *Gospel*, 553.

18. Michaels, *Gospel*, 961–63.

19. Lamb, *Text, Context*, 163n83. This interpretation is supported by Thyen (*Das Johannesevangelium*, 748) and Michaels (*Gospel*, 970–75).

20. However, Randolph Bynum argues that John 19:37 was based on the Greek scroll of the Minor Prophets, 8HevXIIgr (R). Wm. Randolph Bynum, *The Fourth Gospel and the Scriptures: Illuminating the Form and Meaning of Scriptural Citation in John 19:37*, NovT Sup 144 (Leiden: Brill, 2012).

21. Barrett, *Gospel*, 564.

22. Michaels, *Gospel*, 993; cf. Wengst, *Das Johannesevangelium*, 2:298n26; Zumstein, *L'Évangile*, 2:273.

23. Brent Nongbri argues that there may be some evidence that John 21 is a later addition, based on his reading of a particular reconstruction of the fragments of P66 (Papyrus Bodmer 2). See Brent Nongbri, "P.Bodmer 2 as Possible Evidence for the Circulation of the Gospel according to John without Chapter 21," *Early Christianity* 9:3 (2018): 345–60. However, owing to the fragmentary state of the final chapters of John in P.Bodmer 2, Nongbri does concede that his hypothesis cannot be proved unless further evidence comes to light (355).

24. Cynthia Long Westfall, "A Method for the Analysis of Prominence in Hellenistic Greek," in *The Linguist as Pedagogue: Trends in the Teaching and Linguistic Analysis of the Greek New Testament*, ed. Stanley E. Porter and Matthew Brook O'Donnell, New Testament Monographs 11 (Sheffield: Sheffield Phoenix Press, 2009), 92–93.

25. Tenney, "Footnotes," 359.

26. Michaels, *Gospel*, 1041–42.

An Annotated List of Narrative Comments in the Gospel of John    123

27. The only other instances of first person (plural) verbal forms in the narrative framework, as opposed to discourse material, are in the Prologue: 1:14 (καὶ ὁ λόγος σὰρξ ἐγένετο καὶ ἐσκήνωσεν ἐν ἡμῖν, καὶ ἐθεασάμεθα τὴν δόξαν αὐτοῦ) and (unless they are a continuation of John the Baptist's words in v.15) 1:16 (ὅτι ἐκ τοῦ πληρώματος αὐτοῦ ἡμεῖς πάντες ἐλάβομεν).

28. See, for example, Bultmann, *Gospel*, 717–18; Brown, *Gospel*, 2:1124–26; R. Alan Culpepper, *John, the Son of Zebedee: The Life of a Legend* (Edinburgh: T & T Clark, 2000), 71.

29. In Lamb, *Text, Context*, 169n102, I noted Sanders's comment: "'We know his witness is true,' is not the comment of a kind of editorial committee (as the *Muratorian Canon* appears to understand it), but an instance of the author taking his readers into his confidence, and assuming that they share his opinion." See Joseph N. Sanders, *A Commentary on the Gospel According to St John* (ed. B. A. Mastin; BNTC; London: Adam and Charles Black, 1968), 48.

30. Andreas J. Köstenberger, "'I Suppose' (οἶμαι): The Conclusion of John's Gospel in Its Literary and Historical Context," in *The New Testament in Its First Century Setting: Essays on Context and Background in Honour of B. W. Winter on His 65th Birthday*, ed. P. J. Williams, Andrew D. Clark, Peter M. Head, and David Instone-Brewer (Grand Rapids, Eerdmans: 2004), 87.

31. Tenney, "Footnotes," 351.

32. Tenney, "Footnotes," 351.

33. Brant, *Gospel*, 58.

34. See Bultmann, *Gospel*, 171; Zumstein, *L'Évangile*, 131n29; Theobald, *Das Evangelium*, 283.

35. Barrett *Gospel*, 220–21; Bauckham, "John for Readers of Mark," 154–55.

36. Michaels, *Gospel*, 215.

37. Barrett, *Gospel*, 232.

38. Michaels, *Gospel*, 238.

39. Brant, *Gospel*, 83.

40. Michaels, *Gospel*, 271.

41. A parallel in the Synoptics may be Jesus' family's attempt "to restrain him" when he is accused of being demon-possessed (Mark 3:21–22). However, the interpretation of οἱ παρ' αὐτοῦ in 3:21 as Jesus' "family," including his brothers, depends on seeing the verse as linked to 3:31.

42. See Barrett, *Gospel*, 312. The Contemporary English Version (CEV) has: "Even Jesus' own brothers had not yet become his followers."

43. "The reader can only conclude that it is to be read as Jesus correcting himself" (Michaels, *Gospel*, 445). Brant states, "[Jesus] includes a self-correction that underscores both that the practice of circumcision is older than Moses and that Jesus is knowledgeable" (*Gospel*, 137).

44. See, for example, Brown, *Gospel*, 1:xcii–xcviii; Culpepper, *John*, 56–85; Richard Bauckham, *Jesus and the Eyewitnesses: The Gospels as Eyewitness Testimony*, 2nd ed. (Grand Rapids: Eerdmans, 2017), 358–411.

45. Brown, *Gospel*, 1:517.

124 *Chapter 3*

46. 16:2, 4 refer to a different sort of ὥρα, the time of the persecution of Jesus' disciples.

47. Michaels, *Gospel*, 553.

48. Many recent scholars regard this comment regarding expulsion from the synagogue as "anachronistic" and therefore reflecting the time when the Gospel was written. It forms the basis for Martyn's influential "two-level" interpretation: J. Louis Martyn, *History and Theology in the Fourth Gospel*, 3rd ed. (Louisville: Westminster John Knox, 2003), 35–66. Lincoln states, "The anachronistic nature of the narrator's comment provides an important clue for reading this account, and by extension the Gospel as a whole, as a two-level drama" (*Gospel*, 284).

*Chapter 4*

# The Process of Composition

An important element of the asides/comments raised in chapter 1, "The Survey of Literature," was the question of to what extent these literary features reveal a process of composition in the Gospel, in particular, whether they are the result of the redaction of earlier material. The subject of redaction was considered in the works of Flowers and Garvie in the 1920s and continued to be prominent until the rise of more synchronic methods of interpretation from the 1970s onwards. We see this shift in emphasis reflected in the work of Raymond Brown, who in the original introduction to his commentary (1966) spoke of notes that "are often indicative of the editing process at work in the composition of the Gospel," but who in his revised introduction (2003) is less certain about this editing process and is more willing to consider the narrative function of these notes.[1]

The process of the Gospel's composition—that is, the relationship between the words and actions of Jesus and those whom he encountered and the Koiné Greek texts of the following centuries—is a complex and disputed one. It seems reasonable to suggest that it involves an interaction between the memories of witnesses, ongoing oral traditions, and writing in a variety of forms. It also involves the social contexts of those involved, which for many scholars has become of deeper concern than the attempt to retrieve the *ipsissima verba et facta Jesu*. Indeed, some regard the latter as a misguided quest in relation to what they regard as primarily literary and theological creations.[2]

In this chapter, I will consider the place of narrative comments in this process of composition and, in particular, whether some or all should be considered as the work of later redactors of the text, who may not necessarily share the same perspective as the original author. As an example of this, I referred in chapter 1 to Macgregor, who, is his 1928 commentary, states, "Parenthetical comments occur which so clearly misunderstand the real point of the

126                                   *Chapter 4*

context as to prove that they are due to a later hand."[3] Macgregor gives the
examples of John 2:21; 6:46; 8:27; 12:16; 18:9, and supports his proposition
with a quote from Wellhausen, "A writer may be negligent and maladroit, and
once in a way even a little forgetful, but he must know what he himself means
and cannot lose forthwith all idea of what he himself said."[4]

So, are there, as Macgregor and others believe, multiple "voices" in the
Gospel indicated by addition of narrative comments? In seeking to answer
this question, I begin by looking at the work of two critics noted for their
focus on the process of composition—namely, the foundational work of Bultmann and the more recent contribution of Urban von Wahlde.

## BULTMANN: *DAS EVANGELIUM DES JOHANNES* (1941)

Bultmann's highly influential commentary *Das Evangelium des Johannes*
was first published in 1941, with an English translation in 1971. Bultmann's
form-critical method of NT interpretation, drawing on the work of Schmidt
and Dibelius, lays emphasis on the units of oral tradition that lie behind the
NT texts, but his analysis of the Gospel concentrates more on written stages
of composition. He specifically proposes various written "traditions" or
"sources" (revelatory discourses, signs, passion-resurrection), the use of these
sources by "the Evangelist," and the subsequent modification of this material
by "the Ecclesiastical Redactor."[5]

I noted in chapter 2 the variety of terms which Bultmann uses to refer
to parenthetical material. These include terms which specifically indicate
a process of redaction: *Einfügungen, Glossen, Zusätze* (insertions, glosses,
additions). However, he also speaks of explanations (*Erläuterungen*) or comments (*Anmerkungen*) that the Evangelist makes regarding his source material. So, for example, Bultmann believes that in John 1:1–18, verses 6–8, 13,
and 15 "stand out as interruptions" ("treten . . . störend dazwischen") from
"the verse rhythm" of the Prologue, as well as conflicting with its character
as "a hymn of the community."[6] This leads him to conclude, "There lies at
the basis of the Prologue a source document to which the Evangelist has
added his own comments."[7] He goes on to state, "These insertions are not
to be eliminated as interpolations: they are the Evangelist's own comments
(the ancient world has no knowledge of notes placed under the text), as is
confirmed by the way he works throughout the Gospel."[8] As such, they are to
be distinguished from "glosses of a secondary redaction."[9] Regarding the purpose of these comments in the Prologue, Bultmann suggests that verses 6 to
8 and 15 were inserted into an existing "hymn of the Baptist-Community" to
make it clear that it is Jesus and not John the Baptist who is "the Revealer."[10]

The Process of Composition                                127

Verse 13 serves as an interpretation of the phrase τέκνα θεοῦ in the preceding verse.[11] Bultmann also regards the final phrases in verse 12 and verse 17 and (possibly) verse 18 along with "other small corrections" as additions to the source material.[12]

It is worth noting that Bultmann also considers the role of comments in the delivery of the text: "One has to suppose that in oral recitation the 'comments' would be distinguishable by the tone of the speaker."[13] I will consider the implications of this later.

Other examples Bultmann provides of comments by the Evangelist on his source material include:

2:9:   καὶ οὐκ ᾔδει πόθεν ἐστίν, οἱ δὲ διάκονοι ᾔδεισαν οἱ ἠντληκότες τὸ ὕδωρ: He understands this as "the Evangelist's addition" to the verse, primarily on stylistic grounds, observing that "the antithesis between knowing and not knowing sounds Johannine."[14]

4:9:   οὐ γὰρ συγχρῶνται Ἰουδαῖοι Σαμαρίταις: "The enmity between the Jews and the Samaritans noted by the gloss at the end of v. 9, was common knowledge to the original narrator and his audience."[15] He notes the textual uncertainty of this sentence and adds, "If originally it was contained in the text, then of course it comes from the Evangelist."[16] I will consider this "gloss" in more detail below.

4:44v: "a note added by the Evangelist to remind the reader of a saying spoken by Jesus on another occasion, and which was known to the reader from another tradition."[17] Bultmann is referring here to synoptic parallels (Mark 6:4; Matthew 13:57; Luke 4:24) and Papyrus Oxyrhynchus 1.[18]

7:5v:  He states, "The motivation given in v. 5 is typical of the Evangelist."[19]

12:6v: "a composition of the Evangelist's."[20] Bultmann suggests that the Evangelist has undermined the real point of the story ("this extravagant act of love") by this explanation.[21]

Other "notes" attributed to the Evangelist are 2:21–22; 7:39; 11:13; 12:16; and 12:33.[22]

However, Bultmann also perceives the influence of another "voice" behind the additions, which he attributes to the ecclesiastical redactor. These include:

128                           *Chapter 4*

3:24v:    Rather than being an addition by the Evangelist, "it is even more
          probable that 3.24 (like 7.39b) is a gloss inserted by the ecclesiasti-
          cal editor."[23] This is done in order to harmonize with the synoptic
          account.

7:38b:    καθὼς εἶπεν ἡ γραφή, ποταμοὶ ἐκ τῆς κοιλίας αὐτοῦ ῥεύσουσιν
          ὕδατος ζῶντος: This "makes an inadmissible break between Jesus'
          words in vv. 37.38a and v.39," which the ecclesiastical editor is
          responsible for.[24] As Bultmann notes, the exact basis of this "scrip-
          tural" quotation is uncertain.[25]

18:32v:   "a comment of the ecclesiastical redactor, which harks back to
          12.33."[26] I note that this is an example of a comment within the
          narrative framework.

19:35v:   Bultmann sees this claim to eyewitness testimony as character-
          istic of the ecclesiastical redactor, alongside the references to
          baptism and the Lord's Supper in 19:34b (καὶ ἐξῆλθεν εὐθὺς αἷμα
          καὶ ὕδωρ), 3:5, and 6:52b–58.[27] In the latter cases, I observe that
          his decision to categorize them as later additions is made on the
          grounds of theological content rather than style or structure.

21:19:    τοῦτο δὲ εἶπεν σημαίνων ποίῳ θανάτῳ δοξάσει τὸν θεόν: This
          explanation of the "proverb" in v. 18 is, along with the rest of
          chapter 21, the work of the Redactor.[28]

Despite Bultmann's customary confidence in allocating the text of the Gospel
to particular sources or layers of redaction, we need to note his uncertainty
as to whether to assign certain remarks to the Evangelist or Redactor, as in
the case of the so-called "translation asides" in 1:38, 41, 42; 4:25; 9:7; 11:16;
19:13; 20:16.[29] Similarly, he is unsure whether 4:2, the parenthetical verse
which "corrects the statement in 3:22," is part of the Evangelist's introduction
to the account of Jesus' encounter with the Samaritan woman or an "editorial
gloss."[30] Moreover, in some cases, such as the phrase "in order to fulfil the
scripture" in 19:28, he sees remarks as integral to the source material.[31] This
is true of 19:24, "This was to fulfil what the scripture says," for "the Evangelist does not have a primary concern for proof from Scripture, although
occasionally he does give it room."[32]

   Overall, we can say that Bultmann makes a distinction between the "comments" of the Evangelist and the "glosses" of the Redactor, while some
asides are attributed to the Gospel's source material. Bultmann makes his

The Process of Composition                               129

distinctions on the grounds of both style and (theological) content, but does admit to a degree of uncertainty.

## URBAN VON WAHLDE: *THE GOSPEL AND LETTERS OF JOHN* (2010)

To some extent, von Wahlde bucks the trend of much recent Johannine scholarship by taking up the mantle of a diachronic approach as central to the correct interpretation of the Gospel. It is the aporias, the "various inconsistencies, disjunctures, and breaks in sequence," described by von Wahlde as "a hallmark of the Gospel of John," which expose the literary seams of this composite work.[33] He sees three distinct literary layers in the Gospel, which are the product of three distinct individuals. These editions relate to specific periods in the history of the Johannine community. The first edition (AD 55–65?) presents a complete narrative of Jesus' ministry including the miracles and was probably written in Judea. The second edition (AD 60–65?) shows a deeper theological understanding of Jesus's ministry and the role of the Spirit that puts the community at odds with fellow Jews in the synagogue. This edition also originated in Judea. The third edition (AD 90–95) enshrines the understanding of the Jesus tradition articulated by the Elder ("the Beloved Disciple") and was written in Asia Minor (possibly in Ephesus) after the composition of the Johannine Epistles and schism within the community.[34] As von Wahlde believes that we can have a reasonable degree of confidence in assigning the text of the Gospel to these three editions (1E, 2E, 3E), it is worth noting how he deals with asides/comments and to which of his three editions he attributes them. Using as a sample the NRSV's 25 phrases or sentences in brackets or dashes and the categorization labels I suggested for them in chapter 2, we can determine something of von Wahlde's understanding of their relation to the three-stage process of composition.[35]

He allocates the comments which are looking forward (prolepsis) or which are possible references to existing tradition in 1:15; 3:24; 4:44; 12:4 to 3E:

1:15v:    This is one of four "additions" to the Prologue's "hymn." As the language of these additions is not typical of either the Gospel or Letters, von Wahlde concludes that "the author is not one of those involved in the composition of the remainder of the Gospel or Letters."[36] It "lacks the brevity, the parallelism, and the catchword-linking characteristic of the hymnic sections" of the Prologue.[37] In addition, like Bultmann, he sees it as interrupting the sequence of the hymn. It is modelled on 1:30 (also from 3E), echoing its theology of Christ's pre-existence.[38]

130                                     *Chapter 4*

3:24v:    An "awkward" insertion "intended to relate the Johannine material
          to elements of the Synoptic tradition."[39]

12:4:     "(the one about to betray him)": this is part of a section of material
          (12:3–8) which has also been adapted from the synoptic tradition in
          an awkward manner. After surveying evidence for this adaptation,
          von Wahlde concludes: "The Johannine account is a less-than-
          perfect conflation of both the Marcan and Lucan anointing traditions
          by someone who apparently did not fully understand the meaning
          of either."[40] Presumably, the aside that Judas Iscariot was "the one
          about to betray him" relates to the fact that the Markan anointing
          pericope (and its parallel in Matthew) is followed by the account of
          Judas's betrayal, although von Wahlde does not mention this. He
          does suggest that, as with other adaptations of synoptic material,
          the editor's aim was "to attempt to give the reader a greater sense
          that the Johannine Gospel was indeed similar in many obvious ways
          to the other Gospel accounts."[41] Although, if we agree with von
          Wahlde, it seems that he made a poor job of this.

4:44v:    The primary purpose of this "brief modification" to the account in
          4:43–54 is "to reflect the Synoptics," although, as in other instances
          where the author incorporates material from the synoptic tradition,
          this is done "poorly."[42]

Regarding *explanations or clarifications of narrative*, von Wahlde makes the
following observations:

2:9:      "(but the servants who had drawn the water knew)": possibly from
          2E, but more likely part of 1E.[43]

4:2v:     Almost certainly belongs to 3E, being "marked as an editorial addi-
          tion by the way it interrupts the narrative in which it stands and by
          the way it contradicts two other statements from the first edition
          (3:22 and 4:1), which indicate Jesus did in fact have a baptizing
          ministry."[44] He sees it as being "inserted for a specific theological
          purpose," both to indicate Jesus' superiority to John the Baptist and
          to bring the account into line with the Synoptics.[45] Although von
          Wahlde regards Jesus' "superiority" to John the Baptist as a charac-
          teristic of 2E, he believes that this addition belongs to 3E.[46]

4:8v:     This is part of 4:4–9, found in 1E, and receives no special comment.

## The Process of Composition

7:5v:    This is from a section of material (7:3–10) full of "idiosyncrasies" that can be attributed to 3E. Regarding the brothers' lack of faith in Jesus, von Wahlde states, "In the third edition, the primary focus is on the correctness of belief rather than on belief being 'easy'."[47]

7:22:    "—not that it is from Moses but the patriarchs—": is part of 7:21–24, coming from 2E.[48]

10:35:    "and if scripture cannot be contradicted": is part of a long section (10:22–29) from 2E and receives no special comment.

12:6:    (whole verse): like 12:4, is from a 3E section (12:3–8) that is poorly adapted from the synoptic tradition, although "only here do we hear that Judas was a thief."[49]

13:23:    "whom Jesus loved": is from a 3E section (13:21–27). Von Wahlde states, "In the Greek, this clause occurs awkwardly at the end of the verse after the disciple had been identified earlier in the verse simply as 'one of his disciples.'"[50]

14:22:    "not the Iscariot": the whole verse, including this comment, is from 2E.

18:32v:    Part of a short section (18:30–32) from 3E. This "formula of fulfilment . . . is typical of the third edition."[51]

21:19:    "He said this signifying by what type of death he would glorify God": belongs to the 3E ending to the Gospel (21:15–25). Von Wahlde puts it in brackets.

The *translations of Hebrew/Aramaic terms* in 1:38, 41, 42; 4:25; 9:7; 19:17; 20:16 all belong to 1E, whereas 20:24 ("the one called Didymus"), along with the whole section relating to Thomas (20:24–29), belongs to 3E. The other references to Thomas as "Didymus" are attributed to 2E in 11:16 and 3E in 21:2. In the latter instance the author has incorporated traditional written material not found in the two earlier editions.[52]

Regarding the *explanation of Jewish customs*, von Wahlde states that the clause "For Jews do not associate with Samaritans" in 4:9 is "an explanation of customs typical of the first edition."[53]

Regarding the *fulfilment of scripture*, he describes 19:28, with its clause "so that the Scripture might be completed," as an "awkward" reference belonging to 3E that is part of the theological interpretation in 19:28b–30a: "the author

132                                        *Chapter 4*

intends to present Jesus as being in complete control and conscious of his role in the divine plan right to the end."[54]

Regarding the *authority of the narrator/witness*, the assertion in 19:35 is seen as a reference to the Beloved Disciple and his theological understanding of the meaning of Jesus' death.[55] As such it is part of the narrative in 19:32–37 that comes from 3E, a section which also includes two references to the fulfilment of scripture (verses 36–37). However, von Wahlde does not regard such quotations from the OT/HB as exclusive to 3E. Indeed, of the 20 quotations or references that he considers, he attributes two to 1E, nine to 2E, and nine to 3E.[56]

From this survey, we see that von Wahlde attributes generally recognized asides/comments to all three of the editions of the text which he claims to be able to isolate, so they cannot be universally attributed to later redaction. For example, he regards John 20:30–31 (with the exception of the final clause "and that believing you may have life in his name," added in 2E) as "the conclusion to *the first edition* of the Gospel."[57] However, the majority of asides/comments do belong to 3E, although they are often incorporated into larger sections of material from this edition. On the process of "annotating or ('glossing')" in 3E, von Wahlde asserts, "The final author works within the structure of the previous editions, appending and inserting comments (sometimes lengthy ones) in order to clarify, at appropriate points, his interpretation of various theological issues, particularly those disputed by the opponents within the community."[58]

## THE WEAKNESS OF THE SOURCE AND REDACTION CRITICISM APPROACH TO ASIDES

Both Bultmann and von Wahlde, with some confidence, assign comments to various different stages in the composition of the Gospel. However, the weakness of their approach and that of other proponents of source and redaction criticism is the paucity of textual evidence to support their proposals. We do not have shorter early editions of the Gospel for comparison, editions which may then have been subjected to additions and amendments, possibly reflecting the theological and political concerns of particular individuals or groups. Commenting on such possible stages of redaction of the text and their relation to the history of a hypothetical Johannine community, Luke Timothy Johnson writes:

> The putative discovery of seams and sources is sometimes also connected to "stages in the community's life." The text is thereby treated as an archaeological site whose layers reveal buried social history. The reconstructions are, however, sufficiently numerous and unconvincing to diminish confidence in the method itself. The FG we now read does not

## The Process of Composition

have the look of composition by committee or of a haphazard outcome of heavy-handed editing. Only to minds obsessively concerned with a certain level of consistency are seams always indicators of sources.[59]

Similarly, Bauckham, in drawing attention to Van Belle's work, says of the parentheses that "in both style and content, they are homogenous both with each other and with the rest of the Gospel."[60] Bauckham concludes:

> The habit of critics, prior to recent literary studies, of attributing many of them to later redactors or glossators is unjustified. The presence of explanatory parentheses of various kinds in the Gospel is not evidence of redactional processes in the history of the composition of the Gospel or of later additions to the text of the Gospel, but is simply a characteristic literary feature of the Fourth Gospel as such. The parentheses in general must be regarded as integral to the Gospel, and to treat any particular parenthesis as a gloss requires a very good argument in that particular case if it is to be convincing.[61]

The work of source and redaction critics of the Gospel depends much on the detection of so-called aporias, as von Wahlde explicitly states regarding his own analysis of the text: "The starting point for this analysis is recognition of the aporias. These various inconsistencies, disjunctures, and breaks in sequence are used to identity the literary seams. These seams indicate where the material from one author ends and another begins."[62] However, an awareness of the processes of transmission in predominantly oral cultures, such as the first-century Mediterranean world, should make us wary of this modern perception of aporias. As Craig Koester observes, listeners "are much less likely to notice occasional breaks in logical and narrative sequence than those who study the printed page."[63] Similarly, Joanna Dewey states, "Our modern tools for separating source from redaction often rely on subtle analytic distinctions that are incompatible with the additive and aggregative nature of oral narrative and the style of most first-century writing."[64] She concludes, "We need to take less seriously the aporias of the FG."[65]

On the other hand, Dewey and others are perhaps overly sceptical of the use of written sources and have not given sufficient attention to the complex literary structure of the Gospel, which suggests deliberate written composition rather than just "the additive and aggregative nature of oral narrative."[66] Culpepper, in his pioneering study of the literary design of the Gospel, describes it as "magnificent in its complexity, subtlety, and profundity," albeit "oddly flawed in some of its transitions, sequences, and movements."[67]

Regarding the use of written sources, we have in the OT/HB scrolls a major example of authoritative written texts in first-century Palestine that find their

134 *Chapter 4*

way into John as with the other Gospels. As Rafael Rodríguez points out, "Beyond questions pertaining to the Gospels' sources and their handling of those sources—questions that have yet to find final resolution even in the early 21st century!—there were texts that undoubtedly did factor into the development of the Jesus tradition and the textualization of our written Gospels: Hebrew biblical texts."[68] Furthermore, Craig Keener argues that the author of the Gospel of John would have drawn on both accurately transmitted oral sources and the sort of written accounts of Jesus that are attested in the Prologue to Luke's Gospel (Luke 1:1–4).[69]

Why John chose to commit a particular understanding of Jesus' ministry to writing is a contested issue in NT scholarship. One traditional explanation, recorded in the seventh- or eighth-century Latin text of the *Muratorian Canon*, is that it was at the prompting of "his fellow-disciples and bishops" and the result of revelation.[70] Regarding revelation, Keener emphasizes the author's self-understanding of being inspired by the Holy Spirit in the composition of the Gospel, proposing that, "John's voice is in some sense linked with that of the Paraclete."[71] He draws attention to the role of the Paraclete in serving "to bring to memory the sayings of Jesus (John 14:26)" and guiding in God's truth (16:13–15).[72] Furthermore, he sees the working out of this inspiration to be in "John's activity as an omniscient narrator who has special insight into the thoughts and deeds of his characters, and who frequently informs his readers by narrative asides."[73] While we are not in a position to decide whether or not the author of the Gospel was in fact inspired and guided by the Holy Spirit, we can, nevertheless, agree with Keener's conclusion that "the writer and first readers of the Fourth Gospel undoubtedly assumed its inspiration, and thus ceded the document authority because they affirmed that Jesus stood behind and spoke in the document."[74]

Keener's view of Paraclete-led inspiration need not necessarily militate against the modern consensus that the Gospel originates from a particular social group, the Johannine community, responding to a particular social situation, one of conflict and disagreement over the nature of Christ.[75] So, for example, Thatcher, writing from a social memory perspective and drawing on his understanding of the "antichrists" of the Johannine Epistles, argues:

> It appears that John wished to capitalize on the rhetorical value of writing by converting the fluid memory of Jesus to a fixed history book, a move that would at once preserve his unique vision of Jesus, freeze that vision in a perpetually nonnegotiable medium, and assert the special authority of that vision against competing claims.[76]

I do not find Thatcher's arguments altogether convincing. For example, the many variants found in the early manuscripts of the Gospel hardly imply the

The Process of Composition 135

sort of "perpetually nonnegotiable medium" that we expect in our modern era of author copyright. However, at least Thatcher is making the point that at some stage oral (and written) sources were in some way fixed. Whether this is through inspiration by the Paraclete and/or the literary creation of someone with intense theological insight and conviction responding to a particular social situation, the Gospel we now have includes the narrative comments as an essential part of its text.

I will look again later in this chapter at the relation of the narrative comments to oral stages of composition, but I want first to consider their relation to written composition in the light of my statement that there is a paucity of textual evidence to support the proposals of Bultmann, von Wahlde, and other proponents of source and redaction criticism.

## TEXTUAL EVIDENCE FOR ASIDES AS GLOSSES?

Is there any textual evidence to support the idea that at least some of the comments are additions to the text? The editors of NA28 indicate a few cases where generally accepted asides/comments are missing from certain early manuscripts:

4:9: οὐ γὰρ συγχρῶνται Ἰουδαῖοι Σαμαρίταις: missing from the first scribal hand of the fourth-century Codex Sinaiticus (ℵ*) and the fifth-century Codex Bezae (D), as well as from four fourth- to sixth-century Old Latin manuscripts.[77] BDF calls it "a spurious addition."[78]

7:50: ὁ ἐλθὼν πρὸς αὐτὸν [τὸ] πρότερον: missing from ℵ*, as well as occurring in varying word order, and with the adverb νυκτος in some manuscripts. Raymond Brown states, "An additional indication like 'previously,' 'at night,' or 'first' appears in many witnesses, but the variance suggests we are dealing with copyists' clarifications."[79]

18:5: ὁ παραδιδοὺς αὐτὸν: probably missing from the original text of P66 (Papyrus Bodmer 2) (mid-second century?).[80] It is omitted from the fourth-/fifth-century Syriac manuscript Syrus Sinaiticus (sys).

19:28: ἵνα τελειωθῇ ἡ γραφή: missing from the original text of P66. It is also omitted from some Coptic manuscripts (ly, boms).

21:4: εἰς τὸν αἰγιαλόν, οὐ μέντοι ᾔδεισαν οἱ μαθηταὶ ὅτι Ἰησοῦς ἐστιν: missing from the fourth-/fifth-century Codex Washington (W).

21:25v: This is missing from ℵ*. Brown makes the following comment:

136                           *Chapter 4*

Tischendorf thought that this verse was omitted by the original scribe of Codex Sinaiticus. However, ultra-violet examination of the codex after it was acquired by the British Museum in 1934 has clarified the situation. . . . At first the original scribe brought the Gospel to a close with vs. 24, as signified by a coronis (flourish of penmanship) and a subscription. But later the same scribe washed the vellum clean and added vs. 25, repeating the coronis and subscription in a lower position on the page. Was the omission in the first instance an act of carelessness or was the scribe copying from a ms. that did not have vs. 25 (which he subsequently got from another ms.)? Even if the latter is the case, the textual evidence for treating vs. 25 as a scribal gloss is very slim.[81]

The evidence for asides as textual additions is clearly thin and would seem to be the result of copyists' errors or corrections rather than editorial work by a later "voice."[82] However, I will consider the instances of 4:9 and 7:50 (both missing from א*) in more detail later in this chapter.


## A LATER FOOTNOTE?

I have dismissed the textual evidence of omissions in 4:9; 7:50; 18:5; 19:28; 21:4, 25 as indicating later additions. However, there is one example of an explanatory comment that was almost certainly added to the text. This is 5:4, which is found in the fifth-century Codex Alexandrinus (A) and many later Greek manuscripts (with minor variations), but omitted by all earlier manuscripts.[83] It is found in Tyndale and the KJV, but is put in a footnote in the Revised Version (1881), as it is in the RSV and NRSV. It occurs in the main text of the Jerusalem Bible (1966), with the footnote, "The best witnesses omit 'waiting for the water to move' and the whole of v.4," but is placed in a footnote in the New Jerusalem Bible (1985). It serves, along with the likely additional clause at the end of 5:3, as an explanation of why the sick man and other invalids were gathered by the pool in Jerusalem known as Bethzatha (alternatively Bethesda or Bethsaida) (5:2–3, 5) and specifically the sick man's mention of the water being "stirred up" (5:7):

> [2] Now in Jerusalem by the Sheep Gate there is a pool, called in Hebrew Bethzatha, which has five porticoes. [3] In these lay many invalids—blind, lame, and paralysed.

> *waiting for the stirring of the water;* [4] *for an angel of the Lord went down at certain seasons into the pool, and stirred up the water; whoever stepped in first after the stirring of the water was made well from whatever disease that person had.*

The Process of Composition                                    137

⁵One man was there who had been ill for thirty-eight years. ⁶When Jesus
saw him lying there and knew that he had been there a long time, he said
to him, "Do you want to be made well?" ⁷The sick man answered him,
"Sir, I have no one to put me into the pool when the water is stirred up;
and while I am making my way, someone else steps down ahead of me."
(NRSV, including footnote)

The fact that the comment in 5:4 is used by Tertullian in *De Baptismo*,
chapter 5, indicates that if it was a textual gloss, it was added at a relatively
early stage (late second to early third century). It is also cited in other early
writings, such as John Chrysostom, *Homily 36 on John* (late fourth century).
Indeed, in a recent article, Tobias Nicklas and Thomas Kraus have tried
to defend the authenticity of the comment through a text-critical survey of
its use by the Church Fathers.[84] However, their arguments are rejected by
Michael Theobald as inconclusive.[85] Indeed, the consensus view that 5:4 is
an addition to the text is summed up by Metzger in his *Textual Commentary*,
who rejects it on the basis of "its absence from the earliest and best witnesses"; "the presence of asterisks or obeli to mark the words as spurious in
more than twenty Greek witnesses"; "the presence of non-Johannine words
or expressions"; and "the rather wide diversity of variant forms in which the
verse was transmitted."[86] Metzger's argument is supported by Fee, who adds
his own theological reasons for rejecting its authenticity.[87]

Nevertheless, it is an addition and it is a comment, so it worth asking what
prompted it. J. B. Lightfoot, in his notes on the Gospel, asks, "What was the
motive of the interpolator?" and answers, "To explain vs. 7 which seemed to
need explaining and to heighten the effect."[88] He also states, "The interpolation reflects a belief that all physical changes, whether regular or irregular
were produced by angelic agency," a belief found "in Jewish writers and
again in early Apologists" and he suggests that it may have "emanated from
St John's own school in Asia Minor."[89] By contrast, Michaels argues that the
focus on the "angel of the Lord" in this addition ("based on a scribe's imagination or local legend") would be contrary to the original author's intention in
this miracle story given that "angels play only a very minor role in this Gospel."[90] So, although it provides an explanation of verse 7, it is an explanation
which could be seen as detracting from the christological focus of the Gospel
and which was, therefore, not widely accepted in the early textual traditions.
I am inclined to follow Michael's reasoning, and his argument seems relevant
to the question of whether there are conflicting voices in the text, as Flowers
and Hedrick (and von Wahlde?) have proposed. The omission of 5:4 (and the
extra clause at the end of 5:3) militates against the perception of conflicting
voices in the Gospel.

## CASE STUDY 1: 4:9: AN EXTERNAL ASIDE?

In the section on "Textual Evidence for Asides as Glosses?", I said I would consider the instances of 4:9 and 7:50 in more detail. I begin with 4:9, which I have already touched on in chapter 2 in discussing the distinction between telling and showing:

λέγει οὖν αὐτῷ ἡ γυνὴ ἡ Σαμαρῖτις· πῶς σὺ Ἰουδαῖος ὢν παρ' ἐμοῦ πεῖν αἰτεῖς γυναικὸς Σαμαρίτιδος οὔσης; οὐ γὰρ συγχρῶνται Ἰουδαῖοι Σαμαρίταις.
The Samaritan woman said to him, "How is it that you, a Jew, ask a drink of me, a woman of Samaria?" (Jews do not share things in common with Samaritans.)

I pointed out above that the phrase οὐ γὰρ συγχρῶνται Ἰουδαῖοι Σαμαρίταις is missing from the first scribal hand of Codex Sinaiticus (ℵ*) and from Codex Bezae (D), as well as various Old Latin and Coptic manuscripts. It is, however, included in the majority of early manuscripts (including P63 P66 P75 P76 ℵ¹ A B C) and is found in all NT editions prior to Tischendorf's eighth edition of 1869.[91] The marginal annotation by the first corrector of Codex Sinaiticus (ℵ¹) is shown in figure 4.1.

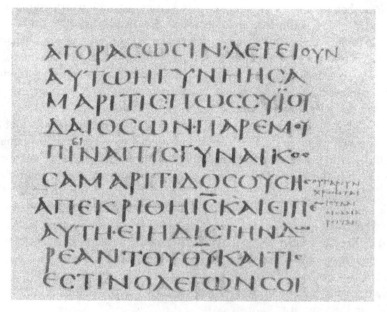

Figure 4.1. Section from one column of the Codex Sinaiticus showing an extract from John 4:8–10 with the marginal annotation ου γαρ συγχρωνται ϊουδαιοι σαμαριταις.
By permission of The British Library and Llyfrgell Genedlaethol Cymru/The National Library of Wales.

## The Process of Composition 139

Tischendorf relied heavily on the Codex Sinaiticus as the basis for his rejection of this clause. It is put in square brackets in Westcott-Hort, who provide a discussion of interpolations and the "Western tradition" (which includes the Codex Bezae) in support of their belief that it might be a later addition.[92] Westcott-Hort's use of square brackets is followed in the first 25 editions of Nestle/Nestle-Aland, but these are dropped in subsequent editions. The phrase is put in (curved) brackets in NRSV, although it was not marked in this way in the KJV and RSV.

Van Belle devotes a whole chapter to this parenthesis.[93] First, he looks at evidence for it being a later addition to the text. He considers the external evidence, including the possibilities either that it may have been intentionally omitted by scribes who did not understand the unusual verb συγχράομαι or else that it was accidentally omitted.[94] He then proceeds to examine internal stylistic evidence against its authenticity. These include the fact that συγχράομαι is a NT hapax legomenon and that the substantive adjectives Ἰουδαῖοι and Σαμαρίταις lack the article, something unique in John.[95] Van Belle rejects these arguments, noting the frequent use of other compound verbs with συν- in the Gospel and suggesting that the omission of the article with Ἰουδαῖοι and Σαμαρίταις may result from the gnomic quality of the phrase.[96] His decisive argument in favour of its authenticity as an integral part of the text is that such explanatory comments are characteristic of the author.[97] He supports this argument on the basis of the content and style of the phrase and its place in the dramatic structure of the whole pericope (4:1–42).[98]

Van Belle also points out that in early exegesis the words were generally attributed to the Samaritan woman, even though more recent scholarship almost unanimously rejects this supposition.[99] Indeed, the consensus of 20th- and early 21st-century scholarship is that it is a comment made by the narrator or the evangelist or a later redactor and that as such it is certainly a comment on the narrative and possibly an addition to the text. Bultmann categorically states, "The gloss is omitted by ℵ* D and the ancient Latin authorities; if originally it was contained in the text, then of course it comes from the Evangelist."[100]

In addition to Bultmann, there are a number of others who attribute the clause in 4:9 to the evangelist (or John). Bernard (1928) states, "The comment is not that of the Samaritan woman, but of the evangelist, and is quite in his manner."[101] Barrett (1978) says, "The sentence if genuine is in any case to be regarded as a gloss; it is not part of the woman's speech. . . . On the whole it is best to suppose that John has added to his material an editorial note applicable to his own day."[102] Carson (1991) notes, "John parenthetically . . . explains why the woman is so suspicious."[103] Wengst (2004) describes it as an explanatory comment (*Anmerkung*) by the evangelist, and Schnelle (2009) calls it an interjection (*Zwischenbemerkung*) by the evangelist.[104]

140 *Chapter 4*

Schnackenburg (1968) regards it as an explanation by the evangelist or possibly "a later interpolation."[105] Others who regard it as the work of a later redactor include Macgregor (1928): "probably added by the Redactor" (97); and R. H. Lightfoot (1956): "The last words of this verse are an editorial note and do not form part of the woman's words to the Lord."[106] Brown (1966) puts the clause in brackets, but does not comment on whether or not it is an addition, although he states that there is "respectable Western evidence" for its omission.[107] Theobald (2009) states that this comment (*Kommentarsatz*), which has in mind the reader who is unaware of the historical circumstances in Palestine, may belong to a redaction of the Gospel.[108]

Amongst those who, perhaps owing to the influence of narrative approaches to interpretation, attribute the clause in 4:9 to the narrator include Moloney (1993), Thyen (2005), Lincoln (2005), and Zumstein (2014).[109]

However, we do not need to see this comment as a narrative aside added to the text either by the original author or by a later redactor. It could equally be regarded as the words of the Samaritan woman herself. In fact, there is some willingness in recent scholarship to return the earlier view that the clause is, in fact, part of the Samaritan woman's dialogue with Jesus, and the question is raised of how to understand the significance of her response. In chapter 2, I noted that Calvin wrote in his 1553 commentary: "I think the woman spoke these words. . . . Others take them as an interpolation by the Evangelist in explanation. It is of little importance which meaning you choose, but it seems to me to fit in best that the woman is jeering at Christ like this: 'Oh! You're sure it's all right to ask me for a drink, when you think we are so irreligious?'"[110]

J. B. Lightfoot, in his notes on the Gospel (dating from the mid-19th century), is unsure how to interpret the phrase: "If this is part of the woman's own reply, it is a rude irony, perhaps it is one of the interjectional explanations of the Evangelist. But in either case, what exactly does it mean?"[111] The idea that the woman's response is a form of jeering or a "rude irony" is supported by Keener (2003), who notes, "In contrast to the common ideals of antiquity, the woman speaks boldly and forthrightly with Jesus; in view of the expectation generated by the woman-at-the-well-type scene (esp. Gen 24:18), her lack of deference would strike much of John's audience as rude."[112] Keener does, however, acknowledge that she was "possibly probing Jesus' motives" in uttering this observation.[113] Brant (2011) writes of the Samaritan woman, "Her question delivers an insult by marking the two boundaries of gender and ethnicity that Jesus has breached. Jesus is a Jew, but not a good one by the Jews' standards."[114] However, quite why the woman's words are an example of "jeering," or "rude," or an "insult" is not altogether clear to me. Surely, she could simply be expressing surprise at Jesus' request given the socio-political circumstances?

The Process of Composition 141

Uncertainty about how to take the Samaritan woman's response is reflected in other commentators. Thus, McHugh (2009) states, "The words are omitted in ℵ* D a b e j and by Tischendorf ('loyal to his codex Sinaiticus', Schnackenburg), probably because they sound odd on the lips of the Samaritan. They certainly read more like an explanatory gloss to help the reader than as an utterance of the woman of Samaria."[115] Quite why the words sound odd on the lips of the Samaritan woman, he does not explain.

A more positive appreciation of the woman's response is found in the commentary of Milligan and Moulton (1880), and I think it is worth quoting their observations in full:

It is usually assumed that the last sentence is inserted by the Evangelist in the interest of Gentile readers. It may be so, as such short parenthetical explanations are certainly to be found elsewhere in this Gospel. There seems, however, no sufficient reason for removing the clause from the woman's answer. The repetition of a well-known maxim gives a piquant emphasis to her words, bringing out with sharp distinctiveness the contrast between the principles of the countrymen of Jesus and the request which necessity had extorted. The use of the present tense ("have no dealings") adds some support to this view; and one can hardly avoid the conviction that, had John himself given such an explanation, he would so have expressed himself as to avoid all appearance of discordance with his statement in ver. 8.[116]

Maybe the reluctance of most scholars to attribute the remark to the woman, or else attribute it in a positive way, is because they do not have a high opinion of her likely intellectual (and linguistic?) capabilities. Even Michaels (2010), who does accept it as part of the woman's response to Jesus, sees it as possibly an unreliable comment from the author's perspective:

Her comment is commonly viewed as that of the Gospel writer, explaining to the reader why she said what she did. Yet the writer seems to attribute it to the woman herself . . . just as he attributed 3:16–21 to Jesus and 3:31–36 to John, and just as he will attribute to Jesus the comment that "salvation is from the Jews" (v. 22b). In this instance, however, the writer may regard the comment as unreliable, because he has already told us that the disciples are off to town precisely to deal with the Samaritans (v. 8).[117]

If we accept Michaels's view, we are dealing here not with an "unreliable narrator" but an "unreliable character" in the narrative and Jesus is challenging

142                                Chapter 4

her view that Jews and Samaritans cannot come together in true worship (4:23–24). However, whether or not we follow Michaels's interpretation, if we accept the words as an integral part of the narrative, we are less likely to regard it primarily as a comment on the author's own situation, including potential friction with the wider Jewish world caused by the acceptance of Samaritans into a Johannine community, as Raymond Brown proposed.[118]

So, does it matter whether this verse is a narrative comment or not? For, ultimately whether the author/narrator is putting the explanation into the mouth of the Samaritan woman or is directly addressing the reader at this juncture, the same information is provided. I think that it does matter in that if we accept it as part of the woman's response then we are less likely to be swayed by arguments for the omission of οὐ γὰρ συγχρῶνται Ἰουδαῖοι Σαμαρίταις (as Brown seems to have been). However, we are then faced with the interpretation of the significance of the phrase within the dialogue between Jesus and the woman. I would argue that there is no need to take the woman's words as rude or ironic, rather they have a "piquant emphasis" (Milligan and Moulton) and reflect a genuine surprise at Jesus' request of her. She may equally well have been surprised at Jesus' disciples buying food in a Samaritan city (4:8), but we are not told this. I can see no reason why it should be considered as later interpolation and I have not included it as a narrative comment in my own list.

### CASE STUDY 2: 7:50: AN INTERNAL COMMENT?

The other comment missing from the first scribal hand of the Codex Sinaiticus (א*) is from 7:50:

> λέγει Νικόδημος πρὸς αὐτούς, ὁ ἐλθὼν πρὸς αὐτὸν [τὸ] πρότερον, εἷς ὢν ἐξ αὐτῶν
> Nicodemus, who had gone to [Jesus]* before, and who was one of them, asked
>
> (* "him" in NRSV footnote)

The phrase ὁ ἐλθὼν πρὸς αὐτὸν [τὸ] πρότερον is missing from א*, as well as occurring in varying word order and with the adverb νυκτος in other manuscripts.

In the previous chapter I gave the examples of the comments ὁ ἐλθὼν πρὸς αὐτὸν [τὸ] πρότερον (in 7:50) and ὁ ἐλθὼν πρὸς αὐτὸν νυκτὸς τὸ πρῶτον (in 19:39), which both refer back to the introduction of Nicodemus in 3:1–10, as asides that are *internal* to the narrative, suggesting that they act as "stage

## The Process of Composition

asides." Zumstein refers to the phrase in 7:50 as an example of analepsis.[119] Thyen sees the phrases in both verses as deliberate reminders by the narrator of the need for the reader to call to mind the earlier scene.[120]

There are variant readings of both phrases, including a considerable number of variants of 7:50 and some of 19:39. In 7:50, το προτερον is replaced with νυκτος το πρωτον (corresponding to 19:39) in Codex Bezae (D); το προτερον is omitted and νυκτος added in a number of later codices (K N Δ Ψ);[121] and there is variation in the word order in P75, the Codex Vaticanus (B) and Codex Borgianus (T).

Commentators have made a number of suggestions regarding the omission and variants of the phrase. Bultmann proposes, "The description of Nicodemus as ὁ ἐλθὼν κτλ. which is omitted by ℵ* may have found its way in here via 19.39."[122] Brown states, "The variance suggests that we are dealing with copyists' clarifications," whereas the "parenthesis is an instance of the common Johannine practice of identifying characters already encountered."[123] Lindars goes so far as to say, "It is nothing unusual for the glossator to provide the obvious cross-reference, and so it should probably be omitted."[124]

However, I suggest that it is not sufficient to see the two comments in 7:50 and 19:39 simply as stage asides, prompts to the listeners' memories. Rather they are significant reflections on an important character in the narrative. In both cases, translators and commentators usually take the adverbs πρότερον and πρῶτον simply as indicating that Nicodemus had previously come to Jesus. Although, I note that Michaels is more nuanced in suggesting that πρότερον is used in 7:50 as it refers to just the one earlier incident (3:2), whereas τὸ πρῶτον refers to the first of the two earlier appearances (3:2 and 7:50).[125] Nevertheless, it is also possible that the author is stressing that Nicodemus is the *first* person in the Gospel who had *actively come* to speak to Jesus of his own accord rather than simply responding to Jesus' summons (as with the disciples in 1:35–51, who either respond directly to Jesus or else to those who urge them to respond). Although πρότερον is normally used in the sense of "earlier" or "previously" in the NT, it may well have the meaning "first" in 2 Corinthians 1:15 and Galatians 4:13. Commentating on the Galatians reference, Richard Longenecker states, "The adjective πρότερος in classical Greek functioned as a comparative (the 'former' of two) in distinction from πρῶτος (the 'first' of a series), but in Koine Greek πρότερος if often equivalent to πρῶτος."[126] If it is the case that 7:50 and 19:39 are using both the adverbs πρότερον and πρῶτον to emphasize that Nicodemus was the *first* person in the Gospel to actively approach Jesus, then maybe these comments serve as an indication that Nicodemus was notable by his action.

144                                   *Chapter 4*

Furthermore, as many commentators have noticed, light and dark/day and night are prominent motifs in the Gospel, and we are probably right to see the indication in 3:2 that Nicodemus first came to Jesus "by night" and the reminder of that in 19:39 (and possibly 7:50) as having a symbolic significance beyond just a desire to avoid public disclosure. Brown, regarding the mention of Nicodemus's visit "at night" in 3:2, observes, "John consistently recalls this detail . . . because of its symbolic import."[127]

I conclude that ὁ ἐλθὼν πρὸς αὐτὸν [τὸ] πρότερον in 7:50 in some sense serves as a stage aside, reintroducing Nicodemus to the reader/hearer (as 19:39 also does), but, in addition, it indicates something of Nicodemus's status in the narrative, notably that he was the first to go directly to Jesus of his own accord. I would classify it as an *internal* comment, that is integral to narrative and in no way a later addition to the text.

I have considered 4:9 and 7:50 in some detail as they are both missing from ℵ*. I also listed 21:25 as missing from ℵ*. However, as Brown noted, the textual evidence for its omission even by the original scribe is thin.

## CASE STUDY 3: 4:2: A CONTRADICTORY VOICE?

Although there is no textual evidence for this verse as missing in any manuscripts, it is nevertheless seen by many commentators as a parenthesis that is indicative of the compositional process of the Gospel. It is shown with dashes/hyphens in NA28 and NRSV:

—καίτοιγε Ἰησοῦς αὐτὸς οὐκ ἐβάπτιζεν ἀλλ᾽ οἱ μαθηταὶ αὐτοῦ—
—although it was not Jesus himself who was baptizing but his disciples—

Bultmann regards 4:1–3 (or possibly 4:1–4) as "the editor's introduction" to the account of Jesus in Samaria (4:1–42), and I noted above his uncertainty as to whether verse 2 is a correction by the Evangelist or an editorial gloss.[128] By contrast, von Wahlde confidently states, "It is long recognized that this verse is not part of the original Gospel. It is a curious comment since it stands alongside the other two statements that Jesus was in fact baptizing."[129] Indeed, 4:2 is regarded by many scholars as a flat contradiction of what is directly stated in 3:22 (ὁ Ἰησοῦς . . . ἐβάπτιζεν), what is reported by John the Baptist's disciples in 3:26 (οὗτος βαπτίζει), and what was heard by the Pharisees (as Jesus knew) in 4:1 (ἔγνω ὁ Ἰησοῦς ὅτι ἤκουσαν οἱ Φαρισαῖοι ὅτι Ἰησοῦς πλείονας μαθητὰς ποιεῖ καὶ βαπτίζει ἢ Ἰωάννης). It is, therefore, seen as a later addition to the text.

Regarding the view that 4:2 represents a contradictory voice, I noted in chapter 1 the comments of Flowers, who regarded it as "a clear case of the feeling of the Christian church obtruding itself into the Gospel tradition" and a probable instance of a scribe's marginal note being incorporated into the

The Process of Composition                          145

text.[130] Dodd, referring to the statement in 3:22 that Jesus himself was baptizing, notes, "The statement is repeated in iv. 1, but immediately corrected in iv. 2, in a parenthesis which ruins the sentence, and perhaps has a better claim to be regarded as an 'editorial note' by a 'redactor' than anything else in the gospel except the colophon, xxi. 24–5."[131] Similarly, Brown states:

> This is clearly an attempt to modify iii 22, where it is said that Jesus did baptize, and serves as almost indisputable evidence of the presence of several hands in the composition of John. Perhaps the final redactor was afraid that the sectarians of John the Baptist would use Jesus' baptizing as an argument that he was only an imitator of John the Baptist. The unusual word for "however" (*kaitoi ge*) may be another indication of a different hand.[132]

As well as the perceived contradiction with the statements in 3:22, 26 and 4:1, evidence that this is the work of a redactor is usually found in two stylistic features: the use of the NT *hapax legomenon* καίτοιγε and the rare occurrence in John of Ἰησοῦς without the article.[133] The refutation of the statement that Jesus was himself baptizing (3:22) is seen as an attempt to put the Gospel more in line with the Synoptics, which make no mention of Jesus baptizing, and to make clearer the distinction between the work of Jesus, "the one who baptizes with the Holy Spirit" (1:33), and John, who baptizes with water only (1:31).[134]

However, other commentators are less sure that this is a later redaction. Lincoln states, "It is not impossible that the clause is a narratorial gloss, which is meant also to apply retrospectively to the earlier verses and to indicate that there too mention of Jesus baptizing was actually shorthand for the disciples baptizing."[135] Certainly, 3:26 can be interpreted as a misunderstanding on the part of John's disciples, paralleling a similar misunderstanding on the part of the Pharisees (4:1), who had only "heard" that Jesus was baptizing but had not actually seen him do so. Moreover, the imperfect ἐβάπτιζεν in 3:22 may have no more than a general sense that is inclusive of the disciples, whom Jesus was spending time with (διέτριβεν). So that 4:2 is simply what Craig Blomberg describes as a "clarifying remark": "In this context, John offers a clarifying remark that Jesus did not personally baptize people; instead, his disciples acted as his agents (v. 2). This clarification scarcely deserves to be called a contradiction. Paul will insert a similar kind of caveat into his discussion in 1 Corinthians 1:14–17."[136] Likewise, Beasley-Murray states, "The tradition of Jesus baptizing need not be resisted. . . . That Jesus remitted the task of baptizing to his disciples is comprehensible. Paul did the same (1 Cor. 1:14–17)."[137]

Regarding the idea that the disciples were acting on Jesus' behalf, Keener states, "It may have been common practice that the leader of the party did

146                                   *Chapter 4*

not baptize."[138] Michaels, too, argues, "If Jesus sponsored and supervised a ministry of baptism in Judea, it is fair to say he 'was baptizing,' whether he personally anointed or dipped candidates in the waters of the region or whether his disciples did it for him."[139]

Another perspective is that of McHugh, who asserts that the suggestions that 4:2 "was inserted in order to correct 3:22 on a matter of historical fact" or that the so-called correction in 4:2 itself should be deleted, both "reflect modern preoccupations ('What really happened?'), rather than those of first-century Ephesus."[140] He believes that "the purpose of 4:2 is to ensure that 3:22 is not understood as implying that Jesus had during his earthly life admitted people to what was later called Christian baptism (7:39), for the first-century disciples knew instinctively that there was a genuine difference between baptisms before, and Christian baptism after, Jesus' death."[141] This may be true, but 4:2 does seem to suggest a concern for some historical accuracy.

Overall, I think the fact that to speak of "Jesus baptizing" may be a short-hand way of describing the actual means of baptism (that is, by his disciples) is a good reason to understand 4:2 as a clarification and not a correction of the (possible) references to Jesus baptizing in 3:22, 26 and 4:1, even though it may well also serve to highlight theological concerns, such as distinguishing Jesus' ministry from that of John the Baptist or concerning the nature of baptism itself. Therefore, it is not necessary to regard it as a later addition and a contradictory voice. We must also take into consideration the style of writing in John, the to-ing and fro-ing that I have already indicated as a feature of the internal comments (or the instances of *analepsis* and *prolepsis* to use the narratological terminology). As Michaels, points out regarding the comment, "Like certain other narrative asides in the Gospel, the disclaimer comes very belatedly, as if to say, 'Oh, I forgot to tell you this before' (compare 1:24, 28; 3:24)."[142] Although, I think that he is rather overstating the case to say that this aside is made "very belatedly." It follows on from the previous verse, and the first reference to Jesus baptizing (3:22) is only 15 verses before.

In none of these three case studies (4:9; 7:50; 4:2) do I see any compelling evidence for later redaction and for understanding these comments as *insertions, glosses*, or *additions* to an existing written text. I think it is important, therefore, to give consideration both to the oral transmission of the narrative and also to comments as a written stylistic feature of the Gospel. I begin with the issue of oral transmission.

## ORAL TRANSMISSION AND COMMENTS

We do not possess enough evidence to determine accurately the levels of literacy in first-century Palestine. Although Kim Haines-Eitzen states, "That

The Process of Composition 147

literacy remained restricted to a very small elite throughout the ancient and late antique world seems now a given" and Joanna Dewey believes that "perhaps 95 percent" of the first-century world were not literate at all, there is also evidence that literacy rates may have been higher amongst Jewish people given the influence of the written scriptures in education and daily life.[143] So, for example, Meir Bar-Ilan, in his contribution to a survey of Jewish literacy in Ancient Israel and Early Judaism, states, "In the Hellenistic and Roman periods the book and the written letter reached all Jewish classes. Beyond the precinct of the Temple and the administrative courts the book, the stylus and the ink became commonplace means of communication."[144]

Whatever the extent of literacy in first-century Palestine, it seems most likely that there was a continuing interaction between oral and written traditions. I noted earlier in this chapter Bultmann's remark on the relationship of comments to the reading of the text: "One has to suppose that in oral recitation the 'comments' would be distinguishable by the tone of the speaker."[145] This seems to me a significant observation in the light of Burton-Roberts's remark that all *parentheticals* "are marked off from their hosts" by punctuation in writing or "special intonation contour in speech."[146] It raises the question of whether this "intonation contour" would have been operative not only at readings of the finished Gospel of John, but also at its original dictation, if we assume that the author did not do the actual writing. Even if we cannot know the precise physical process of its original composition, we nevertheless need to take some account of what Paul Achtemeier has described as the "oral environment" in which the NT documents were composed. Achtemeier makes a distinction between "print" and "oral environments" in relation to the NT writings' use of sources:

> One implication of this orality of the NT documents concerns the problem of the identification of sources. One wonders if it can so quickly be assumed that where there are discrepancies or inconsistencies in a Gospel or a letter, it is the result of the combination of divergent written sources. It may well be the case that such inconsistencies are the result of the need to provide oral/aural clues to the one who listens to the document. Of course the NT documents were written down, but they were written, and would be read, as we have seen, in a way far different from that to which we are accustomed, and much closer to an oral than to a print environment.[147]

One possible implication of this for the Gospel of John is the connection between the "voice" of characters within the narrative, including the words of Jesus, and the comments of the author/narrator. These may have been distinguished far more easily in spoken discourse than in the written text. We see

148 *Chapter 4*

this, for example, in our uncertainty as to where to set the quotation marks in 3:13–21 (are they the words of Jesus or the narrator?) and 3:31–36 (are they the words of John the Baptist or the narrator?), which I looked at in chapter 2. Regarding the ambiguities in these passages, Thatcher writes:

> The blending of voices in John 3 is the natural result of a composi-tional technique based on what might be called "dual vocalization" or, more specifically here, "dual visualization." When presenting Jesus's speeches in live performance (or when writing a book by dictation), the oral composer always speaks in two voices to two audiences at once: as Jesus to other characters in the story, and as himself to his own audience/reader.[148]

So, we can assume that 3:13–21 and 3:31–36 would have been marked with a "special intonation contour" (Burton-Roberts) if they were the remarks of the speaker/narrator.

Tenney makes a similar point to Thatcher, alongside his suggestion that John's parenthetical style indicates the oral teaching of an old man: "The random nature of these comments and the diversity of their nature convey the impression that they may have been oral parentheses in material that was either repeated frequently in public teaching or that was dictated to an amanu-ensis for writing, or both."[149]

Certainly, asides/parentheses/comments are a notable feature of spoken discourse, often involving syntactical anomalies. They are a natural part of the way we speak. As Robert Fowler, writing about the occurrences of anaco-luthon in the Gospel of Mark and their relation to oral transmission, observes, "Even hopelessly literate people, who regard a breakdown in syntax in for-mal, written communication as an inexcusable fault, punctuate their own informal, oral utterances with numerous ruptures in syntax."[150] Moreover, as Boomershine, also writing about the Gospel of Mark, points out:

> In a performance of a story, audience asides are one of the most impor-tant storytelling techniques, since they allow the storyteller to pause the account of what is happening, to lean in and speak directly to the audience. This may be a step to the audience, a hand to the side of the mouth, a wink and a smile, or a change of tone. Whatever the particular move, the storyteller gives some sign that indicates the statement to follow is inside information that will help the members of the audience understand what is going on in the story.[151]

These observations lead me to ask at what stage in the transmission of oral discourse to written text were the comments most likely to have been added?

*The Process of Composition*  149

Before writing down was considered? At the actual the moment of transcription? Or in a complex interaction between writing, performance, and rewriting?

Barnabas Lindars, in his 1972 commentary, presents a scenario in which the asides/comments are the result of adapting spoken material to a written text. He states that the author of the Gospel made use of "large self-contained pieces as the basis of his work" and that it "is very likely that most of these underlying pieces were homilies which he gave to the Christian assembly, possibly at the eucharist."[152] He mentions Barrett, Braun, Brown, Schnackenburg, and Sanders in support of this homily idea.[153] This oral material (unless, of course, John was preaching from written notes!) was then linked together to form the Gospel narrative. So, for example, in the account of Jesus' discourse with the Samaritan woman (4:1–26), the sentence "His disciples had gone into the town to buy food" (4:8) is an "interpolation" added "in the process of dovetailing the homily into the book."[154]

Another way of thinking about the possible spoken origins of narrative comments is elegantly expressed by R. T. France concerning the "aside" in Mark 5:8, "For he had said to him, 'Come out of the man, you unclean spirit!'" and its relation to the pericope of Mark 5:1–20, Jesus' healing of the demon-possessed Gerasene man:

> Commentators seem to have an irresistible tendency to take any such "aside" as an indication of an originally composite story, inelegantly stitched together. . . . But it is not at all out of character for a storyteller to insert a piece of useful information to provide essential (or interesting) background, or to enable the hearer more easily to follow the development of the story, and repetition is a regular stock-in-trade of effective storytelling. The whole pericope reads well as a unity, provided that it is understood as a well-told story rather than the meticulous product of a scholar's desk.[155]

All this suggests to me that we need to be careful when we speak of *interpolations, glosses,* and *additions* to the text and that when we engage in questions of the text's integrity and unity, we must take into account the process of oral transmission. Who precisely is doing the "adding" and when?

## COMMENTS: WRITTEN STYLISTIC FEATURES?

However, in addition to an awareness of the "oral environment" (Achtemeier) in which the NT documents were composed, we must also take into account the Gospel's emphasis both on the process of writing and on the final form

150                                   *Chapter 4*

of the document, which are expressed in 20:31 and 21:24–25, alongside the references to existing written scriptures in 1:45; 2:17; 5:46; 6:31, 45; 8:17; 10:34; 12:14, 16; and 15:25. The force of "what is written" is also conveyed in the description of Pilate's sign on the cross: "What I have written, I have written" (19:22). The implication is that written words cannot be changed and this would give some support to Thatcher's idea of the rhetorical value of the written word as "fixed history."[156]

I suggested earlier in this chapter that Dewey and others who have high-lighted the oral aspect of the Gospel's composition have not given sufficient weight to the use of written sources and to the complex literary structure of the Gospel, which suggests careful composition rather than simply "the additive and aggregative nature of oral narrative."[157] Moreover, as Rodríguez points out, "written language can be just as additive, aggregative, and tradi-tionalist as oral language."[158]

Certainly, the internal comments, those instances of analepsis and pro-lepsis, can be understood as characteristic of the Gospel's particular *style*, notably its use of repetition. Writing of this style, Margaret Davies concludes, "The leisurely and repetitive manner serves a didactic purpose and creates a respectful dignity and deliberate solemnity."[159] Similarly, Schnackenburg states, "The solemn and monotonous diction is rather due to the meditative and long-pondered theology of John, which gave rise to stereotyped expres-sions which may be abstract and colourless, but remain impressive and memorable."[160]

In a collection of essays based on a 2006 colloquium at the University of Leuven on "Repetitions and Variations in the Fourth Gospel: Style, Text, Interpretation," Van Belle argues that the use of *repetition*, alongside *varia-tion* and *amplification*, are central features of the Evangelist's style, which serve his overall purpose of engaging with and guiding the reader:

> The secret of the Fourth Evangelist is to be found precisely in his use of various forms of repetition (variation and amplification), whereby he endeavours to keep the attention of his reader time and again. . . . By recapitulating, varying and expanding upon ideas, the Evangelist reveals his capacity to draw his readers into the mystery of the Word of God made flesh. . . . The literary art of repetition, variation and amplifica-tion fits hand in glove with Johannine theology and the latter's goal of strengthening the faith of the reader (20, 30–31).[161]

Van Belle describes the rhetorical function of repetitions in John, stressing that the author does not simply repeat the same words and phrases, but rather provides a measure of "conceptual development and expansion" in the repeti-tion, hence Van Belle's use of the terms *variation* and *amplification*.[162]

The Process of Composition 151

We can see this *variation* and *amplification* at work in some of the internal comments, such as the references to Nicodemus in 7:50 and 19:39, which I have suggested are indicative of a development of ideas and a deepening of the reader's understanding. The fact that some of the many variant readings of 7:50 add νυκτός (by night), which is used in the account of Nicodemus's initial visit to Jesus (3:2) and in the comment in 19:39, suggests that conformity, rather than variation, is a feature of this later editorial work. As Brown remarks about 7:50, "The variance suggests we are dealing with copyists' clarifications."[163]

Other comments can be seen as integral to the structure of the text. The commentary in 1:1–5, 7–14, 16–18 serves as an introduction to the Gospel, and 20:30–31 and 21:23–25 provide summarizing conclusions (alongside considerable debate amongst scholars as to whether or not 20:30–31 is the "original" ending). The comments in 2:11 and 4:54, which include a numbering of the "signs," also provide a structural element. Why the numbering was not continued with other miracles/signs in the narrative (5:2–9; 6:1–14; 9:1–7; 11:1–44) is uncertain. Maybe it was enough for the narrator/author to establish a sequence in the mind of the listener/reader, while aware that, in fact, there were many other miraculous signs which Jesus did (20:30), so enumeration has a limited value.

Those comments which concern the fulfilment of scripture in the ministry of Jesus (2:17; 12:14b–15, 38–41; 19:24, 28, 36–37; 20:9) also suggest the importance of written text. They could be comments added at an oral stage of composition, which depended on the author's memory of the scriptures, but seem to me to belong more naturally to a written stage. In this respect, it is worth noting that, with the exception of 2:17, these comments are found in two main clusters, associated with the account of Jesus' entry into Jerusalem in chapter 12 and the crucifixion narrative in chapter 19. Did the author have particular access to the relevant scriptures at the time these accounts were written?

Overall, I suggest that we need to take into account both the oral transmission of the narrative and the function of comments within that narrative and also the role of comments as a written stylistic feature of the Gospel. On balance, I would give more weight to their function as part of the written text, while conceding that at least some may have been introduced at an oral stage of composition. While John relies on oral traditions about Jesus—some shared with the Synoptics, others seemingly independent—one aspect of its literary character is its distance from those traditions and a greater reliance on the creative thinking of the author. I am not making this a question of the historicity of the Gospel, but I do think that it implies a written rather than oral work.

152                                   *Chapter 4*

## CONCLUSIONS

It seems to me that in the light of what I have covered in this chapter there are
three main possibilities regarding the relation of comments to the composition of the Gospel.

1.  The comments are part of the storytelling process, a natural concomi-
    tant of how narrators tell stories with the use of explanation, repetition,
    prolepsis, and analepsis.[164] They form an integral part of the Gospel's
    composition at an oral stage, prior to the transcription of the text.

2.  The comments were added to an existing narrative at the time the text
    was written down—that is, they are part of its actual composition.
    They provide the author's particular understanding, which would be
    perceived to be guided by the Holy Spirit/Paraclete. The scribe included
    these comments at the time of writing.

3.  The comments were added after an initial copy of the text was written and
    form part of a later edition/s of the text. In this case, they may be considered
    as *glosses* or *interpolations*. They may reflect the viewpoint of the original
    author and/or of the author's school/community. Or they may, in places,
    reflect the different or even contrary perspective of a later editor.

Regarding the third option, I have argued that, with the exception of 5:4,
none of the asides/comments are the work of a later redactor and therefore
a reflection of a viewpoint distinct from the main author of the work. I used
my case studies, a more detailed examination of the comments in 4:9; 7:50;
4:2 to support this argument. I also referred to Luke Timothy Johnson's
rejection of a general process of redaction linked to the activities of a proposed Johannine community and to Bauckham's rejection of redaction in
respect of the "explanatory parentheses." I would add to these the thorough
examination made by Van Belle, who insists that the asides are an integral
part of the text:

> Il est difficile, semble-t-il, d'attribuer les parenthèses à une autre main
> qu'à celle d'évangéliste. Qui veut les attribuer à un éditeur éventuel, devra
> concéder que celui-ci aurait joué un rôle important dans la composition
> de tout l'évangile et que son propre point de vue aurait été le même que
> celui de l'évangéliste. Mais l'homogénéité du style et du contenu des
> parenthèses ainsi que la consistance de celles-ci avec le reste de l'évangile
> nous dissuadent d'accepter une telle méthode de travail. (It would seem
> difficult to attribute the parentheses to another hand than that of the

## The Process of Composition

153

evangelist. Whoever wants to attribute them to a possible editor will have to admit that he would have played an important role in the composition of the whole gospel and that his own point of view would be the same as that of the evangelist. But the homogeneity of the style and the contents of the parentheses as well as their consistency with the rest of the gospel dissuade us from accepting such a method of working.)[165]

Similarly, Culpepper observes:

The narrator's intrusive and interpretive comments cannot easily be attributed to an editor unless the editor is given a significant formative role in the gospel's composition or is virtually indistinguishable from the evangelist in his perspective. There is no evidence that they are later (or scribal) glosses, for they express a consistent point of view.[166]

Moreover, given the effort and expense of the writing of manuscripts, I think we should be wary of envisaging multiple early editions of the Gospel with additions by different hands. Admittedly, we do not have the dire warnings against amending the text that are found at the end of Revelation (22:18–19), but the Gospel of John takes its written form seriously. As Thatcher suggests, "As a Jewish person immersed in an oral media culture, John may have felt that a written version of his gospel message would carry more weight in debates over the correct understanding of Jesus. The Fourth Gospel would thus both preserve John's memory of Jesus and, more important, add authority to that memory."[167] In this context it is worth noting the symbolic power of written texts in predominantly illiterate societies that is stressed in the Canadian historian Brian Stock's influential concept of "textual communities."[168]

We may not be able to reconstruct a definitive "final form" of the Gospel, but, on balance, I believe that it is best to try and identify the function of its narrative comments on the basis that they are integral to the text and not later (and, at times, contradictory) additions. Such additions are not supported by the textual evidence that we have, nor do the comments indicate the sort of theological diversity proposed by Hedrick and others. Some of them may have been added at an oral level of composition/transmission, but I have suggested that the repetitive style and complex structure of the narrative imply instead that the comments are primarily part of the literary process. Indeed, we may have to accept that it is not completely possible to differentiate between options one and two: the text of the Gospel we possess is a complex interaction between the memories of witnesses, oral traditions, and actual writing. However, I would stress that the author has a deep personal commitment to this text as a *written* text, believing that its composition was inspired by the Holy Spirit. Moreover, the comments are integral to the text: as

154                                        *Chapter 4*

Tenney writes, "They are not interpolations . . . and are an essential part of the inspired text of the Gospel."[169] So, I would argue that the so-called "asides" in the Gospel of John cannot be considered peripheral or evidence of later editorial work on an otherwise smooth text. Rather they are an essential part of the text, even if we are not always able to determine their exact purpose.

It is my intention, in the next chapter, to consider further the purpose of the narrative comments from both literary and linguistic perspectives, dealing with the role of the *narrator* and the *author*.

## NOTES

1. Brown, *Gospel*, 1:cxxxvi; Brown, *Introduction*, 290.

2. See, for example, Thomas Brodie, "Three Revolutions, A Funeral, and Glimmers of a Challenging New Dawn," in *What We Have Heard from the Beginning: The Past, Present, and Future of Johannine Studies*, ed. Tom Thatcher (Waco: Baylor University Press, 2007), 78–79.

3. Macgregor, Gospel, xliv.

4. Macgregor, *Gospel*, xliv. See J. Wellhausen, *Das Evangelium Johannis* (Berlin: Georg Rimmer, 1908), 4: "Ein Schriftsteller mag sorglos und ungeschickt, auch wohl einmal ein bißchen vergeßlich sein, er muß sich aber selber verstehen und kann nicht alsbald von dem Inhalt seiner eigenen Aussagen keine Vorstellung mehr haben."

5. Moody Smith provides a helpful summary of Bultmann's analysis and critical reaction to it, including the work of scholars such as Noack and Dodd, who defend the significance of oral traditions behind the Gospel. D. Moody Smith, "The Sources of the Gospel of John: An Assessment of the Present State of the Problem," *NTS* 10, no. 3 (2009): 336–51.

6. Bultmann, *Gospel*, 15.

7. Bultmann, *Gospel*, 16.

8. Bultmann, *Gospel*, 16–17.

9. Bultmann, *Gospel*, 17.

10. Bultmann, *Gospel*, 17–18.

11. Bultmann, *Gospel*, 17, 59–60.

12. Bultmann, *Gospel*, 17.

13. Bultmann, *Gospel*, 16n3.

14. Bultmann, *Gospel*, 121, 118n5.

15. Bultmann, *Gospel*, 178.

16. Bultmann, *Gospel*, 178n6.

17. Bultmann, *Gospel*, 204.

18. Bultmann, *Gospel*, 204n3. He cites *P. Oxyrhynchus* 1.5, but it is logion 1.6 (= *Gospel of Thomas* 31) in Grenfell and Hunt. See Bernard P. Grenfell and Arthur S. Hunt, *ΛΟΓΙΑ ΙΗϹΟΥ: Sayings of Our Lord from an Early Greek Papyrus* (London: Egypt Exploration Fund/Henry Frowde, 1897), 14.

The Process of Composition

155

19. Bultmann, *Gospel*, 290n6

20. Bultmann, *Gospel*, 415n7.

21. Bultmann, *Gospel*, 415.

22. Bultmann, *Gospel*, 303n5.

23. Bultmann, *Gospel*, 171n2. Later on, Bultmann appears less certain about attributing 7:39b to the ecclesiastical redactor (see 303n5).

24. Bultmann, *Gospel*, 303n5.

25. Bultmann, *Gospel*, 303n5. As Andrew Lincoln observes re vv. 37–38: "Precisely what Jesus is presented as saying about the water symbolism is one of the most disputed syntactical and exegetical issues in the whole Gospel" (*Gospel*, 254).

26. Bultmann, *Gospel*, 653.

27. Bultmann, *Gospel*, 678.

28. Bultmann, *Gospel*, 714n1, 706.

29. Bultmann, *Gospel*, 192n2; cf. 333.

30. Bultmann, *Gospel*, 176n2; cf. 168n1. Bultmann states that the use of καίτοιγε (unique in the NT) in 4:2 may suggest that the verse is "an editorial gloss" (176n2).

31. Bultmann, *Gospel*, 674.

32. Bultmann, *Gospel*, 671.

33. Urban C. von Wahlde, *The Gospel and Letters of John*, 3 vols., ECC (Grand Rapids: Eerdmans, 2010), 1:23.

34. Von Wahlde, *Gospel and Letters*, 1:50–54.

35. Where I have quoted the Gospel in this section, I have employed von Wahlde's own translation.

36. Von Wahlde, *Gospel and Letters*, 2:24.

37. Von Wahlde, *Gospel and Letters*, 2:23.

38. Von Wahlde, *Gospel and Letters*, 2:23.

39. Von Wahlde, *Gospel and Letters*, 2:157.

40. Von Wahlde, *Gospel and Letters*, 2:534.

41. Von Wahlde, *Gospel and Letters*, 2:536.

42. Von Wahlde, *Gospel and Letters*, 2:208–9.

43. Von Wahlde, *Gospel and Letters*, 2:84.

44. Von Wahlde, *Gospel and Letters*, 2:177.

45. Von Wahlde, *Gospel and Letters*, 2:178.

46. Von Wahlde, *Gospel and Letters*, 2:178.

47. Von Wahlde, *Gospel and Letters*, 2:341.

48. Von Wahlde, *Gospel and Letters*, 2:353–54.

49. Von Wahlde, *Gospel and Letters*, 2:528.

50. Von Wahlde, *Gospel and Letters*, 2:607.

51. Von Wahlde, *Gospel and Letters*, 2:775.

52. Von Wahlde, *Gospel and Letters*, 2:884n1.

53. Von Wahlde, *Gospel and Letters*, 2:178.

54. Von Wahlde, *Gospel and Letters*, 2:814.

55. Von Wahlde, *Gospel and Letters*, 2:820.

56. Von Wahlde, *Gospel and Letters*, 3:316–18.

57. Von Wahlde, *Gospel and Letters*, 2:875.

156 *Chapter 4*

58. Von Wahlde, *Gospel and Letters*, 1:357.

59. Luke Timothy Johnson, *The Writings of the New Testament: An Interpretation*, rev. ed. (London: SCM, 1999), 526. Johnson has particularly in mind here both Bultmann's ecclesiastical redactor and Raymond Brown's five-stage reconstruction.

60. Bauckham, "John for Readers of Mark," 151.

61. Bauckham, "John for Readers of Mark," 151–52. He proceeds to defend the literary integrity of 3:24 and 11:2, commonly regarded as glosses.

62. Von Wahlde, *Gospel and Letters*, 1:23.

63. Craig R. Koester, *Symbolism in the Fourth Gospel* (Minneapolis: Fortress Press, 1995), 231.

64. Joanna Dewey, "The Gospel of John in Its Oral-Written Media World," in *Jesus in Johannine Tradition*, ed. Robert T. Fortna and Tom Thatcher (Louisville: Westminster John Knox, 2001), 249. The terms "additive" and "aggregative" come from Walter Ong's much-used list of characteristics of oral thought and expression. Walter Ong, *Orality and Literacy: The Technologizing of the Word*, 30th anniversary ed. (New York: Routledge, 2012), 37–39.

65. Dewey, "Gospel of John," 251.

66. Somewhat as an aside: I find it hard to comprehend Dewey's statements that Jesus "as a village artisan . . . would not have been literate," given that Luke records Jesus reading from the scroll of Isaiah (Lk. 4:16–20), and that, "as a nonliterate oral teacher Jesus himself probably had no concept of verbatim repetition or 'memorization'" ("Gospel of John," 240, 246). So, presumably Jesus was neither reading from Isaiah nor repeating it from memory.

67. Culpepper, *Anatomy*, 231.

68. Rafael Rodríguez, "Reading and Hearing in Ancient Contexts," *JSNT* 32, no. 2 (2009): 174.

69. Keener, Gospel, 1:60.

70. See James Stevenson, *A New Eusebius: Documents Illustrating the History of the Church to AD 337*, rev. William Hugh Clifford Frend (London: SPCK, 1987), 123.

71. Keener, *Gospel*, 1:117.

72. Keener, *Gospel*, 1:120.

73. Keener, *Gospel*, 1:121.

74. Keener, *Gospel*, 1:122.

75. Although this is still the consensus in recent Johannine scholarship, it has been questioned. See Lamb, *Text, Context*, 15–27.

76. Tom Thatcher, *Why John Wrote a Gospel: Jesus-Memory-History* (Louisville: Westminster John Knox, 2006), 145. Against those who would detect different "voices" in our texts of the Gospel, Thatcher rejects the idea of there being multiple editions (159–64).

77. Both Metzger and Comfort state that it is also omitted from copfay, which is a Coptic manuscript of the Fayyumic dialect, but the precise manuscript is not cited. See Bruce M. Metzger, *A Textual Commentary on the Greek New Testament*, 2nd ed. (London: United Bible Societies, 1994), 177; Philip Wesley Comfort, *A Commentary*

The Process of Composition 157

*on the Manuscripts and Text of the New Testament* (Grand Rapids: Kregel Academic, 2015), 253.

78. Blass, Debrunner, and Funk, *Greek Grammar,* 104.

79. Brown, *Gospel,* 1:325.

80. For the dating of P66, see Comfort, *Commentary,* 69–70.

81. Brown, *Gospel,* 2:1125. Michaels suggests that is may have been added by the compiler of "the fourfold Gospel" (*Gospel,* 1058).

82. Van Belle notes that certain witnesses also omit phrases from 4:23; 5:25; 9:18; 13:10, 11; and 19:20, as well as the whole verses 6:4 and 19:35 (*Les Parenthèses,* 211). However, apart from 6:4 and 19:35, these are somewhat tenuous examples of asides, and the textual evidence is again slight. In the case of 6:4, the possible omission depends on patristic evidence and 19:35 is missing only in the Old Latin manuscript e (fifth century) and the Codex Fuldensis of the Vulgate (sixth century). See Barrett, *Gospel,* 273, 558.

83. Brown, *Gospel,* 1:207. It is omitted even by those early manuscripts such as Codex Bezae (fifth century) that include the extra clause ἐκδεχομένων τὴν τοῦ ὕδατος κίνησιν (waiting for the stirring of the water) at the end of v.3.

84. Tobias Nicklas and Thomas J. Kraus, "Joh 5,3b–4. Ein längst erledigtes textkritisches Problem?" *Annali di Storia dell'Esegesi* 17, no. 2 (2000): 537–56.

85. Theobald, *Das Evangelium,* 376.

86. Metzger, *Textual Commentary,* 179.

87. Gordon D. Fee, "On the Inauthenticity of John 5:3b–4," *EvQ* 54, no. 4 (1982): 207–18; cf. Barrett, *Gospel,* 253; Brown, *Gospel,* 1:207. Zumstein agrees, although he notes some commentators who have defended the verse's authenticity, such as Boismard, Léon-Dufour, and Mollat (*L'Évangile,* 176n11). See Nicklas and Kraus, "Joh 5,3b–4," 537–38n3, for other supporters of its originality.

88. J. B. Lightfoot, *The Gospel of St. John: A Newly Discovered Commentary,* ed. Ben Witherington III and Todd D. Still, assisted by Jeanette M. Hagen (Downers Grove, IL: IVP Academic, 2015), 145. Lightfoot's notes for his commentary on John were incomplete at the time of his death in 1889.

89. Lightfoot, *Gospel,* 145.

90. Michaels, *Gospel,* 291n20.

91. Other editors had, however, noticed its omission in some of the manuscripts they listed. See Van Belle, *Les Parenthèses,* 211–13.

92. Brooke Foss Westcott and Fenton John Anthony Hort, *The New Testament in Original Greek: II Introduction and Appendix* (New York: Harper and Brothers, 1882), 175–77, 294–95. They conclude, "We find ourselves wholly unable to believe some of the clauses and sentences omitted by Western documents to be genuine" (176).

93. Van Belle, *Les Parenthèses,* 211–35.

94. Van Belle, *Les Parenthèses,* 211–19. Van Belle cites Metzger's comment: "The omission, if not accidental, may reflect scribal opinion that the statement is not literally exact and therefore should be deleted" (*Les Parenthèses,* 218–19). See Metzger, *Textual Commentary,* 177. It can be seen as contradicting the mention in

158                                    *Chapter 4*

4:8 of the disciples going into the Samaritan city of Sychar to buy food and thereby associating with Samaritans.

95. Van Belle, *Les Parenthèses*, 219–20. McHugh states, "The absence of the article before both Ἰουδαῖοι and Σαμαρίταις, even when both are definite, is unique in John and points with fair certainty to an editorial insertion." John F. McHugh, *A Critical and Exegetical Commentary on John 1–4*, ed. Graham N. Stanton, ICC (London: T & T Clark, 2009), 268.

96. Van Belle, *Les Parenthèses*, 220–22.

97. Van Belle, *Les Parenthèses*, 222–24.

98. Van Belle, *Les Parenthèses*, 224–34.

99. Van Belle, *Les Parenthèses*, 225.

100. Bultmann, 178n6.

101. Bernard, *Gospel*, 1:138.

102. Barrett, *Gospel*, 232.

103. Carson, *Gospel*, 218.

104. Wengst, *Das Johannesevangelium*, 1:167; Udo Schnelle, *Das Evangelium nach Johannes*, 4th ed., THKNT 4 (Leipzig: Evangelische Verlagsanstalt, 2009), 99.

105. Schnackenburg, *Gospel*, 1:425.

106. R. H. Lightfoot, *St John's Gospel: A Commentary*, ed. C. F. Evans (Oxford: Clarendon, 1956), 134.

107. Brown, *Gospel*, 1:166, 170.

108. Theobald, *Das Evangelium*, 311.

109. Francis J. Moloney, *Belief in the Word: Reading the Fourth Gospel: John 1–4* (Minneapolis: Fortress Press, 1993), 139; Thyen, *Das Johannesevangelium*, 247; Lincoln, *Gospel*, 172; Zumstein, *L'Évangile*, 1:147.

110. Calvin, *Gospel according to St John 1–10*, 90.

111. J. B. Lightfoot, *Gospel*, 136.

112. Keener, *Gospel*, 1:598–99.

113. Keener, *Gospel*, 1:599.

114. Brant, *John*, 84.

115. McHugh, *John 1–4*, 268. He also makes the point that "modern editions can signify the ending of direct speech by quotation marks or (as here in UBS) by the insertion of brackets; ancient scholars not blest with such conventions would sometimes be perplexed about the point at which direct speech ended" (268n15).

116. William Milligan and William F. Moulton, *Commentary on the Gospel of St. John* (Edinburgh: T & T Clark, 1898), 46. (This is a reprint of the work first published in 1880 in the *Popular Commentary* series. The text here is accompanied by a fine engraving of the "Woman at a Well.")

117. Michaels, *Gospel*, 239n34. He cites Hoskyns and Lindars in support of the view that the writer attributes the remark to the woman herself. However, both Hoskyns and Lindars are equivocal in their judgements. Hoskyns writes, "The words *For Jews have no dealings with Samaritans* belong most naturally to the speech of the woman; they may, however, be taken as an explanatory comment of the Evangelist; or, since they are absent from Codex Bezae, Codex Sinaiticus, and from four

The Process of Composition    159

manuscripts of the Old Latin Version, they may perhaps be a gloss added by a later hand." Edwyn Clement Hoskyns, *The Fourth Gospel*, ed. Francis Noel Davey, 2nd ed. (London: Faber & Faber, 1947), 242. In his own translation, he puts the phrase in brackets. Lindars states, "It accords with John's habit of elucidating points unfamiliar to Gentile readers. It could, in fact, be taken as part of the woman's speech." Barnabas Lindars, *The Gospel of John*, NCB (London: Marshall, Morgan & Scott, 1972), 181.

118. Raymond E. Brown, *The Community of the Beloved Disciple* (New York: Paulist Press, 1979), 36–40.

119. Zumstein, *L'Évangile*, 1:274.

120. Thyen, *Das Johannesevangelium*, 412.

121. The KJV translates the phrase as "he that came to Jesus by night" (which it puts in brackets along with "being one of them"), indicating its reliance on a Greek edition which used manuscripts with the alternative reading.

122. Bultmann, *Gospel*, 311n1.

123. Brown, *Gospel* 1:325; cf. 2:940.

124. Lindars, *Gospel*, 304.

125. Michaels, *Gospel*, 981n148. Maybe. Bultmann sees no difference in the two adverbs (*Gospel*, 680n1).

126. Richard Longenecker, *Galatians*, WBC 41 (Dallas: Word, 1990), 190.

127. Brown, *Gospel*, 1:130. However, Schnackenburg states, "It is not an unmistakably symbolic allusion" (*Gospel*, 1:366).

128. Bultmann, *Gospel*, 176n2, 168n1. He believes that the evangelist's references to Jesus' baptizing in 3:22, 26 "may be his own invention" (168).

129. Von Wahlde, *Gospel and Letters*, 2:169.

130. Flowers, "Interpolations," 153–54.

131. C. H. Dodd, *The Interpretation of the Fourth Gospel* (Cambridge: Cambridge University Press, 1953), 311n3.

132. Brown, *Gospel*, 1:164. It should be observed that καίτοιγε is printed as one word in modern Greek editions. As such, it is a *hapax legomenon* in the NT. The particle καίτοι is found in Acts 14:17 (majority of texts) and Heb. 4:3.

133. However, as Schnackenburg notes, these features are not decisive, although he accepts it as a probable redaction on other grounds: "Signs of redactional composition in v. 2 are: καίτοι γε is singular, Ἰησοῦς without the article is at least remarkable, if not a criterion of the style of the redaction (cf. also 4:44; 12:16), as Jeremias, 'Johanneische Literarkritik," pp. 44f., tries to prove. The intrinsic reasons for a subsequent emendation by the 'redaction' are readily understood" (*Gospel*, 1:422n6). See Joachim Jeremias, "Johanneische Literarkritik," *TBl* 20 (1941): 33–46.

134. See Barrett, *Gospel*, 230; Brown, *Gospel*, 1:164; Lincoln, *Gospel*, 171; Schnelle, *Das Evangelium*, 97; Theobald, *Das Evangelium*, 297; Thyen, *Das Johannesevangelium*, 239–40; Zumstein, *L'Évangile*, 1:138.

135. Lincoln, *Gospel*, 171.

136. Craig L. Blomberg, *The Historical Reliability of John's Gospel* (Leicester: Inter-Varsity Press, 2001), 98. Blomberg does concede that "John 4:2 may suggest that John is editing a source here and does not feel free to omit altogether reference to Jesus' baptismal ministry. And in keeping with his concern to avoid an overly

160 *Chapter 4*

sacramental theology . . ., he qualifies his source's remarks." He contrasts the work of the author with that of a proposed redactor, suggesting that a "redactor not constrained by traditional data could surely have written more smoothly" (98).

137. George R. Beasley–Murray, *John*, WBC 36 (Waco: Word, 1987), 58.

138. Keener, *Gospel*, 1:587–88.

139. Michaels, *Gospel*, 234.

140. McHugh, *John 1–4*, 262.

141. McHugh, *John 1–4*, 262–63.

142. Michaels, *Gospel*, 233.

143. Kim Haines-Eitzen, "Textual Communities in Late Antique Christianity," in *A Companion to Late Antiquity*, ed. Philip Rousseau with the assistance of Jutta Raithal (Malden: Wiley-Blackwell, 2009), 256; Dewey, "Gospel of John," 239. Haines-Eitzen cites the influential studies of William Harris, *Ancient Literacy* (1989) and Harry Y. Gamble, *Books and Readers in the Early Church* (1995).

144. Aaron Demsky and Meir Bar-Ilan, "Writing in Ancient Israel and Early Judaism," in *Mikra: Text, Translation, Reading, and Interpretation of the Hebrew Bible in Ancient Judaism and Early Christianity*, ed. Martin Jan Mulder and Harry Sysling (Philadelphia: Fortress Press, 1988), 37.

145. Bultmann, *Gospel*, 16n3.

146. Burton-Roberts, "Parentheticals," 180.

147. Paul J. Achtemeier, "Omne verbum sonat: The New Testament and the Oral Environment of Late Western Antiquity," *JBL* 109, no. 1 (1990): 26. Rodríguez believes that Achtemeier overstates his case regarding a cultural bias in favour of the oral over written communication in late Western antiquity. See Rafael Rodríguez, *Oral Tradition and the New Testament: A Guide for the Perplexed* (London: Bloomsbury, 2014), 42–43. However, it seems to me that Achtemeier and others are correct in alerting us to the dangers of certain modern literary assumptions.

148. Tom Thatcher, "John's Memory Theatre: A Study of Composition in Performance," in *The Fourth Gospel in First-Century Media Culture*, ed. Anthony Le Donne and Tom Thatcher, LNTS 426 (London: T & T Clark, 2011), 89. Thatcher's preference for the description of this process as "dual visualization" follows from his argument that techniques of memory for performance in the Graeco-Roman world emphasized the importance of visual images.

149. Tenney, "Footnotes," 362. By "random nature," Tenney is presumably indicating the "random" distribution of asides in the text.

150. Robert M. Fowler, *Let the Reader Understand: Reader-Response Criticism and the Gospel of Mark* (Minneapolis: Fortress Press, 1991), 113. Fowler argues that "the abundance of anacolutha is yet another characteristic of Mark's narrative that suggests that it was intended for oral performance" (92).

151. Thomas E. Boomershine, "Audience Asides and the Audiences of Mark: The Difference Performance Makes," in *Narrative and Performance Criticisms in Dialogue and Debate*, ed. Kelly R. Iverson (Cambridge: Lutterworth Press, 2014), 88–89.

152. Lindars, *Gospel*, 51.

153. Lindars, *Gospel*, 52.

154. Lindars, *Gospel*, 180.

The Process of Composition 161

155. R. T. France, *The Gospel of Mark: A Commentary on the Greek Text*, NIGTC (Grand Rapids: Eerdmans, 2002), 229n10.

156. Thatcher, *Why John Wrote a Gospel*, 145.

157. Dewey, "Gospel of John," 249.

158. Rodríguez, *Oral Tradition*, 69. "Traditionalist" or "conservative" is another of Walter Ong's characteristics of oral expression.

159. Margaret Davies, *Rhetoric and Reference in the Fourth Gospel*, JSNTSup 69 (Sheffield: Sheffield Academic Press, 1992), 275.

160. Schnackenburg, *Gospel*, 1:111–12.

161. Gilbert Van Belle, "Theory of Repetitions and Variations in the Fourth Gospel," *in Repetitions and Variations in the Fourth Gospel: Style, Text, Interpretation* ed. Gilbert Van Belle, Michael Labahn, and Petrus Maritz, BETL 223 (Leuven: Uitgeverij Peeters, 2009), 30.

162. Van Belle, "Theory of Repetitions and Variations," 25, 22–26. He draws particular attention to the work of Thomas Popp on repetition, variation, and amplification. See Thomas Popp, *Grammatik des Geistes: Literarische Kunst und theologische Konzeption in Johannes 3 und 6*, ABG 3 (Leipzig: Evangelische Verlagsanstalt, 2001).

163. Brown, *Gospel*, 1:325.

164. Although, as Rodríguez argues, repetition is a feature of both oral and written narratives (*Oral Tradition*, 63–64).

165. Van Belle, *Les Parenthèses*, 209–10.

166. Culpepper, *Anatomy*, 49n65.

167. Thatcher, *Why John Wrote a Gospel*, 43. Thatcher contrasts John's *rhetorical* purpose in writing with Luke's more *archival* purpose (43–46).

168. See Brian Stock, *The Implications of Literacy: Written Language and Models of Interpretation in the Eleventh and Twelfth Centuries* (Princeton: Princeton University Press, 1983), 88–92.

169. Tenney, "Footnotes," 362.

*Chapter 5*

# Whose Comments

## *The Narrator's or the Author's?*

Commentators employ a variety of terms to describe the primary composer of the Fourth Gospel. (I use the word "primary" to distinguish that person from possible later redactors of the text). Earlier commentators refer exclusively to John (or even Saint John) or to the Evangelist; modern commentators often speak of the narrator (*der Erzähler, le narrateur*) and when they do use the name "John," they sometimes include a disclaimer to the effect that this need not refer to a particular historical figure. For example, Brant writes in the introduction to her commentary, "In this commentary, the name 'John' is used to refer to the author of the Fourth Gospel. This habit reflects the historical attribution of the Gospel to the disciple John and is not an assertion of the validity of the attribution."[1]

In the past things were simpler. A book had an author and if an author chose to enlist the help of a narrator in telling the story, then this would be a character within that story. Even the Gospels were once seen as having authors. Thus, John wrote the Gospel bearing his name and, even if we could not be sure exactly who this John was (the Apostle, the Beloved Disciple, the Elder?), there were no such complications as an implied author or a narrator (and possibly an unreliable narrator) distinct from the characters in the story. Times have changed. For those working within the historical-critical paradigm, the author of the Gospel has generally been replaced by a Johannine editorial team, assorted members of a Johannine community, one of whom may have had particular creative theological insight and who provided a solid basis for the work, even if this was later modified by and added to by others in the community. On the other hand, for those influenced by modern literary critical theory, focus on the author has also been replaced, but in this case by the figure of the narrator and the distinctive *voice* or *point of view* of this narrator.

164                               Chapter 5

Up till now, I have hedged my bets by tending to use the nomenclature "author/narrator" when referring to the composer of the Gospel, but the time has come to examine this author-narrator distinction or dichotomy in more detail and also some of the implications of this for understanding the function of the narrative comments. So, in this chapter, I provide a brief overview of how the narrator and point of view have been understood in modern literary critical approaches to the NT and I look more closely at scholars' presentation of the narrator in John with regard to *omniscience, intrusiveness,* and *reliability.* I then consider some of the limitations of these narratological methods, before returning to the *author* and looking at linguistic approaches to the relationship between the author and reader. Finally, I offer another case study, this time an analysis of the so-called "translation asides" and determine what they might tell us about the author-reader dynamic.

## NARRATIVE CRITICISM, THE NARRATOR AND POINT OF VIEW

Mark Stibbe, an author who has applied literary critical theory to the Gospel of John, traces the emergence within NT studies of what is usually called "narrative criticism" to the publication of Erich Auerbach's *Mimesis: The Representation of Reality in Western Literature* in 1953, a wide-ranging work which includes a close examination of Peter's denial in the Gospel of Mark.[2] Gradually, this narrative critical approach came to be adopted by a number of NT scholars, initially focussing on Mark, but later moving to the other Gospels including John.[3] In my "Survey of Literature" in chapter 1, I noted references to the narrator in the works of Olsson, Culpepper, Lombard, Hedrick, Sheeley, and Thatcher and this chapter makes use of some of their observations as well as those of a number of other Johannine scholars who have written on the function of the narrator in the Gospel, including David Wead, Jeffrey Lloyd Staley, Mark Stibbe, James Resseguie, and Jo-Ann Brant. I consider how the observations of these authors relate to the function of the narrative comments.

Birger Olsson was a pioneer in the use of literary critical theory as part of his "text-linguistic" methodology. I noted his reference to the concept of *point of view* in literary theory and his simplified definition of it as "the position from which the narrative is presented to the reader."[4] In the case of John's narrative, he agrees with David Wead that this presents "a post resurrection point of view."[5] Olsson sees this point of view communicated in both an "external" and "internal" manner, stating, "The external position tends to allow the narrator much greater freedom. He can use several means of conveying information, he can comment on the events he describes etc."[6]

*Whose Comments*  165

However, although the narrator in John is "standing at a distance from the events," he also "possesses an insight and a knowledge which makes him a constantly present, although invisible witness."[7]

Culpepper makes an extensive and eclectic use of literary critical theory in his *Anatomy of the Fourth Gospel*, drawing on the work of Wayne Booth, Frank Kermode, Boris Uspensky, Wolfgang Iser, Seymour Chatman, Meir Sternberg, and Gérard Genette, amongst others. He outlines the distinctions Chatman makes between the real author, implied author, narrator, narratee, implied reader, and real reader and Genette's distinction between discourse and story.[8] He argues that the narrator communicates indirectly through narrative time, plot, and characters, but also in a more intrusive way through the use of explicit commentary.[9] Regarding *point of view*, Culpepper refers to Genette's concept of "focalization," regarding the narrator's relation to the author and to characters within the narrative, but relies mainly on Uspensky's "planes" of the ideological, phraseological, spatial and temporal, and psychological points of view.[10] In terms of these planes, he proposes that the narrator in John is omniscient (psychological plane); omnipresent (spatial plane); broadly retrospective, with "an acute sensitivity to the history and struggles of the Johannine community" (temporal plane); and reliable and "stereoscopic" (ideological plane).[11] By "stereoscopic," Culpepper means that "the narrator views Jesus and his ministry from the twin perspectives of his 'whence' and his 'whither,' his origin as the pre-existent *logos* and his destiny as the exalted Son of God."[12] Culpepper cites a number of commonly designated asides/comments in support of his argument, particularly with respect to the *omniscience* of the narrator.[13]

Lombard, like Culpepper, draws on the work of a range of scholars in his overview of literary criticism and its application to the Gospel. In addition to Iser, Chatman, and Genette, he also refers to the work of Stanley Fish, Roger Fowler, and Shlomith Rimmon-Kenan. He stresses literary criticism's focus on the narrator in the "textual world" and the "elusive 'paper readers'" created within this text.[14] He is thus dealing with the narrator and implied readers, although I think there is some lack of clarity in his discussion of "the reader" as to when he is referring to the implied reader and when the real reader. Overall his intention is to bridge literary-critical and historical-critical approaches, but I suggested earlier that too much is assumed rather than argued for in his paper. Perhaps unintentionally, he highlights the complexity of narrative criticism's concepts and terminology and the problem of reconciling them with more traditional understandings of the author and reader. He is certainly right to see the limitations of only dealing with the closed world of the text itself.

Hedrick draws on the work of Booth, Chatman, Genette, and Rimmon-Kenan. His exploration centres on the distinction between telling and showing

166                                     Chapter 5

in his definition of asides.[15] He also uses a distinction between the implied author and the narrator in his proposal that where there is a discrepancy between the asides and the narrative, it is the implied author of the asides who is (inadvertently?) setting up a contradictory voice in the text.[16] Although Hedrick cites Booth in his article, he does not do so with reference to the telling-showing distinction. Thatcher, on the other hand, refers to "Wayne Booth's acclaimed distinction between telling and showing."[17] However, this distinction is found in narrative theorists before and after Booth.

Sheeley's work centres on Luke-Acts, but he also considers the function of the asides in John. He cites Booth, Chatman, Genette, and Rimmon-Kenan in developing a methodology that makes use of the work of both modern narrative critics and ancient rhetoricians.[18] From the modern narrative critics, he derives a focus on narrative voice and the levels of the narrator's *intrusion* into the text.[19]

A number of other writers on John have employed terminology and definitions from modern literary criticism, sometimes including reference to the asides/comments. One of the first applications of literary approaches to the Gospel, published in 1970 (and, therefore, prior to the work of a number of the literary theorists mentioned above) is David Wead's *The Literary Devices in John's Gospel*, which I have already referenced on a number of occasions. The book was republished in a revised and expanded edition, with a foreword by Culpepper, in 2018, and it is this edition that I refer to here. Wead deals with a number of issues that are relevant to our discussion of narrative criticism, although it should be noted that he uses the terms *the author, the evangelist*, and *the narrator* somewhat interchangeably, with emphasis on *the author*.

Wead has a chapter on "The Post-Resurrection Point of View" of the author/narrator, in which he draws on the work of Lubbock (1921) and Connolly (1953).[20] He traces the foundation and development for work on point of view (or *Erzählungssituation*) to Henry James and his pupil Percy Lubbock and states, "Point of view shows the position where the author stands in relation to the events he is relating to his readers."[21] He then refers to the three questions posed by Francis Connolly in *A Rhetoric Case Book*: "Who is telling the story? From what physical point of view or angle of narration is he telling the story? From what mode, or mental point of view, is he telling the story?"[22] His answers to these three questions are that it is the Beloved Disciple who is telling the story (on the basis of John 21:24); the physical point of view is "panoramic" or "omniscient," so that the author separates himself from the events of the narrative; and the mental point of view is reflected more in "the author's choice and presentation of material," rather than his "breaking into the text itself."[23] In connection with the physical point of view, Wead believes that John's post-resurrection perspective is distinct from that of the writers of the Synoptics.[24] For example, he states, "John's panoramic view of the life of Christ is indicated with his first words in the prologue—a marked difference between this Gospel and the others."[25] He includes a number of examples of the ways in which the author intrudes into the narrative "to illuminate the text before us": these include the explanations of "customs and times"; the noting of the disciples' lack of understanding; the "many little notes which give us insight into the meaning of the words of Jesus as they were later (and, more correctly, the author believes) understood"; and the provision of information about characters in the narrative, such as Mary and Caiaphas.[26] Wead lists many of these narrative comments as examples of "John's panoramic view."[27]

Both of Wead's categories, physical and mental, relate to the author's post-resurrection point of view, and I see support in this for my definition of the narrative comments as that which lies outside the narrative framework in a temporal or spatial sense. I also note Wead's assertion of the literary unity of the Gospel:

> An exploration into the literary point of view also reveals the overall unity of the Gospel. Following the unity of grammatical style—as has been demonstrated by Schweizer, Ruckstuhl, and Noack—the literary point of view becomes another factor that speaks for the unitive composition of the Gospel.[28]

If, as Wead asserts, the author's point of view is consistent across both the narrative and the comments on the narrative, then this lends support to the view that the comments are not later glosses.

Another application of literary theory Wead makes is in his chapter on "Irony in the Fourth Gospel."[29] He states that one of the approaches to irony which the author employs is "the so-called 'wink,' . . . a device wherein the author takes pains to step aside and explain the irony he or she puts into the text. This is done from the author's godlike position."[30] He explains that "the so-called 'wink' comes when the author relates to the readers that there is a second and fuller meaning to what has been said."[31] He gives the example of 11:50–52, in which Caiaphas's "prophecy" is given a deeper meaning by the author. I included 11:51–52 in my list of comments as an example of dramatic irony.

In an Epilogue, which was added in the second edition of *The Literary Devices*, Wead considers the likely influence of Greek drama on John and sees parallels between the prologue and endings of Euripides's plays and the prologue and epilogues (20:30–31; 21:24–25) in the Gospel. In both cases, they serve to indicate the author's perspective on the narrative.[32]

Jeffrey Lloyd Staley, in *The Print's First Kiss* (1988), considers the rhetorical significance of the printed text of the Gospel on the implied reader

168                                   *Chapter 5*

through the "sequence" of both the story and the discourse. He refers to the work of Olsson and, especially, Culpepper.[33] He is critical of Culpepper for confusing the narrator, implied author, and author/editor.[34] Staley generally takes a much stricter approach to Chatman's rhetorical levels, including the implied author-narrator distinction.[35] Although he believes that the narrator in John is the Beloved Disciple and hence a witness to the events, he is also omniscient "in a general way."[36] The narrator is also reliable, as the translation asides in 1:38, 41, 42 establish, but "his is a sort of reliability that is not above surreptitiously leading the implied reader astray, nor above putting stumbling blocks in the way—just so that he can, as it were in mild admonishment, lead the implied reader back once again to the right path."[37] Using terms drawn from literary theory, Staley speaks of the implied author as "victimizing the reader" or employing a "rhetoric of entrapment," which, "first presents the reader with the narrative 'facts' in such a way that the reader is induced to commit the character's or narrator's errors, then . . . forces the reader to recognize his or her misjudgements by supplying or implying the corrective perspective."[38] He uses 4:1–2 as an example of this. Noting that "the vast majority of scholars" regard 4:2 as "a later editorial gloss," Staley focuses instead on the rhetorical impact of this verse and its juxtaposition with the narrator's statements in 3:22, 26 and 4:1.[39] He concludes that the tension created is a deliberate rhetorical strategy on the part of the implied author, through which "the implied reader is forced . . . to reevaluate his relationship to the narrator and the story."[40]

In *John as Storyteller* (1992), Mark Stibbe undertakes to integrate literary and historical approaches to the Gospel. He is critical of Culpepper for being overreliant on theory based on the study of the modern novel (and hence "anachronistic") and for neglecting the historical dimension, especially as it relates to a "community history."[41] He specifically accuses Culpepper and others of being overly indebted to "New criticism" and failing to take into account more sociologically based approaches.[42] His own method is an eclectic one, drawing on structuralism in literary theory, alongside insights from the sociologies of knowledge and of religion (as reflected in the writings of Meeks and Malina) and from the philosophy of history regarding the relationship between narrative and history. Nevertheless, Stibbe does consider "some of the literary strategies which help to give the gospel its unity and which indicate a single, artistic imagination behind the narrative."[43] These strategies include "narrator's asides" and the "narrator's point of view." Of the asides, Stibbe states:

> In John's gospel one often finds explanatory asides from the narrator. These explain names (1.38,42), and symbols (2.21/12.33/18.9), they

*Whose Comments* 169

correct possible misunderstandings (4.2/6.6), they remind the reader of related events (3.24/11.2), and reidentify the characters of the story (7.50/21.20). There are approximately sixty of these asides, and they are further evidence of a uniform literary style.[44]

Regarding the narrator's point of view, Stibbe asserts:

> The same narrator and the same voice speaks throughout the gospel. His voice is always in the third person. He stands outside the action, and has a privileged view and understanding of the words and works of Jesus. . . . He sees matters from an enlightened, post-resurrection stance . . . which has clearly been influenced by Old Testament Scripture and by the Spirit-Paraclete.[45]

Although Stibbe is reluctant to label the narrator "omniscient" ("he is not, after all, a divine figure"), he "everywhere . . . works obviously—though not clumsily—to coax the reader around to the point of view or ideological stance he embraces."[46]

James Resseguie, as well as publishing a broad overview of narrative criticism of the NT and a glossary of terms, has also applied a narrative critical approach to the Gospel in *The Strange Gospel: Narrative Design and Point of View in John* (2001).[47] Resseguie defines point of view both as "the mode or angle of vision from which characters, dialogue, actions, setting, and events are considered or observed" and also as "the narrator's attitude towards or evaluation of characters, dialogue, actions, setting, and events."[48] It is this latter definition, which he calls the "subjective point of view" and which he equates with Uspensky's ideological plane, that forms the focus of his study.[49] He sees this ideological plane as "determined by a close analysis of other aspects of point of view—phraseological, spatial, temporal, and psychological." [50] For example, from his analysis of the temporal aspect, he concludes, "The narrator of John uses posterior narration to recount events that are viewed from a post-resurrection perspective."[51] To support this argument, he gives the example of the comments in 2:22; 7:39; 12:16; and 20:9.[52]

Resseguie understands the subjective or ideological point of view of the narrator to be summed up in 1:14, of which he writes, "The glory is revealed in the flesh. This is not only the paradox of the gospel, but also the dilemma for everyone who encounters the Word."[53] In contrast to those, such as the "representatives of the dominant culture—the religious authorities," who see only the surface, material, and literal, the Gospel's ideological viewpoint (reflected, for example, in the words of the man born blind) "judges correctly, exegetes at a deeper level, sees beyond the material point of view, and focuses on the spiritual."[54]

170                                   *Chapter 5*

In regard to the omniscience and reliability of the narrator, Resseguie states,

> The narrator of the Fourth Gospel is an invisible, roving narrator who has privileged access to the inner consciousness of characters. He knows their beliefs, emotions, and motivations. He is also what Wayne Booth calls a "reliable" narrator who "speaks for or acts in accordance with the norms of the work," making his point of view congruent with the point of view of the main character, Jesus.[55]

In regard to intrusiveness, he states, "When the narrator intrudes into the narrative to speak with his own voice he reveals an ideological position."[56] Resseguie sees an example of this in the Prologue, in the phrases "the Word became flesh . . . and we have seen his glory" (1:14), where an "ideological perspective" is expressed.[57] He goes on to speak of the narrator "using annotations to clarify misunderstandings," as in 2:21 ("But he was speaking of the temple of his body"). Here the narrator is correcting a superficial "material" understanding of Jesus' words about the destruction and raising up of the Temple and applying it to Jesus himself.[58]

From a different perspective, Brant considers the role of the narrator in *Dialogue and Drama* (2004), her comparison of the Gospel with elements of classical Greek tragedy.[59] She believes that "the narrator in the Fourth Gospel plays a more limited role than, or a qualitatively different role from, that in the Synoptic Gospels" and suggests that this more limited or different role is partly to do with the greater dependence on dialogue in John.[60] However, she also points out that the narrator in John has particular insight into the motives of Jesus and other characters, as well as into "the interior disposition of belief."[61] In this way "the Johannine narrator violates the limits of his witness by claiming the ability to see into the minds of others."[62] She lists various examples of these insights, many of which would be considered narrative asides by commentors, such as John 2:11 and 2:22. She separates this "ideal if not exactly an omniscient narrator" from the Beloved Disciple.[63]

Brant provides an overview of narrative critical approaches in her essay, "The Fourth Gospel as Narrative and Drama" (2018). She highlights the distinction between diegesis (telling) and mimesis (showing), suggesting that "the Gospel uses mimesis to a significant degree," through its abundance of dialogue.[64] However, she notes that diegesis is evident in the "narrator asides" or "narrative asides": "the narrator tells the reader what to think by explaining terms or by telling us what Jesus (e.g. 4:1; 11:33) and other characters (e.g. 9:22) are thinking so that we can understand motivations and interpret actions."[65]

*Whose Comments* 171

## THE NARRATOR IN JOHN: OMNISCIENT, INTRUSIVE, RELIABLE/UNRELIABLE?

From this survey of the application of narrative criticism, we can draw some general conclusions about what sort of narrator we have in John, focussing on the characteristics of omniscience, intrusiveness, reliability, and point of view.

### An Omniscient Narrator?

Most of the scholars I have surveyed agree that the narrator in John is in some sense omniscient. Using Uspensky's "planes," Culpepper states that the narrator is omniscient from a psychological point of view and omnipresent from a spatial point of view.[66] Similarly, Resseguie speaks of "an invisible, roving narrator who has privileged access to the inner consciousness of characters."[67]

This omniscience fits with a Gospel that is almost all in third-person narration (the exceptions being 1:14, 16 and 21:24–25). It would also seem to fit with the ability to provide narrative comments to help explain the story. As Genette remarks: in contrast to "rigorous focalization," which "excludes on principle every kind of intervention by the narrator . . . the use of commentarial discourse is somewhat the privilege of the 'omniscient' narrator."[68] This omniscience would seem to be especially true of those comments which reveal insights even into the mind of Christ himself, what Van Belle calls the "connaissance surnaturelle de Jésus" and Köstenberger, "references to Jesus' supernatural insight or foreknowledge of events."[69] Van Belle gives the examples of 2:24–25; 6:6, 64; and 13:11, to which Köstenberger adds 13:1, 3; 16:19; 18:4; and 19:28.[70] Both scholars are emphasizing the supernatural insight of Jesus himself, but narrative critics would also see them as examples of the narrator's omniscience, what Culpepper calls "inside views of Jesus' mind."[71] Indeed, with the exception of 13:3, Culpepper includes all the above examples in his own list of these "inside views."[72]

However, even Culpepper acknowledges that "omniscience in narrators is not a monolithic quality. . . . There are various types of omniscience, since the source and extent of a narrator's knowledge may vary."[73] Indeed, if we focus more on the narrator's (or author's) post-resurrection perspective, then these insights are not so much signs of omniscience, but rather the perceptions of someone who has reflected on the nature and ministry of Jesus and come to the realization that, for example, Jesus "himself knew what was in everyone" (2:25). Looking back at Jesus' interactions with others, the writer has come to understand that Jesus had a unique insight into human character and motives. So that, for example, Jesus knew that Nicodemus was genuine in his quest for truth, as Nicodemus's subsequent actions demonstrated.

Similarly, Jesus knew that Judas would betray him and that Peter would deny him, as subsequent events confirmed. So, it is not supernatural insight that the narrator/author has into the mind of Jesus, but rather insight that has been gained from observation (if an eyewitness of the events) and/or a long period of reflection. Thus, when, with reference to the comment in 6:6, Westcott writes, "Throughout the Gospel the Evangelist speaks as one who had an intimate knowledge of the Lord's mind," he has in mind not an omniscient narrator but an author whose knowledge results from his being an eyewitness of the events.[74] I suggest that even if not an eyewitness, the Evangelist could be drawing on the testimony of those who had such knowledge.

Indeed, the term "omniscient narrator" is one that is not liked by all literary critics, as it implies a knowledge that is beyond that of any single individual. More recent studies of the narrator have sought to qualify or replace the term *omniscience*. For example, Jonathan Culler (2004) sees the understanding of the term as derived from the concept of an omniscient God and is critical of this as a theological idea and of its application to narratology.[75] He draws attention to the fact that where the narrator is not a specified character in the narrative, then readers have a mistaken tendency to personify the narrator and then label this narrator as omniscient: "It is above all when there is no primary character through whom narration is focalized that our proclivity leads us astray: we invent a person to be the source of textual details, but since this knowledge is not that which an ordinary person could have, we must imagine this invented person to be godlike, omniscient."[76]

Culler concludes that what is commonly referred to in narratology as omniscience, is in fact "a fantasy," a blanket term for a range of practices employed by the author, and he argues that the terms omniscience and omniscient narrator should be abandoned.[77]

The recent essay by Annjeanette Wiese "Replacing Omniscience: Superior Knowledge and Narratorial Access" (2021) responds to Culler's challenge and seeks an alternative critical lexicon.[78] She introduces the concept of "superior knowledge," which she defines as "knowledge that could not typically be known by either a narrator of nonfiction or a (non-supernatural) fictional character who narrates from within a given storyworld."[79] This "superior knowledge" comprises "knowledge of characters and events (including interior thoughts and consciousness), knowledge of temporality (past, present, and future), and knowledge of spatial location (such as being present in two places at once, or being where one should not be able to be)."[80] Wiese distinguishes between superior knowledge and omniscience in stating that the former is "based on its relevance to the author's rhetorical strategies and is therefore not necessarily comprehensive."[81]

Of course, a number of scholars have tried to equate the narrator in John with a particular character in the narrative—namely, the "Beloved Disciple"—

*Whose Comments*                                                              173

but I do not find this argument convincing. For example, Resseguie, having stated that the narrator is "an invisible, roving narrator," surprisingly goes on to say, "The narrator is the beloved disciple, which means that he is also a character within the narrative."[82] Although, he immediately qualifies this by adding, "However, he does not limit his point of view by narrating from the perspective of the beloved disciple."[83] Resseguie believes that the parenthetical remarks in 19:35 and 21:24 represent a coming together of the narrator and the Beloved Disciple, but he does not really argue his case and there are other explanations for these narrative comments.[84] Culpepper also regards 19:35 and 21:24 as "the key references for discussion of the relationship between the Beloved Disciple, the narrator, the implied author, and the author."[85] He regards the Beloved Disciple as "an idealized characterization of an historical figure" and the "implied author" of the Gospel.[86] As such, the implied author and the narrator are separate, something which Culpepper believes "is without parallel in ancient literature."[87] However, in practice, Culpepper does not distinguish between the narrator and implied author: "There is no real difference between the point of view of the narrator, i.e., the voice which tells the story, and the perspective of the implied author which is projected by the text."[88] I have noted above Staley's criticism of Culpepper's reluctance to differentiate the two figures.

### An Intrusive Narrator?

The scholars I have surveyed generally have less to say about the intrusiveness of the narrator than about omniscience, but where they do, they are agreed that the narrator in John is intrusive to a lesser or greater extent and that this intrusiveness is demonstrated in the asides/comments. For example, Culpepper states:

> The narrator guides the reader through the narrative, introduces the reader to the world of the narrative and the characters which populate it, and provides the proper perspective from which to view the action. In John, the narrator is the one who speaks in the prologue, tells the story, introduces the dialogue, provides explanations, translates terms, and tells us what various characters knew or did not know. In short, the narrator tells us what to think. Because he, or she, makes comments to the reader which interrupt the flow of the narrative, the narrator is *intrusive*. We have a clear sense of his presence and relate to him as a person.[89]

Similarly, Resseguie speaks of the narrator as intruding "into the narrative to speak in his own voice."[90] In addition to the example from the Prologue noted above, "we have seen his glory" (1:14), Resseguie also cites the instances of

174                                        *Chapter 5*

the narrator intruding to draw attention to the fact that Jesus' ministry caused division: 7:43; 9:16; 10:19.[91] (He highlights the use of the word σχίσμα in these verses.) However, these seem to me fairly weak examples, which again raise the difficulty of deciding what we mean by intrusive. In chapter 2, I referred to Sheeley's definition of narrative asides in his study of Luke-Acts, where he speaks of them "as parenthetical remarks addressed directly to the reader which interrupt the logical progression of the story."[92] I made the point that it is not easy to determine what interrupts "the logical progression of the story" or to agree to what extent the narrative asides are, in fact, a more "direct address" to the reader than the rest of the text. We certainly have nothing in the Gospel of John comparable to the intrusive narrator that we find in 19th century novels. For example, in the following extract from Thackeray's *Vanity Fair* (1848), the narrator addresses the reader directly with a (tongue-in-cheek) apology:

> I know that the tune I am piping is a very mild one (although there are some terrific chapters coming presently), and must beg the good-natured reader to remember that we are only discoursing at present about a stockbroker's family in Russell Square, who are taking walks, or luncheon, or dinner, or talking and making love as people do in common life, and without a single passionate and wonderful incident to mark the progress of their loves.[93]

This intrusion is primarily for comic effect. By contrast, a far more serious tone is established in the Prologue to Luke's Gospel (1:1–4):

> Since many have undertaken to set down an orderly account of the events that have been fulfilled among us, just as they were handed on to us by those who from the beginning were eyewitnesses and servants of the word, I too decided, after investigating everything carefully from the very first, to write an orderly account for you, most excellent Theophilus, so that you may know the truth concerning the things about which you have been instructed.

The nearest we come to such self-conscious address to the reader in John are the comments 21:24–25:

> This is the disciple who is testifying to these things and has written them, and we know that his testimony is true. But there are also many other things that Jesus did; if every one of them were written down, I suppose that the world itself could not contain the books that would be written.

*Whose Comments* 175

However, nowhere in John is "the reader" referred to directly, although the plural pronoun "you" (ὑμεῖς) is used in 19:35:

(He who saw this has testified so that you also may believe. His testimony is true, and he knows that he tells the truth.)

In chapter 2, I referred to the "scale of narrative features," which Richardson employs in his study of the narrator in Homer, a scale "ranging from the most covert signs of the narrator's presence to the most overt."[94] Richardson states, "Self-conscious narration is the furthest extreme of narrator-prominence. Not only does the narrator come out into the open, but he also exposes something of the creative process, of which we normally see only the final product without reflecting on its genesis."[95] The most overt sign of the narrator's presence is in 21:24–25 and these verses expose "something of the creative process." However, what the precise relationship between the disciple who testifies (the Beloved Disciple?), the "we" who know his testimony is true, and the "I" who supposes is the subject of considerable debate and disagreement amongst scholars. Michaels sums up the dilemma well:

The distinction introduced at the last minute, as it were, between the Gospel writer and the narrator or narrative voices, complicates the literary reading of the Gospel at least to some degree. . . . Readers of modern literature are accustomed to authors creating for themselves narrative voices—sometimes more than one—to tell their stories for them, but here we have a narrative voice, introduced abruptly at the end, telling us at last who the true author is. So who is the true author? Whose voice are we hearing throughout? This final narrative voice, or the person this voice explicitly identifies as the author of the Gospel? It is not an easy question, nor does it in the end make an enormous difference.[96]

I have given some thoughts on these matters in chapter 3, but whatever conclusions we come to about the persons indicated in these verses, the fact remains that even here the narrator (author?) remains relatively hidden, just like the elusive Beloved Disciple. Indeed, by and large, despite the high number of asides/comments listed by some commentators, the narrator in John is not overly intrusive, so I am puzzled by Culpepper's observation that we have a clear sense of the narrator's presence and relate to him as a person.

In fact, some instances of supposed narrative asides seem to me to have no intrusive aspect whatsoever and are simply integral to the narrative. I regard 6:10 as a case in point:

176　　　　　　　　　　　　　　　*Chapter 5*

εἶπεν ὁ Ἰησοῦς, Ποιήσατε τοὺς ἀνθρώπους ἀναπεσεῖν. ἦν δὲ χόρτος πολὺς ἐν τῷ τόπῳ. ἀνέπεσαν οὖν οἱ ἄνδρες τὸν ἀριθμὸν ὡς πεντακισχίλιοι. Jesus said, "Make the people sit down." Now there was a great deal of grass in the place; so they sat down, about five thousand in all.

Van Belle puts the sentence ἦν δὲ χόρτος πολὺς ἐν τῷ τόπῳ in brackets and finds support for its listing as a parenthesis in various early scholars.[97] Many commentators note the parallels to Mark 6:39 (especially "the green grass") and Matthew 14:19, and Zumstein sees a possible allusion to Psalm 23:2.[98] Theobald calls it "eine Notiz" (a note) and suggests that it might indicate the time of year (Spring) and hence the approaching Passover festival.[99] However, whatever its possible allusions and whether or not it was part of an existing oral tradition or, as Carson suggests, a "personal recollection of detail," there seems no good reason for treating it as a separate narrative comment.[100] The same applies to other supposed narrative comments which function as part of the scene setting, such as the note that "the Jewish festival of Booths was near" (7:2) or that "Bethany was near Jerusalem, some two miles away" (11:18).

Maybe too much is made of the distinction between *showing* and *telling*, the distinction that Thatcher and others use in their attempt to define asides. As Genette has pointed out, the concept of *showing* in narrative is problematic: "The very idea of *showing*, like that of imitation or narrative representation . . . is completely illusory: in contrast to dramatic representation, no narrative can 'show' or 'imitate' the story it tells."[101] Similarly, as I noted in chapter 2, Boomershine remarks, "In storytelling . . . the performer . . . is always addressing the audience, sometimes directly and sometimes indirectly."[102] Or as Rimmon-Kenan states, "The crucial distinction . . . is not between telling and showing, but between different degrees and kinds of telling."[103] The narrator is always there in the text, whether intrusive or not. The whole discourse (the "how" of the story) is the narrator's production: the choice of material narrated, the speed of the narrative's flow (sometimes paused, sometimes speeded up), the ordering of events. Indeed, the narrator (author?) of the Gospel is quite explicit in stating that the composition is selected from an overwhelming choice (20:30; 21:25).

At a more theoretical level, I wonder if the distinction between story and discourse (a core principle of structuralist narratology) is in fact a valid one. Does a story ever actually exist? Or do we only have the interpretations (the discourses) of different narrators? This issue has led to considerable debate among narratologists. As the literary scholar Dan Shen notes:

> The distinction between story and discourse as "an indispensable premise of narratology" has attracted a lot of critical attention, leading to challenges, defenses, as well as applications. The heatedness of the critical

*Whose Comments* 177

debate is in part attributable to the fact that the nature of the distinction and what it involves are not yet fully clarified.[104]

### Intrusion and Dramatic Irony

Returning to the intrusive narrator, we can compare this intrusion with the phenomenon of parabasis or "breaking the fourth wall" in drama, which I referred to in chapter 2. In the theatre or on screen, we may observe one of the actors turn to face the audience and address them directly for dramatic or comic effect.[105] Do the asides/comments in John have this quality of direct address and do they contribute to the use of dramatic irony in the text? For, certainly, it has long been noted that the Gospel of John has dramatic qualities.[106] Moreover, some of the comments highlight the ignorance of some of the participants in the narrative regarding the meaning of what Jesus says and does, a meaning which is then made explicit for the reader/hearer. A few examples are:

- In 2:18–20, "the Jews" take Jesus' destruction and raising of the temple in three days as literal. In 2:21, the narrator turns to the audience and says, "But he was speaking of the temple of his body."

- In 11:11–12, the disciples seem to think that Jesus' statement "Our friend Lazarus has fallen asleep, but I am going there to awaken him" is an indication that Lazarus is in deep sleep (a coma?) and that "he will be all right." In 11:13, the narrator again turns to the audience and says, "Jesus, however, had been speaking about his death, but they thought that he was referring merely to sleep."

- In 20:3–8, Peter and "the other disciple" run to the tomb and find it empty. The narrator points out that despite all that Jesus had said to them previously they still did not "understand the scripture, that he must rise from the dead" (20:9).

Such instances of dramatic irony can be used for comic or tragic effect, yet is that the case in John? Brant claims to find humour in the Gospel's dramatic ironies. For example, she refers to "the disciples' humorous lack of understanding" in their "occasional interruptions" during Jesus' Farewell Address (13:31–17:26), comparing them to the comedy routines of Abbott and Costello and others.[107] I am not so sure. Maybe in 11:11–12, "the disciples are portrayed here as so dense as not to be able to understand the most obvious metaphor" (Lincoln) and there is a comic irony in this, but the subject is a serious one and humour seems inappropriate.[108] Admittedly, elsewhere Brant speaks of John as displaying a "propensity to appropriate

178                                   *Chapter 5*

genre by maneuvering through humor and gliding from plain to grand prose."[109]

In an early essay on the role of irony in John, George MacRae (1973) distinguishes the Gospel's irony from humour or satire as well as from Socratic, tragic (or Sophoclean), and "metaphysical" forms of irony and states, "The Johannine irony is first of all dramatic irony in that it presumes upon the superior knowledge of the reader to recognise the true perspective within which the Gospel's assertions are ironical."[110] I would argue that it is this "true perspective," the narrator's point of view, that is fundamental in determining the function of those comments which indicate dramatic irony. As Lincoln states, "The narrative characters who are victims of misunderstanding serve as foils to enable the reader to come to the right interpretation."[111] Wengst speaks of the misunderstanding disciples as being a mirror for the reading and hearing community.[112]

## A RELIABLE NARRATOR?

Although most of the commentators I have reviewed do not specifically comment on the reliability of the narrator, we can assume that they accept that the information provided in the narrative comments is reliable and is intended to guide the reader/hearer to a better understanding. Certainly, the narrator wishes to be seen as reliable. Hence the comment in 19:35:

καὶ ὁ ἑωρακὼς μεμαρτύρηκεν, καὶ ἀληθινὴ αὐτοῦ ἐστιν ἡ μαρτυρία, καὶ ἐκεῖνος οἶδεν ὅτι ἀληθῆ λέγει, ἵνα καὶ ὑμεῖς πιστεύ[σ]ητε.
(He who saw this has testified so that you also may believe. His testimony is true, and he knows that he tells the truth.)

Culpepper includes "an unreliable narrator" as being amongst the "modern" literary devices that we should not expect to find in "literary art in the first century."[113] Staley speaks of "the modern invention of the 'unreliable narrator'."[114] Resseguie goes so far as to say that "New Testament narrators are reliable narrators—that is, their perspectives and judgments coincide with those of the implied author. An unreliable or fallible narrator," that is "one whose perspectives and judgments are at odds with the implied author . . . is not found in the New Testament."[115] Resseguie also affirms, "An unreliable narrator is entirely a modern invention," referring to Scholes and Kellogg, *The Nature of Narrative* (1966).[116] Scholes and Kellogg state, "The unreliable or semi-reliable narrator in fiction is quite uncharacteristic of primitive or ancient narrative . . . the idea of creating an unreliable fictional eye-witness is the sophisticated product of an empirical and ironical age."[117]

*Whose Comments* 179

In fact, I would argue that the concept of an "unreliable narrator" is not entirely a recent literary phenomenon. It can be applied, for example, to the character Pyrgopolynices, the "boastful soldier" of the Latin comic writer Plautus's play *Miles Gloriosus*, dating from ca. 200 BC/BCE, the model for many later such characters. Erik Gunderson states, "Pyrgopolynices offers a spectacularly inaccurate summary of his own story and the moral conclusion to be drawn from it."[118]

However, if commentators believe that it is an entirely modern concept, then it is obvious that none of them will speak of an *unreliable narrator* in John. Hedrick comes closest to this in proposing a divergence between the "author" of the asides and the "narrator" of the main narrative and suggesting that the (implied) author is actually subverting the principal narrator.[119] Moreover, Staley, while accepting that the narrator is fundamentally reliable, sees instances of the narrator temporarily "leading the implied reader astray," before restoring him or her "to the right path."[120] Others reject the idea that the narrator acts even in this way. For example, Francis Moloney states, "While some modern and contemporary narratives may use the technique to lead the reader astray temporarily, this never happens in the Gospel of John. What the narrator communicates directly to the reader through commentary is a reliable representation of the overall point of view of the omniscient author."[121]

We can, in fact, contrast the reliability of the narrator in John with the unreliability of some of its characters: the disciples who fail to understand, who (in the case of Peter) deny Jesus and who hide in fear after the crucifixion; or the religious authorities who misunderstand and persecute Jesus; or Nicodemus, who fails to understand Jesus even though he is a "teacher of Israel" (3:10); or the Samaritan woman who is evasive (4:17, 20) and naïve (4:11, 15). Humans are by their nature not fully reliable, as the narrative comment in 2:24–25 suggests. However, the one who tells the story in this gospel, although human, is passionately committed to truth (19:35) and believes that "the Spirit of truth" is guiding his testimony (15:26; cf. 21:24). We may not share this conviction, but we are justified in seeing the narrative comments as part of a strategy to present a reliable picture. The narrator is a reliable and effective guide, comparable to the narrator in Homer described by Richardson:

> Part of providing a clear and accurate picture of the story is to be an effective guide: to highlight by various techniques the important features of a scene or an episode, to capture the essential nature of a speech or a character's predicament, to clarify the meaning or purpose of an action that might be opaque if left unexplained.[122]

180                                                 *Chapter 5*

Or, as Gary Burge comments about the "author" of the Gospel of John, "He is like the director of a great drama who stands on the sidelines coaching our understanding. In fact, we are more informed than the apostles when we read this Gospel because John is slipping us notes."[123]

## Point of View

I would argue, contrary to most commentators, that if we are to speak of a narrator in John then it is one that is not omniscient, although able to provide an insight beyond the characters in the narrative, with the exception of Jesus himself. Nor is this narrator overly intrusive. The narrator is, however, reliable. This insight and the reliability derive from a particular perspective: the post-resurrection point of view that is highlighted by Wead, Culpepper, Stibbe, Resseguie, and others.

Of course, this point of view is shared by the other Gospels, in the sense that they were all written after the event. Moreover, all four Gospels have a subjective or ideological point of view—that is, an evaluation of Jesus' teaching and ministry—which they wish the reader/hearer to share. Whether this evaluation differs somewhat across the Gospels is a matter of critical debate, but it seems reasonable to accept that the voice of the narrator in each Gospel is consistent with its author's perspective. Resseguie states, "All characters within the Gospels are judged from the point of view of the narrator, which also coincides with Jesus' point of view."[124] In the case of John, support for this statement can be found in the various comments which show insight into the mind of Jesus (such as 2:24–25; 6:6, 64; 13:1, 3, 11; 18:4; 19:28) and those passages where the words of Jesus appear to morph into the voice of the narrator (3:16–21, 31–36). However, I think we need to qualify Resseguie's statement somewhat if we accept that the narrator is not omniscient, but rather seeking an insight into "Jesus' point of view," based on the author's post-resurrection reflections. I see a tension between the rather nebulous concept of an infallible narrator and an actual author who, although guided by "the Spirit of truth," is still a fallible human being. There are limitations to the author's omniscience, as 21:25 indicates. This is still an author who is grappling with the inconceivable implications of the Word made flesh.

## NARRATOR AND AUTHORS

Following on from my judgement that if we are to speak of a narrator in John, then it is one who is neither omniscient nor overly intrusive, but who is reliable and speaks from a particular (post-resurrection) point of view, I want now to move beyond a focus on the narrator. For although there is value in the narrative critical approaches that have produced the insights I have reflected on, the narrator remains something of an artificial construct. Modern literary theory has arisen primarily from study of the novel and, whatever else it might be, the Gospel of John is not a novel, as Stibbe indicates.[125] Indeed, although Brant believes that "serious consideration of John within the genre of the ancient novel is a worthwhile expenditure of intellectual capital," this is not the same as imposing on ancient texts a methodology derived from study of the modern novel.[126] The modern novelist is often consciously playing with the narrator in a way that we should not expect of one of the authors of the Gospels, such as employing an unreliable narrator. As Culpepper has shown, care must be taken in applying literary concepts to ancient literature, and we should not expect to "find such modern devices as an unreliable narrator, distance between the narrator and the implied author, or between the narratee and the implied reader."[127] Similarly, Stibbe is right to stress that "the sophistications of gospel narratives are quite different from the subtleties of modern novels. Gospel narratives share in the subtleties of ancient Hebrew and Graeco-Roman narratives, not in the more self-conscious subtleties of modern novels."[128]

For some, the "narrative turn" in Johannine scholarship has been a cause of great joy, a return to treating the text as a unified whole against the fragmentary tendencies of the dead hand of historical-criticism.[129] However, there is also the consequence that it can leave us with a work of literature that is divorced from any historical context. As Cor Bennema forcefully points out:

> Too often, narrative critics restrict themselves to the text of the Gospel and the narrative world it evokes, effectively reading the Gospel as a fictional narrative that is disconnected from reality. Instead, we need a form of *historical narrative criticism* that takes a text-centred approach but examines aspects of the world outside or 'behind' the text if the text invites us to do so.[130]

Even taking into account many modern commentators' doubtful views of its historicity, the Gospel of John was not intended as a literary fiction. Indeed, as the historian Hayden White has emphasized, narrative is as much an integral part of historiography as of fictional writing. Indeed, "Far from being one code among many that a culture may utilize for endowing experience with meaning, narrative is a meta-code, a human universal on the basis of which transcultural messages about the nature of a shared reality can be transmitted."[131] Furthermore, "Every historical narrative has as its latent or manifest purpose the desire to moralize the events of which it treats."[132] The author of the Gospel of John has to narrate its signs and speeches and by the very choice of these is making a "comment," quite apart from the *telling* indicated by the various narrative comments.

182                                Chapter 5

So, can we move from a focus on the narrator to a focus on the author? And, if so, are we dealing with an implied author or a real "flesh and blood" author?

The term *implied author*, to be distinguished from the actual, historical author of a text, was introduced by Wayne Booth in *Rhetoric of Fiction* (1961). Booth describes it as the author's "second self" (borrowing a term from Kathleen Tillotson) that is created in a particular writing to convey the values and norms in which the author wants the reader to stand.[133] Booth understands the narrator to be only a part of the implied author's identity.[134] Using Booth's term, Staley says the implied author "describes the unifying sense that the reader makes of a narrative, irrespective of how many real authors or editors may lie behind it."[135]

However, as Nünning notes, "Whether narratology is well served by such a problematic concept as the implied author, be it of the personalised or deper-sonalised, or the textual or reader-response variety, remains an open question which continues to generate controversial debate."[136] Be that as it may, the term is used by NT narrative critics, although I have already noted that some of the commentators I have looked at do not want to distinguish between the *narrator* and the *implied author*. So Resseguie observes, "Generally, New Testament narrative critics do not identify the narrator as a separate party from the implied author—just as they do not separate the narratee from the implied reader."[137] Regarding the Gospel of John, Culpepper states, "In John it is difficult to say what the relationship between the real author and the implied author is, but there is no real difference between the point of view of the narrator, i.e., the voice which tells the story, and the perspective of the implied author which is projected by the text."[138]

I will not to go into the complex arguments concerning the author in modern critical scholarship associated with Roland Barthes and Michel Fou-cault.[139] Nor the various criticisms of Booth's concept of the implied author. However, even if we are committed to a narratological approach, the ques-tion of the author or the author's intention remains. As Elizabeth Shively expresses:

> Those who employ narrative criticism have not, in fact, abandoned "authorial" intention but have taken it from the actual author and relo-cated it within the text by assigning intentionality either to a textually constructed implied author, to the text/story, or to the narrator, which guides the implied (and real) reader toward certain responses.[140]

As far as the Gospel of John is concerned, given that we are dependent on the uncertain and conflicting accounts of authorship in the early church writings, the best we can do is speak of "the author" (in quotation marks). However, I would stress that this author is not simply an abstract conjecture, but rather a real and therefore fallible human being. Even if we do not know who the (primary) author was, we should take to heart Staley's comment, "In contrast to the narrators which they might create, all real authors are finite human beings and thus can be neither omniscient nor omnipresent."[141]

## AUTHOR AND READER: SOCIAL CONTEXT AND LINGUISTIC INSIGHTS

In chapter 2, I examined some of the complexity of linguistic definitions of parentheticals. Here, I am more concerned with the pragmatics of the author-reader relationship and how this is reflected in parenthetical comments. If we accept that the narrator is the author (or the final redactor or whatever), then we can scrutinize the comments not merely as examples of narrative technique, but as insights into the relationship between the author and intended readers. In this context, it is worthwhile to examine the methodology of *evaluation* or *appraisal*, a developing area of study within linguistics. Geoff Thompson and Susan Hunston define *evaluation* as "the expression of the speaker or writer's attitude or stance towards, viewpoint on, or feelings about the entities or propositions that he or she is talking about."[142] In practice, linguists use a range of methodologies and terminologies relating to evaluation/appraisal, and these overlap with the narratologists' concepts of *point of view* or *focalization*.[143] We see this, for example, in Resseguie's emphasis on the subjective or ideological point of view, in which he speaks of "the narrator's attitude towards or evaluation of characters, dialogue, actions, setting, and events."[144] Resseguie quotes Uspensky in stating, "The ideological point of view is 'the most basic aspect of point of view,'" but it is also "'the least accessible to formalization, for its analysis relies, to a degree, on intuitive understanding.'"[145] However, the methodologies of evaluation or appraisal in linguistics attempt to put the manner in which an author conveys attitude or stance towards a subject on a more empirical footing.[146]

One way that linguists have analysed texts in seeking to establish an author's evaluation is through focussing on *metadiscourse*. A major exponent in this field is Ken Hyland, whose book *Metadiscourse: Exploring Interaction in Writing* was first published in 2005. Hyland uses the concept of metadiscourse to define aspects of discourse that are either self-referential or refer to the reader or the text. He explains in more detail the thinking behind the concept:

> Essentially metadiscourse embodies the idea that communication is more than just the exchange of information, goods or services, but

184                                    *Chapter 5*

also involves the personalities, attitudes and assumptions of those who are communicating. Language is always a consequence of interaction, of the differences between people which are expressed verbally, and metadiscourse options are the ways we articulate and construct these interactions. This, then, is a dynamic view of language as metadiscourse stresses the fact that, as we speak or write, we negotiate with others, making decisions about the kind of effects we are having on our listeners or readers.[147]

Hyland's definition of metadiscourse is that it is a "cover term for the self-reflective expressions used to negotiate interactional meanings in a text, assisting the writer (or speaker) to express a viewpoint and engage with readers as members of a particular community."[148] In short, it can be described as that which distinguishes the way the propositional content of a text (the discourse) is presented to take into account the reader of the text and the aims of the author.[149] The "self-reflective expressions" Hyland refers to can take many different forms and he divides them into those that are *interactive*, helping to guide the reader through the text, and *interactional*, involving the reader in the text.[150] I believe we can apply examples from both these categories to the *external* and *internal* comments in John that I have listed.

Three of the examples of *interactive* expressions Hyland gives are *frame markers*, *endophoric markers*, and *evidentials*, where *frame markers* refer to "discourse acts, sequences or stages," such as "finally . . . ," "to conclude . . . ," or "my purpose is . . ."; *endophoric markers* refer to "information in other parts of the text"; and *evidentials* refers to "information from other texts."[151] From this perspective, the Gospel's Prologue (1:1–18, excluding the references to John the Baptist), the "endings" in 20:30–31 and 21:24–25, as well as the "numbered" comments in 2:11 and 4:54 can be considered as *frame markers*. I have denoted these as *external* comments as they relate to information beyond the narrative framework, but they also have some of the function of *internal* comments in the structuring of the narrative.

The various analeptic and proleptic *internal* comments in the Gospel can be considered as *endophoric markers* as they refer to "information in other parts of the text." However, if some of the proleptic comments relate to earlier (synoptic) traditions (3:24; 4:44), then they can be regarded as *evidentials*, although this would depend on the reader's knowledge of these sources, given that no explicit citation is made. More certain cases of *evidentials* are the various references to the OT/HB (2:17; 12:14b–15; 12:38–41; 19:24, 28, 36–37), although only in the instance of 12:38–41 is a specific writing denoted ("the word spoken by the prophet Isaiah"). Those comments which possibly or definitely relate to "information from other texts," I have labelled *external*.

*Whose Comments* 185

Other examples of narrative comments in the Gospel fit Hyland's category of *interactional* expressions. These expressions include *self-mentions*, which provide "explicit reference to author(s)" and *engagement markers*, which "explicitly build relationship with reader." In fact, as we have already noted in considering the *intrusive narrator*, such comments are rare in the Gospel and I believe we can only designate 1:16–18 ("we have seen his glory"; "From his fullness we have all received") and 21:23–25 ("we know that his testimony is true"; "I suppose that the world itself . . .") as *self-mentions* and 19:35–37 (". . . so that you also may believe") and 20:30–31 (". . . so that you may come to believe") as *engagement markers*. This suggests that although the author wishes to guide the reader through the text by means of *interactive* expressions, the involvement of the reader in the text through *interactional* expressions is more limited.

However, it would be wrong to infer from the fact that there are very few examples of *interactional* expressions that the involvement of the reader is unimportant to the author of the Gospel. Elsewhere, in a study of stance and engagement in academic discourse, Hyland examines a number of the strategies writers use to engage with their readership—including reader pronouns, personal asides, appeals to shared knowledge, directives and questions.[152] Of the specific category of personal asides, he observes:

> *Personal asides* allow writers to address readers directly by briefly interrupting the argument to offer a comment on what has been said. While asides express something of the writer's personality and willingness to explicitly intervene to offer a view, they can also be seen as a key reader-oriented strategy. By turning to the reader in mid-flow, the writer acknowledges and responds to an active audience, often to initiate a brief dialogue that is largely interpersonal. As we can see, such comments often add more to the writer–reader relationship than to the propositional development of the discourse.[153]

In my annotated list of external asides, I described 21:24–25 as the most striking example of narrator/author intrusion into the narrative. We can also recognize it, in Hyland's terminology, as an instance of a "personal aside" and thus "a key reader-oriented strategy." These verses contain the only example of a first-person singular verb in the narrative framework: οἶμαι (I suppose), although the significance of this verb in interpersonal terms is difficult to determine.[154] In chapter 3, I noted Köstenberger's comparative study of the verb and suggested that the author of the Gospel may simply be adopting a relatively common stylistic feature in the conclusion of the text.

186                                    *Chapter 5*

In fact, the *interactional* expressions or *personal asides* in John tell us little about the author (not even the gender) or the hearer/reader. However, they do suggest that the author is passionately committed to the message of this Gospel. The author wants hearers/readers to believe that Jesus is the Christ, the Son of God, and for them to have "life in his name": that is why the book was written (20:31). The *interactive* expressions, including the analeptic and proleptic *internal* comments, are also part of this process. As we have seen, Wendy North speaks of John as "a born pedant," who "when it comes to getting his message across to his readers" makes sure that "everything necessary is explicitly communicated, false impressions are carefully ruled out, and nothing is left to chance."[155] I would not go quite as far as that, in that ambiguities still remain, such as the comment on Jesus' manner of dying in 12:33, but I do believe that we have an author who does not want to just present the perceived facts of the case in a dispassionate manner. Everything is focussed on the key message that we should not just observe or hear Jesus but also believe in him. All the narrative comments are an integral part of that key message. It is with that in mind that I conclude this chapter with an analysis of what may not seem the most obvious category of comments with regard to the author-reader dynamic, but which nevertheless may have greater significance than is at first apparent.

## A CASE STUDY ON FUNCTION: THE "TRANSLATION" COMMENTS

In my categorization of the NRSV's 25 phrases or sentences in brackets or dashes, I placed the category "Translations" in quotation marks to indicate a degree of uncertainty as to whether these asides/comments are actually intended simply as straightforward translations of Hebrew or Aramaic terms into Greek or whether they have more significance. Similarly, in my own list of narrative comments, I referred to "what are commonly designated 'translation asides.'" They nevertheless provide a helpful case study in that they belong to a distinct category that is included by all the scholars who provide categorization lists and they can be readily identified by lexico-grammatical features.

The seven occurrences indicated by punctuation in the NRSV are 1:38, 41, 42; 4:25; 9:7; 20:16, 24. (The phrase "[who was called the twin]," found in 20:24, also occurs in 11:16 and the similar "called the twin" in 21:2, but these are not marked by brackets or dashes in the NRSV.) This is the same as the list provided by Tenney, except that he is unsure about the reference to Thomas "the twin" in 20:24 and he also includes 19:13 and 17. O'Rourke agrees with Tenney's list but suggests that 5:2 ("called in Hebrew

*Whose Comments* 187

Bethzatha") should be added, "although these words could be placed under some other heading."[156] Van Belle (1985) includes all 12 instances mentioned above. Hedrick gives seven occurrences, including 6:1b ("also called the sea of Tiberias"). Köstenberger provides 11 instances, all of which overlap with those of the other scholars. In my own list, I include eight examples: 1:38, 41, 42; 4:25; 9:7; 19:13, 17; and 20:16. This brief overview provides the following cumulative list of 13 occurrences:

1:38: ῥαββί, ὃ λέγεται μεθερμηνευόμενον Διδάσκαλε
Rabbi (which translated means Teacher)

1:41: τὸν Μεσσίαν, ὅ ἐστιν μεθερμηνευόμενον Χριστός
Messiah' (which is translated Anointed)

1:42: Κηφᾶς, ὃ ἑρμηνεύεται Πέτρος
Cephas (which is translated Peter)

4:25: Μεσσίας ἔρχεται ὁ λεγόμενος Χριστός
Messiah is coming (who is called Christ)

5:2: κολυμβήθρα ἡ ἐπιλεγομένη Ἑβραϊστὶ Βηθζαθὰ
a pool, called in Hebrew Bethzatha

6:1: πέραν τῆς θαλάσσης τῆς Γαλιλαίας τῆς Τιβεριάδος.
the other side of the Sea of Galilee, also called the Sea of Tiberias

9:7: τοῦ Σιλωάμ (ὃ ἑρμηνεύεται Ἀπεσταλμένος).
of Siloam (which means Sent)

11:16: Θωμᾶς ὁ λεγόμενος Δίδυμος
Thomas, who was called the Twin

19:13: εἰς τόπον λεγόμενον Λιθόστρωτον, Ἑβραϊστὶ δὲ Γαββαθα.
at a place called the Stone Pavement, or in Hebrew Gabbatha

19:17: εἰς τὸν λεγόμενον Κρανίου Τόπον, ὃ λέγεται Ἑβραϊστὶ Γολγοθα,
to what is called the Place of the Skull, which in Hebrew is called Golgotha

188                                    Chapter 5

20:16:       Ἑβραϊστί, ραββουνι, ὃ λέγεται Διδάσκαλε
             in Hebrew, "Rabbouni!" (which means Teacher)

20:24:       Θωμᾶς . . . ὁ λεγόμενος Δίδυμος
             Thomas (who was called the Twin)

21:2:        Θωμᾶς ὁ λεγόμενος Δίδυμος
             Thomas called the Twin

With the exception of 6:1, these are all marked with a distinctive lexical term,
a verb in the passive voice which indicates an alternative way of noting the
referent (a "translation"):

• λέγω: 1:38; 4:25; 11:16; 19:13, 17; 20:16, 24; 21:2

• μεθερμηνεύω: 1:38 (with λέγω); 1:41

• ἑρμηνεύω: 1:42; 9:7

• ἐπιλέγω: 5:2

The latter three terms are rare in the NT. The verb μεθερμηνεύω is also found
in Matthew 1:23; Mark 5:41; 15:22, 34; Acts 4:36; 13:8. The only other
occurrence of ἑρμηνεύω is in Hebrews 7:2 and of ἐπιλέγω in Acts 15:40,
where it is used in the middle voice with the meaning "choose."
     As far as grammatical/syntactical features are concerned, 6 of the 13 asides
are relative clauses using a form of the relative pronoun (1:38, 41, 42; 9:7; 19:17;
20:16); 5 are attributive participle phrases with the article (4:25; 5:2; 11:16; 20:24;
21:2); 2 are nouns (with the article) in apposition (6:1; 19:13).[157]
     At face value, most of these lexico-grammatically defined comments/asides
suggest that the author is providing a Greek equivalent for unfamiliar Hebrew
or Aramaic words (ραββί, Μεσσίας, Κηφᾶς, Σιλωάμ, Γαββαθα, Γολγοθα,
ραββουνι), with the implication that the intended audience, or at least some
part of it, would not know the meaning of these words in the (transliterated)
Hebrew/Aramaic. This was certainly the view of some earlier commentators.
Thus, Frédéric Godet, in his commentary on John (1899–1900), writes regarding the use of διδάσκαλε for ραββί in 1:38, "The translation of the name, added
by the evangelist, proves that the author writes for Greek readers."[158] Bernard
(1928), too, thinks that the author "translated it for the benefit of his Greek
readers, but preserved the original word."[159] This view has persisted into more
recent scholarship. Culpepper states, "The reader knows Greek and only Greek.
Such common terms as 'Rabbi' (1:38), 'Messiah' (1:41), and 'Rabbouni'

*Whose Comments* 189

(20:16) must be translated."[160] Lombard states, "The implied reader is unfamiliar with and stands outside the Jewish-Palestinian world. This can be observed in footnotes which translate Hebrew/Aramaic words and names into Greek."[161]

Other scholars are more nuanced in their understanding of John's readership. Westcott makes the observation re 1:38, 41, 42 that "the fresh recollection of the incident seems to bring back the original terms which had almost grown to be foreign words."[162] Tenney believes that the "translation asides," alongside other explanations of place and custom, indicate that whereas the author is familiar with Palestinian language and culture, some of his intended audience are not. He writes:

> These translation footnotes presuppose a bilingual environment for the writer of John. He stood halfway between the Aramaic-speaking group of Palestine and the Greek-speaking mission of the Gentile world. The footnotes locate the Gospel in a period of the transition from one to the other, written after the understanding of the Palestinian culture had diminished in the growing Gentile church, yet before the contacts with the eyewitnesses of Jesus had passed completely out of reach of first-century Christians.[163]

Bauckham, too, suggests, "the translations of the words 'Rabbi' and 'Messiah' (1:38, 41) are unlikely to have been needed by any Jewish reader/hearer, even in the diaspora, but their presence in the Gospel does not indicate that only Gentile readers/hearers are expected. They are included for the sake of those readers/hearers who may need them."[164]

Looking more closely at 1:38, the translation of ῥαββί into the Greek διδάσκαλε (with a vocative ending)[165] would at first glance seem to imply a writer who understands Jewish terminology but wishes also to communicate to a non-Jewish, or else a non-Hebrew- or non-Aramaic-speaking audience. The term ῥαββί is certainly used infrequently in the NT: four times in Matthew, three in Mark, none in Luke, and eight in John (mostly referring to Jesus, but also used of John the Baptist in 3:26).[166] The Aramaic equivalent, ραββουνι, is only found twice: in Mark 10:51 and John 20:16. So, it would seem sensible to provide a Greek equivalent for this Semitic word. However, we might reasonably ask why other Hebrew/Aramaic terms are not explained or translated. For example, why are ῥαββί/ραββουνι interpreted, but not συναγωγή (6:59; 18:20) or ἀποσυνάγωγος (9:22; 12:42; 16:2), a key Johannine term in the view of many commentators?[167] So, there may be other reasons why the author provides Greek equivalents in 1:38 and elsewhere. As Michaels remarks on 1:38:

> This is one of many authorial comments or narrative asides in this Gospel intended to help the reader understand what is going on. In this instance the comment implies that John's disciples are now Jesus'

190                                    *Chapter 5*

disciples because they consider him their "Teacher." It is the first of three such translations of Hebrew expressions in the immediate context (see vv. 41, 42). We cannot assume that the Greek-speaking readers of the Gospel actually needed the translations. Quite possibly the writer simply wants to accent his own credibility as someone familiar with Jewish terms and customs.[168]

Michaels's statement that the writer may have wanted to "accent his own credibility" could imply that he is "showing off" his erudition: he knows Jewish words, but he also knows their Greek equivalents. This reminds me of a conversation I had with someone about doing research on *glossolalia*, who immediately followed her use of the term with the explanation, "that means speaking in tongues." The implication being: this is information that I know and I want you to know that I know! However, I think this is unlikely for a writer who rarely indulges in self-projection into the narrative, and the idea of such "coquetterie d'érudit" is rejected by Loisy, who, commenting on the author's use of Semitic terms in 1:38, 41, 42, states:

> L'usage qu'il fait de termes sémitiques (1,38) ne prouve pas qu'il soit lui-même d'origine palestinienne, mais qu'il avait une certaine connaissance des choses juives et surtout qu'il attachait de l'importance aux noms en tant que symboles mystiques. C'est à raison de cette valeur mystique, et non par coquetterie d'érudit, que la forme sémitique des noms lui a paru bonne à garder.[169] (The use he makes of Semitic terms [1:38] does not prove that he himself is of Palestinian origin, but that he had a certain knowledge of Jewish matters and, above all, that he attached importance to names as mystical symbols. It is because of this mystical value, and not out of scholarly coquetry, that the Semitic form of names seemed to him worth keeping.)

I am not sure what Loisy means by "symboles mystiques" with reference to ῥαββί, Μεσσίας and Κηφᾶς, but ῥαββί and Μεσσίας are certainly significant titles for Jesus. Indeed, I would argue that these "translations" serve not only to emphasize the author's credibility, but also to highlight the fact that Jesus is "the teacher" and "the Christ." Indeed, regarding the former, "teacher" should be seen an interpretation rather than a translation of ῥαββί. As Thyen perceptively observes:

> Daß unser Erzähler der hebräischen Anrede „Rabbi" erläuternd hinzufügt: ὃ λέγεται μεθερμηνευόμενον διδάσκαλε, hat sicher nicht den vordergründigen Zweck, griechischen Lesern ein fremdes Lexem zu übersetzen. Vielmehr dient in nahezu allen literarischen Erzählungen die

*Whose Comments* 191

Einführung von Lexemen in der Muttersprache der handelnden Personen dem Gesetz des *Verisimile*. Zudem wird in unserem Fall der kurzen und schnell verklungenen Anrede ῥαββί durch ihr μεθερμηνεύειν zusätzliches Gewicht verliehen und klargestellt, daß es sich hier nicht um eine bloße Höflichkeitsfloskel, sondern um die respektvolle Anrede von hörbereiten *Schülern* handelt.[170] (That our narrator adds to the Hebrew form of address 'Rabbi' the explanatory: ὃ λέγεται μεθερμηνευόμενον διδάσκαλε, surely does not have the superficial purpose of translating for Greek readers an unknown word. Rather, in nearly all literary narratives, the introduction of words in the mother-tongue of the dramatis personae serves the rule of *verisimilitude*. Moreover, in our case, the short and quickly fading form of address ῥαββί is lent additional weight through its μεθερμηνεύειν and it is made clear that it is here not a matter of a polite empty phrase, but a respectful form of address from *disciples* ready to listen.)

So we have in 1:38 not so much a "translation" for Greek hearers/readers (although it does have that function too), but a significant comment on a central aspect of Jesus' ministry, his role as a teacher. As Brown states, "In John, the frequency of the terms 'rabbi' and 'teacher,' used by the disciples in addressing Jesus, seems to follow a deliberate plan: these terms appear almost exclusively in the Book of Signs, while in the Book of Glory the disciples address Jesus as '*kyrios* [lord].' In these forms of address John may be attempting to capture the growth of understanding on the disciples' part."[171]

In the case of Jesus as the Messiah/the Christ (1:41; 4:25), we need to note that John alone of the NT writers uses the (transliterated) Aramaic Μεσσίας and that he may be drawing together both the OT background for the Aramaic term and the early church's development of the Greek term as the principal title for Jesus.

The other observation that Thyen makes—namely, that the use of "words in the mother-tongue of the dramatis personae serves the rule of *verisimilitude*"—is echoed by a number of other commentors. Thus, Margaret Davies says, "Readers were interested in reading Hebrew and Aramaic words, which gives local colour to the narrative."[172] Similarly, McHugh states, "The use of 'Rabbi', together with the gloss that it means in translation 'Teacher', reveals a desire on the part of the writer to retain authentic local colour and at the same time to explain its meaning to readers unfamiliar with such terms."[173] This retention of "local colour" is perhaps particularly the case for the various place names that are given a Greek equivalent: Σιλωάμ (9:7), Γαββαθα (19:13), and Γολγοθα (19:17). The same applies to Βηθζαθά (5:2), which we are told is "in Aramaic/Hebrew" (Ἑβραϊστί) but is not "translated."[174] Culpepper states the presence of these "foreign words . . . adds credibility to the account."[175]

192                                    *Chapter 5*

However, as I have already stated, not all Hebrew and Aramaic terms are "translated." Some scholars see this as evidence of the process of composition, with the author using sources where (in some cases) such translations were already provided. For example, Lincoln states that John's "topographical note" in 19:17 (εἰς τὸν λεγόμενον Κρανίου Τόπον, ὃ λέγεται Ἑβραϊστὶ Γολγοθα) "is taken from the tradition."[176] Zumstein, too, believes that it derives from John's source, which here coincides with that in the Synoptic tradition.[177] Margaret Davies goes so far as to argue that the author did not know any Hebrew or Aramaic, so where these interpretations are provided, they are from the source material:

> The most likely explanation of the evidence is that the translation of only some of the Aramaic terms had been handed down in the tradition inherited by the Evangelist. In other words, the author did not know Hebrew or Aramaic but took up what tradition made available, in order to give colour and veracity to the narrative.[178]

Another explanation for why only some terms are "translated" is that the author has a diverse audience in mind. So, for example, Koester sees the fact that some Jewish words and practices are explained, while others are not, as one of the features of the Gospel implying a mixed audience of Jewish, Samaritan, and Greek background.[179] I am not sure how this works in practice. Does the author sometimes have one audience in mind and sometimes another? Sometimes translating/explaining, sometimes not? Moreover, even if a diverse audience is intended, I would argue that the comments on rabbi/teacher (1:38) and Messiah/Christ (4:25) have a deeper significance within the narrative. The same is true of the comments in 1:42 and 9:7:

1:42:          Κηφᾶς, ὃ ἑρμηνεύεται Πέτρος
               Cephas (which is translated Peter)

Schnackenburg states, "The translation of Κηφᾶς . . . is given, not just to mention the well-known name of Peter for the benefit of Greek readers, but to explain it."[180] However, in contrast to Matthew, John attaches no obvious significance to this new name for Simon. Whereas Matthew records Simon Peter's declaration of faith and Jesus' response, "You are Peter and on this rock I will build my church" (16:16–18), John "shows no interest in the wordplay" (Michaels).[181] Lincoln suggests that "the change of name to Cephas (Aramaic) or Peter (Greek) with its meaning of 'rock', signals the leadership role Simon will have in the church," even though "that significance is not developed and the name change functions more as a way of underlining Jesus' foreknowledge of Simon's later role."[182] Zumstein also sees a proleptic function in the name Cephas and its translation at this point in the narrative:

> La traduction de « Céphas » en « Pierre » est porteuse de sens : elle renvoie à l'identité ecclésiale de Pierre et dit par avance sa fonction de fondement (jeu de mots entre le nom propre et le nom commun « pierre » !). Le narrateur trace ici un portrait « proleptique » de Pierre.[183] (The translation of Cephas to Peter is meaningful: it reflects the ecclesiastical identity of Peter and states in advance his foundational function (a play on the proper name and the common name "rock"!). The narrator paints here a "proleptic" portrait of Peter.)

Brant comments that, in contrast to Matthew, "John does not make Jesus's purpose clear" in the giving of the new name, "but the silence at this point may be a narrative strategy to generate suspense rather than polemic against Simon Peter's role as a leader."[184] I think she goes too far in her suggestion that "the nickname Cephas (Aramaic for *rock*) seems to signify intransigence or thickheadedness more than a firm foundation; this Gospel never identifies Peter as the central leader of the church."[185]

9:7:      τοῦ Σιλωάμ (ὃ ἑρμηνεύεται Ἀπεσταλμένος)
          of Siloam (which means Sent)

As a "translation" of Siloam, "sent" is something of a puzzle.[186] The "waters of Shiloah" (מֵי הַשִּׁלֹחַ) are mentioned in Isaiah 8:6 and translated in the LXX as τὸ ὕδωρ τοῦ Σιλωαμ and the Hebrew שָׁלַח would seem to be related to the root שׁלח (meaning "to send").[187] However, as Brown point out, "'Shiloah' is not a passive participial form, as would be required by John's etymology," so "the evangelist is either following a different reading of the consonants . . . or exercising liberty in adapting the etymology to his purposes."[188] Keener draws attention to the "wordplay" aspect of John's association of "Siloam" with "sent": "John either revocalizes and modifies the term or adapts the etymology freely. The matter is less the nature of 'Siloam's' original etymology than the function of the wordplay in this context."[189] Indeed, as Michaels points out, "The etymology of the name (whatever its origin and whatever its merits) is not strictly necessary to the story, but for that very reason is important to the author—and consequently to the reader."[190] This is not an irrelevant aside, but a comment that is intended to convey significant information from author to reader. Michaels traces the concept of being "sent" in the Gospel as it applies to Jesus, the disciples, the Spirit, and John the Baptist and concludes that here the waters of Siloam should be understood as being sent "from

194 *Chapter 5*

heaven" or "from God."[191] Zumstein also draws attention to the link between Jesus as the sent one and the name of the place of healing: "Pour le lecteur de l'évangile, l'effet de sens est clair : le lieu de la guérison est mis en relation avec le christologie de l'envoyé."[192] (For the reader of the Gospel, the effect of the meaning is clear: the place of the healing is related to the christology of the sender.) Similarly, Lincoln states:

> [The narrator's] translation of the Hebrew name of the pool into a Greek equivalent indicates that he considers its derivation significant. He expects readers to make a connection with his distinctive characterization of Jesus in terms of the one who is "sent" as the Father's uniquely authorized agent, and they have just been reminded of this formulation in v. 4—"We must work the works of *him who sent me.*" Through this play on etymology the point is underlined that the man's enlightenment comes both via a source that means "sent" and ultimately from a source who is the sent one par excellence, sent to carry out the life-giving works of God.[193]

So, in the case of both 1:42 and 9:7, the author is highlighting the significance of particular words in relation to the narrative's overall purpose, rather than providing translations for an audience who did not understand Aramaic or Hebrew terms. This, as we have seen, is also the case for the other so-called "translation" asides/comments in 1:38, 41; 4:25; and 20:16, whereas the asides/comments in 5:2; 19:13 and 17 may serve to "to retain authentic local colour" (McHugh). As far as the other "translation" asides/comments are concerned, I have suggested in my annotated list that the comment in 6:1 ("also called the Sea of Tiberias" ) is an example of providing an alternative name rather than a translation. Similarly, the three references to Thomas as Δίδυμος (the Twin) (11:16; 20:24; 21:2) are not so much translations ("Thomas" was not an Aramaic or Hebrew name) as the use of a "label" to clarify which disciple is being referred to.[194] Thomas may have been a Greek name that was adopted for Semitic use.[195]

Overall, I conclude that the category of "translation" comments/asides is something of a misnomer and that while some of the comments provide "local colour" and thus a degree of verisimilitude, others are used to highlight the significance of terms in relation to the Gospel's overall purpose—that is, they have a christological function: Jesus is the teacher (1:38; 20:16), the Christ (4:25), the sent one (9:7). In terms of the author-reader dynamic, these comments do not necessarily imply either a solely Greek-speaking readership or for that matter a diverse audience (although this seems more likely), but they do support the credibility and authority of the author in relation to the intended audience. This is an author who knows particular terms and their significance. In short, an author who is reliable.

## CONCLUSIONS

Study of the narrative comments in the Gospel of John over the past 40 years (using Culpepper's *Anatomy* as a marker) has been particularly influenced by modern literary criticism and the growing impact of narrative criticism in NT studies. This influence has not been universally welcomed, and I think we do well to heed the warnings of Stibbe and others about the risks of applying methodologies that have been developed primarily in the study of the modern novel. So, the various understandings of the narrator, in particular the concepts of the *omniscient narrator* and the *unreliable narrator* have to be treated with caution. I have, for example, noted the questioning of the concept of *omniscience* by some recent literary critics. Wiese's category of "superior knowledge" seems to me a more helpful one and it fits with the post-resurrection point of view (or perspective) of the writer of the Gospel, looking back on the events of Jesus' life after time to reflect on their meaning. This is not necessarily supernatural knowledge, though the writer may well claim to be inspired by the Spirit of truth—as a linking of 15:26 and 21:24 suggest, whoever's *voice* (narrator or author?) is being referred to.

Whatever its source, human and/or divine, it is this "superior knowledge" that the writer wishes the hearer/reader to share and which leads to instances of dramatic irony, such as the comments in 2:21, 11:13, and 20:9, which rather than having the comic function that is sometimes associated with dramatic irony, introduce perhaps a note of pathos as they seek to guide the hearer/reader to a deeper insight, while acknowledging the lack of comprehension of those involved in the events.

Regarding the categories of *intrusiveness* and *reliability*, I conclude that the narrator in John is not overly intrusive when compared with examples from the Victorian novel or even the Prologue to Luke's Gospel. There is little "self-conscious narration," with 21:24–25 being the only clear instance. However, the narrator is presented as reliable and authoritative through the various comments, including the so-called "translation asides." I see this reliability as derived from the post-resurrection perspective, as well as the belief in the guidance of the Spirit of truth.

In fact, while I admit that I have spent a large part of this chapter interacting with those who have focussed on the narrator in John, I am not ultimately convinced that we can distinguish between the author and the narrator. If we adopt a purely narratological approach, then we restrict the narrative to a closed world removed from any historical context. Or as Bennema puts it: "a fictional narrative that is disconnected from reality."[196] Indeed, what I have concluded about the nature of a proposed narrator in terms of omniscience, intrusiveness, reliability, and point of view apply equally to an author of the Gospel, even though we do not know who that

196                                   *Chapter 5*

author was. For that reason, although I have chosen to use the term "narrative comments" rather than "authorial comments," I reject the term "narrator's comments."

I think it is important to give attention to how the narrative comments are used in the relationship between the author and intended readers of texts. In this respect I have drawn attention to those working with the methodology of *evaluation* or *appraisal* within linguistics and have drawn comparisons with the analysis of point of view. In particular, I refer to the work of the linguist Ken Rylands on *metadiscourse* and argue that despite the paucity of overt author-reader comments in the Gospel (namely 1:16–18; 19:35–37; 20:30–31; 21:23–25), we can nevertheless see these comments as indicating a definite author-reader dynamic in which the author is resolved to guide the reader to a particular understanding of Jesus as "the Messiah, the Son of God" (20:31). This is done partly through the use of *internal* comments—that is, analepsis and prolepsis—which enable the author to keep a tight hold on the overall structure of the narrative. It is done even more so through the use of *external* comments (*temporal* and/or *spatial*), by which the author conveys a credible and authoritative perspective to a possibly diverse intended readership. So, for example, I have suggested that the "translation asides/comments" do not imply a readership which cannot understand particular Hebrew or Aramaic terms, but rather they support the credibility and authority of the author in relation to the Gospel's intended audience. In the final chapter, I make some comparison of the use of narrative comments in John with that in the Synoptic Gospels and I suggest reasons why there are more such comments in John. For now, I make the tentative suggestion that the author "John" may have been aware that his Gospel is different from the increasing popular and well-circulated Synoptics and, therefore, possibly open to challenge. The greater number of narrative comments may reflect a concern to be understood and accepted.

Returning to the question posed by the title of this chapter, "Whose Comments?" and reflecting on the various literary and linguistic analyses of the relationship between the narrative comments and the narrator and/or author, alongside the vexed question of who the author might be (the Apostle, the Beloved Disciple, the Elder?), I conclude that they are the work of a real "flesh and blood" author who, although not omniscient, is nevertheless knowledgeable, reflective, inspired, and passionately committed to a particular understanding of Jesus, with a determination that hearers/readers will share this understanding. The overall function of the narrative comments is to guide into the truth as the author sees it, following the words of Jesus recounted in 16:13: "When the Spirit of truth comes, he will guide you into all the truth."

*Whose Comments* 197

## NOTES

1. Brant, *Gospel*, 5.
2. Mark W. G. Stibbe, *John as Storyteller: Narrative Criticism and the Fourth Gospel* (Cambridge: Cambridge University Press, 1992), 6; cf. Mark Allan Powell, *What Is Narrative Criticism?* (Minneapolis: Fortress Press, 1990), 4. See Eric Auerbach, *Mimesis: The Representation of Reality in Western Literature* (Princeton: Princeton University Press, 1953), 40–49. Elizabeth Shively also cites as an earlier "seminal" work the form-critical approach of Herman Gunkel, *The Legend of Genesis* (1901). See Elizabeth E. Shively, "Literary Approaches," in *Cambridge Companion to the New Testament*, ed. S. B. Chapman and M. A. Sweeney (Cambridge: Cambridge University Press, 2021), 369. Shively attributes the coining of the phrase "narrative criticism" to David Rhoads in his work on the Gospel of Mark (371); cf. Powell, *Narrative Criticism*, 6; James L. Resseguie, *Narrative Criticism of the New Testament: An Introduction* (Grand Rapids: Baker Academic, 2005), 18n4. Resseguie notes that the term is not used by "secular modern literary critics and theorists" (18n4).
3. Stibbe, *John as Storyteller*, 5–9.
4. Olsson, *Structure and Meaning*, 92.
5. Olsson, *Structure and Meaning*, 93.
6. Olsson, *Structure and Meaning*, 92.
7. Olsson, *Structure and Meaning*, 94.
8. Culpepper, *Anatomy*, 6, 53. See Chatman, *Story and Discourse*, 147–51, 267; Gérard Genette, *Narrative Discourse*, trans. Jane E. Lewin (Oxford: Basil Blackwell, 1980), 189–211.
9. Culpepper, *Anatomy*, 17.
10. Culpepper, *Anatomy*, 20–21. See Boris Uspensky, *A Poetics of Composition: The Structure of the Artistic Text and Typology of a Compositional Form*, trans. Valentina Zavarin and Susan Wittig (Berkeley: University of California Press, 1973), 8–100.
11. Culpepper, *Anatomy*, 21–34. He does not explicitly make use of Uspensky's phraseological plane, although his discussion of the "historic presents" in John (30–32) could fit into this category.
12. Culpepper, *Anatomy*, 33.
13. Culpepper, *Anatomy*, 22–25.
14. Lombard, "John's Gospel," 398.
15. Hedrick, "Authorial Presence," 76.
16. Hedrick, "Authorial Presence," 93. Sheeley criticizes Hedrick for assuming that "intrusion equals correction" and for his over-reliance on what he regards as Wayne Booth's somewhat confused distinction between the implied author and the narrator (*Narrative Asides*, 23n2).
17. Thatcher, "New Look at Asides," 430.
18. Sheeley, *Narrative Asides*, 31–39.
19. Sheeley, *Narrative Asides*, 32–34.

198       *Chapter 5*

20. Wead, *Literary Devices*, rev. ed., 1–14. See Percy Lubbock, *The Craft of Fiction* (New York: Charles Scribner's Sons, 1921); Francis X. Connolly, *A Rhetoric Case Book* (New York: Harcourt, Brace & Co., 1953).

21. Wead, *Literary Devices*, rev. ed., 1.

22. Wead, *Literary Devices*, rev. ed., 2.

23. Wead, *Literary Devices*, rev. ed., 3–11.

24. Wead, *Literary Devices*, rev. ed., 4–5. Olsson is critical of Wead's differentiation between John and the Synoptics, stating, "All the Gospels were written in the light of the resurrection and the existence of the Church" (*Structure and Meaning*, 93).

25. Wead, *Literary Devices*, rev. ed., 5.

26. Wead, *Literary Devices*, rev. ed., 6–7.

27. Wead, *Literary Devices*, rev. ed., 5–8.

28. Wead, *Literary Devices*, rev. ed., 11.

29. Wead, *Literary Devices*, rev. ed., 59–88.

30. Wead, *Literary Devices*, rev. ed., 67.

31. Wead, *Literary Devices*, rev. ed., 67.

32. Wead, *Literary Devices*, rev. ed., 122–28.

33. Staley, *Print's First Kiss*, 8, 10–15.

34. Staley, *Print's First Kiss*, 13.

35. As Chatman states, "That it is essential not to confuse author and narrator has become a commonplace of literary theory" (*Story and Discourse*, 147).

36. Staley, *Print's First Kiss*, 38–39, 41.

37. Staley, *Print's First Kiss*, 41.

38. Staley, *Print's First Kiss*, 95–96.

39. Staley, *Print's First Kiss*, 97.

40. Staley, *Print's First Kiss*, 98.

41. Stibbe, *John as Storyteller*, 9–12.

42. Stibbe, *John as Storyteller*, 67.

43. Stibbe, *John as Storyteller*, 16.

44. Stibbe, *John as Storyteller*, 20.

45. Stibbe, *John as Storyteller*, 20.

46. Stibbe, *John as Storyteller*, 28.

47. Resseguie, *Narrative Criticism*; Resseguie, "Glossary," 1–39; James L. Resseguie, *The Strange Gospel: Narrative Design and Point of View in John*, BibInt 56 (Leiden: Brill, 2001).

48. Resseguie, *Strange Gospel*, 1.

49. Resseguie, *Strange Gospel*, 2–4. He also draws on the work of Lanser, who distinguishes between "standpoint," which she defines as "an 'objective' position, the subject's relation to some external reality" and "attitude," which "denotes some 'subjective' response or evaluation of that reality." See Susan Sniader Lanser, *The Narrative Act: Point of View in Prose Fiction* (Princeton: Princeton University Press, 1981), 16.

50. Resseguie, *Strange Gospel*, 4.

51. Resseguie, *Strange Gospel*, 8.

52. I note that elsewhere Resseguie refers to 2:22, "After he was raised from the dead, his disciples remembered that he had said this; and they believed the scripture

*Whose Comments* 199

and the word that Jesus had spoken," as an example of Uspensky's *spatial* point of view, whereby "the spatial position of the narrator is as an omniscient and intrusive presence that corrects the misperception of the hearers" ("Glossary," 22). This dual categorization of *temporal* and *spatial* for 2:22 corresponds to that in my own list of comments.

53. Resseguie, *Strange Gospel*, 201.

54. Resseguie, *Strange Gospel*, 201.

55. Resseguie, *Strange Gospel*, 21–22.

56. Resseguie, *Strange Gospel*, 15.

57. Resseguie, *Strange Gospel*, 15.

58. Resseguie, *Strange Gospel*, 15.

59. Brant, *Dialogue and Drama*, 202–8.

60. Brant, *Dialogue and Drama*, 202.

61. Brant, *Dialogue and Drama*, 205.

62. Brant, *Dialogue and Drama*, 202.

63. Brant, *Dialogue and Drama*, 202.

64. Brant, "Fourth Gospel," 190.

65. Brant, "Fourth Gospel," 189, 190.

66. Culpepper, *Anatomy*, 21, 26.

67. Resseguie, *Strange Gospel*, 21.

68. Gérard Genette, *Narrative Discourse Revisited*, trans. Jane E. Lewin (Ithaca, NY: Cornell University Press, 1988), 130.

69. Van Belle, *Les Parenthèses*, 112; Köstenberger, *Theology*, 137. Köstenberger also includes "God's providential ordering of events" in this category.

70. I have omitted (from Köstenberger's list) 7:30 and 8:20, as they would seem to belong to the category of "God's providential ordering of events."

71. Culpepper, *Anatomy*, 22.

72. Culpepper, *Anatomy*, 22.

73. Culpepper, *Anatomy*, 21.

74. Westcott, *Gospel*, 1:212. See 1:xxxix for Westcott's belief that the author was an eyewitness of what he describes.

75. Jonathan D. Culler, "Omniscience," *Narrative* 12, no. 1 (2004): 23.

76. Culler, "Omniscience," 28.

77. Culler, "Omniscience," 37.

78. Annjeanette Wiese, "Replacing Omniscience: Superior Knowledge and Narratorial Access," *Narrative*, 29, no. 3 (2021), 321–38.

79. Wiese, "Replacing Omniscience," 322.

80. Wiese, "Replacing Omniscience," 322.

81. Wiese, "Replacing Omniscience," 326.

82. Resseguie, *Strange Gospel*, 21, 22.

83. Resseguie, *Strange Gospel*, 23.

84. Resseguie, *Strange Gospel*, 23.

85. Culpepper, *Anatomy*, 43. Elsewhere, Culpepper asserts regarding 19:35 that it is "virtually indisputable that the passage is referring to the Beloved Disciple" (*John*, 65).

86. Culpepper, *Anatomy*, 47.

200                                    Chapter 5

87. Culpepper, *Anatomy*, 48. A further example of equating the narrator and the Beloved Disciple is that of Cynthia Westfall, who suggests that "in the Gospel of John, the narrator is the 'beloved disciple,' and the implied narrator John," where the "implied narrator" is her term for "the perspective from which the text is written." Cynthia Long Westfall, "Narrative Criticism," in *Dictionary of Biblical Criticism and Interpretation*, ed. Stanley E. Porter (London: Routledge, 2007), 238. I am not sure that it is helpful to bring yet another category, "the implied narrator," into the discussion.

88. Culpepper, *Anatomy*, 7.

89. Culpepper, *Anatomy*, 16–17.

90. Resseguie, *Strange Gospel*, 15.

91. Resseguie, *Strange Gospel*, 15.

92. Sheeley, *Narrative Asides*, 36; cf. 177.

93. William Thackeray, *Vanity Fair*, ed. J. I. M. Stewart (London: Penguin, 1968), 87–88. For a helpful study of the narrator in *Vanity Fair*, see Harriet Blodgett, "The Rhetoric of the Narrator in Vanity Fair," *Nineteenth-Century Fiction* 22, no. 3 (1967): 211–23.

94. Richardson, *Homeric Narrator*, 169. He is drawing on Chatman, who writes, "It is less important to categorize types of narrators than to identify the features that mark their degrees of audibility" (*Story and Discourse*, 196).

95. Richardson, *Homeric Narrator*, 170.

96. Michaels, *Gospel*, 1056.

97. Van Belle, *Les Parenthèses*, 263, 75.

98. Zumstein, *L'Évangile*, 1:212; cf. Theobald, *Das Evangelium*, 433.

99. Theobald, *Das Evangelium*, 433; cf. Schnackenburg, *Gospel*, 2:16.

100. Carson, *Gospel*, 270. Michaels writes, "Grass need not have been mentioned, yet it seems to have been part of the story from the start, perhaps already in oral tradition" (*Gospel*, 347). Bultmann believes that the details given in 6:10 serve "to raise the tension here" (*Gospel*, 213). In other words, they have a narrative function.

101. Genette, *Narrative Discourse*, 163–64.

102. Boomershine, "Medium and Message," 101.

103. Shlomith Rimmon-Kenan, *Narrative Fiction: Contemporary Poetics*, 2nd ed. (New York: Routledge, 2002), 111.

104. Dan Shen, "Defense and Challenge: Reflections on the Relation between Story and Discourse," *Narrative* 10, no. 3 (2002): 241.

105. Just as in the popular TV series *Morecombe and Wise* (BBC, 1968–77; ITV 1978–83), Eric Morecombe would put his hand to the side of his mouth, turn to the camera, and say, "This boy's a fool!"—intended for the audience not his dialogue partner. A similar turn to the audience can be found in the programmes of Miranda Hart (influenced by Eric Morecombe). A more "highbrow" example is Puck's address to the audience at the end of Shakespeare's *Midsummer Night's Dream* (Act 5, Scene 1, lines 440–55).

106. Stibbe traces studies on the "dramatic qualities of John" back to an essay published by Hitchcock in 1923 (*John as Storyteller*, 9). See F. R. M. Hitchcock, "Is the Fourth Gospel a Drama?" *Theology* 7 (1923): 307–17; repr. in *The Gospel of John as*

*Literature: An Anthology of Twentieth Century Perspectives*, ed. Mark W. G. Stibbe, 15–24. NTTSD 17 (Leiden: Brill, 1993).

107. Brant, *John*, 210.

108. Lincoln, *Gospel*, 320.

109. Jo-Ann A. Brant, "John among the Ancient Novels," in *The Gospel of John as Genre Mosaic*, ed. Kasper Bro Larsen, Studia Aarhusiana Neotestamentica 3 (Göttingen: Vandenhoeck & Ruprecht, 2015), 161.

110. George W. MacRae, "Theology and Irony in the Fourth Gospel," in *The Gospel of John as Literature: An Anthology of Twentieth Century Perspectives*, ed. Mark W. G. Stibbe, NTTSD 17 (Leiden: Brill, 1993), 107. Originally published in *The Word in the World: Essays in Honour of F.L. Moriarty*, ed. R. J. Clifford and G. W. MacRae (Cambridge, MA: Weston College, 1973), 83–96.

111. Lincoln, *Gospel*, 321.

112. Wengst, *Das Johannesevangelium*, 2:25.

113. Culpepper, *Anatomy*, 9.

114. Staley, *Print's First Kiss*, 27.

115. Resseguie, "Glossary," 17.

116. Resseguie, *Narrative Criticism*, 132n35.

117. Robert Scholes and Robert Kellogg, *The Nature of Narrative* (New York: Oxford University Press, 1966), 264.

118. Erik Gunderson, *Laughing Awry: Plautus and Tragicomedy* (Oxford: Oxford University Press, 2015), 75.

119. Hedrick, "Authorial Presence," 93.

120. Staley, *Print's First Kiss*, 41.

121. Francis J. Moloney, "Who Is the Reader in/of the Fourth Gospel?" in *The Interpretation of John*, ed. John Ashton, 2nd ed. (Edinburgh: T & T Clark, 1997), 221; repr. from *Australian Biblical Review* 40 (1992): 20–33. Moloney is critical of Staley's "over-subtle introduction of an implied author who plays tricks with the implied reader" (231n16).

122. Richardson, *Homeric Narrator*, 198.

123. Burge, *Interpreting*, 93.

124. Resseguie, *Narrative Criticism*, 169.

125. Stibbe suggests that Auerbach's *Mimesis* may be partly responsible for the influence of the "novel-based model" on interpreting the gospel narratives (*John as Storyteller*, 11).

126. Brant, "John among the Ancient Novels," 158.

127. Culpepper, *Anatomy*, 9.

128. Stibbe, *John as Storyteller*, 11.

129. We also need to note that literary theory has also moved on, with a shift to reader-response theory and the growing influence of feminist, postcolonial, and gender approaches. To some extent, neither the narrator nor the author is seen as that important for understanding the Gospel of John.

130. Cornelis Bennema, "A Comprehensive Approach to Understanding Character in the Gospel of John," in *Characters and Characterization in the Gospel of John*, ed. Christopher W. Skinner, LNTS 461 (London: Bloomsbury T & T Clark, 2013), 45.

202                                Chapter 5

131. Hayden White, *The Content of Form: Narrative Discourse and Historical Representation* (Baltimore: John Hopkins University Press, 1987), 1.

132. White, *Content of Form*, 14.

133. Booth, *Rhetoric*, 71, 73.

134. Booth, *Rhetoric*, 73.

135. Staley, *Print's First Kiss*, 27.

136. Ansgar Nünning, "Implied Author," in *Routledge Encyclopedia of Narrative Theory*, ed. David Herman, Manfred Jahn, and Marie-Laure Ryan (New York: Routledge, 2005), 240.

137. Resseguie, "Glossary," 17. He does, however, note that Malbon "argues that the implied author is an identifiable party from the narrator, and the narratee is separate from the implied reader" (17). See Elizabeth Struthers Malbon, "Narrative Criticism: How Does the Story Mean?" in *Mark & Method: New Approaches in Biblical Studies*, ed. Janice Capel Anderson and Stephen D. Moore, 2nd ed. (Minneapolis: Fortress Press, 2008), 33; Elizabeth Struthers Malbon, "Characters in Mark's Story: Changing Perspectives on the Narrative Process," in *Mark as Story: Retrospect and Prospect*, ed. Kelly R. Iverson and Christopher W. Skinner, SBLRBS 65 (Atlanta: Society of Biblical Literature, 2011), 68.

138. Culpepper, *Anatomy*, 7.

139. "Roland Barthes and Michel Foucault have each written epitaphs—words on the tomb—for the author. According to Barthes, the author is a modern invention, the product of an individualism that accompanied Enlightenment rationalism and Reformation piety"; "Foucault is interested primarily in how the concept of an author *functions*. The idea of an author functions as a unifying principle that allows one to group certain texts together and treat them as though they constituted a coherent group." Kevin J. Vanhoozer, *Is There a Meaning in This Text? The Bible, the Reader and the Morality of Literary Knowledge* (Grand Rapids: IVP/Apollos, 1998), 69, 70. Vanhoozer references Roland Barthes, "The Death of the Author" (1977) and Michel Foucault, "What Is an Author?" (1980).

140. Shively, "Literary Approaches," 375.

141. Staley, *Print's First Kiss*, 23.

142. Geoff Thompson and Susan Hunston, "Evaluation: An Introduction," in *Evaluation in Text: Authorial Stance and the Construction of Discourse*, ed. Susan Hunston and Geoff Thompson (Oxford: Oxford University Press, 2000), 5.

143. See Martin Cortazzi and Lixian Jin, "Evaluating Evaluation in Narrative," in *Evaluation in Text: Authorial Stance and the Construction of Discourse*, ed. Susan Hunston and Geoff Thompson (Oxford: Oxford University Press, 2000), 103–4.

144. Resseguie, *Strange Gospel*, 1.

145. Resseguie, *Strange Gospel*, 4. See Uspensky, *Poetics*, 8. Uspensky himself describes this point of view as "ideological or evaluative."

146. See, for example, David A. Lamb and Thora Tenbrink, "Evaluating Jesus and other 'heroes': An application of appraisal analysis to Hellenistic Greek texts in the 'Lives' genre," *Language, Context and Text* 4, no. 2 (2022): 227–58. This compares the Gospel of John with two other roughly contemporaneous "biographies," Plutarch's Life of Cato the Younger and Lucius of Samosata's *Life of Demonax*, employing

*Whose Comments* 203

a methodology based on Martin and White's *The Language of Evaluation*. Lamb and Tenbrink conclude that there are notable differences in the way the central characters of these three texts are evaluated. Martin and White's functional linguistic approach has been widely adopted in evaluation/appraisal studies. See James R. Martin and Peter R. R. White, *The Language of Evaluation: Appraisal in English* (Basingstoke: Palgrave Macmillan, 2005).

147. Ken Hyland, *Metadiscourse: Exploring Interaction in Writing*, 2nd ed. (London: Bloomsbury Academic, 2019), 3–4.

148. Hyland, *Metadiscourse*, 43–44.

149. There is a parallel here to the categories of the *ideational, interpersonal*, and *textual metafunctions* in Hallidayan systemic functional linguistics (SFL), as Hyland acknowledges (*Metadiscourse*, 30–31). However, as Hyland notes, "While Halliday's terminology lends a certain theoretical respectability to the idea of metadiscourse, the concept plays no part in his thinking" (31). I have elsewhere drawn on SFL and other methodologies to examine some of the narrative asides in John "where the author appears to be directly addressing the readers and where the act of writing is consciously highlighted" (Lamb, *Text, Context*, 159). The asides I analyse are 2:21–22; 12:16; 19:35–37; 20:30–31; 21:23–25 (159–71).

150. Hyland, *Metadiscourse*, 57–58. Hyland has adapted this distinction from Geoff Thompson and Puleng Thetela, "The Sound of One Hand Clapping: The Management of Interaction in Writing Discourse," *Text* 15, no. 1 (1995): 103–27.

151. Adapted from Hyland, *Metadiscourse*, 58.

152. Ken Hyland, "Stance and Engagement: A Model of Interaction in Academic Discourse," *Discourse Studies* 7, no. 2 (2005): 182.

153. Hyland, "Stance and Engagement," 183.

154. See Lamb, *Text, Context*, 171.

155. North, *Journey Round John*, 149.

156. O'Rourke, "Asides," 206.

157. In the "participle phrases," the participle is being used in an attributive sense, which normally occurs with the article.

158. Frédéric Louis Godet, *Commentary on the Gospel of St. John with a Critical Introduction*, trans. M. D. Cusin, 3rd ed., 3 vols. (Edinburgh: T & T Clark, 1899–1900), 1:441.

159. Bernard, *Gospel*, 1:56.

160. Culpepper, *Anatomy*, 218; cf. Lindars, *Gospel*, 113; Carson, *Gospel*, 155; Wengst, *Das Johannesevangelium*, 1:95n36.

161. Lombard, "John's Gospel," 406.

162. Westcott, *Gospel*, 1:48.

163. Tenney, "Footnotes," 352–53.

164. Bauckham, "John for Readers of Mark," 150.

165. ῥαββί is indeclinable. The vocative διδάσκαλε is also used in 20:16 to "translate" the Aramaic term ραββουνι, but in 1:41 the nominative Χριστός is used for the accusative τὸν Μεσσίαν. I do not know why this is.

166. Mt. 23:7, 8; 26:25, 49; Mk. 9:5; 11:21; 14:45; Jn. 1:38, 49; 3:2, 26 (of John the Baptist); 4:31; 6:25; 9:2; 11:8.

204                                   *Chapter 5*

167. It is worth noting that συναγωγή is only used twice in John, whereas it occurs much more frequently in the Synoptics (Matthew: 9 times; Mark: 8 times; Luke: 15 times).

168. Michaels, *Gospel of John*, 119–20.

169. Alfred Loisy, *Le quatriéme Évangile. Les épitres dites de Jean*. 2nd ed. (Paris: Émile Nourry, 1921), 130.

170. Thyen, *Das Johannesevangelium*, 130.

171. Brown, (*Gospel*, 1:75).

172. Margaret Davies, *Rhetoric and Reference*, 368; cf. 273, 275.

173. McHugh, *John 1–4*, 150–51. He cites the "new Schürer" for evidence that "the use of 'Rabbi' as a title seems to have originated around the life-time of Jesus. Thus to address Jesus as 'Rabbi' is to accord him the highest status as a teacher of Israel." The reference is to Emil Schürer, *The History of the Jewish People in the Age of Jesus Christ*, rev. and ed. Geza Vermes et al., 4 vols. (Edinburgh: T & T Clark, 1973–1987), 2:326.

174. There is considerable textual uncertainty concerning the reading Βηθζαθά in 5:2. See Metzger, *Textual Commentary*, 178–79; Comfort, *Commentary*, 254.

175. Culpepper, *Anatomy*, 219.

176. Lincoln, *Gospel*, 474.

177. Zumstein, *L'Évangile*, 1:242n6. However, I note that Mark (15:22) uses μεθερμηνεύω rather than λέγω. Matthew (27:33) does use λέγω. Luke (23:33) only provides the Greek name.

178. Davies, *Rhetoric and Reference*, 273; cf. 368–69.

179. Koester, *Symbolism in the Fourth Gospel*, 18–23.

180. Schnackenburg, *Gospel*, 1:311–12.

181. Michaels, *Gospel*, 124n29.

182. Lincoln, *Gospel*, 119.

183. Zumstein, *L'Évangile*, 1:88.

184. Brant, *John*, 52.

185. Brant, *John*, 52.

186. The only other NT occurrence of "Siloam" is in Lk. 13:4, where it refers to "the tower of Siloam" and is not "translated."

187. Bultmann thinks it possible that the Evangelist may have had Is. 8:6 in mind with regard to "the Jews' unbelief" in this section of the narrative (*Gospel*, 333n4).

188. Brown, *Gospel*, 1:373.

189. Keener, *Gospel*, 1:782.

190. Michaels, *Gospel*, 547.

191. Michaels, *Gospel*, 547.

192. Zumstein, *L'Évangile*, 1:319.

193. Lincoln, *Gospel*, 281–82.

194. The label ο λεγομενος Διδυμος is also a variant reading in 14:5 in the fifth-century Codex Bezae (D).

195. Brown, *Gospel*, 1:424; Michaels, *Gospel*, 623n42.

196. Bennema, "Character," 45.

*Chapter 6*

# Towards a Comparative Study

Writing about the genre of the canonical Gospels, David Aune gives this warning: "There are many perils in any comparative enterprise: what do we compare with what and how do we go about making the comparison?"[1]

In my survey of literature in chapter 1, I discussed two authors who compare the use of parentheses in the NT writings with other roughly contemporaneous literature. Bjerkelund refers to parallels to his Johannine *Präzierungssätze* in the first-century Greek writings of Philo and Josephus as well as (more problematically, I suggest) some of the Hebrew/Aramaic Samaritan literature, which is harder to date.[2] Sheeley compares the asides in Luke/Acts with a selection of Graeco-Roman romances, histories, and biographies from the period 100 BC/BCE to AD/CE 250.[3] I also noted Hedrick's remark that "explanatory 'asides' are a common narrative feature in ancient Greek and Roman novels and historical narrative" and Bauckham's assertion that parentheses comparable to those used in John "are common in Greco-Roman historiography and biography."[4] Similarly, Keener, in a section on "Greco-Roman Biography and History" in the introduction to his commentary on the Gospel of John, states, "Historians frequently included moralizing narrative asides to interpret history's meaning for their readers, illustrate the fulfillment of prophetic utterances, or provide the author's perspective."[5]

In fact, despite Richard Bauckham's observation, which I noted in chapter 1, that there has been very little comparison of the functions of narrative asides in John with those in other ancient narrative literature, I remain hesitant about comparing their use in John with that in extrabiblical Greek and Roman literature, simply because we lack evidence of any direct dependence on such writings.[6] As Larry Hurtado notes in a comparison of the NT writers'

206                                  *Chapter 6*

use of biblical (OT) and extracanonical Jewish texts with their use of classical literature:

> It is really striking that the NT authors so clearly align themselves with the
> biblical/Jewish literary traditions, and make so little effort to draw con-
> sciously on and to cite the larger literary world of their time. Clearly, they
> were either unable to do so, or uninterested in justifying and articulating their
> intended messages with reference to the literature of classical antiquity.[7]

Likewise, Austin Busch, even though he seeks to make a number of literary
connections between NT and Graeco-Roman narratives, acknowledges that
"New Testament writers treat Old Testament literature with extraordinary
esteem," but "show much less deference toward classical Greek literature."[8]
To be sure, there have been comparative studies of the Gospels with contemporary (non-Jewish) Greek and Roman literature, particularly in relation to
genre, but we cannot be sure of the wider (extrabiblical) milieu in which the
Gospels were composed and it may have little resemblance to reconstruc-
tions based on the those texts of classical literature that have survived.[9] So,
even if we examine the use of narrative comments in other historiographical
and biographical works with the Gospel of John, this does not imply that the
author purposely followed widely accepted practice.[10]

   Moreover, to provide a comprehensive study of narrative comments in
literature that either predates or is contemporary with the Gospel of John lies
beyond the scope of this book in terms of space, which is why I have given
this chapter the title "Towards a Comparative Study." I have chosen to focus
on an exploration of the use of comments in some of the OT/HB's historical writings (using 2 Samuel as a case study), and in the Synoptic Gospels
(without engaging in debate as to whether or not John was dependent on the
Synoptics). I interact more briefly with two other Greek historical writings,
the works of Herodotus and Thucydides. I hope to take this research further
in the future.


## PARENTHESES IN THE OLD TESTAMENT/
## HEBREW BIBLE

A pioneering study of narratology in the OT/HB is Robert Alter, *The Art of
Biblical Narrative* (1981).[11] In his examination of narrative in the Pentateuch
and the Former Prophets, Alter concludes that it is necessary to speak of
"the reticence of the biblical narrator" and "the Bible's highly laconic mode
of narration," especially when contrasted with those 18th- and 19th-century

*Towards a Comparative Study* 207

novelists who "flaunt their knowledge by stepping out in front of the prosce-
nium arch to chat with or lecture to the audience."[12] Although the biblical
narrator is "omniscient," with a distinct insight into "God's assessments and
intentions," he must also be self-effacing in order not to deflect attention
away from God.[13]

However, against this general pattern of reticence, Alter notes that the narrator does occasionally intrude into the narrative and that "we should direct
special attention to those moments when the illusion of unmediated action
is manifestly shattered."[14] He gives the examples of the narrator breaking
"the time-frame of his story" to either look back in history or forward to
the time of his own audience; of summarizing statements; and of a slowing
down of the narrative's tempo in order to focus on particular details.[15] So,
for instance, regarding the breaking of the time-frame, he regards the use
of summarized background material at the opening of stories (e.g., those of
Ruth, Job, Samuel, Saul) as "pretemporal, statically enumerating data that are
not bound to a specific moment in time: they are facts that stand before the
time of the story proper."[16] In an analysis of various chapters in the story of
Joseph and his brothers in Genesis 37–50, Alter homes in on 42:23, "They did
not know that Joseph understood them, since he spoke with them through an
interpreter," as an instance of where we are made aware of "the knowing eyes
of the omniscient narrator."[17] He regards all such "relaxations of reticence" as
important for our reading of the texts, although he does not draw any specific
conclusions about their functions.[18]

Alter makes little use of current literary critical theory, preferring instead
to rely on his own close reading of the text. He admits to being "particularly
suspicious of the value of elaborate taxonomies and skeptical as whether our
understanding of narrative is really advanced by the deployment of bristling
neologisms like *analepsis, intradiegetic, actantial.*"[19] Moreover, he does
not provide many actual examples of narrator's intrusions, which perhaps
unintentionally supports his proposal that such intrusions are rare. However,
his observation that where such intrusions do occur, the "omniscient" narrator does not want to be seen as detracting from emphasis on God seems to
me an important one when we compare these intrusions with the occasional
glimpses into the feelings and motivations of Jesus in John (and the other
Gospels). For example, we have this narrative comment in John 2:24–25:
"But Jesus on his part would not entrust himself to them, because he knew all
people and needed no one to testify about anyone; for he himself knew what
was in everyone." This is immediately followed by the arrival of Nicodemus
who to some extent "testifies" about Jesus (3:2: "Rabbi, we know that you
are a teacher who has come from God; for no one can do these signs that you
do apart from the presence of God"). The link between the verses is more
obvious in the Greek through the repeated use of ἄνθρωπος at the end of 2:25

208                                   Chapter 6

and the beginning of 3:1: αὐτὸς γὰρ ἐγίνωσκεν τί ἦν ἐν τῷ ἀνθρώπῳ. Ἦν δὲ ἄνθρωπος ἐκ τῶν Φαρισαίων, Νικόδημος ὄνομα αὐτῷ. So, the implication of the comment in 2:24–25 is clear in the case of Nicodemus: Jesus does not need Nicodemus's testimony. However, I suggest that there is a sense in which this is also true of the author/narrator of the Gospel. Jesus does not need the testimony of John (the author). John only has insight into the mind of Jesus through the guidance of the "Spirit of truth," who "testifies" on Jesus' behalf, as 15:26 makes clear.

A more focussed and comprehensive study of parentheses in the HB is Tamar Zewi, *Parenthesis in Biblical Hebrew* (2007), which draws on linguistics, discourse studies, text linguistics, philology, comparative Semitics, and literary approaches in seeking "to offer a complete description of parenthetical units in Biblical Hebrew."[20] She acknowledges that "the identification and definition of a parenthetical unit is elusive from a linguistic viewpoint, and that it is often more productive to pinpoint parenthesis by employing functional-pragmatic and literary perspectives."[21]

Her introductory chapter includes an overview of various linguistic definitions, starting with the classic work of Leonard Bloomfield (1933) and his observation that parenthesis is "a variety of parataxis in which one form interrupts the other," through to a paper by the generative grammatist Gunther Kaltenböck (2005), who states that parenthetical clauses "have no syntagmatic (i.e. paratactic, hypotactic) link to their host clauses. They are related to their host by linear adjacency but are not part of any larger syntactic unit, i.e. they do not form constituents."[22] Zewi notes that there is a vagueness in the linguistic definitions of parentheses and parenthetical clauses and, moreover, that the use of prosodic marking or typographic signs (such as punctuation marks, brackets, and dashes) is not available for Biblical Hebrew.[23] She concludes that given "the complexity in establishing formal criteria for parenthetical units," she is left with "only two formal criteria as fundamental for identifying parenthesis," namely that "(1) parenthetical units are relatively independent syntactically, and (2) they frequently enjoy flexible positioning in a sentence."[24] To these she adds a third, "functional-pragmatic" criterion, which "relies on contextual considerations."[25] This functional-pragmatic criterion takes account of Biblical Hebrew syntax, discourse studies, and textual philology as well as literary approaches. In regard to the latter, she refers briefly to the work of various scholars, including Robert Alter, Adele Berlin, and Meir Sternberg, and their observations regarding the insertion of expository information or commentary into the text and its relation to the point of view of the narrator.[26]

In the two main chapters of *Parenthesis in Biblical Hebrew*, Zewi categorizes and analyses a large selection of parenthetical clauses, phrases, and words drawn mainly from the Book of Genesis and the Deuteronomic histories. The clauses include references to a speaker (often "the LORD");

Towards a Comparative Study

expressions of appealing and pleading; affirmations of God's existence, identity, and status; oath patterns; recurring narrative formulas; and external information, such as background information, foreshadowing, explanatory information, and theological and historical remarks.[27] The phrases and words include references to a speaker (again, often "the LORD"); the observer's identity; "God's standpoint"; expressions of appealing and pleading; expressions of address; and a variety of time indicators.[28] Some of the examples Zewi gives would certainly fit my own definition of what lies outside the narrative framework in temporal or spatial terms. This is true, for instance, of expressions involving time indicators such as עַד הַיּוֹם הַזֶּה found in Genesis 26:33 and 32:32 (MT 32:33):[29]

> He called it Shibah; therefore the name of the city is Beer-sheba *to this day.* (Genesis 26:33, my emphasis)

> Therefore *to this day* the Israelites do not eat the thigh muscle that is on the hip socket, because he struck Jacob on the hip socket at the thigh muscle. (Genesis 32:32, my emphasis)

Similarly, much of the "external information" belongs to my category of outside the narrative framework in *spatial* terms. Examples are the "theological remarks" in Judges 14:4 and 2 Samuel 17:14:[30]

> *His father and mother did not know that this was from the LORD*; for he was seeking a pretext to act against the Philistines. At that time the Philistines had dominion over Israel. (Judges 14:4, my emphasis)

> Absalom and all the men of Israel said, "The counsel of Hushai the Archite is better than the counsel of Ahithophel." *For the LORD had ordained to defeat the good counsel of Ahithophel, so that the LORD might bring ruin on Absalom.* (2 Samuel 17:14, my emphasis)

As with my discussion of Alter's "omniscient" narrator, we can compare Zewi's examples here to John's comments giving insight into the mind of Jesus and other characters.

However, many of the examples Zewi gives seem to me to be integral to the narrative and cannot be considered as comments of the author or narrator. Similarly, I would discount her various references to "God's existence, identity, and status," all of which occur in direct speech rather than the narrative framework.[31]

In a recent article, "Parenthesis in Biblical Hebrew as Noncoordinative Nonsubordination" (2020), Robert Holmstedt interacts with the work of Zewi alongside other linguistic analyses.[32] He believes, "It is clear from the linguistic literature that parenthesis consists of a clause or phrase that is

210                                    *Chapter 6*

linearly integrated *within* a host clause."[33] He, therefore, rejects Zewi's many examples of full clauses that are not clearly integrated into a host clause.[34] Indeed, he is critical of Zewi for her "lack of linguistic criteria."[35]

Holmstedt is aware that much recent linguistic work relies on the study of intonational features such as "surrounding pauses, lowered pitch, diminished loudness, increased tempo" in analysing the "extraordinary range of linguistic expressions" that "fall under the parenthesis umbrella," an option that is not available in the study of an ancient language such as Biblical Hebrew.[36] However, he is convinced that there are enough syntactic and semantic indicators to determine that parentheses are linearly integrated into their host clause from a syntactical perspective, but at the same time they "present a proposition that is distinct, 'sealed off,' from the proposition of the host clause."[37] Holmstedt, therefore, accepts as a parenthesis Zewi's example of Genesis 23:19, where the phrase "that is Hebron" offers "a brief explanatory comment":

After this, Abraham buried Sarah his wife in the cave of the field of Machpelah facing Mamre (that is, Hebron) in the land of Canaan.[38]

On the other hand, he questions many of Zewi's other examples of parentheses in as much as that they are not linearly integral to a host clause. He gives Zewi's example of Genesis 26:14–16 as a case in point, where verse 15 provides background information that does not move the narrative forward:

[14] He had possessions of flocks and herds, and a great household, so that the Philistines envied him. [15] (Now the Philistines had stopped up and filled with earth all the wells that his father's servants had dug in the days of his father Abraham.) [16] And Abimelech said to Isaac, "Go away from us; you have become too powerful for us."[39]

It is clear that Holmstedt's concern to define parentheses solely in linguistic terms radically reduces the number of such instances in the HB. However, in chapter 2, I noted that linguistic definitions are complex and contested, and I attempted to broaden the scope of parentheses/asides/comments in terms of their function.

Christopher Paris, in *Narrative Obtrusion in the Hebrew Bible* (2014), makes no reference to Zewi's work. His focus is on those instances where the narrator breaks the framework of the narrative in order "to shape the response of the reader."[40] He regards these narrative obtrusions as significant features in the interpretation of the narrative:

*Towards a Comparative Study* 211

The significance of narrative obtrusions lies in the fact that they bring the narrator, the text, and the reader together at crucial points within the narrative where the narrator has broken or reframed the text and inserted a comment that specifically attempts to influence the reader's response. Therefore, narrative obtrusions serve as important intersections in interpretation.[41]

Paris marks out these narrative obtrusions, which he considers to be "relatively rare," as a subset of "omniscient comments" that "aid reader understanding," a wider group which he also refers to as "asides" or "narrative interruptions."[42] He further distinguishes the narrative obtrusions from "comments that narrators may put into the mouths of characters."[43] His approach derives primarily from narrative criticism with its emphasis on the unity of the text, although he aims to build bridges with redaction criticism and reader-response methods.

Regarding his distinction between omniscient comments and narrative obtrusions, Paris looks in some detail at the beginning of Genesis 22, "After these things God tested Abraham."[44] After a lengthy investigation in which he seems to waver between the two categories, he concludes that this sentence is an obtrusion on the basis of its location in the account of the Aqedah and its purpose in pre-empting reader questions: "The narrator of Genesis 22 acts obtrusively by intervening at the beginning of the text with the specific goal of influencing reader response."[45] His major distinction, therefore, is between "asides, historical information, and essential information," which "are often the narrator's endeavours to assist reader understanding through general omniscience" and obtrusions, which may represent "nonessential narrative comments that could be omitted from the story" or "essential comments that are intrusive based on their location and the narrator's intent to intervene."[46] Paris also notes that narrative obtrusions are often linked to the issue of divine causality and help increase trust in the narrator, who has "insight into God's actions and motivations."[47] Indeed, "Statements about God often prove more obtrusive than general comments about history or characters."[48]

Another of Paris's key examples is Judges 14:4 ("But his father and his mother did not know that it was of the Lord. He was seeking an occasion/pretext against the Philistines, for at that time the Philistines were ruling over Israel") and he devotes a whole chapter to his analysis of its function:[49] He concludes that this verse contains both an omniscient remark ("at that time the Philistines were ruling over Israel") and an obtrusion in the narrator's pre-empting of reader: "The narrator tries to remove questions from the reader's mind by intruding with nonessential information."[50] In a chapter on "Reader Response, Narrator Foresight and Foreclosure," Paris examines further the ways in which the narrator attempts to restrict the reader's response to the

212 *Chapter 6*

narrative, through obtrusions that break the frame and others which instead take advantage of natural interruptions in the plot.[51] He deduces, "The obtrusive narrator limits the reader's power in both types of obtrusions, restricting the reader's control over the text by blocking undesired interpretations."[52]

Paris acknowledges that there are varying levels of narrative intrusion and he does not find any examples of *apostrophe* ("the highest level of obtrusiveness") in Hebrew biblical narrative.[53] He also admits that his methodology is not foolproof and that "considering the subtlety and laconic nature of the narrator," interpreters and translators may have other reasons for "characterizing a narrative comment as an obtrusion."[54] He also considers the use of omniscient comments and narrative obtrusions in comparative Ancient Near Eastern literature and sees parallels between the obtrusive narrator in the Deuteronomistic writings and that in the writings of the Mesopotamian scribe Kabti-ilāni-Marduk (eighth century BCE?).[55]

Overall, in terms of function, Paris is concerned with the content of narrative obtrusions and what they suggest about the narrator-reader dynamic.

In conclusion, the main lesson to draw from this brief look at some of the scholarly writings on parentheses in the HB is that this feature is indeed present in the historical narratives. However, the extent of these parentheses depends on definition, which as Zewi admits is complex and uncertain. Her own definition is very wide and Holmstedt's linguistic definition radically reduces it, whereas Alter and Paris focus on a particular category of parenthesis, that of the narrator's intrusions/obtrusions. Alter notes that one of the features of the narrator's intrusions is that they break the time frame of the narrative and Zewi has "time indicators" (such as "to this day") as one of her categories. This fits with my own temporal definition. Other categories used by Zewi fit my spatial definition. Similarly, Paris speaks of obtrusions that break or reframe the text. Of particular importance is the observation by Alter, Zewi, and Paris that some of the parentheses relate the omniscience of the narrator to insight into the mind of God, although Alter stresses that the narrator remains "self-effacing."[56] I have questioned the validity of the concept of an omniscient narrator in respect to the Gospel of John, but it seems to me that the narrator's comments in the historical narratives of the HB provide something of a paradigm for John's insights into the mind and motives of Jesus. We can compare comments such as John 6:6, "He said this to test him, for he himself knew what he was going to do," and Genesis 22:1, "After these things God tested Abraham. . . ."[57]

## A Case Study: 2 Samuel

To illustrate instances of narrative comments in the HB, I have chosen to focus on the Second Book of Samuel as it is of comparable length to the

Gospel of John and is also an example of historiography focussing on one character, in this case, David during his time as king. The NRSV marks seven parentheses with brackets as follows:

1:18:     (He ordered that The Song of the Bow be taught to the people of Judah; it is written in the Book of Jashar.)

4:3v:     (Now the people of Beeroth had fled to Gittaim and are there as resident aliens to this day.)

11:4:     (Now she was purifying herself after her period.)

13:18:    (Now she was wearing a long robe with sleeves; for this is how the virgin daughters of the king were clothed in earlier times.)

14:26:    (for at the end of every year he used to cut it; when it was heavy on him, he cut it)

18:13:    (and there is nothing hidden from the king)

52.92 pt  (Now the Gibeonites were not of the people of Israel, but of the remnant of the Amorites; although the people of Israel had sworn to spare them, Saul had tried to wipe them out in his zeal for the people of Israel and Judah.)

I acknowledge all these as external comments with the exception of 18:13, which seems to belong to the speech of Joab's unnamed interlocutor. In addition, I include another 27 external comments in 2:1; 3:1, 2–5; 4:2; 5:4–5, 8, 10, 12, 14–16, 20; 6:2, 8; 8:10, 14, 15–18; 11:1, 27; 12:24–25; 17:14; 18:18; 20:3, 23–26; 21:14; 23:1; 24:1, 15–16, 25. (I have omitted the material in 23:8–39, the references to "the Three" and "the Thirty" warriors, which seems to be an addition to the text.)[58] This gives a total of 33 comments, 24 spatial, 3 temporal, and 6 temporal/spatial.

Of particular note are the comments which give insight into the divine, in line with Alter's observation that the biblical narrator is "omniscient," with a distinct insight into "God's assessments and intentions."[59] These comments are found in 5:10, 12; 8:14; 11:27; 17:14; 21:14; 24:1, 15–16, 25.[60] (I referred above to 17:14 as one of Zewi's examples of a "theological remark." Auld describes this as an instance in which "Yahweh demonstrates his own independence and sovereignty."[61]) There is also insight into the mind of David in 5:12: "David then perceived that the LORD had established him king over Israel, and that he had exalted his kingdom for the sake of his people Israel."

214           *Chapter 6*

There is nothing comparable in John to the aetiological explanations of place names (2:16; 5:20; 6:8; 18:18) or the alternative personal name for Solomon (12:24–25), but these serve to enhance the reliability of the narrator/author in the same way that the "translation" of words and explanation of customs do in the Gospel.

The narrator is most intrusive in the various references to "to this day" (עַד הַיּוֹם הַזֶּה) in 4:3; 6:8; 18:18).

I have also included a number of summaries and lists of names (3:1, 2–5; 5:4–5, 14–16; 8:15–18) and other explanatory comments, such as the note that "the ark of God" is "called by the name of the LORD of hosts who is enthroned on the cherubim" (6:2) or the reference to spring being "the time when kings go out to battle" (11:1).

Overall, we can see in this brief survey of narrative comments in 2 Samuel an author/narrator who is usually nonintrusive but who has insight into the character and purposes of the divine. There is a limited amount of explanatory material, which may serve the theological purposes of the author/narrator and contribute to a sense of reliability. It is also worth observing that some of the comments in 2 Samuel are repeated or adapted in parallel passages in 1 Chronicles 10–22, a process which is paralleled in Matthew and Luke's use of Mark. The comments which are shared are:

| 2 Samuel | 1 Chronicles |
|---|---|
| 5:10 | 11:9 |
| 5:12 | 14:2 |
| 5:14–16 | 14:3–5 |
| 5:20 | 14:11 |
| 6:2 | 13:6 |
| 6:8 | 13:11 |
| 8:10 | 18:10 |
| 8:14 | 18:13 |
| 8:15–18 | 18:14–17 |
| 11:1 | 20:1 |
| 24:1 | 21:1 |
| 24:15–16 | 21:14–15 |
| 24:25 | 21:27 |

Of particular interest are the adaptations which the author of Chronicles has made to the source material (assuming that the Chronicler had some form of the Samuel text, rather than the two texts sharing a common source).[62] The most striking example is the switch from "Again the anger of the LORD was kindled against Israel, and he incited David against them" (2 Samuel 24:1)

## Towards a Comparative Study

to "Satan stood up against Israel, and incited David to count the people of Israel" (1 Chronicles 21:1). This may be the result of a change in theological perspective or evidence of the Chronicler's use of an earlier text of Samuel or of shared source material.[63]

## PARENTHESES IN THE SYNOPTIC GOSPELS

For my investigation of narrative comments in the Synoptic Gospels, I begin by listing instances of sentences and phrases put in brackets or set apart with dashes in the Greek editions NA28, UBS5, and SBLGNT and in the NRSV English translation. I also add my own list of other comments that are external on a temporal or spatial basis and I consider some of the relevant secondary literature. I begin with the Gospel of Mark, following the widely accepted source-critical chronology.

### The Gospel of Mark

NA28 has no phrases or sentences in brackets, but three marked with dashes: 2:10 (—λέγει τῷ παραλυτικῷ), 7:3–4vv, and 11:32 (—ἐφοβοῦντο τὸν ὄχλον· ἅπαντες γὰρ εἶχον τὸν Ἰωάννην ὄντως ὅτι προφήτης ἦν). UBS5 has the same three phrases/sentences with dashes. SBLGNT has one phrase/sentence in brackets: 3:17 (καὶ ἐπέθηκεν αὐτοῖς ὀνόματα Βοανηργές, ὅ ἐστιν Υἱοὶ Βροντῆς). It has four in/with dashes: 2:10, 7:3–4, and 11:32 (as NA28/USB5); and also 7:19 (—καθαρίζων πάντα τὰ βρώματα).[64] NRSV has nine phrases or sentences in brackets (3:16, 17; 5:42; 7:3–4vv, 11, 19; 13:14; 15:16, 22) and six in dashes or introduced with a dash (1:16; 2:10, 15; 3:30; 10:30; 11:32). In line with my definition of narrative comments as what lies outside the narrative framework in a temporal or spatial sense, I accept eight of the NRSV asides in brackets as external comments in the spatial category: 3:16; 3:17; 7:3–4vv, 11, 19; 13:14; 15:16, 22.[65] I regard the NRSV's six phrases/sentences marked with dashes as integral to the narrative. However, I would also include the following 11 as external comments: 1:1v, 2–3vv; 2:8 (καὶ εὐθὺς . . . ἐν ἑαυτοῖς); 4:33–34vv; 5:41 (ὅ ἐστιν μεθερμηνευόμενον· τὸ κοράσιον); 6:52v; 7:34 (ὅ ἐστιν, Διανοίχθητι); 9:9–10vv, 30–32vv; 12:18 (οἵτινες λέγουσιν ἀνάστασιν μὴ εἶναι); 15:34 (ὅ ἐστιν . . . ἐγκατέλιπές με;).

I note that Mark rarely has the sort of comments indicating insight into the mind of Jesus or other protagonists that we find in John. As France states, "Jesus' supernatural powers of discernment are not made explicit in Mark as often as in the other gospels."[66] Indeed, in most cases (for example 5:30; 6:6, 48; 12:15 re Jesus; and 9:6 re Peter with James and John) these seem to me to be no more than part of the narrative and there is nothing remarkable

216                                   *Chapter 6*

about the depth of insight required by the author (or "omniscient narrator").[67] However, in the case of 2:8, the use of the phrase τῷ πνεύματι αὐτοῦ suggests that this is a more significant insight, and Guellich picks up Pesch's suggestion that Jesus is here depicted as a prophet in God's stead, just as, in the OT, God is a "knower of hearts."[68] I also note that the comments I have listed include a number of "translations" of Hebrew or Aramaic words: 5:41; 7:11, 34; 15:22, 34, comparable to the "translation comments" in John.[69] The comment in 12:18 ("who say there is no resurrection") is an explanatory comment about the beliefs of the Sadducees. As France observes, "The present tense of the clause οἵτινες λέγουσιν ἀνάστασιν μὴ εἶναι indicates that it is not a specific description of this particular group but characterises the Sadducean position in general."[70]

Overall, I have observed a total of 19 external narrative comments in Mark: 16 spatial, 1 temporal, and 2 temporal/spatial.[71] So, even taking into account the shorter length of Mark compared with John, such comments appear to be a less frequent feature of the text. However, other writers have referred to considerably more asides/parentheses/comments in the Gospel, and I briefly examine here the work of Hedrick, Fowler, and Boomershine.

In his article, "Narrator and Story in the Gospel of Mark: *Hermeneia* and *Paradosis*" (1987), Hedrick follows on from his research on the Gospel of John by conducting what he believes to be the first systematic investigation of *hermeneiai* in Mark.[72] Hedrick equates his term *hermeneiai* with other terms such as footnotes, parentheses, and explanatory comments, and uses the same definition that he used in his work on John—namely that "it is comprised of intrusive word(s), sentence(s), or paragraph(s) of explanatory or clarifying commentary included in the narrative as direct address to the reader."[73] He regards the primary function of the *hermeneiai* as to "simply enhance the story, or clarify aspects of plot or action inside the story."[74] Hedrick lists 67 examples of this feature, dividing them into 13 categories.[75] He regards it as striking that over half of his listed *hermeneiai* are "unique to Mark."[76] Given that he regards the many comments of the narrator as a major aspect of the Gospel's literary composition, he questions the value of redaction criticism in being able to isolate early traditions: "How confident can the redaction critic be of possessing the ability to sort out early and independent tradition from the imagination and interpretation of the evangelists, if the gospel narrative has been shaped by the author's imagination and literary skill."[77]

Robert Fowler, in his study of narrative strategies in the Gospel of Mark, *Let the Reader Understand* (1991), notes, "The parenthetical comment has long been recognized as a typical characteristic of Mark's Gospel" and "the narrator of this Gospel makes numerous parenthetical comments."[78] Fowler examines these parenthetical comments in a chapter on "Explicit Commentary by the Narrator."[79] He uses Chatman's distinction between *implicit* and *explicit commentary*, while widening the definition of *implicit commentary* beyond just the use of irony to include "any guidance provided by the narrator in the course of telling the story that helps to direct the reading experience without explicitly invoking the narrator's voice."[80] In effect, this includes the speech of characters within the story and the plotting of the narrative.[81] However, it is Chatman's category of *explicit commentary*, which Fowler regards as parenthetical to the narrative, that we are concerned with here. Chatman states that explicit commentary includes "interpretation, judgment, generalization, and 'self-conscious' narration," of which the first three are comments on the story and the latter comment on the discourse.[82]

Fowler provides four examples of self-conscious narration—that is, explicit commentary *on the discourse*: 1:1, 2–3, 14–15; 13:14.[83] Regarding 13:14: "(let the reader understand)," he writes, "This parenthetical comment by the narrator to the reader, which occurs abruptly in the midst of words supposedly uttered by Jesus, lays bare the narrative situation obtaining throughout the entire Gospel."[84] Fowler discusses who this "reader" might be, rejecting "the modern image of a solitary, individual reader of the Gospel, reading silently in private," but acknowledging that it could be an individual reader of the Gospel and/or of the Jewish scriptures (the Book of Daniel) or else an "*anagnostes*, a professional reader reciting the Gospel of Mark before an assembled audience."[85]

Regarding explicit commentary *on the story* (that is, Chatman's subcategories of interpretation, judgment, and generalization), Fowler observes that much of the judgment and generalization in the Gospel is found in the words of Jesus and should therefore be considered as *implicit commentary*. However, that still leaves "numerous instances of what Chatman calls 'interpretation,'" that is, "commentary on the story by the narrator."[86] Fowler states, "Many of the narrator's interpretations are offered smoothly and unobtrusively in the course of his narration; they contribute inconspicuously to the narrator's exposition of the action in the story. Others are noticeable, however, because they disrupt the flow of the story."[87] Following the analysis in Blass, Debrunner, and Funk's grammar, he divides these disruptions into two categories: *parenthesis*, where the disruption is "conducted with a degree of gracefulness," and *anacoluthon*, where it is "ungrammatical and awkward."[88] He then gives various examples of both parenthesis and anacoluthon according to grammatical categories.[89] He lists a total of approximately 55 examples of parentheses marked grammatically in these ways.[90] He also examines 3 examples of anacoluthon (2:10; 7:19; 11:32).[91]

I suggest that overall Fowler's survey relies on an understanding of parenthesis based on a narrator showing/telling distinction that is largely subjective (what constitutes "a degree of gracefulness"?) and that his separation into various grammatical sub-categories does not add much to our understanding. Indeed, I

218                                         *Chapter 6*

would argue that it is not the presence of a particular grammatical feature that is the marker of parenthesis. For example, although Fowler detects 4 examples of parenthesis beginning with *kai*, he also acknowledges that "*kai* parataxis is ubiquitous in Mark's Gospel."[92] Overall, his survey of over 50 examples of parenthesis indicates that they are mostly explanatory in function, although the "inside views" can also act as a challenge to the reader.[93] Clearly, Fowler has a much broader understanding of parentheses than fits my own definition.

Thomas Boomershine, in his essay "Audience Asides and the Audiences of Mark: The Difference Performance Makes" (2014), which I referred to in chapter 4, views Fowler's work as reflecting "Mark as read by Enlightenment readers" rather than its performance to audiences of hearers.[94] He gives close attention to three "audience asides": 7:3–4, the explanation of Jewish purification customs; 13:14 ("let the reader understand"); and 15:21 ("the father of Alexander and Rufus"), as well as providing a list of six categories with "representative examples of each type of audience aside."[95] His categories and examples are:

1. Translations of Aramaic words into Greek: 5:41; 15:22, 34.
2. Explanations of Jewish customs and practices: 7:3–4; 15:42.
3. Introduction of characters by naming their children or parents: 1:19; 2:14; 3:17, 18; 10:47; 15:21, 40.
4. Explanations of "things that are puzzling in the previous statement": 3:10, 21; 5:28; 14:56; 15:10.
5. Inside views of the feelings or motives of a character: 9:6.
6. "Explanations that raise more questions than the puzzle [Mark] has just reported": 6:52; 16:8. Boomershine sees these as cases of the Markan storyteller being "more of a provocateur than a helper."

Boomershine's performance-critical analysis of the Markan audience indicates to him that it was predominantly Jewish, but with explanations, such as 7:3–4, provided in order to include Gentiles.[96] The naming of Simon of Cyrene's sons in 15:21 "creates a sense of authenticity of the storyteller and his story," rather than naming people who would actually be known by his audience.[97] While I accept that some of the "audience asides" in Mark (and the other Gospels) may have originated in the telling of the story, at some point they became embedded in a written text, so I do not see the storyteller's performance as a sufficient explanation for the function of the narrative comments. This is something I have already considered in chapter 4.

### The Gospel of Matthew

NA28, UBS5, and SBLGNT have no phrases or sentences in brackets and only one marked with a dash: 9:6 (—τότε λέγει τῷ παραλυτικῷ).[98] NRSV has two

*Towards a Comparative Study*     219

phrases or sentences in brackets (24:15; 27:33) and one in dashes (9:6).[99] All three of these comments are found in Mark (13:14; 15:22; 2:10), and I accept the first two as external comments in the spatial category. In addition, I would include another 20 phrases/sentences as external comments: 1:1–17vv, 18 (Τοῦ δὲ . . . οὕτως ἦν), 22–23vv; 2:15 (ἵνα πληρωθῇ . . . προφήτου λέγοντος), 17–18vv, 23 (ὅπως πληρωθῇ . . . Ναζωραῖος κληθήσεται); 4:14–16vv; 7:29v; 8:17v; 9:8v; 12:17–21vv; 13:34v, 35v, 58v; 21:4–5vv; 27:8v, 9–10vv, 46 (τοῦτ' ἔστιν . . . με ἐγκατέλιπες;), 52–53vv; 28:15 (καὶ διεφημίσθη . . . τῆς σήμερον [ἡμέρας]).[100] Of these comments, I make the following observations. The genealogy in 1:1–17 belongs outside the narrative framework both temporally and, I think, spatially as a distinct genre within the Gospel.[101] I find support for this in the assessment of Alter, who, writing of genealogies in OT narrative, calls them "an extreme form of summary," which cannot be construed as "narrative event" as "the ratio between narrating time and time narrated is too drastically disproportionate."[102] There are two "translation comments" in my list: 1:22–23 and 27:46, the latter paralleling Mark 15:34, and these are amongst the few instances in Matthew that we can compare with the frequent explanatory type of comment that we find in the Gospel of John. After 24:15, "(let the reader understand)," 27:8 and 28:15 are the most intrusive comments in the Gospel, with their references to the author's own time (27:8: ἕως τῆς σήμερον; 28:15: μέχρι τῆς σήμερον [ἡμέρας]). They can be compared with the examples of "time indicators" in the HB that Zewi gives, such as Genesis 26:33 and 32:33 (MT), and the examples I noted in 2 Samuel 4:3, 6:8, and 18:18. Davies and Allison note, "'Until this day' . . . , a standard formula in OT aetiologies, lends a biblical aura to the passage and posits a substantial passing of time between Jesus' death and our Gospel."[103]

A particular feature of the Gospel of Matthew is the number of so-called "formula quotations" or "fulfilment quotations"—that is, scripture citations introduced with a form of words indicating that the author regards them as being fulfilled in the events related. For example, Τοῦτο δὲ ὅλον γέγονεν ἵνα πληρωθῇ τὸ ῥηθὲν ὑπὸ κυρίου διὰ τοῦ προφήτου λέγοντος (All this took place to fulfil what had been spoken by the Lord through the prophet) (1:22). There are 10 such formula quotations in the narrative framework (1:22–23; 2:15, 17–18, 23; 4:14–16; 8:17; 12:17–21; 13:35; 21:4–5; 27:9–10), and France states that they are "presented as editorial comments on the events being narrated."[104] I include all of them, with the accompanying citations, as external comments in the spatial/temporal category, with the fulfilment formula as spatial and the scripture citation as temporal, as with the various such citations in the Gospel of John.

I have not included as comments those few references which would seem to provide some insight into the mind of Jesus (one of the categories of asides used by Hedrick alongside Sheeley's more general "inside view

220                                    *Chapter 6*

of some person within the story").[105] On occasion, the narrator/author
does refer to Jesus knowing what his opponents were discussing (9:4 re
the scribes; 12:25 re the Pharisees; 22:18 re the Pharisees and the Herodi-
ans), but there does not seem to me to be anything miraculous about these
insights. Similarly, there is nothing miraculous about the disciples' coming
to understanding in 16:12 and 17:13, although Resseguie gives 16:12 as
an example to support his assertion that "Matthew's narrator uses asides
to place the disciples in a more favorable light than in Mark."[106] Along the
same lines, I have not included the "insight" into the mind of Pilate (27:18;
cf. Mark 15:10).

In other cases, there is uncertainty as to what is intended to be the
words of Jesus and what is the narrator/author's own commentary. An
example is 21:44: Καὶ ὁ πεσὼν ἐπὶ τὸν λίθον τοῦτον συνθλασθήσεται·
ἐφ᾽ ὃν δ᾽ ἂν πέσῃ λικμήσει αὐτόν (The one who falls on this stone will
be broken to pieces; and it will crush anyone on whom it falls). As
France points out, "In the absence of quotation marks it is impossible to
be sure whether Matthew intends this verse to be read as a continuation
of Jesus' speech or his own editorial comment."[107] The verse is omitted
by Codex Bezae (D) and placed in square brackets in NA28 and UBS5.
Davies and Allison regard it as "secondary," and Metzger notes, "Many
modern scholars regard this verse as an early interpolation (from Lk
20.18) into most manuscripts of Matthew."[108] However, in support of the
retention of 21:44, Luz points out, "The textual evidence is overwhelm-
ingly strong."[109]

Overall, I have counted 22 external comments in Matthew, including the
10 fulfilment quotations. Of these 11 are in the temporal/spatial category, 8
in the spatial category and 3 in the temporal category. The total number is
comparable with the 19 in Mark, although Matthew's emphasis is clearly on
the fulfilment of scripture. Four of the comments I have included are parallels
of Mark, as follows:

| Matthew | Mark |
|---------|------|
| 13:34v  | 4:33–34vv |
| 24:15   | 13:14 |
| 27:33   | 15:22 |
| 27:46   | 15:34 |

In Matthew 24:15/Mark 13:14, the wording is identical: ὁ ἀναγινώσκων
νοείτω.[110] In two of the other examples, the wording is similar, but not identical (with some textual variants):

| Matthew 27:33: | ὅ ἐστιν Κρανίου Τόπος λεγόμενος |
| Mark 15:22: | ὅ ἐστιν μεθερμηνευόμενον Κρανίου Τόπος |

| Matthew 27:46: | τοῦτ' ἐστιν· θεέ μου θεέ μου, ἱνατί με ἐγκατέλιπες; |
| Mark 15:34: | ὅ ἐστιν μεθερμηνευόμενον· ὁ θεός μου ὁ θεός μου, εἰς τί ἐγκατέλιπές με; |

This suggests that the author of Matthew, although not copying word-for-word from a written Markan text, was certainly incorporating Markan comments. What does this imply about the role of these comments in the process of composition? I suggest that although some of Mark's comments may have originated at an oral stage of composition, as Boomershine and others argue, these comments quickly became part of the written text. Moreover, while Matthew adds his own comments, notably regarding the fulfilment of scripture, he also incorporates existing comments or, as in the case of 22:23, makes a comment a more integral part of the narrative.

## The Gospel of Luke

NA28 and UBS5 have no phrases or sentences in brackets, but four marked with dashes: 2:35 (—καὶ σοῦ [δὲ] αὐτῆς τὴν ψυχὴν διελεύσεται ῥομφαία—); 5:24 (—εἶπεν τῷ παραλελυμένῳ); 19:25v; 23:51 (—οὗτος οὐκ ἦν συγκατατεθειμένος τῇ βουλῇ καὶ τῇ πράξει αὐτῶν—). SBLGNT has three phrases in brackets and three marked with dashes. The phrases in brackets are 2:2v, 36 (αὕτη προβεβηκυῖα ἐν ἡμέραις πολλαῖς, ζήσασα ⸆μετὰ ἀνδρὸς ἔτη⸇ ἑπτὰ ἀπὸ τῆς παρθενίας αὐτῆς, καὶ αὐτὴ χήρα ⸆ἕως ἐτῶν ὀγδοήκοντα τεσσάρων); 7:29–30vv. The phrases with dashes are 5:24; 19:25; 23:51 (all as NA28/UBS5). The NRSV has seven phrases or sentences in brackets (2:23v; 3:23; 5:17; 7:29–30vv; 8:29; 19:25; 23:19v) and four with dashes (2:35; 5:24; 9:33; 16:28).

Following my definition of narrative comments as what lies outside the narrative framework in a temporal or spatial sense, I accept five of the NRSV asides in brackets as external comments, three in the temporal category (2:23; 8:29; 23:19) and two in the spatial category (3:23; 7:29–30). It could be argued that the events in 8:29 and 23:19 occurred during Jesus' lifetime, but they are not recorded elsewhere in the Gospel and they provide essential background information for the hearer/reader.

Sheeley, in his survey of "narrative asides" in Luke-Acts, which I looked at in chapter 1, discusses a total of 23 asides in Luke. He sets out a list of these in four categories as follows:[111]

222                                    *Chapter 6*

- Provide Essential Information (18 examples): 1:8–9; 2:2, 4, 22–23; 3:23; 4:16; 6:16; 8:29; 9:14, 33, 45; 14:7; 17:16; 18:1; 20:27; 22:1; 23:18–19, 50–51.[112]
- Provide General Information (1 example): 23:12.
- Provide Inside Views (2 examples): 7:29–30; 9:45
- Reflect Self-Conscious Narration (4 examples): 1:1–4; 2:22–23; 5:24; 14:35.[113]

I do not accept all of his asides. For example, in his examination of the category of "Self-Conscious Narration," Sheeley argues that the remark "He who has ears to hear, let him hear" in 14:35 (echoing Jesus' words in 8:8), "has been loosened from the preceding text enough . . . to allow one to interpret it as an aside to the reader."[114] He finds support for his argument in Boomershine's emphasis on the "reading" of the text as an aural experience.[115] However, the remark as it stands can equally be considered as a suitable conclusion to Jesus' words to the crowd in this section of the narrative. Indeed, with the exception of his Prologue (1:1–4), Luke is far from being an intrusive narrator, and I disagree with Sheeley's judgement that "the narrator of Luke's Gospel falls somewhere in the middle of the continuum in terms of overt presence."[116]

Regarding my own list of comments, I note that Luke makes frequent use of summaries—for example, in the infancy narrative there are summaries in 1:80; 2:40, and 2:52. While such summaries certainly alter the tempo of the narrative, they do not go beyond the narrative framework in a temporal sense. So, I only include as narrative comments those summaries where the author/narrator adds information that in some way belongs outside the framework in a spatial sense. I see 2:52 as an example of this:

Καὶ Ἰησοῦς προέκοπτεν [ἐν τῇ] σοφίᾳ καὶ ἡλικίᾳ καὶ χάριτι παρὰ θεῷ καὶ ἀνθρώποις.

And Jesus increased in wisdom and in years, and in divine and human favour.

There is a parallel here with 1 Samuel 2:26, with both examples proving insight into the divine "favour" of the protagonist. I consider Luke 2:52 as an external comment in the spatial category.

In addition to five of the comments in brackets in the NRSV and 2:52, I also accept as external comments the following: 1:1–4vv, 9 (κατὰ τὸ ἔθος τῆς ἱερατείας); 2:2–3vv, 4 (διὰ τὸ . . . πατριᾶς Δαυίδ), 19v, 51 (καὶ ἡ μήτηρ . . . καρδίᾳ αὐτῆς); 3:1–2vv, 4–6vv, 23–38vv; 4:41 (ὅτι ᾔδεισαν . . . αὐτὸν εἶναι); 6:14; 9:45v; 16:14 (φιλάργυροι ὑπάρχοντες); 18:34v; 19:11 (διὰ τὸ . . . θεοῦ ἀναφαίνεσθαι); 20:27 (οἱ [ἀντι]λέγοντες ἀνάστασιν μὴ εἶναι); 22:1 (ἡ λεγομένη πάσχα); 23:12v. I note that nine of the latter coincide with Sheeley's asides (1:1–4, 9; 2:2, 4; 3:23; 9:45; 20:27; 22:1; 23:12).[117]

## Towards a Comparative Study

Regarding the comment in 1:9, "according to the custom of the priesthood," which is an explanation of sorts but not very informative, William Kurz, in an article on "Narrative Approaches to Luke-Acts," observes:

> Like the Hebrew Bible, the omniscient narrator in Luke-Acts does give normal asides to the implied reader, which are momentary reversions to the *telling* point of view, as Sternberg notes. . . . An early example of such an aside appears in Luke 1,9, "according to the custom of the priesthood." These bits of information give clues to the kind of reader that the narrative implies, and reveal what the reader is expected to know or not to know.[118]

In fact, I am not sure that the aside in 1:9 tells us much about the reader. However, other asides/comments may indicate something about the Gospel's intended readership. For example, the chronological note in 3:1–2vv would seem to go well beyond what is needed for a smooth continuation of the narrative and reflects rather Luke's concern to be regarded as a careful and reliable historian (1:3). Green observes, "Similar lists of contemporary authorities are found in ancient historiography, and this will have had some significance for Luke's audience."[119]

I have included Luke's genealogy of Jesus in 3:23–38vv as an external comment. As with the genealogy in Matthew 1:1–17, I suggest that it lies outside the narrative framework temporally as well as spatially in terms of its genre. I have already noted the NRSV's bracketed phrase in 3:23, "(as was thought)," which introduces the genealogy and which Green describes as "a deliberate aside to his audience."[120] However, the significance of this aside is not entirely clear. Bovon takes it as an indication that Luke was not so much concerned with the negation of the idea that Jesus was the biological son of Joseph, but rather that Jesus was correctly "considered" to be the son of Joseph, "on the basis of an adoption."[121]

I considered in my look at comments in Mark and Matthew, various "insights" into the mind and motives of Jesus and others, questioning the extent to which they indicated a degree of "omniscience" on the part of the author/narrator. For Luke, the only insight into the mind of Jesus that I have included is 2:52. However, I have included the insights into the mind (and heart) of Mary in 2:19 and 2:51. I have also included 9:45, where the insight into the minds of the disciples, especially the remark ἦν παρακεκαλυμμένον ἀπ᾽ αὐτῶν (its meaning was concealed from them), is at a deeper level than the parallel in Mark 9:32. As Marshall comments, "Luke takes over Mark's statement that the disciples did not understand this saying. . . . He develops the thought independently."[122] Like 9:45, the strongly worded comment in 18:34, which is found only in Luke, speaks of what is "hidden" from the disciples (ἦν τὸ ῥῆμα τοῦτο κεκρυμμένον ἀπ᾽ αὐτῶν), suggesting what Marshall calls "a divine 'veiling.'"[123]

224 *Chapter 6*

Overall, I observe a total of 24 external comments in Luke. Of these, 13 are in the spatial category, 7 in the temporal/spatial category, and 4 in the temporal category. The total number compares with 19 in Mark, 22 in Matthew (of which 10 are fulfilment quotations), and 45 in John.

## Conclusions from Comparison with the Synoptic Gospels

What can we learn from this survey of external comments in the Synoptics? One thing to note is that some comments which may have been of help to early hearers/readers are obscure or ambiguous for modern readers. I am thinking particularly (and paradoxically) of ὁ ἀναγινώσκων νοείτω (let the reader understand) in Mark 13:14 and Matthew 24:15 and ὡς ἐνομίζετο (as was thought) in Luke 3:23. These may have been comments which arose at an oral stage of composition and then became incorporated into the written texts, but whose precise significance remains obscure.

Regarding the individual Gospels, Matthew has the fewest comments, if we set aside his 10 fulfilment quotations, and this is reflected in the small number of parenthetical indications in the Greek editions and the NRSV translation. Of the 12 comments apart from the fulfilment quotations, 4 seem to be taken from Mark and the others provide only limited explanatory material. The narrator/author remains largely in the background, with the most intrusive remarks being the references to the present time in Matthew 27:8 and 28:15. Matthew's main aim in his use of comments is to present Jesus' ministry in terms of the fulfilment of scripture.

Mark has proportionally more comments than Matthew and Luke, taking into account the length of the texts.[124] Moreover, as I have noted, some of Mark's comments are adopted by the other Synoptics. Mark provides more explanatory comments of background information than Matthew and Luke, such as the clarification of Jewish customs in 7:3–4. Luke is the most intrusive of the three authors in the Prologue to his Gospel (1:1–4), but apart from this none of the three authors can be considered overly intrusive.

I stated in my summing up of the parentheses in the HB that the narrator's comments in the historical narratives provide something of a paradigm for John's insights into the mind and motives of Jesus. However, whereas comments providing insight into Jesus are fairly frequent in John (2:24–25; 6:6, 15, 64; 13:1, 3, 11; 18:4), they are less so in the Synoptics. I here distinguish between insights that require some "divine insight" (or a post-resurrection point of view) on the part of the author and those that are based on reasonable assumptions. For example, in the case of John, I distinguished between the following two comments:

## Towards a Comparative Study          225

He said this to test him, for he himself knew what he was going to do. (6:6)

But Jesus, being aware that his disciples were complaining about it, said to them, "Does this offend you?" (6:61)

In the first case, the author can only know Jesus' motives through "divine insight" and/or later reflection on the nature of Jesus. In the second case, it is reasonable to assume that Jesus overheard the disciples' complaint (6:60).

Most of the insights into the mind and motives of Jesus in the Synoptics seem to belong to the second category of reasonable assumption. Exceptions are Mark 2:8, with its reference to Jesus perceiving "in his spirit" (τῷ πνεύματι αὐτοῦ) and Luke 2:52, where the author tells us that "Jesus increased in . . . divine . . . favour" (Ἰησοῦς προέκοπτεν . . . χάριτι παρὰ θεῷ).[125]

It is noticeable that of the eight insights into the mind and motives of Jesus which I have accepted as external comments in the Gospel of John, the majority indicate Jesus' own insight into others. The author/narrator has insight that Jesus has insight. Three indicate that Jesus knew who was going to betray him and how (6:64; 13:11; 18:4). The comment in 2:24–25 speaks of Jesus' general insight ("he himself knew what was in everyone"), but this then leads into his insight into Nicodemus (3:1–10). The comments also show Jesus' awareness of God the Father and the Father's plans for him (13:1, 3). Michaels argues that the comment in 6:15, "When Jesus realized that they were about to come and take him by force to make him king, he withdrew again to the mountain by himself," may imply that Jesus had knowledge that was "supernatural, like his knowledge of Nathanael, or of the Samaritan woman, or in general of 'what was in the person' (2.25)," or it may be that the knowledge was acquired naturally.[126] Michaels also notes that "when supernatural knowledge is involved, the writer often prefers the perfect participle εἰδῶς . . . or the pluperfect indicative ᾔδει," rather than the aorist participle (γνούς) used in 6:15.[127] However, I have chosen to accept 6:15 as an example of supernatural knowledge.

What accounts for John's deeper insight into the mind and motives of Jesus, when compared with the Synoptics? Maybe it the result of John's heightened sense of being the author of Scripture, guided by the Spirit of truth (16:13), with the same sort of prophetic insight that guided the writers of the OT historical narratives.

The examination of comments relating to "insights" on the part of the author/narrator also highlights the need for nuance in determining the contents of narrative comments and the complexities of categorization. The same applies to the comparison of so-called "translation asides" in John and the Synoptics. In my case study of 13 such asides in John at the end of chapter 5, I concluded that their function was varied, some providing "local colour" and a degree of verisimilitude; others used to highlight the significance of terms

226                                     *Chapter 6*

in relation to the Gospel's overall christological purpose; all supporting the
credibility and authority of the author in relation to the intended audience.
Further such asides/comments are found in Mark and Matthew, as follows:

Mark 3:17; 5:41; 7:11; 15:22, 34. (14:36 can also be considered a translation, if not an aside.)

Referring to 5:41, France comments that "Mark's preservation (and translation) of the Aramaic words . . . is typical of his interest in vivid recreation of
the scene."[128] France also notes that the somewhat doubtful etymology in 3:17
("the name Boanerges, that is, Sons of Thunder") is comparable to some of
the etymologies of names in the OT.[129]

Mathew 1:23; 27:33, 46.

The two examples in Matthew 27 parallel Mark 15:22, 34. The other, 1:23, is
unique to Matthew as part of his infancy narrative:

Ἐμμανουήλ, ὅ ἐστιν μεθερμηνευόμενον μεθ' ἡμῶν ὁ θεός

"Emmanuel," which means, "God is with us"

This draws out the theological significance of the Hebrew word.[130]

Luke has no "translation asides," and it is interesting to note that in 23:33,
the parallel to Mark's "the place called Golgotha (which means the place
of a skull)" (Mark 15:22; cf. Matthew 27:33), Luke misses out the Aramaic
word altogether.[131] This may support Sheeley's observation about Luke: "The
absence of any asides used to translate unfamiliar terms suggests that his
readers were competent in the language in which the Gospel was written."[132]
Sheeley contrasts this with Mark's use of Aramaic terms, but also notes that
the narrator of Acts does include and translate Aramaic terms, perhaps for
"rhetorical rather than explanatory effect."[133]

Overall, I suggest, about "translation asides" in the Synoptics, that in Mark
they help provide "local colour" and verisimilitude and that in Matthew the
one unique example has a theological purpose relating to his overall christology. Luke may be guided by his potential audience.

## PARENTHESES IN HERODOTUS AND THUCYDIDES

I have already stated a reluctance to compare the use of narrative comments
in John with those in extrabiblical contemporaneous Greek (or Roman)

*Towards a Comparative Study* 227

literature, including historiography and biography, given the lack of obvious dependence on such literature. However, that is not to deny that such comparative study can have value in highlighting certain functions of the Johannine comments, even if the author of the Gospel did not use this literature as a model.

Of the authors who have compared the use of comments in the NT, including John, with extrabiblical literature, I have referred to Bjerkelund and Sheeley. Sheeley's list of comparative texts is the more extensive and he examines the use of narrative asides in 11 works drawn from the genres of romance (novel), historiography, and biography. I note that only some of these works are written in Greek and pre-date or are roughly contemporary with the Gospel of John (if we accept a late first century AD/CE date for the Gospel). Of the historical/biographical writings, these are 1 Maccabees; 2 Maccabees; Josephus, *Jewish War*; and Philo, *Life of Moses*.[134] I have mentioned some of Sheeley's conclusions in my survey of literature in chapter 1, including his acknowledgement that differences in the use of asides in his selected texts may be as much to do with the author's practice as with the actual genre.[135] In connection with this, I would add that it is not necessarily helpful to make a sharp distinction between the genres of Greek historiography and biography. As Philip Stadter states, "We can only speak of separate genres of history and biography if we remain aware of the fluidity of the boundary between them, and the difficulty of drawing any neat demarcation."[136]

Of the extrabiblical writings, it would certainly seem worthwhile to follow Bjerkelund and Sheeley in making a comparison with the works of the Jewish writers Philo and Josephus, given that they were writing in the same period as the Gospels. However, for now I am going to restrict myself to a brief overview of the two major Greek historians of the late fifth century BC/BCE, Herodotus and Thucydides. These writers were pioneers in the "invention" of the authoritative prose of historiography in a deliberate departure from the Homeric epics. As Jonas Grethlein argues, "One of the most striking differences . . . from the epics, which aligns historiography with contemporaneous prose genres, is the establishment of narratorial authority."[137] This narratorial authority has been the subject of some research in the area of authorial/narrator comment and I refer to a number of recent articles. First, I make some observations about the use of narrative comments in Herodotus, *Histories*.

In her essay "Narrative Surface and Authorial Voice in Herodotus' *Histories*" (1987), Carolyn Dewald depicts Herodotus as a "heroic warrior," wrestling with his extensive, diffuse, and largely oral source material to provide "accurate information."[138] Within this struggle, "the role of the authorial 'I' within the third-person narrative" of the *Histories* is particularly striking.[139] Dewald reckons that there are "1087 individual authorial expressions" in the text and she divides these into four categories in respect of the *histōr*'s role in

228                                        *Chapter 6*

these comments: onlooker, eyewitness investigator, critic, writer.[140] She uses the term *"histōr"* to distinguish the "authorial persona of the *Histories*" from "Herodotus himself."[141]

It is clear that Herodotus is a highly intrusive narrator. Indeed, he provides a running commentary throughout his work. For example, on a number of occasions he disowns some of his source material, with remarks such as: "And I have to say what is said, but I do not at all have to believe it, and let this declaration on my account hold good for the whole logos" (*Histories*, 7.152.3).[142] Dewald states, "More than forty times Herodotus interrupts the ongoing narrative to make comments like these which expressly call into question the truth of the version of events he records."[143] She also points out that Herodotus indicates the value of eyewitness interviews and his own observations, even if this is reflected in only 34 of the authorial comments and these investigations often lead to a questioning of the evidence.[144] We might compare this with the occasional remarks in John which highlight "eyewitness testimony": 1:14; 19:35; 21:24.

Dewald does not employ the terminology of asides or parentheses, but she does speak of the *"histōr's* comments" or the *"histōr's* authorial comments" and she describes the comments based on eyewitness interview and observation as "ancient equivalents of the modern-day footnote."[145] It is through these comments that Herodotus seeks to show the "accuracy" (*akribeia*) of his account: "For Herodotus, the way to achieve *akribeia* . . . is carefully to preserve the distinction between his own voice, as an investigator, and the voice of the logoi he investigates."[146] We can contrast this with John's presentation of his proposed source material, where there is often little distinction between the voice of Jesus and the voice of the narrator/author—as we have noted, for example, in the likely commentary in John 3:16–21, 31–36. This is not to say that the author's voice in John does not distinguish itself at all (most notably in 21:25), but this is an author who is committed to his narrative, almost an integral part of it. He is certainly not the "harassed editor of an unruly text," as Dewald describes Herodotus.[147]

Robin Waterfield, who translated the *Histories* for the *Oxford World's Classics* series, makes further observations on the authorial comments.[148] He rejects Alan Griffiths's description of them as "fussy authorial nudges," for he believes that "they play too important a role to be described only as 'fussy.'"[149] I see a parallel here with North's description of the author of John as shepherding readers through the narrative, "fussing the while with explanatory comments on why things happen quite as they do."[150] Like Waterfield with Herodotus, I suggest that they are too important to be described as "fussing," although North does acknowledge "John has striven to communicate with the utmost clarity."[151]

*Towards a Comparative Study*                    229

Waterfield argues that these "authorial nudges," which he also calls authorial intrusions and examples of metanarrative, are the result of the *Histories'* roots in oral performance. Even though it is a written text, with a "hugely intricate architectural unity," it "retains marked features of oral presentation."[152] I note that in Waterfield's own translation of the *Histories*, a number of the comments are placed in brackets or dashes, but most are not, which presumably reflects his own perception of their relation to the written text.[153]

Brant, in her commentary on John, mentions a parallel between one of Herodotus's procedures and the use of what I label *internal* comments in Gospel of John. Regarding the remark in John 3:24 ("For John had not yet been put under guard"), Brant describes it as an example of the narrator pointing to "an unseen, malevolent force" that "casts a shadow over the Baptist's ministry."[154] She goes on to state, "John's narrator employs a technique used with some frequency by Herodotus's narrator. At the moment that he narrates a person's success, he will add a proleptic reference to the person's end in order to point to the instability of fortune or to comment on the significance of an event."[155] However, I doubt that the author of John would have understood John the Baptist's arrest as a consequence of "the instability of fortune."[156]

In her essay on the authorial voice in Herodotus, Dewald contrasts Herodotus's intrusive style with the narrative technique of Thucydides and those historians who followed him, where the *res gestae* are presented in logical connection and almost without comment.[157] She states, "Thucydides almost never interrupts the narrative to comment *in propria persona* on the contents of the narrative or his own procedures as a historian. When he does so, it is further to reinforce the authority of the third-person narrative."[158]

David Gribble, in his essay on "Narrator Interventions in Thucydides," agrees that "the main narrative of Thucydides is characterised by a third person 'objective' style where the signs of the narrator are concealed."[159] However, "This predominant narrative mode is punctuated by passages . . . where the narrator interrupts the main account, referring to himself in the first person and/or time outside that of the main narrative."[160] Gribble suggests that reaction to these interventions has generally fallen into two categories: "They have either been seen as later additions and used as the centrepiece of analyst interpretations of the *History*, or they have been treated as expressions of the 'judgement' of the historian, providing the key to the *History*'s meaning."[161] He admits that an exact definition of these "narrator interventions" is not possible, but he sees a number of "signs" of their presence—namely, "the use of the first person; reference to τις—an implied reader; jumps in time, either retrojections, anticipations, or a more vaguely-defined anachrony . . . ; counter-factuals; and superlatives–statements that something was the greatest or the only instance."[162] He gives 22 examples of these interventions and labels them with his various categories.[163]

230                                    *Chapter 6*

A number of things strike me about Gribble's "signs" in relation to my own definition of external narrative comments in John as what lies outside the narrative framework in a temporal or spatial sense. Regarding the temporal sense, Gribble draws attention to the chronicling of "time" and "time of narration" through the interventions: "Signalling of the narrator also implies a signalling of the time of narration and thus, naturally, many of the interventions in Thucydides involve anticipation. . . . This is important. In historiography, the distinction between the time of narration and the time of the story has a dimension which is not present in fictional narratives."[164] He gives as an example the intervention in Book 3 concerning the "Ambraciot disaster":

> This was the greatest disaster to overtake a single Greek city in an equal number of days in the whole course of this war. I have not written the number of the dead, because the number of those said to have died is not credible when considered in comparison to the size of the city. However I know that if the Acarnanians and Amphilocians had been prepared to take Demosthenes' advice to assault Ambracia, they would have taken it without a struggle. (Thucydides, *History*, 3. 113.6)[165]

We can compare this shift from the time of the story to the time of narration to the use of "to this day" in 2 Samuel 4:3; 6:8; 18:18 and Matthew 27:8; 28:15. It is also comparable with the shift to the author's perspective on events in John 21:23–25.

Other of Gribble's "signs" of intervention seem to me to belong to the spatial category. This is particularly the case with the use of superlatives, as in the quotation above: "This was the *greatest* disaster to overtake a single Greek city in an equal number of days in the whole course of this war" (*my emphasis*). The use of a superlative can lift a statement out of the narrative framework by indicating a knowledge (real or imagined) of *all* instances of a particular event or quality. Gribble speaks of the paradigmatic nature of such statements: "This paradigmatic quality is suggested by the rhetoric of the interventions themselves, which typically signal that the event in question was the first, the greatest, or the only example of some general phenomenon."[166] So, for example, when Thucydides says, "Themistocles was indeed a man who displayed beyond doubt, and *more than any other*, natural genius to a quite exceptional and awesome degree" (*History*, 1:138)[167] (*my emphasis*), he is speaking rhetorically and beyond the bounds of his "objective" history. We can say the same about the author's comment in John 21:25: "There are also many other things that Jesus did; if every one of them were written down, I suppose that the world itself could not contain the books that would be written."

*Towards a Comparative Study* 231

Gribble comes to two main conclusions regarding the function of the narrator interventions in Thucydides, *History*, which relate to the two main reactions to them in existing scholarship. First, he rejects the idea that they are interventions by a later author into "an already-composed text." Even if they were written at another time from the main narrative, "they are consistent with, and indeed central to, the thinking and themes of the whole *History*."[168] This seems to me to be very close to the conclusion of Van Belle regarding the parentheses in the Gospel of John: "Qui veut les attribuer à un éditeur éventuel, devra concéder que celui-ci aurait joué un rôle important dans la composition de tout l'évangile et que son propre point de vue aurait été le même que celui de l'évangéliste" (Anyone who wants to attribute them to a later editor, will have to admit that he would have played an important role in the composition of the whole Gospel and that his own point of view would be the same as that of the evangelist).[169]

Gribble's second main conclusion is to question the belief that the narrator interventions can be separated from the rest of the narrative in such a way as to provide a distinct understanding of the author's point of view, an approach which "equates the narratorial voice of the interventions with an all-authoritative authorial voice."[170] He suggests that the purpose of the interventions "is not to tell the reader what to think (or replace a close reading of the text), but to shape reader reaction in a wider sense."[171] A similar observation is made by Tim Rood in contrasting the narrators in Thucydides and Herodotus: "Thucydides creates a greater sense of a controlling and single-minded purpose in his narrator than Herodotus does."[172] I would argue that, in the same way as in Thucydides, the narrative comments in the Gospel of John must be read as coming from one authoritative voice that is constant throughout the text, rather than conjecturing (with Hedrick and others) a conflict of voices.

## NOTES

1. David E. Aune, *The New Testament in Its Literary Environment*, LEC 8 (Philadelphia: Westminster Press, 1987), 23.
2. Bjerkelund, *Tauta Egeneto*, 23–54.
3. Sheeley, *Narrative Asides*, 40–96.
4. Hedrick, "Authorial Presence," 76; Bauckham, *Testimony*, 105.
5. Keener, *Gospel*, 1:14.
6. Bauckham, *Testimony*, 105n45.
7. Larry Hurtado, "The New Testament and Its Literary Environment," *Larry Hurtado's Blog* (blog), May 27, 2013, https://larryhurtado.wordpress.com/2013/05 /27/the-new-testament-and-its-literary-environment/.

232                                   Chapter 6

8. Austin Busch, "New Testament Narrative and Greco-Roman Literature," in *The Oxford Handbook of Biblical Narrative*, ed. Danna Nolan Fewell (Oxford: Oxford University Press, 2016), 61.

9. For such comparative work regarding the genre of the Gospels, I have found of particular value: Sean A. Adams, *Greek Genres and Jewish Authors: Negotiating Literary Culture in the Greco-Roman Era* (Waco: Baylor University Press, 2020); Aune, *New Testament*; Richard A. Burridge, *What Are the Gospels? A Comparison with Graeco-Roman Biography*, 3rd ed. (Waco: Baylor University Press, 2018); Thomas Hägg, *The Art of Biography in Antiquity* (Cambridge: Cambridge University Press, 2012); and Justin Marc Smith, *Why Βίος? On the Relationship between Gospel Genre and Implied Audience*, LNTS 518 (London: Bloomsbury T & T Clark, 2015).

10. I note Sean Adam's observation: "Unlike history writing, which is found throughout the Hellenistic and Roman eras, all of the extant Jewish biographies come from the first century CE. This concentration is noteworthy, as it suggests that Jewish authors did not previously engage with this genre and that something shifted in their perspective to make participation in biography more desirable. The increased interest in *bios* parallels the rise in biography in the Roman era, suggesting that Jewish authors were influenced by wider literary trends" (*Greek Genres*, 292). Maybe, but presumably the shift in perspective for the Gospel writers was prompted above all by their "encounter" with Jesus and desire to write about him.

11. Robert Alter, *The Art of Biblical Narrative* (London: George Allen & Unwin, 1981).

12. Alter, *Art of Biblical Narrative*, 184.

13. Alter, *Art of Biblical Narrative*, 157–58.

14. Alter, *Art of Biblical Narrative*, 184.

15. Alter, *Art of Biblical Narrative*, 184–85.

16. Alter, *Art of Biblical Narrative*, 80.

17. Alter, *Art of Biblical Narrative*, 167.

18. Alter, *Art of Biblical Narrative*, 185.

19. Alter, *Art of Biblical Narrative*, x.

20. Tamar Zewi, *Parenthesis in Biblical Hebrew*, Studies in Semitic Languages and Linguistics 50 (Leiden: Brill, 2007), 171.

21. Zewi, *Parenthesis*, 171.

22. Zewi, *Parenthesis*, 2, 6. See Leonard Bloomfield, *Language* (Chicago: University of Chicago Press, 1984; first published in 1933 by Rinehart and Winston, New York), 186; Gunther Kaltenböck, "Charting the Boundaries of Syntax: A Taxonomy of Spoken Parenthetical Clauses," *VIEWS, Vienna English Working Papers* 14, no. 1 (2005): 21.

23. Zewi, *Parenthesis*, 8.

24. Zewi, *Parenthesis*, 8.

25. Zewi, *Parenthesis*, 8.

26. Zewi, *Parenthesis*, 25–26.

27. Zewi, *Parenthesis*, 31–101.

28. Zewi, *Parenthesis*, 103–70. Zewi gives only two instances of "God's standpoint": "the LORD being merciful to him" in Genesis 19:16 and "because the LORD loved Israel for ever" in 1 Kings 10:9.

## Towards a Comparative Study

29. See Zewi, *Parenthesis*, 159–60.

30. See Zewi, *Parenthesis*, 86–87.

31. Zewi, *Parenthesis*, 49–52.

32. Robert D. Holmstedt, "Parenthesis in Biblical Hebrew as Noncoordinative Nonsubordination," *Brill's Journal of Afroasiatic Languages and Linguistics* 12 (2020): 99–118.

33. Holmstedt, "Parenthesis in Biblical Hebrew," 103.

34. Holmstedt, "Parenthesis in Biblical Hebrew," 103–4.

35. Holmstedt, "Parenthesis in Biblical Hebrew," 104.

36. Holmstedt, "Parenthesis in Biblical Hebrew," 104–5.

37. Holmstedt, "Parenthesis in Biblical Hebrew," 107.

38. Holmstedt, "Parenthesis in Biblical Hebrew," 100–101.

39. Holmstedt, "Parenthesis in Biblical Hebrew," 101–2.

40. Christopher T. Paris, *Narrative Obtrusion in the Hebrew Bible* (Minneapolis: Fortress Press, 2014), 1.

41. Paris, *Narrative Obtrusion*, 8; cf. his later comment: "Narrative obtrusions are the narrator's reaction to potential questions or problems created by the reader" (32).

42. Paris, *Narrative Obtrusion*, 1.

43. Paris, *Narrative Obtrusion*, 3.

44. Paris, *Narrative Obtrusion*, 48–66.

45. Paris, *Narrative Obtrusion*, 65. He admits that the narrator's obtrusive explanation here is insufficient in answering the ethical questions of modern readers, "but the fact that the narrator obtruded attests to the narrator's foresight into potential reader questions" (172).

46. Paris, *Narrative Obtrusion*, 66. Paris does not help his case by being rather loose in his terminology. For example, *obtrusions*, *intrusions*, and *interruptions* seem to be used interchangeably.

47. Paris, *Narrative Obtrusion*, 47.

48. Paris, *Narrative Obtrusion*, 4.

49. Paris, *Narrative Obtrusion*, 69–99. The translation of Judges 14:4 is Paris's own.

50. Paris, *Narrative Obtrusion*, 77.

51. Paris, *Narrative Obtrusion*, 101–127.

52. Paris, *Narrative Obtrusion*, 127.

53. Paris, *Narrative Obtrusion*, 41–44. He sees examples in Hebrew biblical poetry and the NT—for example, "let the reader understand" (Mk. 13:14; cf. Mt. 24:15). *Apostrophe* is one of Quintilian's figures of speech in ancient rhetoric that Sheeley refers to, defining it as "the act of turning aside from addressing the judge in the courtroom to address some other person" (*Narrative Asides*, 31).

54. Paris, *Narrative Obtrusion*, 65.

55. Paris, *Narrative Obtrusion*, 153–57.

56. Alter, *Art of Biblical Narrative*, 157.

57. A correlation between John 6:6 and Genesis 22:1 (and other OT references to God testing people) is noted by Keener (*Gospel*, 1:665).

234                                    *Chapter 6*

58. The whole section 2 Samuel 21–24 is often regarded as a series of appendices added to the Deuteronomistic history, of which 23:8–39 is a particularly self-contained unit. See A. A. Anderson, *2 Samuel*, WBC 11 (Dallas: Word, 1989), xxxv–xxxvi, 248.

59. Alter, *Art of Biblical Narrative*, 157.

60. I have not included the four references to David inquiring of the Lord, with the Lord's response (2:1; 5:19, 23–24; 21:1) as these seem to form part of the narrative rather than being parenthetical explanations.

61. A. Graeme Auld, *I & II Samuel: A Commentary*, OTL (Louisville: Westminster John Knox, 2011), 536.

62. For a summary of views on the Chronicler's use of sources, see Brevard S. Childs, *Introduction to the Old Testament as Scripture* (London: SCM Press, 1979), 645–46.

63. Auld, *I & II Samuel*, 604–5.

64. I am less sure about the dash SBLGNT uses to introduce 4:32, which may reflect the awkward syntax in 4:31–32. See France, *Gospel of Mark*, 215n30.

65. The three comments in chapter 7 are noteworthy in that they do not occur in the parallel passages in Matthew. Best sees them as the result of Mark's oral process of composition. Ernest Best, "Mark's Narrative Technique," *JSNT* 37 (1989): 53.

66. France, *Gospel of Mark*, 126.

67. I make a similar observation about John 6:61 in my annotated list.

68. Robert A. Guellich, *Mark 1–8:26*, WBC 34A (Dallas: Word, 1989), 88. See Rudolf Pesch, *Das Marcusevangelium*, 2 vols., HTKNT (Freiburg: Herder, 1977), 1:159.

69. The relation between the NT hapax legomenon Βοανηργές (Boanerges) and υἱοὶ βροντῆς (Sons of Thunder) in 3:17 is harder to explain. For a recent discussion, see Hanoch Ben Keshet, "Rethinking Mark 3:17: Did Jesus give both Boanērges and Huioi Brontēs as Apostolic Names?" *Evangelical Quarterly* 89, no. 2 (2018): 162–80.

70. France, *Gospel of Mark*, 473.

71. I have not included the shorter and longer endings of Mark, although if I did, I would probably count the shorter ending and vv.19–20 in the longer ending as temporal/spatial comments.

72. Charles W. Hedrick, "Narrator and Story in the Gospel of Mark: *Hermeneia* and *Paradosis*," *Perspectives in Religious Studies* 14, no. 3 (1987): 242. Hedrick's essay on *hermeneiai* in John, which I looked at in chapter 1, was first published in 1990, but he gave a paper on "Authorial Presence and Narrator in John: *Hermeneia* and *Paradosis*" at the Society of Biblical Literature meeting in Anaheim, California, in 1985.

73. Hedrick, "Narrator and Story," 239.

74. Hedrick, "Narrator and Story," 245.

75. Hedrick, "Narrator and Story," 242–45. He does note that 10 of his examples can be "read as statements of actors in dramatic presentation" rather than "interpretive comments of the narrator" (245).

76. Hedrick, "Narrator and Story," 245.

# Towards a Comparative Study                235

77. Hedrick, "Narrator and Story," 258.

78. Fowler, *Let the Reader*, 91n18; 142.

79. Fowler, *Let the Reader*, 81–126.

80. Fowler, *Let the Reader*, 82.

81. See Fowler, *Let the Reader*, 127–54.

82. Fowler, *Let the Reader*, 81, quoting Chatman, *Story and Discourse*, 228. I note that these are close to the four categories of aside that Sheeley uses in his analysis of Luke-Acts and other contemporaneous works.

83. Fowler, *Let the Reader*, 82–91.

84. Fowler, *Let the Reader*, 83.

85. Fowler, *Let the Reader*, 83–84.

86. Fowler, *Let the Reader*, 91.

87. Fowler, *Let the Reader*, 91.

88. Fowler, *Let the Reader*, 91.

89. Fowler, *Let the Reader*, 104–112.

90. Fowler, *Let the Reader*, 92n19; 98n27; 101n30, n31; 103n34; 105n36; 109–12; 112n51. He is uncertain as to whether to include some of his examples as comments by the narrator—for example, the phrase "as it is written of him" in Mark 9:13 (112).

91. Fowler, *Let the Reader*, 112–16.

92. Fowler, *Let the Reader*, 117.

93. Fowler, *Let the Reader*, 126. However, the main example Fowler gives of this challenge to the reader is what he calls the "interior debate by the high priests, scribes, and elders in 11:31–32," and it is not obvious to me in what sense this is parenthetical.

94. Boomershine, "Audience Asides," 87.

95. Boomershine, "Audience Asides," 82–83, 89–94.

96. Boomershine, "Audience Asides," 92–93.

97. Boomershine, "Audience Asides," 93–94. This contrasts sharply with Bauckham's thesis that Simon of Cyrene's sons were providing eyewitness testimony for the early Christian movement. Bauckham, *Jesus and the Eyewitnesses*, 51–52.

98. SBLGNT uses dashes in 7:9, 10; 23:37, but these do not indicate parentheses.

99. Some phrases at the end of sentences are introduced with a dash and it is unlikely that the editors intend them as asides: 4:18; 6:30; 7:27; 10:42.

100. Whether or not we accept 27:52–53 as belonging outside the narrative framework, which ends with the appearance of Jesus to the Eleven in Galilee (28:16–20), depends to some extent on the force of the phrase μετὰ τὴν ἔγερσιν αὐτοῦ (after his resurrection) in v.53. Although it is accepted in nearly all the manuscript evidence, Davies and Allison suspect it of being "an early gloss" inserted in order to avoid the troubling impression that these resurrections and/or appearances took place before the resurrection and appearances of Jesus himself. W. D. Davies and Dale C. Allison Jr., *The Gospel According to Saint Matthew*, 3 vols., ICC 3 (Edinburgh: T & T Clark, 1988, 1991, 1997), 3:634.

101. Luz calls genealogy "a frequent genre in biblical as well as Hellenistic sources." Ulrich Luz, *Matthew 1–7: A Commentary*, trans. James E. Crouch, ed. Helmut Koester, Hermeneia (Minneapolis: Fortress Press, 2007), 81.

236                                    *Chapter 6*

102. Alter, *Art of Biblical Narrative*, 63.

103. Davies and Allison, *Gospel*, 3:672–73.

104. R. T. France, *The Gospel of Matthew*, NICNT (Grand Rapids: Eerdmans, 2007), 12. Davies and Allison write, "With the possible exception of 1:22–3, they are editorial commentary; the characters do not speak them" (*Gospel*, 3:574). 1:22–23 could be considered as the words of the "angel of the Lord" (1:20). Another fulfilment quotation, 13:14–15, is found in Jesus' dialogue.

105. Hedrick, "Authorial Presence," 82; Sheeley, *Narrative Asides*, 38.

106. Resseguie, *Narrative Criticism*, 183.

107. France, *Gospel of Matthew*, 818.

108. Davies and Allison, *Gospel*, 3:186n65; Metzger, *Textual Commentary*, 47.

109. Ulrich Luz, *Matthew 21–28: A Commentary*, trans. James E. Crouch, ed. Helmut Koester, Hermeneia (Minneapolis: Fortress Press, 2005).

110. In Mark 13:14, Codex Bezae (D) adds τι αναγινωσκει. Much has been written about the significance of ὁ ἀναγινώσκων νοείτω. A recent comparative study by Jeffrey Hubbard examines the phrase in relation to teaching communities: Jeffrey M. Hubbard, "'Let the Reader Understand': Ancient Pedagogy and the Social Setting of Mark," *NovT* 65 (2023): 285–305. He comes to the broad conclusion that possibly "Mark's Gospel was written to be read and studied in a pedagogical setting comprised of Jesus followers" (305). However, Matthew's use of the identical phrase suggests to me that it need not be indicative of a community (Lamb, *Text, Context*, 206n25).

111. Sheeley, *Narrative Asides*, 186–88. I note that 2:22–23 and 9:45 are listed in two of his categories.

112. Sheeley divides these further into the sub-categories of explanation, identification, context, commentary (on the story and on the characters), and custom (*Narrative Asides*, 98).

113. Sheeley divides these into the sub-categories of the narrator's relationship to the story, the narrator's relationship to the reader, and the reader relationship to the story (*Narrative Asides*, 98).

114. Sheeley, *Narrative Asides*, 118. I am using the author's own translation of the remark.

115. Sheeley, *Narrative Asides*, 118.

116. Sheeley, *Narrative Asides*, 97.

117. Sheeley also includes a number of the asides marked in the Greek texts and/ or NRSV: 2:2, 23; 3:23; 5:24; 7:29–30; 8:29; 9:33; 23:19, 51. He also includes asides in 4:16; 6:16; 9:14; 14:7, 35; 17:16; 18:1, which are not in the Greek texts, NRSV, or my own list. See *Narrative Asides*, 186–88.

118. William S. Kurz, "Narrative Approaches to Luke-Acts," *Biblica* 68, no. 2 (1987): 206.

119. Joel B. Green, *The Gospel of Luke*, NICNT (Grand Rapids: Eerdmans, 1997), 167.

120. Green, *Gospel*, 189.

121. François Bovon, *Luke 1: A Commentary on the Gospel of Luke 1:1–9:50*, trans. Christine M. Thomas, ed. Helmut Koester, Hermeneia (Minneapolis: Fortress

Press, 2002), 136–37; cf. Darrell L. Bock, *Luke*, 2 vols., BECNT (Grand Rapids: Baker Academic, 1994, 1996), 1:352.

122. I. Howard Marshall, *The Gospel of Luke: A Commentary on the Greek Text*, NIGTC (Grand Rapids: Eerdmans, 1978), 394.

123. Marshall, *Gospel*, 691.

124. I have used the word counts, based on NA27, in Todd L. Price, *Structural Lexicology and the Greek New Testament: Applying Corpus Linguistics for Word Sense Possibility Delimitation Using Collocational Indicators*, Perspectives on Linguistics and Ancient Languages 6 (Piscataway, NJ: Gorgias Press, 2015). Price gives the following number of "tokens" in the Gospels as follows: Matthew: 18,348; Mark: 11,306; Luke: 19,488, where "tokens" is the term used in Corpus Linguistics of the "running words" in a text, in contrast to "types," which are the "unique words in a text" (*Structural Lexicology*, 46, 27). This gives a percentage of comment (not taking into account the length of each comment) of: Matthew: 0.12%; Mark: 0.17%; Luke: 0.12%. The figures for John are 15,640 tokens and 0.28% of comment. There are too many variables to draw any statistical significance from these figures.

125. Sheeley gives examples of "Asides which Provide Inside Views" in Luke 7:29–30 and 9:45, but neither of these are insights into Jesus (*Narrative Asides*, 114–15).

126. Michaels, *Gospel*, 353–53.

127. Michaels, *Gospel*, 353n66.

128. France, *Gospel of Mark*, 240.

129. France, *Gospel of Mark*, 161–62.

130. France, *Gospel of Matthew*, 49.

131. I do not consider 22:1, ἡ λεγομένη πάσχα (which is called the Passover), as a "translation aside," but rather an identification of the Passover with the festival of Unleavened Bread. Sheeley notes, "One may assume that Luke's readers were aware of the term 'Passover', as the narrator had already used the term to chronicle another part of Jesus' life (2.41)" (*Narrative Asides*, 107).

132. Sheeley, *Narrative Asides*, 168.

133. Sheeley, *Narrative Asides*, 168n1.

134. Most scholars believe that 1 Maccabees was originally written in Hebrew, although there are no surviving manuscripts. David A. DeSilva, *Introducing the Apocrypha: Message, Context, and Significance* (Grand Rapids: Baker Academic, 2002), 247.

135. Sheeley, *Narrative Asides*, 95.

136. Philip Stadter, "Biography and History," in *A Companion to Greek and Roman Historiography*, ed. John Marincola, Blackwells Companions to the Ancient World (Oxford: Wiley Blackwell, 2011), 528.

137. Jonas Grethlein, "The Rise of Greek Historiography and the Invention of Prose," in *The Oxford History of Historical Writing: Volume 1: Beginnings to AD 600*, ed. Andrew Feldherr and Grant Hardy (Oxford: Oxford University Press, 2011), 149. Grethlein argues that Herodotus and Thucydides developed their new genre of historiography both in sharing features of oratory and scientific writing, but also in reacting against them.

238 *Chapter 6*

138. Carolyn Dewald, "Narrative Surface and Authorial Voice in Herodotus' *Histories*," *Arethusa* 20, no. 1/2 (1987): 147.

139. Dewald, "Narrative Surface," 149.

140. Dewald, "Narrative Surface," 150n10, 154–67. The large number of authorial comments must be seen in relation to the size of the *Histories*, which *Thesaurus Linguae Graecae* gives as 185,472 words ("Statistics: Largest Works," accessed February 27, 2024, https://stephanus.tlg.uci.edu/Iris/demo/stat.jsp). Even so, this implies a percentage of comment of about 0.59%, over twice that of the Gospel of John.

141. Dewald, "Narrative Surface," 153. Presumably, this is equivalent to the distinction between a *narrator* and an *implied author*, given that we know little of Herodotus outside of the *Histories*. However, the expression "*histōr*'s authorial comments" (165) would seem to conflate the narrator and author.

142. Dewald, "Narrative Surface," 151. This is Dewald's own translation.

143. Dewald, "Narrative Surface," 151.

144. Dewald, "Narrative Surface," 156–59. John Marincola detects 42 statements of such "autopsy and enquiry." John Marincola, "Herodotean Narrative and the Narrator's Presence," *Arethusa* 20, no. 1/2 (1987): 122.

145. Dewald, "Narrative Surface," 156.

146. Dewald, "Narrative Surface," 153.

147. Dewald, "Narrative Surface," 166.

148. Robin Waterfield, "On 'Fussy Authorial Nudges' in Herodotus," *The Classical World* 102 (2009): 485–94.

149. Waterfield, "Authorial Nudges," 488. See Alan Griffiths, "Stories and Storytelling in the *Histories*," in *The Cambridge Companion to Herodotus*, ed. Carolyn Dewald and John Marincola (Cambridge: Cambridge University Press, 2006), 131.

150. North, *Journey Round John*, 149.

151. North, *Journey Round John*, 149.

152. Waterfield, "Authorial Nudges," 487.

153. Herodotus, *The Histories*, trans. Robin Waterfield, with intro. and notes Carolyn Dewald; Oxford World's Classics (Oxford: Oxford University Press, 1998).

154. Brant, *John*, 79. This is Brant's own translation.

155. Brant, *John*, 80. Brant is here citing an essay by Irene de Jong, who gives an example from Herodotus, *Histories* 7.213, "where, at the moment Ephialtes is ingratiating himself with the Persian king, the narrator reveals that he will later be killed." See Irene J. F. de Jong, "Herodotus," in *Narrators, Narratees, and Narratives in Ancient Greek: Studies in Ancient Greek Narrative, Volume 1*, ed. Irene J. F. de Jong, René Nünlist, and Angus M. Bowie, Mnemosyne Supplements 257 (Leiden: Brill, 2004), 106.

156. Brant modifies her phrase "the instability of fortune" from de Jong's "the instability of fate" ("Herodotus," 106).

157. Dewald, "Narrative Surface," 148.

158. Dewald, "Narrative Surface," 149–50.

159. David Gribble, "Narrator Interventions in Thucydides," *The Journal of Hellenic Studies* 118 (1998): 41.

160. Gribble, "Narrator Interventions," 41.

Towards a Comparative Study

161. Gribble, "Narrator Interventions," 41.

162. Gribble, "Narrator Interventions," 47. He adds to this list the use of rhetorical questions (on two occasions) (49n50).

163. Gribble, "Narrator Interventions," 47–49.

164. Gribble, "Narrator Interventions," 50.

165. Gribble, "Narrator Interventions," 51. I assume this is his own translation, but he does not say.

166. Gribble, "Narrator Interventions," 54.

167. Thucydides, *The Peloponnesian War*, trans. Martin Hammond, with intro. and notes P. J. Rhodes, Oxford World's Classics (Oxford: Oxford University Press, 2009), 67.

168. Gribble, "Narrator Interventions," 62, 63.

169. Van Belle, *Les Parenthèses*, 209–10

170. Gribble, "Narrator Interventions," 63.

171. Gribble, "Narrator Interventions," 62.

172. T. Rood, "Thucydides," in *Narrators, Narratees, and Narratives in Ancient Greek: Studies in Ancient Greek Narrative, Volume 1*, ed. Irene J. F. de Jong, René Nünlist, and Angus M. Bowie, Mnemosyne Supplements 257 (Leiden: Brill, 2004), 121.

# Conclusions

## *The Function of Narrative Comments in the Gospel of John*

So what exactly is the function (or are the functions) of narrative comments in the Gospel of John?

In attempting to find answers to this question, I began by looking at articles and monographs on the subject from the past 100 years or so. I focussed particularly on the influential essay by Tenney (1960) and the major works by Van Belle (1985), Bjerkelund (1987), and Sheeley (1992), and I also looked more briefly at sections in the introductions to the commentaries by Bernard (1928) and Brown (1966, 2003) and at various Greek grammars. This survey raised further questions. Indeed, the sheer number of examples considered by scholars, at its most extreme with Van Belle's cumulative and overlapping list of 700, strongly implies that there is a considerable subjective element in determining what an aside/parenthesis/comment is and raised the question of whether there are any objective criteria for distinguishing such phenomena from the main narrative of the text. This formed the basis for further examination in chapter 2 and my own list of comments in chapter 3. The survey also raised the questions of the relation of the narrative comments to the process of the Gospel's composition and their relation to the narrator or author of the text, which formed the basis for chapters 4 and 5. Finally, the use of a comparative approach by Bjerkelund and Sheeley, as well as the observations by Bauckham (2007), prompted my "Towards a Comparative Study" in chapter 6, which concentrates on some of the historical writings in the OT/HB and on the Synoptic Gospels, as well as making a brief glance at the writings of Herodotus and Thucydides, alongside a health warning about the dangers of comparative study with extrabiblical Graeco-Roman literature.

In chapter 2, I focussed on the *terminology, definition,* and *categorization* of asides, arguing that this is an area in which too much has been assumed rather than argued for. As well as considering the findings of the scholars

241

242 *Conclusions*

in my initial survey, I also adopted an "inductive" approach based on those asides indicated with punctuation marks in recent editions of the Greek NT and the NRSV translation, as well as insights from narratology, drama, and linguistic theory. I noted that there is a considerable degree of complexity and uncertainty, which is probably why NT scholars have often shied away from consideration of these issues. In regard to the variety of *terminology* for phrases and sentences which commentators regard as in some way distinct from their co-text, I distinguished between those terms which emphasize a perceived redactional process in the composition of the text, terms such as *interpolations, insertions*, and *glosses*, and those terms which reflect the influence of modern narrative criticism and the point of view of the narrator, terms such as *asides, comments*, and *remarks*. I also noted the problem with the term *asides* and other spatial metaphors, such as *footnotes* or *parentheses*, in that they imply that these phrases and sentences are of lesser value than the "real" narrative. On this basis, I argued that it is helpful to employ the more neutral term *narrative comments*.

Regarding *definition*, I proposed that in the Gospel of John the comments make some form of interjection into the narrative, although there remains a subjective element in determining the force of this interjection. I also concluded that although their principal function is explanatory, this is not their sole function: they also indicate a more direct form of address and thus help establish a relationship between the author/narrator and reader/narratee. Through consideration of the range of definitions in literary, dramatic, and linguistic theory, I observed that they can fulfil a rhetorical function in conveying the values of the narrator/author and can also be used as part of a strategy of dramatic irony. However, their definition remains complex and contested, especially with regard to lexical, grammatical, or syntactical definitions. Indeed, I have chosen to give relatively little attention to such linguistic indicators of comments, as, in practice, I believe that phrases and sentences have to first be defined as parenthetical before we can consider lexical/grammatical/syntactical features, rather than it being the other way round. For example, some if not most of the "asides" in John are relative clauses, but then so are even more "non-asides." So, I agree with Van Belle that we cannot be bound by a grammatical definition.[1]

In an attempt to overcome some of the element of subjectivity in the definition of parenthetical material, while acknowledging their interjectory and explanatory functions, I have provided my own definition of narrative comments as those phrases or sentences which lie outside the narrative framework of the Gospel, thus making a distinction between *external* and *internal* comments. I further classify the external comments as those which belong outside the narrative framework in a *temporal* sense and those which belong outside in a *spatial* sense (by providing extra information for the reader), although in some cases I admit that there is an overlap between these sub-categories. Although many scholars would include various internal comments in their lists of asides, I question whether such examples of *analepsis* and *prolepsis,* integral to the overall structure of the narrative, can truly be considered as parenthetical. My definitions, which are based on content and function, are not foolproof, but I would encourage readers to consider if they can improve on them, given the complexity and subjectivity of the definition of parenthetical material. A continuing debate on this subject would be of value not just for Johannine studies, but for literary and linguistic methods generally.

I am less sure of the value of *categorization,* but I analysed the lists of categories used by Tenney, O'Rourke, Van Belle, Hedrick, and Köstenberger, comparing them with the broader categories used by Thatcher and Sheeley. I concluded that there is general agreement over the following categories: explanation—of words, places, times, and customs; structuring of the narrative; theological insights; reference to external sources; the self-awareness of the author/narrator.

In chapter 3, I provide a numbered list of narrative comments in the Gospel of John based on my own definitions as set out in the previous chapter. These are the comments which I regard as *external* to the narrative framework in contrast to those which are *internal,* which I list separately. I have annotated my list of 45 narrative comments with the sub-category of *temporal, spatial* or *temporal-spatial,* and explained why I have included them. I also note a number of sentences or phrases marked with dashes or brackets in the NRSV which I regard as integral to the narrative or discourse and have, therefore, not included in my list of external narrative comments. Readers will observe that I have fewer narrative comments in my list than those of the scholars in my survey, but the number in my list still indicates that the comments are a notable feature of the Gospel.

In chapter 4, I returned to the question of the relation of the comments to the process of the Gospel's composition. I noted that the earlier scholars in my survey all raised the issue of layers of redaction within the text, using terms such as *interpolations* or *glosses* to imply that they are the work of an editor or editors adding material to an existing text. Indeed, in the case of Flowers's essay, he claimed to be able to detect conflicting voices in the narrative, and I observed how this idea is echoed in the writings of scholars such as Hedrick.

The importance of a process of redaction in relation to asides continues to be found in some Johannine commentaries, such as those of Bultmann (1941) and von Wahlde (2010), but I suggested that from roughly the 1960s onwards there has been a shift in focus to a more synchronic approach and an increasing interest in the literary function of asides as an integral part of the text. Through various case studies, including an examination of textual

244                                   *Conclusions*

variants, I argued that none of the narrative comments should be treated as later additions, with the exception of 5:4. I also spent some time looking at the relationship between oral and written methods of transmission and concluded that we should be wary of envisaging multiple early editions of the Gospel with additions by different hands. Although we cannot reconstruct a definitive "final form" of the Gospel, and we cannot be sure at what stage in the process of transmission and composition the comments were integrated into the narrative, I suggested that its repetitive style and complex structure imply that they are primarily part of the literary process. Moreover, we should take seriously the author's commitment to the Gospel as a *written* text and the author's possible belief that its composition was inspired by the Holy Spirit.

Overall, I argued that the so-called "asides" in the Gospel of John cannot be considered peripheral or as evidence of later editorial work. Rather they are an essential part of the text, even if we cannot be sure of their exact purpose.

Following on from my observation about the shift from diachronic to synchronic approaches in the interpretation of the Gospel and the growing impact of narrative criticism in NT studies, I noted in chapter 5 how this has brought to the fore the matter of the relation between the *author* and the *narrator*. I spent the bulk of this chapter looking at various understandings of the narrator in John, although aware of the warnings of Stibbe and others about the risks of applying methodologies that have been developed primarily in the study of the modern novel, so that concepts such as the *unreliable narrator* have to be treated with caution. I questioned the widely held belief that the narrator in John is *omniscient* and suggested that the literary critic Annjeanette Wiese's concept of the narrator's "superior knowledge" is more helpful and fits with the post-resurrection point of view of the writer of the Gospel, looking back on the events of Jesus' life after time to reflect on their meaning. I stated that this "superior knowledge" is not necessarily a supernatural knowledge, although the writer may well have claimed to be inspired by the Spirit of truth. In terms of *intrusiveness* and *reliability*, I concluded that the narrator in John is not overly intrusive and that there is little "self-conscious narration." However, I stressed that the narrator is shown as reliable and authoritative through the comments, including the so-called "translation asides."

While I spent a large part of chapter 5 interacting with those who have focussed on the narrator in John, I am not, in fact, convinced that we can distinguish between the author and the narrator. So what I concluded about the nature of a proposed narrator in terms of omniscience, intrusiveness, reliability, and point of view applies equally to the author of the Gospel, even if that author remains unknown to us. I also stressed the importance of noting how the narrative comments are used in the relationship between the author and intended hearers/readers of texts. In this respect, I drew attention to the methodology of *evaluation* or *appraisal* within linguistics. I also referred

*Conclusions*                                                                                        245

to the work of the Ken Rylands on *metadiscourse* and argued that although there are only a few direct author-reader comments in the Gospel (1:16–18; 19:35–37; 20:30–31; 21:23–25), these comments indicate an author-reader dynamic in which the author seeks to guide the reader to a particular understanding of Jesus. This is done partly through the use of *internal* comments (analepsis and prolepsis), through which the author maintains a hold on the overall structure of the narrative, but even more so through the use of *external* comments (temporal and/or spatial), by which the author conveys a credible and authoritative perspective to a possibly diverse intended readership.

I concluded that the narrative comments are the work of a real "flesh and blood" author who, although not omniscient, possesses a "superior knowledge" from a post-resurrection perspective and who is committed to sharing a particular understanding of Jesus with hearers/readers. Given my emphasis on the author rather than the narrator, I rejected the term *narrator's comments*, but as we do not know who the author was and as I do not think we can distinguish between the author and the narrator in John, I have chosen to use the term *narrative comments* rather than *authorial comments*.

In the final chapter, I made comparisons of the use of narrative comments in John with those in some of the OT/HB historical narratives, notably in 2 Samuel, and I looked at the work of Robert Alter, Tamar Zewi, Robert Holmstedt, and Christopher Paris. I noted similarities with my own definitions of temporal and spatial comments and I drew particular attention to the insights that the OT narrators have into the mind of God, suggesting that they provide something of a paradigm for John's insights into the mind and motives of Jesus.

I also made comparisons with the Synoptic Gospels and listed all the examples of external narrative comments in them that fit my own definition. I decided that there are 19 in Mark, 22 in Matthew (of which 10 are fulfilment quotations), and 24 in Luke. This compares with the 45 in John. With the exception of the Prologue in Luke (1:1–4), I noted that none of the Synoptic narrators are overly intrusive. I also noted that one particular difference between John and the Synoptics is that whereas comments providing insight into Jesus are fairly frequent in John, they are less so in the Synoptics. I speculated as to whether this might be accounted for by John's heightened sense of being the author of Scripture, guided by the Spirit of truth (16:13), with the same sort of prophetic insight that guided the writers of the OT historical narratives.

I also made some tentative comparisons with the use of narrative comments in extrabiblical Greek literature, despite my reluctance to do so given the lack of obvious dependence on such literature. I briefly glanced at the two major Greek historians of the late fifth century BC/BCE, Herodotus and Thucydides, pioneers in the "invention" of the authoritative prose of

246  *Conclusions*

historiography. I referred to the work of Carolyn Dewald and Robin Water-field on Herodotus and David Gribble and Tim Root on Thucydides and noted that whereas Herodotus is a highly intrusive author, Thucydides is much less so.

That is the ground that I have covered in this book and whether or not my own definitions and deductions are widely accepted, I hope that I have been able to provide a helpful overview of the subject of narrative comments in the Gospel of John. I have not intended to tie up all the loose ends of asides/comments/parentheses in the Gospel, but I trust that I have been able to give sufficiently comprehensive coverage to their function to stimulate further debate not just on the comments themselves, but on the wider issues of literary and linguistic approaches to the text and the importance of terminology. Perhaps the major insight that has come across in the course of this study is that we cannot dismiss the comments as somehow of lesser value than their co-text. Indeed, the evidence of sociolinguistic work on parentheticals suggests that such material can have a major function in the communitive process. So, returning to the question as to what exactly are the functions of narrative comments in the Gospel of John, I draw the following main conclusions:

1. The narrative comments in John are an integral, indeed essential, part of the text. They are not later additions to an already written composition and they do not represent conflicting voices. They may well have been added to the narrative at some point in the complex process of oral transmission and dictation, but they are representative of the style of the author, rather than being the work of redactors. What historical critics label as *asides*, *glosses*, or *additions*, seeing them as fitting awkwardly into a desired smooth narrative, reflects rather the problem that linguists (both formal and functional) have in defining parenthetical material. I also see the historical critics' approach as undermining something of the joy of freedom of expression in language.

2. The internal comments, as examples of analepsis and prolepsis, have a structural function in the narrative and can be seen as part of the strategy of guiding the hearer/reader. However, we have to be careful not to over-label and treat as parenthetical those remarks which are simply part of the author's discursive style, moving back and forth during the narrative, picking up and sometimes clarifying earlier details. This is important, as determining what is and is not an aside/comment has implications for exegesis, as we have seen in the case of 4:9 and the question of whether the words "Jews do not share things in common with Samaritans" should be attributed to the Samaritan woman or the author/narrator.

*Conclusions* 247

3. The external comments are those which lie outside the framework of the narrative in a temporal or spatial sense. That is, they concern sayings or events either before or after the ministry of Jesus on earth or are outside the common perception of those who were involved in that ministry. Their primary function is explanatory in what David Ford describes as "this thoroughly pedagogical Gospel."[2] Some commentators dislike this pedagogical function. They do not like being told what to think. However, the author of John was vitally concerned that hearers/readers should believe that Jesus is the Christ, the Son of God, and that they might have "life in his name" (20:31). All the narrative comments are an integral part of that key message.

4. The narrative comments are also an assertion of the author's authority. This is not an omniscient narrator, but an author who has a particular insight into the mind and motives of Jesus. This insight is not necessarily a supernatural knowledge, although it may be understood as guided by the Spirit of truth, but it is the result of the post-resurrection perspective of the author, who has had time to reflect on the meaning of the events of Jesus' ministry. It may be that the author of John is conscious that this is a different Gospel from the Synoptics and wants to make sure that it is read and understood correctly.

5. Those narrative comments which can be considered more intrusive (1:16–18; 19:35–37; 20:30–31; 21:23–25) indicate a more direct form of address and establish something of a relationship between the author and hearer/reader. However, I am sceptical that any of the comments, including the so-called "translation asides," can be used to determine the actual intended audience of the Gospel or only in the very broad terms of it being a diverse audience.

These are my conclusions and I hope they will lead to further discussion.

## NOTES

1. Van Belle, "Les Parenthèses Johanniques," 1918. Although I suggest that there is an ambivalence in Van Belle's attitude to the value of the grammatical definition of parentheses, hence his long list of parentheses by 29 categories of grammatical classification (*Les Parenthèses*, 113–24) and his criticism of Sheeley for focussing on their function and content rather than "their style and grammatical construction" (review of Sheeley, 468).

2. David F. Ford, *The Gospel of John: A Theological Commentary* (Grand Rapids: Baker Academic, 2021), 66.

# Bibliography

Abbott, Edwin A. *Johannine Grammar*. London: Adam and Charles Black, 1906.

Achtemeier, Paul J. "Omne verbum sonat: The New Testament and the Oral Environment of Late Western Antiquity." *Journal of Biblical Literature* 109, no. 1 (1990): 3–27.

Adams, Sean A. *Greek Genres and Jewish Authors: Negotiating Literary Culture in the Greco-Roman Era*. Waco: Baylor University Press, 2020.

Alter, Robert. *The Art of Biblical Narrative*. London: George Allen & Unwin, 1981.

Anderson, A. A. *2 Samuel*. Word Biblical Commentary 11. Dallas: Word, 1989.

Auerbach, Eric. *Mimesis: The Representation of Reality in Western Literature*. Princeton: Princeton University Press, 1953.

Auld, A. Graeme. *I & II Samuel: A Commentary*. Old Testament Library. Louisville: Westminster John Knox, 2011.

Aune, David E. *The New Testament in Its Literary Environment*. Library of Early Christianity 8. Philadelphia: Westminster Press, 1987.

Bain, David. *Actors and Audience: A Study of Asides and Related Conventions in Greek Drama*. Oxford: Oxford University Press, 1977.

Barrett, Charles K. *The Gospel According to St. John*. 2nd ed. London: SPCK, 1978.

Bauckham, Richard. "John for Readers of Mark." In *The Gospels for All Christians: Rethinking the Gospel Audiences*, edited by Richard Bauckham, 147–71. Edinburgh: T & T Clark, 1998.

Bauckham, Richard. *The Testimony of the Beloved Disciple: Narrative, History, and Theology in the Gospel of John*. Grand Rapids: Baker Academic, 2007.

Bauckham, Richard. *Jesus and the Eyewitnesses: The Gospels as Eyewitness Testimony*. 2nd ed. Grand Rapids: Eerdmans, 2017.

Beasley-Murray, George R. *John*. Word Biblical Commentary 36. Waco: Word, 1987.

Ben Keshet, Hanoch. "Rethinking Mark 3:17: Did Jesus give both Boanērges and Huioi Brontēs as Apostolic Names?" *Evangelical Quarterly* 89, no. 2 (2018): 162–80.

250 Bibliography

Bennema, Cornelis. "A Comprehensive Approach to Understanding Character in the Gospel of John." In *Characters and Characterization in the Gospel of John*, edited by Christopher W. Skinner, 36–58. Library of New Testament Studies 461. London: Bloomsbury T & T Clark, 2013.

Bernard, John Henry. *A Critical and Exegetical Commentary on the Gospel According to St. John.* Edited by A. H. McNeile. 2 vols. International Critical Commentary. Edinburgh: T & T Clark, 1928.

Best, Ernest. "Mark's Narrative Technique." *Journal for the Study of the New Testament* 37 (1989): 43–58.

Bjerkelund, Carl J. *Tauta Egeneto: Die Präzisierungssätze im Johannesevangelium.* Wissenschaftliche Untersuchungen zum Neuen Testament 40. Tübingen: Mohr Siebeck, 1987.

Blass, Friedrich, Albert Debrunner, and Robert W. Funk. *A Greek Grammar of the New Testament and Other Early Christian Literature.* Chicago: University of Chicago Press, 1961.

Blass, Friedrich, Albert Debrunner, and Friedrich Rehkopf. *Grammatik des neutestamentlichen Griechisch.* 18th ed. Göttingen: Vandenhoeck and Ruprecht, 2001.

Blodgett, Harriet. "The Rhetoric of the Narrator in Vanity Fair." *Nineteenth-Century Fiction* 22, no. 3 (1967): 211–23.

Blomberg, Craig L. *The Historical Reliability of John's Gospel.* Leicester: Inter-Varsity Press, 2001.

Bloomfield, Leonard. *Language.* Chicago: University of Chicago Press, 1984. First published 1933 by Rinehart and Winston, New York.

Bock, Darrell L. *Luke.* 2 vols. Baker Exegetical Commentary on the New Testament. Grand Rapids: Baker Academic, 1994, 1996.

Boismard, Marie-Emile, and Arnaud Lamouille. *Synopse des quatre Évangiles en français III: L'évangile de Jean.* Paris: Éditions du Cerf, 1977.

Boomershine, Thomas E. "The Medium and Message of John: Audience Address and Audience Identity in the Fourth Gospel." In *The Fourth Gospel in First Century Media Culture*, edited by Anthony Le Donne and Tom Thatcher, 92–120. Library of New Testament Studies 426. London: Bloomsbury T & T Clark, 2011.

Boomershine, Thomas E. "Audience Asides and the Audiences of Mark: The Difference Performance Makes." In *Narrative and Performance Criticisms in Dialogue and Debate*, edited by Kelly R. Iverson, 80–96. Cambridge: Lutterworth Press, 2014.

Booth, Wayne. *The Rhetoric of Fiction.* 2nd ed. Chicago: University of Chicago Press, 1983.

Bovon, François. *Luke 1: A Commentary on the Gospel of Luke 1:1–9:50.* Translated by Christine M. Thomas. Edited by Helmut Koester. Hermeneia. Minneapolis: Fortress Press, 2002.

Brant, Jo-Ann A. *Dialogue and Drama: Elements of Greek Tragedy in the Fourth Gospel.* Peabody, MA: Hendrickson, 2004.

Brant, Jo-Ann A. *John*, Paideia Commentaries on the New Testament. Grand Rapids: Baker Academic, 2011.

Brant, Jo-Ann A. "John among the Ancient Novels." In *The Gospel of John as Genre Mosaic*, edited by Kasper Bro Larsen, 157–68. Studia Aarhusiana Neotestamentica 3. Göttingen: Vandenhoeck & Ruprecht, 2015.

## Bibliography

Brant, Jo-Ann A. "The Fourth Gospel as Narrative and Drama." In *The Oxford Handbook of Johannine Studies*, edited by Judith M. Lieu and Martinus C. de Boer, 186–202. Oxford: Oxford University Press, 2018.

Brodie, Thomas. "Three Revolutions, A Funeral, and Glimmers of a Challenging New Dawn." In *What We Have Heard from the Beginning: The Past, Present, and Future of Johannine Studies*, edited by Tom Thatcher, 63–81. Waco: Baylor University Press, 2007.

Brown, Raymond E. *The Gospel According to John.* 2 vols. Anchor Bible 29–29A. New York: Doubleday, 1966, 1970.

Brown, Raymond E. *The Community of the Beloved Disciple.* New York: Paulist Press, 1979.

Brown, Raymond E. *Introduction to the Gospel of John.* Edited by Francis J. Maloney. Anchor Bible Reference Library. New York: Doubleday, 2003.

Bultmann, Rudolf. *Das Evangelium des Johannes.* Kritisch-exegetischer Kommentar über das Neue Testament. Göttingen: Vandenhoeck & Ruprecht, 1941.

Bultmann, Rudolf. *The Gospel of John: A Commentary.* Translated by George R. Beasley-Murray. Edited by Rupert W. N. Hoare and John K. Riches. Philadelphia: Westminster Press, 1971.

Burge, Gary M. *Interpreting the Gospel of John: A Practical Guide.* 2nd ed. Grand Rapids: Baker Academic, 2013.

Burridge, Richard A. *What Are the Gospels? A Comparison with Graeco-Roman Biography.* 3rd ed. Waco: Baylor University Press, 2018.

Burton-Roberts, Noel. "Parentheticals." In *Encyclopedia of Language and Linguistics*, edited by Keith Brown, 2nd ed., 14 vols. Amsterdam: Elsevier, 2006.

Busch, Austin. "New Testament Narrative and Greco-Roman Literature." In *The Oxford Handbook of Biblical Narrative*, edited by Danna Nolan Fewell, 61–72. Oxford: Oxford University Press, 2016.

Bynum, Wm. Randolph. *The Fourth Gospel and the Scriptures: Illuminating the Form and Meaning of Scriptural Citation in John 19:37.* Supplements to Novum Testamentum 144. Leiden: Brill, 2012.

Calvin, Jean. *Calvin's Commentaries: The Gospel according to St John 1–10.* Translated by T. H. L. Parker. Edited by David W. Torrance and Thomas F. Torrance. Edinburgh: Saint Andrew Press, 1959.

Carson, Donald A. "Current Source Criticism of the Fourth Gospel: Some Methodological Questions." *Journal of Biblical Literature* 97, no. 3 (1978): 411–29.

Carson, Donald A. *The Gospel According to John.* Leicester: Inter-Varsity Press, 1991.

Chatman, Seymour. *Story and Discourse: Narrative Structure in Fiction and Film.* Ithaca, NY: Cornell University Press, 1978.

Childs, Brevard S. *Introduction to the Old Testament as Scripture.* London: SCM Press, 1979.

Comfort, Philip Wesley. *A Commentary on the Manuscripts and Text of the New Testament.* Grand Rapids: Kregel Academic, 2015.

Connolly, Francis X. *A Rhetoric Case Book.* New York: Harcourt, Brace & Co., 1953.

Cortazzi, Martin, and Lixian Jin. "Evaluating Evaluation in Narrative." In *Evaluation in Text: Authorial Stance and the Construction of Discourse*, ed. Susan Hunston and Geoff Thompson, 102–20. Oxford: Oxford University Press, 2000.

# Bibliography

Credner, Karl August. *Einleitung in das Neue Testament: Erster Theil*. Halle: Waisenhauses, 1836.

Crown, Alan D. "Samaritan Literature and Its Manuscripts." *Bulletin of the John Rylands Library* 76, no. 1 (1994): 21–49.

Culler, Jonathan D. "Omniscience." *Narrative* 12, no. 1 (2004): 22–34.

Culpepper, R. Alan. *The Johannine School: An Evaluation of the Johannine-School Hypothesis Based on an Investigation of the Nature of Ancient Schools*. Society of Biblical Literature Dissertation Series 26. Missoula: Scholars Press, 1975.

Culpepper, R. Alan. *Anatomy of the Fourth Gospel: A Study in Literary Design*. Philadelphia: Fortress Press, 1983.

Culpepper, R. Alan. *John, the Son of Zebedee: The Life of a Legend*. Edinburgh: T & T Clark, 2000.

Davies, Margaret. *Rhetoric and Reference in the Fourth Gospel*. Journal for the Study of the New Testament: Supplement Series 69. Sheffield: Sheffield Academic Press, 1992.

Davies, W. D., and Dale C. Allison Jr. *The Gospel According to Saint Matthew*. 3 vols. International Critical Commentary 3. Edinburgh: T & T Clark, 1988, 1991, 1997.

Dehé, Nicole, and Yordanka Kavalova. "Parentheticals: An Introduction." In *Parentheticals*, edited by Nicole Dehé and Yordanka Kavalova, 1–22. Linguistik Aktuell/ Linguistics Today 106. Amsterdam: John Benjamins, 2007.

De Jong, Irene J. F. "Herodotus." In *Narrators, Narratees, and Narratives in Ancient Greek: Studies in Ancient Greek Narrative, Volume 1*, edited by Irene J. F. de Jong, René Nünlist, and Angus M. Bowie, 101–14. Mnemosyne Supplements 257. Leiden: Brill, 2004, 106.

Demsky, Aaron, and Meir Bar-Ilan. "Writing in Ancient Israel and Early Judaism." In *Mikra: Text, Translation, Reading, and Interpretation of the Hebrew Bible in Ancient Judaism and Early Christianity*, edited by Martin Jan Mulder and Harry Sysling, 1–38. Philadelphia: Fortress Press, 1988.

DeSilva, David A. *Introducing the Apocrypha: Message, Context, and Significance*. Grand Rapids: Baker Academic, 2002.

Dewald, Carolyn. "Narrative Surface and Authorial Voice in Herodotus' *Histories*." *Arethusa* 20, no. 1/2 (1987): 147–70.

Dewey, Joanna. "The Gospel of John in Its Oral-Written Media World." In *Jesus in Johannine Tradition*, edited by Robert T. Fortna and Tom Thatcher, 239–52. Louisville: Westminster John Knox, 2001.

Dodd, C. H. *The Interpretation of the Fourth Gospel*. Cambridge: Cambridge University Press, 1953.

Fee, Gordon D. "On the Inauthenticity of John 5:3b–4." *The Evangelical Quarterly* 54, no. 4 (1982): 207–18.

Flowers, H. J. "Interpolations in the Fourth Gospel." *Journal of Biblical Literature* 40, no. 3/4 (1921): 146–58.

Ford, David F. *The Gospel of John: A Theological Commentary*. Grand Rapids: Baker Academic, 2021.

Fowler, Robert M. *Let the Reader Understand: Reader-Response Criticism and the Gospel of Mark*. Minneapolis: Fortress Press, 1991.

Bibliography 253

France, R. T. *The Gospel of Mark: A Commentary on the Greek Text.* New International Greek Testament Commentary. Grand Rapids: Eerdmans, 2002.

France, R. T. *The Gospel of Matthew.* New International Commentary on the New Testament. Grand Rapids: Eerdmans, 2007.

Garvie, Alfred E. *The Beloved Disciple: Studies of the Fourth Gospel.* London: Hodder and Stoughton, 1922.

Genette, Gérard. *Narrative Discourse.* Translated by Jane E. Lewin. Oxford: Basil Blackwell, 1980.

Genette, Gérard. *Narrative Discourse Revisited.* Translated by Jane E. Lewin. Ithaca, NY: Cornell University Press, 1988.

Godet, Frédéric Louis. *Commentary on the Gospel of St. John with a Critical Introduction.* Translated by M. D. Cusin. 3rd ed. 3 vols. Edinburgh: T & T Clark, 1899–1900.

Grafton, Anthony. *The Footnote: A Curious History.* London: Faber and Faber, 1997.

Grafton, Anthony. "The Footnote from De Thou to Ranke." *History and Theory* 33, no. 4 (1994): 53–76.

*Greek New Testament, The,* edited by Barbara Aland, Kurt Aland, Johannes Karavidopoulos, Carlo M. Martini, Bruce M. Metzger, in cooperation with the Institute for New Testament Textual Research. 5th rev. ed. Stuttgart: Deutsche Bibelgesellschaft/United Bible Societies, 2014.

*Greek New Testament: SBL Edition, The,* edited by Michael W. Holmes. Atlanta: Society of Biblical Literature/Bellingham: Logos Bible Software, 2010.

Green, Joel B. *The Gospel of Luke.* New International Commentary on the New Testament. Grand Rapids: Eerdmans, 1997.

Grenfell, Bernard P., and Arthur S. Hunt. *ΛΟΓΙΑ ΙΗCΟΥ: Sayings of Our Lord from an Early Greek Papyrus.* London: Egypt Exploration Fund/Henry Frowde, 1897.

Grethlein, Jonas. "The Rise of Greek Historiography and the Invention of Prose." In *The Oxford History of Historical Writing: Volume 1: Beginnings to AD 600,* edited by Andrew Feldherr and Grant Hardy, 148–70. Oxford: Oxford University Press, 2011.

Gribble, David. "Narrator Interventions in Thucydides." *The Journal of Hellenic Studies* 118 (1998): 41–67.

Griffiths, Alan. "Stories and Storytelling in the *Histories.*" In *The Cambridge Companion to Herodotus,* edited by Carolyn Dewald and John Marincola, 130–44. Cambridge: Cambridge University Press, 2006.

Guellich, Robert A. *Mark 1–8:26.* Word Biblical Commentary 34A. Dallas: Word, 1989.

Gunderson, Erik. *Laughing Awry: Plautus and Tragicomedy.* Oxford: Oxford University Press, 2015.

Haegeman, Liliane. "Parenthetical Adverbials: The Radical Orphanage Approach." In *Dislocated Elements in Discourse: Syntactic, Semantic, and Pragmatic Perspectives,* edited by Benjamin Shaer, Philippa Cook, Werner Frey, and Claudia Maienborn, 331–47. New York: Routledge, 2009.

Haenchen, Ernst. *A Commentary on the Gospel of John.* Translated by Robert W. Funk. Edited by Robert W. Funk and Ulrich Busse. 2 vols. Hermeneia. Philadelphia: Fortress Press, 1984.

254                                      Bibliography

Hägg, Thomas. *The Art of Biography in Antiquity*. Cambridge: Cambridge University Press, 2012.

Haines-Eitzen, Kim. "Textual Communities in Late Antique Christianity." In *A Companion to Late Antiquity*, edited by Philip Rousseau with the assistance of Jutta Raithal, 246–57. Malden: Wiley-Blackwell, 2009.

Hawthorn, Jeremy. *A Glossary of Contemporary Literary Theory*. 4th ed. London: Arnold, 2000.

Hedrick, Charles W. "Narrator and Story in the Gospel of Mark: *Hermeneia* and *Paradosis*." *Perspectives in Religious Studies* 14, no. 3 (1987): 239–58.

Hedrick, Charles W. "Review of Gilbert Van Belle, *Les Parenthèses dans L'Évangile de Jean: Aperçu Historique et Classification, Texte Grec de Jean*." *Journal of Biblical Literature* 106, no. 4 (1987): 719–22.

Hedrick, Charles W. "Authorial Presence and Narrator in John: Commentary and Story." In *Gospel Origins and Christian Beginnings: In Honor of James M. Robinson*, edited by James E. Goehring, Charles W. Hedrick, and Jack T. Sanders with Hans Dieter Betz, 74–93. Sonoma: Polebridge Press, 1990.

Herodotus, *The Histories*. Translated by Robin Waterfield, with introduction and notes by Carolyn Dewald. Oxford World's Classics. Oxford: Oxford University Press, 1998.

Hitchcock, F. R. M. "Is the Fourth Gospel a Drama?" *Theology* 7 (1923): 307–17. Reprinted in *The Gospel of John as Literature: An Anthology of Twentieth Century Perspectives*, edited by Mark W. G. Stibbe, 15–24. New Testament Tools, Studies and Documents 17. Leiden: Brill, 1993.

Holmstedt, Robert D. "Parenthesis in Biblical Hebrew as Noncoordinative Nonsubordination." *Brill's Journal of Afroasiatic Languages and Linguistics* 12 (2020): 99–118.

Hoskyns, Edwyn Clement. *The Fourth Gospel*. Edited by Francis Noel Davey. 2nd ed. London: Faber & Faber, 1947.

Hubbard, Jeffrey M. "'Let the Reader Understand': Ancient Pedagogy and the Social Setting of Mark." *Novum Testamentum* 65 (2023): 285–305.

Hurtado, Larry. "The New Testament and Its Literary Environment." *Larry Hurtado's Blog* (blog), May 27, 2013. https://larryhurtado.wordpress.com/2013/05/27/the-new-testament-and-its-literary-environment/.

Hyland, Ken. "Stance and Engagement: A Model of Interaction in Academic Discourse." *Discourse Studies* 7, no. 2 (2005): 173–92.

Hyland, Ken. *Metadiscourse: Exploring Interaction in Writing*. 2nd ed. London: Bloomsbury Academic, 2019.

Jeremias, Joachim. "Johanneische Literarkritik." *Theologische Blätter* 20 (1941): 33–46.

Johnson, Luke Timothy. *The Writings of the New Testament: An Interpretation*. Rev. ed. London: SCM, 1999.

Kaltenböck, Gunther. "Charting the Boundaries of Syntax: A Taxonomy of Spoken Parenthetical Clauses." *VIEWS: Vienna English Working Papers* 14, no. 1 (2005): 21–53.

# Bibliography

Keener, Craig S. *The Gospel of John: A Commentary*. 2 vols. Peabody, MA: Hendrickson, 2003.

Klink, Edward W., III. *The Sheep of the Fold: The Audience and Origin of the Gospel of John*. Society for New Testament Studies Monograph Series 141. Cambridge: Cambridge University Press, 2007.

Kluck, Marlies, Dennis Ott, and Mark de Vries. "Incomplete parenthesis: An overview." In *Parenthesis and Ellipsis: Cross-Linguistics and Theoretical Perspectives*, edited by Marlies Kluck, Dennis Ott, and Mark de Vries, 1–21. Studies in Generative Grammar 121. Berlin: De Gruyter, 2015.

Koester, Craig R. *Symbolism in the Fourth Gospel*. Minneapolis: Fortress Press, 1995.

Köstenberger, Andreas J. "'I Suppose' (οἶμαι): The Conclusion of John's Gospel in Its Literary and Historical Context." In *The New Testament in Its First Century Setting: Essays on Context and Background in Honour of B. W. Winter on His 65th Birthday*, edited by P. J. Williams, Andrew D. Clark, Peter M. Head, and David Instone-Brewer, 72–88. Grand Rapids, Eerdmans: 2004.

Köstenberger, Andreas J. *A Theology of John's Gospel and Letters*. Grand Rapids: Zondervan, 2009.

Kurz, William S. "Narrative Approaches to Luke-Acts." *Biblica* 68, no. 2 (1987): 195–220.

Lagrange, Marie-Joseph. "Où en est la dissection littéraire du quatrième évangile?" *Revue Biblique* 33, no. 3 (1924): 321–42.

Lamb, David A. *Text, Context and the Johannine Community: A Sociolinguistic Analysis of the Johannine Writings*. Library of New Testament Studies 477. London: Bloomsbury T & T Clark, 2014.

Lamb, David A., and Thora Tenbrink. "Evaluating Jesus and other 'heroes': An application of appraisal analysis to Hellenistic Greek texts in the 'Lives' genre." *Language, Context and Text* 4, no. 2 (2022): 227–58.

Lanser, Susan Sniader. *The Narrative Act: Point of View in Prose Fiction*. Princeton: Princeton University Press, 1981.

Lee, Dal. *The Narrative Asides in the Book of Revelation*. Lanham, MD: University Press of America, 2002.

Lightfoot, J. B. *The Gospel of St. John: A Newly Discovered Commentary*. Edited by Ben Witherington III and Todd D. Still, assisted by Jeanette M. Hagen. Downers Grove, IL: IVP Academic, 2015.

Lightfoot, R. H. *St John's Gospel: A Commentary*. Edited by C. F. Evans. Oxford: Clarendon, 1956.

Lincoln, Andrew T. *The Gospel According to St John*. Black's New Testament Commentaries. London: Continuum, 2005.

Lindars, Barnabas. *The Gospel of John*. New Century Bible Commentary. London: Marshall, Morgan & Scott, 1972.

Loisy, Alfred. *Le quatriéme Évangile. Les épitres dites de Jean*. 2nd ed. Paris: Émile Nourry, 1921.

Lombard, Herman A. "John's Gospel and the Johannine church: A Mirror of Events within a Text or/and a Window on Events within a Church." *Hervormde Teologiese Studies* 43, no. 3 (1987): 395–413.

256                                    *Bibliography*

Longenecker, Richard. *Galatians*. Word Biblical Commentary 41. Dallas: Word, 1990.

Lubbock, Percy. *The Craft of Fiction*. New York: Charles Scribner's Sons, 1921.

Luz, Ulrich. *Matthew 21–28: A Commentary*. Translated by James E. Crouch. Edited by Helmut Koester. Hermeneia. Minneapolis: Fortress Press, 2005.

Luz, Ulrich. *Matthew 1–7: A Commentary*. Translated by James E. Crouch. Edited by Helmut Koester. Hermeneia. Minneapolis: Fortress Press, 2007.

Macgregor, G. H. C. *The Gospel of John*. London: Hodder and Stoughton, 1928.

MacRae, George W. "Theology and Irony in the Fourth Gospel." In *The Gospel of John as Literature: An Anthology of Twentieth Century Perspectives*, edited by Mark W. G. Stibbe, 103–13. New Testament Tools, Studies and Documents 17. Leiden: Brill, 1993.

Malbon, Elizabeth Struthers. "Narrative Criticism: How Does the Story Mean?" In *Mark & Method: New Approaches in Biblical Studies*, edited by Janice Capel Anderson and Stephen D. Moore, 29–57. 2nd ed. Minneapolis: Fortress Press, 2008.

Malbon, Elizabeth Struthers. "Characters in Mark's Story: Changing Perspectives on the Narrative Process." In *Mark as Story: Retrospect and Prospect*, edited by Kelly R. Iverson and Christopher W. Skinner, 45–69. Society of Biblical Literature Resources for Biblical Study 65. Atlanta: Society of Biblical Literature, 2011.

Marincola, John. "Herodotean Narrative and the Narrator's Presence." *Arethusa* 20, no. 1/2 (1987): 121–37.

Marshall, I. Howard. *The Gospel of Luke: A Commentary on the Greek Text*. New International Greek Testament Commentary. Grand Rapids: Eerdmans, 1978.

Martin, James R., and Peter R. R. White. *The Language of Evaluation: Appraisal in English*. Basingstoke: Palgrave Macmillan, 2005.

Martyn, J. Louis. *History and Theology in the Fourth Gospel*. 3rd ed. Louisville: Westminster John Knox, 2003.

McHugh, John F. *A Critical and Exegetical Commentary on John 1–4*. Edited by Graham N. Stanton. International Critical Commentary. London: T & T Clark, 2009.

Metzger, Bruce M. *Manuscripts of the Greek Bible: An Introduction to Greek Palaeography*. New York: Oxford University Press, 1981.

Metzger, Bruce M. "Persistent Problems Confronting Bible Translators." *Bibliotheca Sacra* 150 (1993): 273–84.

Metzger, Bruce M. *A Textual Commentary on the Greek New Testament*. 2nd ed. London: United Bible Societies, 1994.

Michaels, J. Ramsey. *The Gospel of John*. New International Commentary on the New Testament. Grand Rapids: Eerdmans, 2010.

Milligan, William, and William F. Moulton. *Commentary on the Gospel of St. John*. Edinburgh: T & T Clark, 1898.

Moloney, Francis J. *Belief in the Word: Reading the Fourth Gospel: John 1–4*. Minneapolis: Fortress Press, 1993.

Moloney, Francis J. "Who Is the Reader in/of the Fourth Gospel?" In *The Interpretation of John*, edited by John Ashton, 219–33. 2nd ed. Edinburgh: T & T Clark, 1997. Reprinted from *Australian Biblical Review* 40 (1992): 20–33.

# Bibliography

Neirynck, Frans. *Jean et les Synoptiques: Examen critique de l'exégèse de M.-E. Bosimard.* Bibliotheca Ephemeridum Theologicarum Lovaniensium 49. Leuven: Leuven University Press, 1979.

Neirynck, Frans. "Parentheses in the Fourth Gospel." In *Frans Neirynck. Evangelica II: 1982–1991 Collected Essays,* edited by F. Van Segbroeck, 693–98. Bibliotheca Ephemeridum Theologicarum Lovaniensum 99. Leuven: Leuven University Press, 1991.

Nestle-Aland, *Novum Testamentum Graece,* edited by Barbara Aland, Kurt Aland, Johannes Karavidopoulos, Carlo M. Martini, Bruce M. Metzger, in cooperation with the Institute for New Testament Textual Research. 28th rev. edition. Stuttgart: Deutsche Bibelgesellschaft, 2012.

Nicholson, Godfrey C. *Death as Departure: The Johannine Descent-Ascent Schema.* Society of Biblical Literature Dissertation Series 63. Chico: Scholars Press, 1983.

Nicklas, Tobias, and Thomas J. Kraus. "Joh 5,3b-4. Ein längst erledigtes textkritisches Problem?" *Annali di Storia dell'Esegesi* 17, no. 2 (2000): 537–56.

Nongbri, Brent. "P.Bodmer 2 as Possible Evidence for the Circulation of the Gospel according to John without Chapter 21." *Early Christianity* 9:3 (2018): 345–60.

North, Wendy E. Sproston. *The Lazarus Story within the Johannine Tradition.* Journal for the Study of the New Testament: Supplement Series 212. Sheffield: Sheffield Academic Press, 2001.

North, Wendy E. S. "Why Should Historical Criticism Continue to Have a Place in Johannine Studies?" In *What We Have Heard: The Past, Present, and Future of Johannine Studies,* edited by Tom Thatcher, 19–21. Waco: Baylor University Press, 2007.

North, Wendy E. S. *A Journey Round John: Tradition, Interpretation and Context in the Fourth Gospel.* Library of New Testament Studies 534. London: Bloomsbury T & T Clark, 2015.

Nünning, Ansgar. *Grundzüge eines kommunikationstheoretischen Modells der erzählerischen Vermittlung: die Funktion der Erzählinstanz in den Romanen George Eliots.* Horizonte: Studien zu Texten und Ideen der europäischen Moderne 2. Trier: Wissenschaftlicher Verlag Trier, 1989.

Nünning, Ansgar. "Commentary." In *Routledge Encyclopedia of Narrative Theory,* edited by David Herman, Manfred Jahn, and Marie-Laure Ryan, 74. New York: Routledge, 2005.

Nünning, Ansgar. "Implied Author." In *Routledge Encyclopedia of Narrative Theory,* edited by David Herman, Manfred Jahn, and Marie-Laure Ryan, 239–40. New York: Routledge, 2005.

Nünning, Ansgar. "Metanarrative Comment." In *Routledge Encyclopedia of Narrative Theory,* edited by David Herman, Manfred Jahn, and Marie-Laure Ryan, 304–5. New York: Routledge, 2005.

Olsson, Birger. *Structure and Meaning in the Fourth Gospel: A Text-Linguistic Analysis of John 2:1–11 and 4:1–42.* Translated by Jean Gray. Coniectanea Biblica: New Testament Series 6. Lund: CWK Gleerup, 1974.

258 *Bibliography*

Ong, Walter. *Orality and Literacy: The Technologizing of the Word*. 30th anniversary ed. New York: Routledge, 2012.

O'Rourke, John J. "Asides in the Gospel of John." In *The Composition of John's Gospel: Selected Studies from Novum Testamentum*, compiled by David E. Orton, 205–14. Leiden: Brill, 1999. Reprinted from *Novum Testamentum* 21, no. 3 (1979): 210–19.

Paris, Christopher T. *Narrative Obtrusion in the Hebrew Bible*. Minneapolis: Fortress Press, 2014.

Parkes, Malcolm Beckwith. *Pause and Effect: An Introduction to the History of Punctuation in the West*. Aldershot: Scholar Press, 1992.

Pesch, Rudolf. *Das Marcusevangelium*. 2 vols. Herders theologischer Kommentar zum Neuen Testament. Freiburg: Herder, 1977.

Pfister, Manfred. *The Theory and Analysis of Drama*. Translated by John Halliday. Cambridge: Cambridge University Press, 1988.

Piñero, Antonio, and Jesús Peláez. *The Study of the New Testament: A Comprehensive Introduction*. Translated by David E. Orton and Paul Ellingworth. Leiden: Deo, 2003.

Popp, Thomas. *Grammatik des Geistes: Literarische Kunst und theologische Konzeption in Johannes 3 und 6*. Arbeiten zur Bibel und ihrer Geschichte 3. Leipzig: Evangelische Verlagsanstalt, 2001.

Pourciau, Chuck Aaron. "The Use of Explicit Commentary in the Gospels of Luke and John." PhD diss., New Orleans Baptist Theological Seminary, 1990. ProQuest Dissertations Publishing, Publication No: 9026805.

Powell, Mark Allan. *What Is Narrative Criticism?* Minneapolis: Fortress Press, 1990.

Price, Todd L. *Structural Lexicology and the Greek New Testament: Applying Corpus Linguistics for Word Sense Possibility Delimitation Using Collocational Indicators*. Perspectives on Linguistics and Ancient Languages 6. Piscataway, NJ: Gorgias Press, 2015.

Prince, Gerald. *A Dictionary of Narratology*. Rev. ed. Lincoln: University of Nebraska Press, 2003.

Quintilian. *Institutio Oratoria*. Translated by H. E. Butler. Loeb Classical Library. Cambridge, MA: Harvard University Press, 1921.

Quintilian. *The Orator's Education, Volume IV: Books 9–10*. Edited and translated by Donald A. Russell. Loeb Classical Library 127. Cambridge, MA: Harvard University Press, 2002.

Resseguie, James L. *The Strange Gospel: Narrative Design and Point of View in John*. Biblical Interpretation Series 56. Leiden: Brill, 2001.

Resseguie, James L. *Narrative Criticism of the New Testament: An Introduction*. Grand Rapids: Baker Academic, 2005.

Resseguie, James L. "A Glossary of New Testament Narrative Criticism with Illustrations." *Religions* 10, no. 3 (2019):1–39. https://doi.org/10.3390/rel10030217.

Rhoads, David, Joanna Dewey, and Donald Michie. *Mark as Story: An Introduction to the Narrative of a Gospel*. 3rd ed. Minneapolis: Fortress Press. 2012.

Richardson, Scott. *The Homeric Narrator*. Nashville: Vanderbilt University Press, 1990.

Rieu, E. V. *The Four Gospels: A New Translation from the Greek*. London: Penguin, 1952.

*Bibliography* 259

Rimmon-Kenan, Shlomith. *Narrative Fiction: Contemporary Poetics.* 2nd ed. New York: Routledge, 2002.

Robertson, A. T. *A Grammar of the Greek New Testament in the Light of Historical Research.* 3rd ed. New York: Hodder and Stoughton, 1919.

Rodríguez, Rafael. "Reading and Hearing in Ancient Contexts." *Journal for the Study of the New Testament* 32, no. 2 (2009): 151–78.

Rodríguez, Rafael. *Oral Tradition and the New Testament: A Guide for the Perplexed.* London: Bloomsbury, 2014.

Rood, T. "Thucydides." In *Narrators, Narratees, and Narratives in Ancient Greek: Studies in Ancient Greek Narrative, Volume 1*, edited by Irene J. F. de Jong, René Nünlist, and Angus M. Bowie, 115–28. Mnemosyne Supplements 257. Leiden: Brill, 2004.

Runge, Steven E. *Discourse Grammar of the Greek New Testament: A Practical Introduction for Teaching and Exegesis.* Peabody, MA: Hendrickson, 2010.

Sanders, Joseph N. *A Commentary on the Gospel According to St John.* Edited by B. A. Mastin. Black's New Testament Commentaries. London: Adam and Charles Black, 1968.

Schnackenburg, Rudolf. *Das Johannesevangelium.* 3 vols. Herders theologischer Kommentar zum Neuen Testament 4. Freiburg: Herder, 1965, 1971, 1975.

Schnackenburg, Rudolf. *The Gospel According to St. John.* Translated by Kevin Smyth. 3 vols. Herder's Theological Commentary on the New Testament. London: Burns & Oates, 1968, 1980, 1982.

Schnelle, Udo. *Das Evangelium nach Johannes.* 4th ed. Theologischer Handkommentar zum Neuen Testament 4. Leipzig: Evangelische Verlagsanstalt, 2009.

Scholes, Robert, and Robert Kellogg. *The Nature of Narrative.* New York: Oxford University Press, 1966.

Schuchard, Bruce G. "Form versus Function: Citation Technique and Authorial Intention in the Gospel of John." In *Abiding Words: The Use of Scripture in the Gospel of John*, edited by Alicia D. Myers and B. G. Schuchard, 23–41. Society of Biblical Literature Resources for Biblical Study 81. Atlanta: SBL Press, 2015.

Schürer, Emil. *The History of the Jewish People in the Age of Jesus Christ.* Revised and edited by Geza Vermes, Fergus Millar, Matthew Black, Martin Goodman, and Pamela Vermes. 4 vols. Edinburgh: T & T Clark, 1973–1987.

Sheeley, Steven M. *Narrative Asides in Luke-Acts.* Journal for the Study of the New Testament: Supplement Series 72. Sheffield: Sheffield Academic Press, 1992.

Shen, Dan. "Defense and Challenge: Reflections on the Relation between Story and Discourse." *Narrative* 10, no. 3 (2002): 222–43.

Shively, Elizabeth E. "Literary Approaches." In *Cambridge Companion to the New Testament*, edited by S. B. Chapman and M. A. Sweeney, 369–81. Cambridge: Cambridge University Press, 2021.

Smith, D. Moody. "The Sources of the Gospel of John: An Assessment of the Present State of the Problem." *New Testament Studies* 10, no. 3 (2009): 336–51.

Smith, Justin Marc. *Why Βίος? On the Relationship between Gospel Genre and Implied Audience.* Library of New Testament Studies 518. London: Bloomsbury T & T Clark, 2015.

260 Bibliography

Stadter, Philip. "Biography and History." In *A Companion to Greek and Roman Historiography*, edited by John Marincola, 528–40. Blackwells Companions to the Ancient World. Oxford: Wiley Blackwell, 2011.

Staley, Jeffrey Lloyd. *The Print's First Kiss: A Rhetorical Investigation of the Implied Reader in the Fourth Gospel*. Society of Biblical Literature Dissertation Series 82. Atlanta: Scholars Press, 1988.

Stevenson, James. *A New Eusebius: Documents Illustrating the History of the Church to AD 337*. Revised by William Hugh Clifford Frend. London: SPCK, 1987.

Stibbe, Mark W. G. *John as Storyteller: Narrative Criticism and the Fourth Gospel*. Cambridge: Cambridge University Press, 1992.

Stock, Brian. *The Implications of Literacy: Written Language and Models of Interpretation in the Eleventh and Twelfth Centuries*. Princeton: Princeton University Press, 1983.

Tenney, Merrill C. "The Footnotes of John's Gospel." *Bibliotheca Sacra* 117 (1960): 350–64.

Thackeray, William. *Vanity Fair*. Edited by J. I. M. Stewart. London: Penguin, 1968.

Thatcher, Tom. "A New Look at Asides in the Fourth Gospel." *Bibliotheca Sacra* 151 (1994): 428–39.

Thatcher, Tom. *Why John Wrote a Gospel: Jesus-Memory-History*. Louisville: Westminster John Knox, 2006.

Thatcher, Tom. "John's Memory Theatre: A Study of Composition in Performance." In *The Fourth Gospel in First-Century Media Culture*, edited by Anthony Le Donne and Tom Thatcher, 73–91. Library of New Testament Studies, 426. London: T & T Clark, 2011.

Theobald, Michael. *Das Evangelium nach Johannes: Kapitel 1–12*. Regensburger Neues Testament. Regensburg: Friedrich Pustet, 2009.

Thielman, Frank. "The Style of the Fourth Gospel and Ancient Literary Concepts of Religious Discourse." In *Persuasive Artistry: Studies in New Testament Rhetoric in Honor of George A. Kennedy*, edited by Duane F. Watson, 169–83. Journal for the Study of the New Testament: Supplement Series 20. Sheffield: Sheffield Academic Press, 1991.

Thompson, Geoff, and Susan Hunston. "Evaluation: An Introduction." In *Evaluation in Text: Authorial Stance and the Construction of Discourse*, edited by Susan Hunston and Geoff Thompson, 1–27. Oxford: Oxford University Press, 2000.

Thompson, Geoff, and Puleng Thetela. "The Sound of One Hand Clapping: The Management of Interaction in Writing Discourse." *Text* 15, no. 1 (1995): 103–27.

Thucydides, *The Peloponnesian War*. Translated by Martin Hammond, with introduction and notes by P. J. Rhodes. Oxford World's Classics. Oxford: Oxford University Press, 2009.

Thyen, Hartwig. *Das Johannesevangelium*. Handbuch zum Neuen Testament 6. Tübingen: Mohr Siebeck, 2005.

Turner, Nigel. *Syntax*. Vol. 3 of James Hope Moulton, *A Grammar of New Testament Greek*. Edinburgh: T & T Clark, 1963.

Uspensky, Boris. *A Poetics of Composition: The Structure of the Artistic Text and Typology of a Compositional Form.* Translated by Valentina Zavarin and Susan Wittig. Berkeley: University of California Press, 1973.

Van Belle, Gilbert. *Les Parenthèses dans L'Évangile de Jean: Aperçu Historique et Classification, Texte Grec de Jean.* Studiorum Novi Testamenti Auxilia 11. Leuven: Leuven University Press, 1985.

Van Belle, Gilbert. "Les Parenthèses Johanniques." In *The Four Gospels, 1992: Festschrift Frans Neirynck,* edited by Frans Van Segbroeck, C. M. Tuckett, G. Van Belle, and J. Verheyden, 3:1901–33. 3 vols. Bibliotheca Ephemeridum Theologicarum Lovaniensum 100. Leuven: Leuven University Press, 1992.

Van Belle, Gilbert. "Review of Steven M. Sheeley, Narrative Asides in Luke-Acts." *Ephemerides Theologicae Lovanienses* 71, no. 4 (1995): 465–68.

Van Belle, Gilbert. "Theory of Repetitions and Variations in the Fourth Gospel." In *Repetitions and Variations in the Fourth Gospel: Style, Text, Interpretation,* edited by Gilbert Van Belle, Michael Labahn, and Petrus Maritz, 13–32. Bibliotheca Ephemeridum Theologicarum Lovaniensum 223. Leuven: Uitgeverij Peeters, 2009.

Van Emde Boas, Evert, Albert Rijksbaron, Luuk Huitink, and Mathieu de Bakker. *The Cambridge Grammar of Classical Greek.* Cambridge: Cambridge University Press, 2019.

Vanhoozer, Kevin J. *Is There a Meaning in This Text? The Bible, the Reader and the Morality of Literary Knowledge.* Grand Rapids: IVP/Apollos, 1998.

Van Tilborg, Sjef. *Johannes. Belichting van het bijbelboek.* Boxtel: Katholieke Bijbelstichting, 1988.

Van Tilborg, Sjef. "The Gospel of John: Communicative Processes in a Narrative Text." *Neotestamentica* 23 (1989): 19–31.

Von Siebenthal, Heinrich. *Ancient Greek Grammar for the Study of the New Testament.* Oxford: Peter Lang, 2019.

Von Wahlde, Urban C. *The Gospel and Letters of John.* 3 vols. Eerdmans Critical Commentary. Grand Rapids: Eerdmans, 2010.

Waterfield, Robin. "On 'Fussy Authorial Nudges' in Herodotus." *The Classical World* 102 (2009): 485–94.

Wead, David W. *The Literary Devices in John's Gospel.* Theologische Dissertationen 4. Basel: Friedrich Reinhardt Kommissionsverlag, 1970.

Wead, David W. *The Literary Devices in John's Gospel.* Rev. ed. Edited by Paul N. Anderson and R. Alan Culpepper. Eugene: Wipf & Stock, 2018.

Wellhausen, J. *Das Evangelium Johannis.* Berlin: Georg Rimmer, 1908.

Wengst, Klaus. *Das Johannesevangelium.* 2nd ed. 2 vols. Theologischer Kommentar zum Neuen Testament 4. Stuttgart: Kohlhammer, 2004, 2007.

Westcott, Brooke Foss. *The Gospel According to St. John: The Greek Text with Introduction and Notes.* Edited by Arthur Westcott. 2 vols. London: John Murray, 1908.

Westcott, Brooke Foss, and Fenton John Anthony Hort. *The New Testament in Original Greek: II Introduction and Appendix.* New York: Harper and Brothers, 1882.

Westfall, Cynthia Long. "Narrative Criticism." In *Dictionary of Biblical Criticism and Interpretation,* edited by Stanley E. Porter, 237–39. London: Routledge, 2007.

Westfall, Cynthia Long. "A Method for the Analysis of Prominence in Hellenistic Greek." In *The Linguist as Pedagogue: Trends in the Teaching and Linguistic Analysis of the Greek New Testament*, edited by Stanley E. Porter and Matthew Brook O'Donnell, 75–94. New Testament Monographs 11. Sheffield: Sheffield Phoenix Press, 2009.

White, Hayden. *The Content of Form: Narrative Discourse and Historical Representation*. Baltimore: John Hopkins University Press, 1987.

Wiese, Annjeanette. "Replacing Omniscience: Superior Knowledge and Narratorial Access." *Narrative* 29, no. 3 (2021): 321–38.

Zewi, Tamar. *Parenthesis in Biblical Hebrew*. Studies in Semitic Languages and Linguistics 50. Leiden: Brill, 2007.

Zumstein, Jean. *L'Évangile selon Saint Jean*. 2 vols. Commentaire du Nouveau Testament: Deuxième Série 4. Geneva: Labor et Fides, 2007, 2014.

# Index of Ancient Sources

Hebrew Bible/Old Testament

| Genesis | | 4:3 | 213–14, 219, 230 |
|---|---|---|---|
| 22 | 211 | 5:4–5 | 213–14 |
| 22:1 | 212, 233n57 | 5:8 | 213 |
| 23:19 | 210 | 5:10 | 213–14 |
| 26:14–16 | 210 | 5:12 | 213–14 |
| 26:33 | 209, 219 | 5:14–16 | 213–14 |
| 32:32 | 209 | 5:19 | 234n60 |
| 32:33 (MT) | 209, 219 | 5:20 | 213–14 |
| 37–50 | 207 | 5:23–24 | 234n60 |
| 42:23 | 207 | 6:2 | 213–14 |
| | | 6:8 | 213–14, 219, 230 |
| Exodus | | 8:10 | 213–14 |
| 12:46 | 111 | 8:14 | 213–14 |
| | | 8:15–18 | 213–14 |
| Judges | | 11:1 | 213–14 |
| 14:4 | 209, 211 | 11:4 | 213 |
| | | 11:27 | 213 |
| 1 Samuel | | 12:24–25 | 213 |
| 2:26 | 222 | 13:18 | 213 |
| | | 14:26 | 213 |
| 2 Samuel | | 17:14 | 209, 213 |
| 1:18 | 213 | 18:13 | 213 |
| 2:1 | 213, 234n60 | 18:18 | 213, 219, 230 |
| 2:16 | 213 | 20:3 | 213 |
| 3:1 | 213–14 | 20:23–26 | 213 |
| 3:2–5 | 213–14 | 21:1 | 234n60 |
| 4:2 | 213 | 21:2 | 213 |

263

## 264 Index of Ancient Sources

| | |
|---|---|
| 21:14 | 213 |
| 23:1 | 213 |
| 23:8–39 | 213, 234n58 |
| 24:1 | 213–14 |
| 24:15–16 | 213–14 |
| 24:25 | 213–14 |

1 Chronicles

| | |
|---|---|
| 10–22 | 214 |
| 11:9 | 214 |
| 13:6 | 214 |
| 13:11 | 214 |
| 14:2 | 214 |
| 14:3–5 | 214 |
| 14:11 | 214 |
| 18:10 | 214 |
| 18:13 | 214 |
| 18:14–17 | 214 |
| 20:1 | 214 |
| 21:1 | 214 |
| 21:14–15 | 214 |
| 21:27 | 214 |

Psalms

| | |
|---|---|
| 21:19 | 110 |
| 23:2 | 176 |
| 34:20 | 111 |
| 42:1–2 | 110 |
| 63:1 | 110 |
| 69:9 | 101 |
| 69:21 | 110 |

Isaiah

| | |
|---|---|
| 6:10 | 109 |
| 8:6 | 193, 204n187 |
| 40:9 | 107 |
| 53:1 | 109 |

Zephaniah

| | |
|---|---|
| 3:14–16 | 107 |
| 3:16 | 95n77 |

Zechariah

| | |
|---|---|
| 9:9 | 95n77, 107 |
| 12:10 | 111 |

New Testament

Matthew

| | |
|---|---|
| 1:1–17 | 219 |
| 1:22 | 219 |
| 1:22–23 | 219, 236n104 |
| 1:23 | 188, 226 |
| 2:15 | 219 |
| 2:17–18 | 219 |
| 2:23 | 219 |
| 4:12 | 117 |
| 4:14–16 | 219 |
| 4:18 | 235n99 |
| 6:30 | 235n99 |
| 7:9 | 235n98 |
| 7:10 | 235n98 |
| 7:27 | 235n99 |
| 7:29 | 219 |
| 8:17 | 219 |
| 9:4 | 220 |
| 9:6 | 218–19 |
| 9:8 | 219 |
| 10:42 | 235n99 |
| 12:17–21 | 219 |
| 12:25 | 220 |
| 13:14–15 | 236n104 |
| 13:34 | 219–20 |
| 13:35 | 219 |
| 13:57 | 79, 118, 127 |
| 13:58 | 219 |
| 14:3 | 117 |
| 14:19 | 176 |
| 16:12 | 220 |
| 17:13 | 220 |
| 21:4–5 | 219 |
| 21:44 | 220 |
| 22:18 | 220 |
| 22:23 | 221 |
| 23:37 | 235n98 |
| 24:15 | 73, 219–20, 224, 233n53 |
| 26:6–13 | 86 |
| 27:8 | 219, 224, 230 |
| 27:9–10 | 219 |
| 27:18 | 220 |
| 27:33 | 204n177, 219–21, 226 |

## Index of Ancient Sources

| | | | |
|---|---|---|---|
| 27:46 | 219–21, 226 | 9:30–32 | 215 |
| 27:52–53 | 219, 235n100 | 9:32 | 223 |
| 28:15 | 219, 224, 230 | 10:30 | 215 |
| 28:16–20 | 235n100 | 10:47 | 218 |
| | | 10:51 | 189 |
| Mark | | 11:32 | 215, 217 |
| 1:1 | 215, 217 | 12:15 | 215 |
| 1:2–3 | 215, 217 | 12:18 | 215–16 |
| 1:4 | 75 | 13:14 | 42, 73, 215, 217–20, |
| 1:14 | 117 | | 224, 233n53, 236n110 |
| 1:14–15 | 217 | 14:3–9 | 86 |
| 1:16 | 215 | 14:36 | 226 |
| 1:19 | 218 | 14:56 | 218 |
| 2:8 | 215, 225 | 15:10 | 218, 220 |
| 2:10 | 215, 217, 219 | 15:16 | 215 |
| 2:14 | 218 | 15:21 | 218 |
| 2:15 | 215 | 15:22 | 188, 204n177, 215–16, |
| 3:10 | 218 | | 218–21, 226 |
| 3:16 | 215 | 15:34 | 188, 215–16, 218–21, 228 |
| 3:17 | 215, 218, 226, 234n69 | 15:40 | 218 |
| 3:18 | 218 | 15:42 | 218 |
| 3:21 | 218 | 16:8 | 218 |
| 3:30 | 215 | 16:19–20 | 234n71 |
| 4:31–32 | 234n64 | | |
| 4:32 | 234n64 | Luke | |
| 4:33–34 | 215, 220 | 1:1–4 | 35, 66, 134, 174, 222, |
| 5:1–20 | 149 | | 224, 245 |
| 5:8 | 149 | 1:3 | 223 |
| 5:28 | 218 | 1:8–9 | 222 |
| 5:30 | 215 | 1:9 | 222–23 |
| 5:41 | 188, 215–16, 218, 226 | 1:80 | 222 |
| 5:42 | 215 | 2:2 | 221–22, 236n117 |
| 6:4 | 79, 118, 127 | 2:2–3 | 222 |
| 6:6 | 215 | 2:4 | 220, 222 |
| 6:17 | 117 | 2:19 | 222–23 |
| 6:39 | 176 | 2:22–23 | 35, 53n226, 222, |
| 6:48 | 215 | | 236n111 |
| 6:52 | 215, 218 | 2:23 | 221, 236n117 |
| 7:3–4 | 215, 218 | 2:35 | 221 |
| 7:11 | 215–16, 226 | 2:36 | 221 |
| 7:19 | 215, 217 | 2:40 | 222 |
| 7:34 | 215–16 | 2:51 | 222–23 |
| 9:6 | 215, 218 | 2:52 | 222–23, 225 |
| 9:9–10 | 215 | 3:1–2 | 222–23 |
| 9:13 | 235n90 | 3:4–6 | 222 |

266          *Index of Ancient Sources*

| | | | |
|---|---|---|---|
| 3:19–20 | 117 | 1:7–9 | 76 |
| 3:23 | 221–22, 236n117 | 1:7–14 | 114, 151 |
| 3:23–38 | 222–23 | 1:8–14 | 76 |
| 4:16 | 222, 236n117 | 1:9 | 77 |
| 4:16–20 | 156n66 | 1:9–14 | 76, 100, 115 |
| 4:24 | 79, 118, 127 | 1:12 | 127 |
| 4:41 | 222 | 1:13 | 126–27 |
| 5:17 | 221 | 1:14 | 10, 66, 123n27, 169–70, |
| 5:24 | 35, 221–22, 236n117 | | 173, 228 |
| 6:14 | 222 | 1:15 | 63–64, 67, 75–76, 87, |
| 6:16 | 222, 236n117 | | 95n76, 114, 126, 129 |
| 7:29–30 | 221–22, 236n117, | 1:16 | 10, 171 |
| | 237n125 | 1:16–18 | 76–77, 100, 114–15, 151, |
| 7:36–50 | 86 | | 185, 196, 245, 247 |
| 8:8 | 222 | 1:17 | 127 |
| 8:29 | 221–22, 236n117 | 1:18 | 127 |
| 9:14 | 222, 236n117 | 1:19 | 75, 84 |
| 9:33 | 221–22, 236n117 | 1:19–28 | 24 |
| 9:45 | 222–23, 237n111 | 1:23 | 95n77, 109 |
| 14:7 | 222, 236n117 | 1:24 | 25, 84, 146 |
| 14:35 | 35, 222, 236n117 | 1:28 | 24, 81, 84, 96n88, 121, |
| 16:14 | 222 | | 146 |
| 16:28 | 221 | 1:30 | 87, 129 |
| 17:16 | 222, 236n117 | 1:31 | 145 |
| 18:1 | 222, 236n117 | 1:33 | 145 |
| 18:34 | 222–23 | 1:35–51 | 143 |
| 19:11 | 222 | 1:37 | 84 |
| 19:25 | 221 | 1:38 | 10, 12–13, 29–30, 40, |
| 20:27 | 222 | | 54n269, 55n277, 60, 63– |
| 22:1 | 222, 237n131 | | 64, 66, 87, 101, 105, 115, |
| 23:12 | 222 | | 128, 131, 168, 186–92, |
| 23:18–19 | 222 | | 194, 203n166 |
| 23:19 | 221, 236n117 | 1:40 | 84 |
| 23:33 | 204n177, 226 | 1:41 | 10, 13, 29–30, 40, 60, |
| 23:50–51 | 222 | | 63–64, 87, 101, 105, 115, |
| 23:51 | 221, 236n117 | | 128, 131, 168, 186–90, |
| 24:27 | 111 | | 189, 191, 194, 203n165 |
| | | 1:42 | 10, 12–13, 29–30, 60, 63, |
| John | | | 65, 87, 101, 105, 113, |
| 1–12 | 27 | | 128, 131, 168, 186–90, |
| 1–20 | 6 | | 192, 194 |
| 1:1–5 | 76, 100, 114–15, 151 | 1:45 | 150 |
| 1:1–18 | 66, 99, 126, 184 | 1:48 | 7 |
| 1:6 | 40, 76–77 | 1:49 | 203n166 |
| 1:6–8 | 75–76, 126 | 2:1 | 29, 51n184 |

## Index of Ancient Sources

| | | | |
|---|---|---|---|
| 2:1–10 | 25 | 4:1–2 | 8, 61, 168 |
| 2:1–11 | 84 | 4:1–3 | 40, 144 |
| 2:4 | 120 | 4:1–4 | 144 |
| 2:6 | 36 | 4:1–26 | 149 |
| 2:9 | 41, 65–66, 87, 114, 127, 130 | 4:1–42 | 139, 144 |
| 2:11 | 10, 13, 24, 101, 104, 115, 151, 170, 184 | 4:2 | 6, 8, 12, 29, 40–41, 60, 63–66, 87, 117, 119, 128, 130, 144–46, 152, 155n30, 159n136, 168, 169 |
| 2:13–22 | 14 | | |
| 2:17 | 7, 76, 101, 115, 150–51, 184 | 4:4–9 | 130 |
| 2:18–20 | 177 | 4:4–42 | 82 |
| 2:19 | 78 | 4:6 | 117 |
| 2:21 | 8, 12, 126, 168, 170, 177, 195 | 4:7ff. | 40 |
| 2:21–22 | 1, 6–7, 14, 24, 29, 78– 79, 102, 115, 126–27, 203n149 | 4:8 | 40, 51–52n191, 65–66, 75, 82, 87, 96n91, 117, 119, 130, 141–42, 149, 158n94 |
| 2:22 | 169–70, 198–9n52 | 4:8–10 | 138 |
| 2:24 | 9 | 4:9 | vii, 9–10, 19, 22, 32, |
| 2:24–25 | 7, 102, 105, 115, 171, 179–80, 207–8, 224–25 | | 45n4, 64–65, 68, 80, 87, 117, 127, 131, 135–36,138–42, 144, |
| 2:25 | 171, 207 | | 146, 152, 246 |
| 3:1 | 40, 208 | | |
| 3:1–2 | 83–84, 121 | 4:11 | 179 |
| 3:1–10 | 142, 225 | 4:14 | vii |
| 3:2 | 143–44, 151, 203n166, 207 | 4:15 | 179 |
| | | 4:17 | 179 |
| 3:5 | 128 | 4:20 | 179 |
| 3:10 | 179 | 4:21 | 120 |
| 3:13–21 | 80, 148 | 4:22 | 141 |
| 3:16–21 | 11, 39, 47n76, 102, 115, 141, 180, 228 | 4:23 | 120, 157n82 |
| | | 4:23–24 | 142 |
| 3:22 | 128, 130, 144–46, 159n128, 168 | 4:25 | 10, 60, 65, 87, 101, 104, 115, 128, 131, 186–88, 191–92, 194 |
| 3:24 | 12, 51n191, 65, 87, 117, 119, 128–30, 146, 156n61, 169, 184, 229 | 4:43–45 | 79 |
| | | 4:43–54 | 130 |
| 3:26 | 144–46, 159n128, 168, 189, 203n166 | 4:44 | 7–8, 65, 79, 87, 118, 127, 129, 130, 159n133, 184 |
| 3:31–36 | 7, 11, 39, 47n76, 80, 103, 115, 141, 148, 180, 228 | 4:45 | 79 |
| | | 4:46 | 84 |
| 4:1 | 64, 130, 144–46, 168, 170 | 4:54 | 10, 24, 101, 104, 115, 151, 184 |

Index of Ancient Sources

| | | | |
|---|---|---|---|
| 5:1–15 | 104 | 7:5 | 9, 65, 87, 118, 127, 131 |
| 5:2 | 186–88, 191, 194, | 7:13 | 36 |
| | 204n174 | 7:21–22 | 29 |
| 5:2–3 | 136 | 7:21–24 | 131 |
| 5:2–9 | 151 | 7:22 | 8, 63–66, 87, 118, 131 |
| 5:3 | 65, 136–37 | 7:30 | 120, 199n70 |
| 5:4 | 5, 8, 136–37, 152, 244 | 7:37 | 128 |
| 5:5 | 136 | 7:37–38 | 79 |
| 5:7 | 136–37 | 7:38 | 128 |
| 5:16–18 | 194, 115 | 7:39 | 6–8, 24, 40, 66, 79, 106, |
| 5:17 | 105 | | 108, 115, 127–28, 146, |
| 5:18 | 7 | | 169 |
| 5:19–29 | 7 | 7:39b | 128, 155n23 |
| 5:19–47 | 47n76, 104 | 7:43 | 174 |
| 5:25 | 120, 157n82 | 7:50 | 12, 66, 83–84, 121, |
| 5:28–29 | 6, 120 | | 135–36, 138, 142–44, |
| 5:46 | 150 | | 146, 151–52, 169 |
| 6 | 105 | 7:53–8:11 | 5, 8 |
| 6:1 | 46n23, 60, 105, 115, | 8:17 | 150 |
| | 187–88, 194 | 8:20 | 24, 50n144, 81, 120, |
| 6:1–14 | 151 | | 199n70 |
| 6:1–15 | 84 | 8:27 | 7, 8, 126 |
| 6:6 | 11–12, 102, 105, 115, | 8:58 | 76 |
| | 169, 171–72, 180, 212, | 9:1–7 | 84, 151 |
| | 224–25, 233n57 | 9:4 | 220 |
| 6:10 | 175–76, 200n100 | 9:7 | 10, 29, 61, 63–66, 87, |
| 6:15 | 105–6, 115, 225 | | 101, 106, 115, 128, 131, |
| 6:23 | 8, 66, 81, 84, 105 | | 186–88, 191–94 |
| 6:31 | 95n77, 150 | 9:13 | 84 |
| 6:39 | 6, 121 | 9:14 | 81 |
| 6:40 | 6 | 9:16 | 174 |
| 6:44 | 6 | 9:18 | 84, 157n82 |
| 6:45 | 95n77, 109 | 9:22 | 36, 51–52n191, 170, 189 |
| 6:46 | 126 | 9:22–23 | 120 |
| 6:52b–58 | 128 | 9:24 | 84 |
| 6:54 | 6 | 9:30 | 40 |
| 6:59 | 24, 189 | 10:6 | 24, 26, 50n144 |
| 6:60 | 105, 225 | 10:12 | 63–66 |
| 6:61 | 105 | 10:19 | 174 |
| 6:64 | 11, 105–6, 115, 171, | 10:22–23 | 81 |
| | 180, 224–25 | 10:22–29 | 131 |
| 6:64–71 | 119 | 10:28 | 121 |
| 6:71 | 9, 36 | 10:33 | 104 |
| 7:2 | 81, 96n90, 176 | 10:34 | 74, 109, 150 |
| 7:3–10 | 131 | 10:34–35 | 95n77 |

## Index of Ancient Sources

| | | | |
|---|---|---|---|
| 10:35 | 40, 65, 73, 87, 118, 131 | 12:17 | 84 |
| 10:35–36 | 73–74 | 12:23 | 120 |
| 10:40 | 84, 121 | 12:27 | 120 |
| 11:1–44 | 84–85, 151 | 12:28 | 112 |
| 11:2 | 8, 12, 46n48, 47n77, 66, 85–86, 96n98, 156n61, 169 | 12:32 | 108, 110 |
| | | 12:33 | 6, 8, 12, 24, 108, 110, 112, 116, 127–28, 168, 186 |
| 11:11–12 | 106, 177 | | |
| 11:13 | 8, 106, 115, 127, 177, 195 | 12:37–41 | 7 |
| | | 12:37–43 | 11, 46n49 |
| 11:16 | 101, 118–20, 128, 131, 186–88, 194 | 12:38–41 | 77, 108, 116, 151, 184 |
| | | 12:41 | 24 |
| 11:18 | 176 | 12:42 | 36, 189 |
| 11:30 | 81 | 12:43 | 8 |
| 11:33 | 36, 170 | 13–21 | 27 |
| 11:38 | 36 | 13:1 | 105, 109, 116, 120, 171, 180, 224–25 |
| 11:41 | 7 | | |
| 11:45–57 | 85 | 13:1–3 | 7 |
| 11:49–51 | 84 | 13:2 | 36 |
| 11:49–52 | 121 | 13:3 | 105, 171, 180, 224–25 |
| 11:50–52 | 167 | 13:10 | 157n82 |
| 11:51 | 9, 24 | 13:11 | 11, 105, 109, 116, 157n82, 171, 180, 224–25 |
| 11:51–52 | 7, 107, 115, 167 | | |
| 11:57 | 52n191, 120 | | |
| 12 | 151 | 13:12–17:26 | 114 |
| 12:1 | 85, 97n109 | 13:19 | 7 |
| 12:1–2 | 84 | 13:21–27 | 131 |
| 12:1–8 | 85–86 | 13:21–30 | 87 |
| 12:3 | 46n48, 85 | 13:23 | 10, 65, 87, 119–20, 131 |
| 12:3–8 | 130–31 | 13:23–25 | 84 |
| 12:4 | 36, 65, 87, 118–20, 129, 130–31 | 13:31 | 112 |
| | | 13:31–17:26 | 47, 114, 177 |
| 12:6 | 8, 65, 87, 107, 115, 127, 131 | 14:22 | 60, 65, 87, 118–20, 131 |
| | | 14:26 | 134 |
| 12:9 | 84–85 | 14:29 | 7 |
| 12:12–15 | 78 | 15–17 | 15 |
| 12:12–16 | 14 | 15:25 | 95, 109, 150 |
| 12:14 | 150 | 15:26 | 179, 195, 208 |
| 12:14–15 | 7, 77, 95n77, 107, 116 | 16:2 | 124n46, 189 |
| | | 16:4 | 124n46 |
| 12:14a | 107 | 16:13 | 196, 225, 245 |
| 12:14b–15 | 151, 184 | 16:13–15 | 134 |
| 12:16 | 1, 8, 14, 24, 78–79, 108, 116, 126–27, 150, 159n133, 169, 203n149 | 16:16–18 | 192 |
| | | 16:19 | 171 |
| | | 16:25 | 120 |

| | | | |
|---|---|---|---|
| 16:32 | 120 | 19:35–37 | 1, 196, 203n149, 245, 247 |
| 17:1 | 112, 120 | 19:36 | 7 |
| 17:3 | 7–8 | 19:36–37 | 111, 116, 132, 151, 184 |
| 17:12 | 7, 121 | 19:37 | 7 |
| 18:1–5 | 87 | 19:39 | 83–84, 121, 142–44, 151 |
| 18:4 | 105, 109, 116, 171, 180, 224–25 | 19:42 | 81 |
| | | 20 | 5 |
| 18:5 | 135–36 | 20:2 | 119–20 |
| 18:8–9 | 7 | 20:3–8 | 177 |
| 18:9 | 6, 12, 121, 126, 168 | 20:4 | 84 |
| 18:10 | 36, 84 | 20:8 | 84 |
| 18:14 | 84, 121 | 20:9 | 111, 116, 151, 169, 177, 195 |
| 18:20 | 189 | | |
| 18:22 | 8 | 20:11–18 | 112 |
| 18:24 | 30 | 20:16 | 10, 60, 63, 65, 87, 101, 111, 116, 128, 131, 186–89, 194, 203n165 |
| 18:26 | 84 | | |
| 18:30–32 | 131 | | |
| 18:31–33 | 7 | 20:19–29 | 112 |
| 18:32 | 65, 87, 108–9, 112, 116, 128, 131 | 20:22 | 79, 106 |
| | | 20:24 | 10, 60, 65, 87, 101, 118–20, 131, 186, 188, 194 |
| 19 | 151 | | |
| 19:13 | 10, 101, 110, 116, 128, 186–88, 191, 194 | 20:24–29 | 131 |
| | | 20:30 | 151, 176 |
| 19:17 | 10, 101, 110, 116, 186–88, 194 | 20:30–31 | 1, 10, 66–67, 81, 111, 116, 132, 150–51, 167, 184–85, 196, 203n149, 245, 247 |
| 19:20 | 157n82 | | |
| 19:22 | 150 | | |
| 19:24 | 7, 77, 110, 116, 128, 151, 184 | 20:31 | 27, 75–76, 78, 112, 150, 186, 196, 247 |
| 19:26 | 119–20 | 21 | 5, 7, 15, 21, 105, 112, 122n23, 128 |
| 19:28 | 7, 65, 77, 87, 110, 116, 128, 131, 135–36, 151, 171, 180, 184 | | |
| | | 21:1 | 46n26, 105 |
| | | 21:2 | 101, 118–20, 131, 186, 188, 194 |
| 19:28b–30a | 131 | | |
| 19:29 | 36 | 21:4 | 135–36 |
| 19:31 | 47n77, 65–66, 81 | 21:7 | 47n77, 66, 119–20 |
| 19:32–37 | 132 | 21:8 | 66, 81 |
| 19:34 | 111 | 21:14 | 10, 112, 116 |
| 19:34b | 128 | 21:15–25 | 131 |
| 19:35 | 6–7, 10, 65–66, 70, 81, 87, 110, 116, 128, 132, 157n82, 173, 175, 178–79, 185, 199n85, 228 | 21:18 | 128 |
| | | 21:19 | 65, 87, 110, 112, 116, 128, 131 |
| | | 21:20 | 12, 84, 119–20, 169 |

### Index of Ancient Sources

| | |
|---|---|
| 21:22 | 75 |
| 21:23 | 10, 76, 113 |
| 21:23–25 | 1, 113, 116, 151, 185, 196, 203n149, 230, 245, 247 |
| 21:24 | 113, 166, 173, 179, 195, 228 |
| 21:24–25 | 6, 10, 66–67, 81, 150, 167, 171, 174–75, 184–85, 195 |
| 21:25 | 113, 120, 135, 144, 176, 180, 228, 230 |

**Acts**

| | |
|---|---|
| 1:14 | 118 |
| 4:36 | 188 |
| 13:8 | 188 |
| 14:17 | 159n132 |
| 15:40 | 188 |

**1 Corinthians**

| | |
|---|---|
| 1:14–17 | 46n24, 145 |
| 15:4 | 111 |

**2 Corinthians**

| | |
|---|---|
| 1:15 | 143 |

**Galatians**

| | |
|---|---|
| 4:13 | 143 |

**Hebrews**

| | |
|---|---|
| 4:3 | 159n132 |
| 7:2 | 188 |

**Revelation**

| | |
|---|---|
| 22:18–19 | 153 |

**Classical Authors**

Herodotus
*Histories*

| | |
|---|---|
| 7.152.3 | 228 |
| 7.213 | 238n57 |

Thucydides
*History*

| | |
|---|---|
| 1.138 | 230 |
| 3.113.6 | 230 |

Quintilian
*Institutio Oratoria*

| | |
|---|---|
| 4.1.63 | 53n218 |
| 4.3.12–14 | 53n218 |
| 4.3.23 | 53n218 |
| 9.3.23 | 58 |

**Church Fathers**

Chrysostom
*Homily 36 on John*
137

Tertullian
*De Baptismo*

| | |
|---|---|
| 5 | 137 |

**Other Literature**

Gospel of Thomas

| | |
|---|---|
| 31 | 79, 154n18 |

*Papyrus Oxyrhynchus*

| | |
|---|---|
| 1 | 127 |

# Index of Modern Authors

Abbott, Edwin A., 19, 30, 51–52n191
Achtemeier, Paul J., 147, 149, 160n147
Adams, Sean A., 232n9
Allison, Dale C., Jr., 219–20, 235n100, 236n104
Alter, Robert, 206–8, 212, 219, 245
Anderson, A. A., 234n58
Auerbach, Eric, 164
Auld, A. Graeme, 213
Aune, David E., 37, 205

Bain, David, 70–71, 94n48
Bar-Ilan, Meir, 147
Barrett, Charles K., 79, 82, 86, 105, 110–11, 117, 139, 149
Bauckham, Richard, 37–38, 44, 59, 75, 86, 117, 133, 152, 156n61, 189, 205, 235n97, 241
Beasley-Murray, George R., 145
Ben Keshet, Hanoch, 234n69
Bennema, Cornelis, 181, 195
Bernard, John Henry, 5, 8–9, 19, 43, 57, 96n91, 139, 188, 241
Best, Ernest, 234n65
Bjerkelund, Carl J., 23–28, 30, 32, 38, 43–44, 50n144, 53n223, 54n255, 58, 93, 205, 227, 241
Blass, Friedrich, 40, 217
Blodgett, Harriet, 200n93

Blomberg, Craig L., 145, 159n136
Bloomfield, Leonard, 208
Bock, Darrell L., 237n121
Boismard, Marie-Emile, 20, 49–51n128, 157n87
Boomershine, Thomas E., 68, 148, 176, 216, 218, 221
Booth, Wayne, 33, 36–37, 59, 68, 165–66, 170, 182
Bovon, François, 223
Brant, Jo-Ann A., 68, 71, 76, 82, 85, 107, 117, 122n13, 123n43, 140, 163–64, 170, 177, 181, 193, 229, 238n156
Brodie, Thomas, 154n2
Brown, Raymond E., 2, 5, 12–13, 15, 19, 44, 58, 60, 76, 80–1, 84–85, 96n91, 97n105, 105, 120, 121n1, 125, 135–36, 140, 142–45, 149, 151, 191, 193, 241
Bultmann, Rudolf, 15, 19, 22, 25, 58–60, 82, 86, 92n7, 96n91, 97n114, 101, 126–29, 132, 135, 139, 143–44, 147, 155n23, 155n30, 159n125, 159n128, 200n100, 204n187, 243
Burge, Gary M., 62, 180
Burridge, Richard A., 37, 232n9
Burton-Roberts, Noel, 64, 72, 95n63, 147
Busch, Austin, 206
Bynum, Wm. Randolph, 122n20

273

274 *Index of Modern Authors*

Calvin, Jean, 68, 140
Carson, Donald A., 21, 96n82,
122nn12–13, 139, 176
Chatman, Seymour, 33, 70, 89, 165–66,
168, 198n35, 200n94, 216–17
Childs, Brevard S., 234n62
Comfort, Philip Wesley, 156n77
Connolly, Francis X., 166
Cortazzi, Martin, 202n143
Credner, Karl August, 38, 54n258
Crown, Alan D., 50n151
Culler, Jonathan D., 172
Culpepper, R. Alan, 16–17, 21–22, 28,
32–33, 38–39, 48n89, 49n94, 58,
133, 153, 164–66, 168, 171, 173,
175, 178, 180–82, 188, 191, 195,
197n11, 199n85

Davies, Margaret, 150, 191–92
Davies, W. D., 219–20, 235n100,
236n104
de Bakker, Mathieu, 42
Debrunner, Albert, 40–41, 217
Dehé, Nicole, 72–73
De Jong, Irene J. F., 238nn155–156
DeSilva, David A., 237n134
de Vries, Mark, 73
Dewey, Joanna, 94n41, 133, 147, 150,
156n66
Dewald, Carolyn, 227–29, 246
Dodd, C.H., 145, 154n5

Fee, Gordon D., 137
Flowers, H. J., 2, 5–7, 16, 19, 43,
46n23, 57, 125, 137, 144, 243
Ford, David F., 247
Fowler, Robert M., 148, 160n150, 216–
18, 235n90, 235n93
France, R. T., 149, 215–16, 219–20, 226
Funk, Robert W., 40–41, 217

Garvie, Alfred E., 6–7, 19, 28, 43, 57,
87, 125
Genette, Gérard, 33, 165–66, 171, 176
Godet, Frédéric Louis, 188

Grafton, Anthony, 92n12
Green, Joel B., 223
Grenfell, Bernard P., 154n18
Grethlein, Jonas, 227, 237n137
Gribble, David, 229–31, 246
Griffiths, Alan, 238n149
Guellich, Robert A., 216
Gunderson, Erik, 179

Haegeman, Liliane, 95n62
Haenchen, Ernst, 105
Hägg, Thomas, 232n9
Haines-Eitzen, Kim, 146
Hawthorn, Jeremy, 93n35
Hedrick, Charles W., 23, 28–33, 37–38,
41, 43–44, 50n133, 59–60, 67,
80–82, 87–88, 90–91, 105, 137, 153,
164–66, 179, 187, 197n16, 205, 216,
219, 231, 234n72, 234n75, 243
Hitchcock, F. R. M., 200n106
Holmstedt, Robert D., 209–10, 212, 245
Hort, Fenton John Anthony, 18, 64,
93n22, 95n76, 139, 157n92,
Hoskyns, Edwyn Clement, 158n117
Hubbard, Jeffrey M., 236n110
Huitink, Luuk, 42
Hunston, Susan, 183
Hunt, Arthur S., 154n18
Hurtado, Larry, 205–6
Hyland, Ken, 183–85, 203n149,
203n150

Jeremias, Joachim, 159n133
Jin, Lixian, 202n143
Johnson, Luke Timothy, 132–33, 152,
156n59

Kaltenböck, Gunther, 208
Kavalova, Yordanka, 72–73
Kellogg, Robert, 178
Keener, Craig S., 97n108, 134, 140,
145, 193, 205, 233n57
Klink, Edward W., III, 48n94
Kluck, Marlies, 73
Koester, Craig R., 133, 192

# Index of Modern Authors

Köstenberger, Andreas J., 38–39, 43, 82, 84, 87–88, 90, 113, 171, 185, 187, 199n69
Kraus, Thomas J., 137, 157n87
Kurz, William S., 223

Lagrange, Marie-Joseph, 21
Lamb, David A., 123n29, 156n75, 202n146, 203n149, 236n110
Lamouille, Arnaud, 20, 50n128
Lanser, Susan Sniader, 198n49
Lee, Dal, 37, 54n244
Lightfoot, J. B., 137, 140, 157n88
Lightfoot, R. H., 140
Lincoln, Andrew T., 85, 124n48, 140, 145, 155n25, 177–78, 192–94
Lindars, Barnabas, 15, 143, 149, 158n117
Loisy, Alfred, 190
Lombard, Herman A., 27–28, 30, 44, 59, 164–65, 189
Longenecker, Richard, 143
Lubbock, Percy, 166
Luz, Ulrich, 220, 235n101

Macgregor, G. H. C., 21, 125–26, 140
MacRae, George W., 178
Malbon, Elizabeth Struthers, 202n137
Marincola, John, 238n144
Marshall, I. Howard, 223
Martin, James R., 202–3n146
Martyn, J. Louis, 26, 124n48
McHugh, John F., 141, 146, 158n115, 191, 194, 204n173
Metzger, Bruce M., 64, 137, 156n77, 157n94, 220
Michaels, J. Ramsey, 79, 82, 85, 90, 97n108, 97n128, 106, 110–12, 117–18, 120, 123n43, 137, 141–43, 146, 157n81, 175, 189–90, 200n100, 225
Michie, Donald, 69, 94n41
Milligan, William, 141–42
Moloney, Francis J., 140, 179, 201n121
Moulton, William F., 141–42

Neirynck, Frans, 20, 30–31, 43, 51n189
Nicholson, Godfrey C., 21–22, 33, 52–53n216
Nicklas, Tobias, 137, 157n87
Nongbri, Brent, 122n23
North, Wendy E. S., 62, 75, 83, 86, 186, 228
Nünning, Ansgar, 69–70, 182

Olsson, Birger, 13–15, 19, 24, 44, 47nn76–77, 58, 164, 168, 198n24
Ong, Walter, 156n64, 161n158
O'Rourke, John J., 15–16, 19, 24, 28, 32, 36–38, 43, 48n85, 58, 81–82, 87, 89, 91, 186, 243
Ott, Dennis, 73

Paris, Christopher T., 210–12, 233n41, 233nn45–46, 233n53, 245
Parkes, Malcolm Beckwith, 92n14
Peláez, Jesús, 49n117, 103
Pesch, Rudolf, 216
Pfister, Manfred, 71, 95n52
Piñero, Antonio, 49n117, 103
Price, Todd L., 237n124
Prince, Gerald, 69–70
Popp, Thomas, 161n162
Pourciau, Chuck Aaron, 31
Powell, Mark Allan, 197n2

Rehkopf, Friedrich, 40–41
Resseguie, James L., 69, 164, 169–71, 173–74, 178, 180, 182–83, 197n2, 198n52, 220
Rhoads, David, 69, 94n41, 197n2
Richardson, Scott, 89–91, 175, 179
Rieu, E. V., 60
Rijksbaron, Albert, 42
Rimmon-Kenan, Shlomith, 33, 165–66, 176
Robertson, A. T., 40
Rodríguez, Rafael, 134, 150, 160n147, 161n164
Rood, T., 231
Runge, Steven E., 41–42, 59

## Index of Modern Authors

Sanders, Joseph N., 15, 123n29, 149
Schnackenburg, Rudolf, 19, 58–60, 80, 82, 96n91, 140–1, 149, 150, 159n127, 159n133, 192
Schnelle, Udo, 139
Scholes, Robert, 178
Schuchard, Bruce G., 95n77
Schürer, Emil, 204n173
Sheeley, Steven M., 23, 32–38, 43–44, 52n216, 53n221, 53n223, 53n226, 59–62, 67–70, 74, 80, 89–91, 105, 164, 166, 174, 197n16, 205, 219, 221–22, 226–27, 233n53, 235n82, 236nn111–113, 236n117, 237n125, 237n131, 241, 243, 247n1
Shen, Dan, 176–77
Shively, Elizabeth E., 182, 197n2
Smith, D. Moody, 154n5
Smith, Justin Marc, 232n9
Stadter, Philip, 227
Staley, Jeffrey Lloyd, 30, 164, 167–68, 173, 178–79, 182–83, 201n121
Stevenson, James, 156n70
Stibbe, Mark W. G., 164, 168–69, 180–81, 195, 200–1n106, 201n125, 244
Stock, Brian, 153

Tenbrink, Thora, 202–3n146
Tenney, Merrill C., 1–2, 9–12, 14–16, 19, 24, 27–28, 32, 35–38, 43–44, 46n44, 46n48, 46n49, 47n55, 47n60, 52n216, 57–60, 81–83, 87, 89, 91, 97n128, 112, 114, 148, 154, 160n149, 186, 189, 241, 243
Thackery, William, 174
Thatcher, Tom, 35–38, 41, 59, 67, 80, 87, 89, 91, 96n88, 134–35, 148, 150, 153, 156n76, 160n148, 161n167, 164, 166, 176, 243
Theobald, Michael, 80–82, 86, 137, 140, 176
Thetela, Puleng, 203n150
Thielman, Frank, 31–32

Thompson, Geoff, 183, 203n150
Thyen, Hartwig, 82, 122n19, 140, 143, 190–91
Turner, Nigel, 55n279

Uspensky, Boris, 165, 169, 171, 183, 197n11, 198–99n52, 202n145

Van Belle, Gilbert, 5, 17–24, 28, 30–32, 35, 37–41, 43, 48–49n102, 49–50n128, 50n133, 50n144, 51n167, 51n189, 53n221, 53n223, 54n258, 58, 60–62, 64–65, 67–68, 78, 81–82, 84, 87–88, 90–91, 92n7, 93n30, 96n99, 97n128, 133, 139, 150, 152, 157n82, 157n94, 171, 176, 187, 231, 241–43, 247n1
Van Emde Boas, Evert, 42
Vanhoozer, Kevin J., 202n139
Van Tilborg, Sjef, 30–31
Von Siebenthal, H., 42, 55n289
Von Wahlde, Urban C., 126, 129–33, 135, 137, 144, 243

Waterfield, Robin, 228–29, 246
Wead, David W., 14, 21–22, 79, 164, 166–67, 180, 198n24
Wellhausen, J., 21, 126, 154n4
Wengst, Klaus, 96n91, 139, 178
Westcott, Brooke Foss, 9, 18, 46n37, 64, 86, 93n22, 95n76, 96n92, 97n109, 103–4, 139, 157n92, 172, 189, 199n74
Westfall, Cynthia Long, 112, 200n87
White, Hayden, 181
White, Peter R. R., 202–3n146
Wiese, Annjeanette, 172, 195, 244

Zewi, Tamar, 208–210, 212, 219, 232n28, 245
Zumstein, Jean, 84, 97n105, 140, 143, 157n87, 176, 192–94

# About the Author

**David A. Lamb** is an Honorary Research Fellow in Biblical Studies at the University of Manchester, UK, and a former Visiting Scholar in Linguistics at Bangor University, UK. He is author of *Text, Context and the Johannine Community: A Sociolinguistic Analysis of the Johannine Writings* (Bloomsbury T & T Clark, 2014) and was co-chair of the Johannine Literature Seminar at the British New Testament Conference from 2013 to 2016.